IRRUPTION OF
THE THIRD WORLD

IRRUPTION OF
THE THIRD WORLD

CHALLENGE TO THEOLOGY

**Papers from the Fifth International Conference
of the Ecumenical Association of Third World Theologians,
August 17–29, 1981, New Delhi, India**

**Edited by
Virginia Fabella and Sergio Torres**

ORBIS BOOKS
Maryknoll, New York 10545

Manuscript Editor: William E. Jerman

Unless otherwise noted, all Bible translations are from the New English Bible

Library of Congress Cataloging in Publication Data

International Conference of the Ecumenical Association
    of Third World Theologians (1981: New Delhi, India)
    Irruption of the Third World.

    Includes bibliographical references.
    1. Church and Underdeveloped areas—Congresses.
I. Fabella, Virginia.   II. Torres, Sergio.   III. Title.
BR115. U6I59   1981   230'.09172'4   82-18851
ISBN 0-88344-216-7 (pbk.)

Contents

PART V
FINAL STATEMENT

PART VI
EVALUATION AND INTERPRETATION

Acronyms

ADB	Asian Development Bank
AFP	Agence France Presse
APRA	Alianza Popular Revolucionario Americana
ASEAN	Association of Southeast Asian Nations
CCA	Christian Conference of Asia
CIA	Central Intelligence Agency (U.S.A.)
EATWOT	Ecumenical Association of Third World Theologians
ESCAP	Economic and Social Council for Asia and the Pacific
FAO	Food and Agriculture Organization (UN)
GNP	Gross National Product
IBRD	International Bank for Reconstruction and Development (UN)
IMF	International Monetary Fund
MNC	Multinational Corporation
NATO	North Atlantic Treaty Organization
NIEO	New International Economic Order
NISCO	New International Socio-Cultural Order
OPEC	Organization of Petroleum Exporting Countries
SIPRI	Stockholm International Peace Research Institute
UNCTAD	United Nations Conference on Trade and Development
WCC	World Council of Churches

Preface

Orbis Books offers to the public another book on Third World theology as part of its effort to bring into the theological realm the voices of those who, until recently, were not heard in the First World, or not heard at all. Those who are familiar with Orbis publications will see that this book is a continuation of a concerted and planned endeavor that has been going on for several years. It manifests a further step in the theological work of the Ecumenical Association of Third World Theologians, founded in Dar-es-Salaam in August 1976 at the conclusion of the first Ecumenical Dialogue of Third World Theologians.

The Association, now more familiarly known as EATWOT, is a small group of about fifty theologians from Third World regions: Africa, Asia, and Latin America, as well as from minority groups in the United States. Starting in 1976, the Association has been evolving a particular way of doing theology and articulating some new perspectives for the theological understanding of God and salvation in the world today. One of the major activities of this group of theologians has been to organize international conferences focusing on the contextual theologies emerging in the Third World continents. There have been five conferences in all: two in Africa (Dar-es-Salaam, Tanzania, in 1976; Accra, Ghana, in 1977), one in Latin America (São Paulo, Brazil, in 1980), and two in Asia (Wennappuwa, Sri Lanka, in 1979; New Delhi, India, in 1981).[1]

This new book covers the last of this series of theological events, held in New Delhi from August 17 to 29, 1981 (EATWOT V). Its title, *The Irruption of the Third World: Challenge to Theology*, echoes the central theme of the Delhi meeting.

THE DELHI CONFERENCE

The Delhi Conference brought together a broad range of theologians, both professional and non-professional, from the Third World continents and the Caribbean, and from Black and Hispanic groups of the U.S.A. There were also observers from North America and Europe. It was the task of the fifty participants to examine the commonalities and uniqueness of the efforts to contextualize theology in their different continents and regions and to delve deeper into the significance of this new theological movement not only in the Third World but also in relation to Western theology. For the planners of the Conference, it would be a way of synthesizing the work of EATWOT for the past five years.

EATWOT V was preceded by a year of preparatory work, during which national consultations and other meetings were organized to study the local realities and to review the collective efforts towards a more relevant theology in the regions. The meetings provided the occasion for local Christians to reflect together on the conference theme under four fundamental aspects: (1) the socio-economic reality and political situation in these regions; (2) the existing cultural, ethnic, and religious worldviews; (3) the presence and involvement of Christians; and (4) the influence of Western theology and the local efforts of indigenization, inculturation, or contextualization. Participation at these preparatory meetings was a prerequisite for attendance at the Conference; in only a few cases were exceptions made.

The results of these meetings constituted the nucleus of the regional reports, five of which are reproduced in Part II of this volume.[2] They reveal not only the depth and extent of the preparation for the Conference but also the similarities and variations in Third World contexts and experiences. It was planned that these regional reports would form the basis of the continental discussions at EATWOT V.

The Conference consisted of four distinct but interrelated phases: (1) an exposure to the Indian society; (2) continental sessions; (3) intercontinental dialogue; and (4) the formulation of a conference statement.

The book tells of the process and content of the four phases in a variety of ways, not necessarily in chronological order. During the first three days of the Conference, the participants were provided with the opportunity to visit a rural village, mingle with the teeming population in the Delhi streets and establishments, and listen to five different perspectives of Indian life, religious pluralism, and political visions—Gandhian, Dalit Panther, Sikh, Scheduled Caste Buddhist, and Islamic—in the context of the present historical situation. The exposure, necessarily limited because of the time constraint and language barrier on the one hand, and the vastness and complexity of the Indian reality on the other, proved helpful for the individual participants as they compared this particular Third World life-situation with their own.[3]

The observations and reflections of the delegates from Brazil on the exposure program, which appear in Part IV, give a taste of the first phase.[4] For the Brazilian delegates, their first contact with Asia's widespread poverty and religious traditions was a veritable eye-opener and left them with questions that tormented their minds and hearts. Can it be that the situation of the suffering masses results from the tragic resignation to a "destiny" allotted to them? Or does their attitude reveal great wisdom, expressed in a religious way, in response to pain and misery? Here, the value of human life seems to be calculated so very differently!

A glimpse of the second phase is given in Part II by way of the continental reports prepared by the African and Asian delegates. For two days, the delegates met in their respective continental groups to go over their regional reports, and to see how they had moved closer or further apart since their conferences in Accra, Wennappuwa, or São Paulo. The exchanges, deliberations, and conclusions of each continental grouping were put together in a single report and shared with the rest of the conference participants. This was a helpful and much appreciated phase for the participants.

The core and substance of the Delhi Conference, however, was the intercontinental dialogue that followed. If the Third World was truly irrupting and demanding its rightful place in history, what factors should be taken into account in developing a relevant and authentic theology in the face of this exigency? To help focus the exchange regarding this question, three resource persons were invited to speak on key issues affecting activity in the Third World. Ajit Roy of India spoke on "This Hour of History," a critical overview of the existing global systems and structures with emphasis on the economic and the political. The second speaker, Aloysius Pieris of Sri Lanka, elucidated on the significance of other religions and cultures in the evolution of a Third World theology. The third, Severino Croatto of Argentina, gave some guidelines on biblical hermeneutics from the point of view of the oppressed. Part III features these three presentations.[5]

The discussion that ensued brought about many clarifications while at the same time evoking new questions and posing new problems and challenges. In our theological reflections, are all three components—the socioeconomic, the religio-cultural, and the biblical—given balanced emphasis and approached with equal seriousness? Commonalities and differences emerged, not without heat or passion. It was during this phase of the EATWOT V that the realization came to the participants that "it was premature to talk of the synthesis of the past five years, or to describe Third World theology as one."[6]

The fourth phase consisted mainly in working toward a conference statement, which is reproduced in Part V. It reflects the thoughts, hopes, and concerns shared by the participants in the spirit of fellowship as well as the disagreement and anguish in their two weeks together. The statement makes reference to the daily worship. This included a Eucharistic celebration in authentic Indian style with dance, offering flowers and *arati*, and a worship service by the woman participants which was devotional, prayerful, and theologically challenging. The women's prayer service is included in Part IV of this volume.

The dynamics of the dialogue and the preparation of the Final Statement left no time for a formal evaluation at the end of the conference, for the final day was devoted exclusively to the First General Assembly of EATWOT. Assessments of the Delhi meeting were not altogether absent for they were voiced individually or in groups at different moments, in and out of the scheduled sessions. For the benefit of our readers, six people who went to Delhi, including one from the First World, share their evaluation and interpretation in Part IV of the book.

The concluding articles by the Third World theologians reveal a difference of viewpoints and a gamut of human attitudes and emotions that range from resentment, anger, and sadness, to excitement, gratitude, and eagerness to continue the task and to face the challenges with openness and hope. This only shows that the task of theologizing, though it is talk about God, is a very human endeavor. In Delhi, Christians met to search together how this human endeavor can be both effective and meaningful in the Third World today.

THE IRRUPTION OF THE THIRD WORLD: A HISTORICAL EVENT

The term "Third World," which first came into use two decades ago, is still in popular usage. Unlike faddish expressions destined to fade away after a brief passage of time, "Third World" has acquired instead layers of meaning which vary from the purely geographic ("the South") to the socio-economic ("poor," "underdeveloped") to the political ("non-aligned") and even the theological ("from the underside of history"). To those who met in Delhi, Third Worldness is characterized by massive poverty and oppression.[7]

But beyond its geographic, political, economic, and theological denotations, "Third World" connotes a growing historical force that is threatening the present international order (or disorder). The irruption of the Third World marks the dawning of a new era and the setting of an old one. Just as in the 1500s the "rebirth" in Europe and the "discoveries of new worlds" ushered in modern times and put a close to the Middle Ages, so the irrupting Third World begins a new stage in human history that is evincing the resistance to, and decline of, the dominance of North Atlantic countries and of Western civilization. EATWOT V described this dramatic movement as the "irruption of the exploited classes, marginalized cultures, and humiliated races. They are bursting from the underside of history into the world long dominated by the West. It is an irruption expressed in revolutionary struggles, political uprisings, and liberation movements. It is an irruption of religious and ethnic groups looking for affirmation of their authentic identity, of women demanding recognition and equality, of youth protesting the dominant systems and values. It is an irruption of all those who struggle for full humanity and for their rightful place in history."[8] The implications and consequences of an awakened Third World are not all evident or predictable, but it is clearly unfolding a different scenario with a new set of hitherto unknown and unexpected actors.

The dialectical process behind this drama is well-known. Having become conscious of their wretched condition, the poor and oppressed protest their dehumanization and react against the rule of the dominant classes, who counterreact with greater and more violent forms of repression. The poor and oppressed come back more determined and emboldened to change the existing social order, even at tremendous cost.

This relentless determination of Third World peoples to struggle for their rightful place in history poses both a challenge and a threat to the present international order at all levels: economic, political, cultural, social, and religious. This is clearly pointed out by Ajit Roy[9] and Sergio Torres in their factual expositions.[10] Torres continues to show how the irruption of the Third

World is also challenging the Christian churches and their First World-oriented theology. This is a historical happening that can no longer be denied or disregarded, and it is part of EATWOT's role to act as reminder that this challenge must be faced in all efforts toward a relevant theology and interpretation of Christian mission for our times.

A CHALLENGE TO THEOLOGY

Given the theme of the conference, Asia was an appropriate choice for its site—Asia, where three-fourths of the Third World lives, and where the overwhelming majority of the population adhere to beliefs and religious traditions outside of Christianity. Thus "the irruption of the Third World is also the irruption of the non-Christian world. The vast majority of God's poor perceive their ultimate concern and symbolize their struggle in the idiom of non-Christian religions and cultures."[11]

This assertion by Pieris created an impact on the conference, for it carries far-reaching implications not only for theological renewal but for societal transformations as well—the twin tasks of Third World theologians. Neither theology nor social transformation in the Third World will be truly effective unless it takes the non-Christian majority and their religious experience and aspirations seriously.[12] Pieris also underlined the occidental bias in both the current theology of religions and the revolutionary theories (particularly Marxism), and rued the fact that both are uncritically accepted by many Third World theologians who, at the same time, protest the imposition of Western norms and values in theology and society. A renewed theology of religions needs to incorporate the historical expressions of religiosity, the common thrust of which is liberation.[13] In brief, Pieris suggests that a theology of religions with a Third World perspective should have a unitary perception of religion and revolution. It was clear at the conference that even theologians from the predominantly Christian countries of Latin America and the Philippines felt they were not exempt from the exigencies of the "irruption of the non-Christian world."

Is it not time for a reformulation of the theological basis between Christianity and other world religions, as Torres asks in the initial article of the book. Christianity considers itself the ordinary means of salvation. What does this mean in the midst of many other well-established faiths and religions? It was the Indian regional report that raised the hard questions about the presence of revelation and salvation in the world religions. "As we face this theological task in the context of our wider Indian heritage, we wish to pose ourselves the following questions: Does not the Hindu or Buddhist tradition have its specific role to play, as the Christian has its own, in the common task of building the future? Is there not then a need for mutual criticism? If so, how could Jesus be the norm of critique for all scriptures and realities? Will Jesus also be subject to a critique in the light of Indian experience, past and present?"[14]

These questions threaten the very basis of Christian theology, but they must be asked. Theologians in search of a relevant theology must also play a prophetic role. At the risk of being censured or censored, Third World theologians need to ask hard and even critical questions of religion and society. Did not Jesus and the prophets do this? Does not Sacred Scripture have this critical function, too?

EMERGING THEOLOGIES FROM THE OPPRESSED

As J. Russell Chandran, EATWOT's first president, maintains, the Third World is "the bitter fruit of oppression." Third World theologies can only be theologies from the oppressed, that is, theologies from the vantage point of the oppressed. A Third World theology worthy of the name must arise from reflection on the Gospel of Jesus Christ as "it comes alive in the totality of the struggle of an oppressed people to be fully human."[15]

For EATWOT, this is what distinguishes a Third World theology. Hence, according to the Association's position, not all theologies produced in a Third World region are considered Third World theologies. It does not follow, however that EATWOT has a monopoly in the development of Third World theologies, but it has its particular contribution to the total effort.

One of the purposes of EATWOT V was to determine the commonalities and differences among the emerging Third World theologies. Though this was not done in a systematized manner in Delhi, these commonalities and differences became manifest at every phase of the conference. The more striking ones have been incorporated in the Final Statement. James Cone presents a fine summary in his article in Part VI as he compares Black theology with other Third World theologies.

There was general agreement that the basis of Third World theologies is the struggle of the poor and oppressed against all forms of injustice and domination. Yet upon stating this, one must immediately follow with a caveat that in Delhi, neither poverty nor oppression constituted a univocal term. There were differences in meaning, or at least nuances within the same meaning.

As pointed out in the Final Statement, poverty for most who attended EATWOT V meant material deprivation. For the Africans, however, it had an anthropological significance. As Engelbert Mveng poignantly states in his article in Part VI: "Poverty is defined first of all in function of one's conception of the human being. . . . There is a type of poverty that I call 'anthropological poverty.' It consists in despoiling human beings not only of what they have but of everything that constitutes their being and essence—their identity, history, ethnic roots, language, culture, faith, creativity, dignity, pride, ambitions, right to speak. . . ."

For Latin Americans and Asians, the term signifies material poverty. However, for Latin Americans, poverty is an evil to be eradicated; for the Asians, it is both a sin and a virtue—a sin when it is enforced or imposed from the outside; a virtue when it is voluntarily embraced. For the Buddhist monks, for example, voluntary poverty is both salutary and liberating, for it frees them from greed and overattachment to possessions. Thus Asian poverty cannot be simply reduced to economic categories.[16] Paradoxical as it may seem, in the very sources of agreement also lie the causes of disagreement among Third World theologians.

Prior to the Delhi meeting, it had been accepted that a Third World theology is contextual, liberational, biblically-based, and ecumenical; it is inductive in its method, starting with the faith experience of the poor and oppressed, and it rejects traditional Western theology as inadequate for the Third World. The context is understood to include both the socio-economic-political and the religio-cultural dimensions; liberation is both personal and societal; the text and context are related dialectically in biblical reflection. Though all these elements are held in common, as seen in the Final Documents of the past EATWOT conferences, in Delhi nuances began to surface.

Basic to EATWOT's methodology is the affirmation made in Dar-es-Salaam and reaffirmed in Delhi that commitment to the liberation of the oppressed constitutes the first act of theology.[17] Praxis, then, is an indispensable base of Third World theological activity. Yet from the discussion in Delhi, it becomes doubtful whether all have a common understanding of "commitment" and "praxis."

If Third World theology is truly contextual, then there must be variations in interpretations and conclusions. Moreover, Third World theologians are not entirely culpable in misunderstanding terms and one another. There are several reasons. For one, the meaning they assign a word is conditioned by their experience, their situation, and their history. This is clearly seen in the word "liberation." The term is nuanced differently when used by a Latin American, a black South African, an Indian from the Asian subcontinent, a minority person from the U.S.A., or by a Third World woman. For another, most of the Third World theologians have learned to express themselves theologically in a language other than their mother tongue. They may reject Western domination in all its forms and disclaim the traditional theology of the West as inadequate, yet they have to depend on Western thought patterns and use the language of their former Western colonizers to communicate with one another in their intercontinental dialogues. French, English, Spanish, and Portuguese have been the languages of EATWOT conferences. The question is therefore raised: Can there be genuine, meaningful, and in-depth dialogue among Third World theologians in a First World idiom?

Markedly Western influences remain in the theological production of Third World theologians. To the Asians and Africans, Latin American theologians are the most Westernized of all—and so there is suspicion of, and resistance to, their theology of liberation as the next "universal" theology to dominate the Third World. But Asian and African theologians are equally Westernized though less perceptibly so, perhaps because they are physiognomically more different from Europeans and North Americans. One Canadian anthropologist who worked in Africa for over fifteen years, after translating several of the French articles from *Bulletin of African Theology*,[18] remarked that the writings reflected Louvain more than Africa. The Philippines has often been accused of having cut off its Asian roots in the process of being Christianized. Yet the Philippine Church is only a magnified version of the Christian communities scattered the length and breadth of the Asian continent where many of the Asian theologians live and work.[19]

Though Third World theologians recognize that ostensible differences and even contradictions exist among them in language, concerns, emphasis, and approach to theology, they concur on one factor that uncontestedly unites them all: their faith in the God of life and the kingdom of life.

The Delhi statement devotes one whole section to the God of life and the kingdom.[20] The dialectical relationship between life and death as experienced in countless ways by the poor and oppressed has led Third World theology to a constitutive dimension of our biblical faith: through Jesus' death, God overcame death (2 Tim. 1:10). To believe in this God of life is to say "yes" to love, justice, peace, truth, and human wholeness, and "no" to all causes of dehumanization and all forms of death-dealing structures, situations, and conditions. It is to confirm our faith in the God of the Bible who takes the side of the poor and the oppressed, who enjoins humankind to "choose life," and who sent Jesus that all may have life and life in abundance (Deut. 30:19; John 10:10).

God cannot be separated from the kingdom of God, and this kingdom of God is the kingdom of life. In inaugurating the kingdom, Jesus performed signs of life: healing, feeding, restoring, reconciling, liberating. The kingdom of life is revealed above all in the resurrection of Jesus, which is the central mystery of our faith. We cannot be true disciples of the kingdom unless we witness to Jesus' life, death, and resurrection. Concretely in the Third World, this means, "participation in the struggle of the oppressed for the transformation of social structures and the renewal of cultures. At the same time it demands a conversion of ourselves and of our distorted relationships. This is what it means to love one's neighbor; this is what it means to be a Christian in the Third World today (1 John 3:18)." This is the direction of the reformulation of God in the Third World.

It is astonishing but true that in all EATWOT's intense discussions, confessional divisions have never surfaced. Within EATWOT, there is a wider theological gap between the Latin American and Central African Catholics than there is between Latin American Catholics and Protestants. Dogmas and doctrines that separate denominations have never been a root of disagreement among EATWOT theologians. It is rather the question of worldviews, political visions, or—and this spurred an explosive debate in Delhi—one's attitude towards women.

It was therefore almost expected in Delhi when there occurred an "irruption within the irruption," as Amba Oduyoye aptly describes it in Part IV. Tired of taking second place or being a token percentage in largely male meetings, the women in Delhi claimed their rightful place in EATWOT, in the churches and in society, and openly challenged the heavily male-oriented

Third World theologies. It became clear that just as Third World theologians from Africa, Asia, Latin America, the Caribbean, as well as from minority groups of the U.S.A., cannot be expected to reformulate theology in the selfsame manner, so it cannot be assumed that "African men and African women will say the same things about African reality" or arrive at identical theological conclusions.[21]

From all the foregoing, in no way can it be claimed that Third World theology is identical with the theology of liberation of Latin America, as has been claimed in some First World theological circles, and even by some Third World Christians themselves. In like manner, EATWOT cannot be labeled Latin American either in its origin or in its orientation. To do so would comprise a major distortion as well as an injustice.

Without doubt Third World theology should be liberational in its trust, but liberation theology is not the exclusive work of Latin American theologians nor its first articulators. As Cone points out in his article, both Black and Latin American theologians began to use the term "liberation" as heart of the Gospel and *definiens* of Christian theology almost simultaneously and independently of each other, that is, towards the late 1960s. In his paper, Bonganjalo Goba traces the emergence of the Black consciousness movement and a shift in their theological thinking in South Africa to the end of the same decade.[22] While admitting that Cone was one of the inspirations behind the Black theology movement among Black South Africans, Goba stresses that African traditional values were pertinent to their efforts. In Asia, way back in 1958, a lay group in Sri Lanka started spelling out the liberation praxis in the traditions of Marxism, Buddhism, and Christianity. Though never formally articulated, their reflections on their praxis constitute authentic theology.[23] Feminist theology and a growing number of "people's theologies" are also clearly liberational in their content and approach.

Liberation, then, is not so much a theme of liberation theologies but a *way* of doing theology. Hence, Gutiérrez could rightly conclude that "our method is our spirituality."[24] Writing on the Delhi event in *Vidyajyoti,* Samuel Rayan relates: "In our methodology, practice and theory, action and reflection, discussion and prayer, movement and silence, social analysis and religious hermeneutics, involvement and contemplation, constitute a single process." He likewise concludes, "Our methodology is our spirituality."[25]

The emerging Third World theologies have a sameness, yet with many differences. Is it self-defeating for EATWOT to acknowledge this? On the contrary, the experience in Delhi was a source of enrichment for the participants and a ground for their determination to deepen their theological probing at the regional level. For EATWOT, this search for a relevant theology has become an irreversible process. It does not mean smooth sailing ahead. It could mean further divergences in EATWOT itself; it could mean opposition from the Churches and derision from the traditional theological establishments in both the First and Third Worlds. But at this point, there can be no turning back.

We cannot end this preface without going back to the beginning. This book is about the Delhi Conference, but the Delhi Conference could not have been without the untiring efforts and sacrificial dedication of Samuel Rayan, who coordinated the work of the Local Organizing Committee. To him, and to all who assisted him, we owe our thanks. Our gratitude is also due to countless others who have made it possible to hold EATWOT V: the outgoing Executive Officers of EATWOT, its members, donors, and friends.

We echo the words of the Association's president, Bishop Emilio de Carvalho, in expressing our hope that EATWOT will continue to be at the service of Third World theologies so that these emerging theologies may be more attuned to, and convey, the real aspirations of our struggling peoples.[26] We pray for continued guidance and inspiration to the God of life, justice, love, and peace, whom we praise, worship, and celebrate.

—*Virginia Fabella*

NOTES

1. Orbis Books has published the papers of the first four EATWOT conferences. On the Dar-es-Salaam Conference, see S. Torres and V. Fabella, eds., *The Emergent Gospel* (Maryknoll, New York: Orbis Books, 1977); on the Accra Conference, see K. Appiah-Kubi and S. Torres, eds., *African Theology en Route* (Maryknoll, New York: Orbis Books, 1979); on the Wennappuwa Conference, see V. Fabella, ed., *Asia's Struggle for Full Humanity* (Maryknoll, New York: Orbis Books, 1980); on the São Paulo Conference, see S. Torres and J. Eagleson, eds., *The Challenge of Basic Christian Communities* (Maryknoll, New York: Orbis Books, 1981).

2. See Part II, "Emerging Theologies in Third World Contexts," which include the regional report from South Africa by Bonganjalo Goba, from India by Samuel Rayan, from Peru, by Jorge Alvarez Calderon, and from the American-Hispanics of the U.S.A. by Virgil Elizondo.

3. For participants' comments on their exposure experience, see S. Rayan, "The Irruption of the Third World—A Challenge to Theology," in *Vidyajyoti* (New Delhi), March 1982, pp. 109–115.

4. See "Everyday Life in India: Latin American Impressions," by Ivone Gebara and Zwinglio Dias in Part IV, Chapter 12.

5. See "The Socio-Economic and Political Context of Third World Theology" by Ajit Roy, Chapter 9; "The Place of Non-Christian Religions and Cultures in the Evolution of Third World Theology," by Aloysius Pieris, Chapter 10; "Biblical Hermeneutics in the Theologies of Liberation," by J. Severino Croatto, Chapter 11.

6. See Final Statement, paragraph 7.

7. See Final Statement, paragraphs 9–18.

8. See Final Statement, paragraph 26.

9. See Roy, "Socio-Economic and Political Context."

10. See Sergio Torres, "The Irruption of the Third World: A Challenge to Theology," Chapter 1.

11. See Pieris's article in Part III, p. 113.

12. Just as any Third World theology will be irrelevant if it disregards the experience and aspirations of the majority who are not Christians, so any Christian theology will be irrelevant if it does not take into consideration the experience and aspirations of the Third World, where the majority of Christians now live.

13. This is not to deny the fact that in their historical manifestations world religions have generally contributed to the alienation of the masses. See Final Statement, paragraph 55.

14. See Rayan, "Theological Priorities in India Today" in Part II, p. 37.

15. See J. Russell Chandran, "A Methodological Approach to Third World Theology," in Part III, p. 80.

16. Cf. Aloysius Pieris, "Towards an Asian Theology of Liberation: Some Religio-Cultural Guidelines," in Fabella, *Asia's Struggle,* pp. 81-82. Pieris also points out some of the historical abuses of monastic poverty.

17. Cf. Torres and Fabella, *Emergent Gospel,* for the complete text of the Dar-es-Salaam Final Statement.

18. *Bulletin of African Theology* is published by the Ecumenical Association of African Theologians, B.P. 823, Kinshasa XI, Republic of Zaire.

19. Cf. Pieris, "Towards an Asian Theology of Liberation," in Fabella, *Asia's Struggle,* p. 80.

20. See Final Statement, paragraphs 61-71.

21. See Amba Oduyoye, "Reflections from a Third World Woman's Perspective: Women's Experience and Liberation Theologies," in Part VI, p. 250.

22. See Bonganjalo Goba, "Emerging Theological Perspectives in South Africa," in Part II, Chapter 2.

23. Cf. S. Rayan, in *Vidyajyoti,* March 1982, p. 116.

24. See Gustavo Gutiérrez, "Reflections from a Latin American Perspective: Finding our Way to Talk about God," in Part VI, p. 225.

25. S. Rayan, *Vidyajyoti,* pp. 122, 126.

26. See Emilio J. M. de Carvalho, "Hope for the Future," in Part VI, Chapter 21.

PART I

THE CHALLENGE OF THE THIRD WORLD

1

The Irruption of the Third World: A Challenge to Theology

Sergio Torres

It is in God's name that we come together for the fifth international conference of the Ecumenical Association of Third World Theologians (EATWOT), following those held in São Paulo (1980), Wennappuwa (1979), Accra (1977), and Dar es Salaam (1976). We must be conscious of the responsibility that we assume. We are accountable to the masses of our countries who suffer deprivation and oppression. We represent groups of Christians who share the hope of the resurrection of Jesus Christ. We are committed to articulate a theological synthesis that will include our similarities and differences in dialogue with other world religions.

At the very beginning, I want to draw attention to the overarching twofold theme that we shall be addressing: the irruption of the poor as a challenge to the present international economic order, and as a challenge to theology.

THE IRRUPTION OF THE POOR: A CHALLENGE TO THE PRESENT INTERNATIONAL ECONOMIC ORDER

We call ourselves theologians of the Third World. To be true to this calling, we have to bring the Third World realities of poverty and oppression into our theology. The deterioration of the conditions of the poor, the growing gap between the rich and the poor countries, the confrontation between the northern and the southern hemispheres, the brute facts of racism, sexism, and cultural domination are integral parts of the context in which we live and work. At the same time, we see signs of hope in the struggle of the poor against all forms of oppression and we follow carefully the efforts of our governments toward a New International Economic Order (NIEO).

The Politico-Economic Framework of Reference

Historically the Third World countries have been part of the capitalist system of the West. Even though more and more of them, in the last twenty years, have chosen the socialist political system, still, as a whole, the Third World is caught up in the international economy dominated by Europe, the United States, and, more recently, Westernized Japan.

Today there is a consensus that capitalism is undergoing a worldwide economic and social crisis. It started in 1967 and became more visible with the oil shortage of 1973. This crisis has consequences for all the nations of the First, the Second, and the Third Worlds.

FIRST WORLD

Between 1945 and 1970—the postwar years—the West, spearheaded by the U.S.A., experienced a spectacular economic growth and development. But, as one author commented, "It was a boom for the West and a bust for the South."[1]

Economists and political leaders agree that around 1970 the West entered into a new economic crisis, which could be similar to those of 1869 to 1895 or 1919 to 1932 in the history of capitalism.[2]

The signs of the ongoing crisis are: high level of unemployment, inflation combined with recession (stagflation), slow growth, low profit from investment, protectionism, cuts in welfare allocations, and the like. Technically, it is defined as a crisis of overaccumulation of capital.[3]

Political leaders of the West, advised by business executives and orthodox economists, have reacted against the crisis, adopting various solutions to protect their economies. These measures, in turn, have had negative consequences for the economies of the Third World.[4] All countries attempt to reduce the cost of production through austerity policies, which have resulted in increased unemployment.

But what is more important for us, there is a clear determination of the rich countries to assign, in the international division of labor, a new role to the Third World as low-wage producers in the present world economic crisis.[5]

SECOND WORLD

During the last decade, the socialist countries have increased their trade with the West in order to import Western technology. As a result, they have a deficit in their balance of payments, which is covered with loans from Western banks.[6] The crisis in Poland is a clear sign of this compounded predicament.

There are conflicting views and opinions about the role of the socialist economies at the present time.[7] Some analysts affirm that today there is only one world market—the capitalist. The socialist economies, and particularly those of Eastern Europe, are being integrated into the capitalist market as buyers, sellers, and producers. The socialist East occupies an intermediate place in the international division of labor between the capitalist West and the Third World.

Socialist leaders say that the socialist countries cannot be isolated from the world. It is wise for them to take advantage of the progress of science and technology in favor of their peoples. They also argue that there really are two markets because the socialist countries plan their economies, and not according to the capitalist laws of value and market forces.

There are also conflicting opinions about the consistency of the socialist states with their own basic principles. Some of them have resolved their basic needs in a comparatively short time, which is a major accomplishment. But observers wonder about the quality of life in socialist societies, about freedom and real democracy. It is important to listen to the non-aligned countries when they say that the Soviet Union has been the natural ally of Third World countries. This has been true in many corners of the world. But at the same time the Soviet Union, with its politico-economic policies, sometimes supports bourgeois forces and reactionary states.

For thirty years China has been a model of self-reliance for the masses of the poor of the world.[8] But the Chinese domestic policy of the four modernizations, especially since the death of Mao Tse-tung, and the foreign policy of "the enemy of my enemy is my friend," have also led to Chinese alliances with reactionary forces in other parts of the world.

It is important to be attentive to what is happening in the socialist countries. In the Third World there are Christians who consider scientific socialism to be an objective understanding of nature and history. They tend to believe that socialism will be the next stage of history, after capitalism.

At the same time, however, they say that science cannot be considered a dogma and that the implementation of socialism in their societies is neither mechanical nor automatic. Subjective factors, particularly freedom and religion, play an important role in the historical development of objective factors in the transition to socialism. Those Christians also hope that it will be possible to combine socialism with more participation and more creativity on the part of the people in decisions about their future.

Why should we turn a deaf ear to the worldwide discussion about capitalism and socialism? We follow very carefully the politico-economic crisis in England and other capitalist countries. We also consider very important what is happening in Poland. It is true that there are revisionists there, who want to go back to the past, and there is also Western intervention. But at the same time there is no doubt that the Polish working class is looking for more participation in decisions about its own destiny and is reacting against the bureaucracy of the party and the state.

We hope to see the socialist countries of the Third World—Cuba, Vietnam, Ethiopia, Angola, Mozambique, and others—implement an independent, national model of socialism and advance the process of democratization and participation.

We have high expectations about Nicaragua. We express our solidarity with the pastors, nuns, priests and lay Christians working within the process of reconstruction. They are making an important political and theological contribution to the dialogue between revolution and Christianity.[9]

THIRD WORLD

During the last two decades the world community has been drawn around the reality and the future of the poor of the Third World. The United Nations, voluntary agencies, and the churches have become aware of the growing gap between the rich and poor countries.[10]

Through their own organization, the poor countries have been able to formulate programs for possible solutions and have denounced the injustice of the present international economic order.[11]

It is important for our theological purposes that we discuss some of the issues involved in this context.

Deterioration of the Condition of the Poor. All the efforts of the international organizations and governments of the Third World can give the impression that the condition of the poor has improved. In reality the opposite is true. The poor today are in a worse condition than twenty years ago. Many of the development programs have helped to increase the national wealth but its maldistribution has increased the wealth of an elite and has sunk the poor into deeper poverty.

There is much evidence to confirm this assertion.[12] But what we want to underline here is that the poor themselves are becoming aware of the causes of poverty. Today there is a growing consensus that povery is a *systemic* condition: "Poverty then seems to be the consequence of a process within the operation of a system in which a few economically powerful people wield political power to control institutions for their own private profit."[13]

Racism. Racism is an evil that still exists in many countries of the world. Indians, blacks, and other persons of color, all over the globe but especially in the Third World, undergo discrimination, segregation, and dehumanization because of differences of race and color:

> Racism is seen in every part of the world and in some countries it is more obvious in that it is legally enforced. Racism is also a factor in numerous violations of human rights and fundamental freedoms in many countries.[14]

The churches themselves are not free of the sin of racism: "It is a matter of shame for the Christian churches around the world, which are all too often infested by racism."[15]

We should pay special attention to the study of this form of oppression. There are two mistakes to be avoided in our approach: to reduce racism to its economic dimension of class, or to isolate racism from structural considerations and separate the struggle against racism from the other struggles for integral human liberation.

It is necessary also to develop an organic theology of racial integrity, based on the belief that all human beings are created equal—in the image of God (Gen. 1:27)—and all are called in Christ to the same hope (Col. 1:15).

We salute the World Council of Churches; through its Program to Combat Racism it has awakened the conscience of Christians and churches to fight against the sin of racism in the churches and in society.[16]

Sexism. The subjugation of women in Third World societies is a tragedy that has not been resolved. There is little evidence of progress in overcoming male domination in society and in the churches. The patriarchal pattern of culture and civilization constrains women to be subject to men, to male-defined rules, and to a patriarchal God.[17]

We have to admit that EATWOT does not have a good record on promoting women in theology. We are still a male-dominated organization.

We ask women to help our group and others to move on this issue and to find the determination to work for equality between men and women. Women's participation should be a basic element in articulating the anticapitalist and antipatriarchal struggle.

Women should assume a more active role in theology. We have to read the Bible in a new way. Beyond the cultural and anthropological mediations through which the Bible speaks, we must rediscover the example of Jesus and reformulate christology and ecclesiology from a perspective that is not—consciously or unconsciously—male-centered.[18]

Cultural Domination. Economic domination has resulted in cultural deterioration in Third World countries. Traditional cultures, racial and ethnic values, customs and usages, religious rites, family and clan relationships were disrupted by the colonial powers.[19]

The mass media have been the channel through which the Western influence is carried on now after colonialism. Newspapers, magazines, radio, television, and films are strongly influenced by, and dependent on, the rich countries.[20] Formal education also plays a role in the domestication of indigenous cultures. Cultural domination cannot be separated from economic oppression. The culture and ideology of the dominant classes are socialized through formal education and the media.

It is necessary to react against this new form of domination. The nonaligned countries said in their 1976 declaration that the "establishment of a new international order in the field of information and mass media, for the purpose of forging new international relations in general," is an urgent necessity.[21] Some people are talking about a "New International Socio-Cultural Order" (NISCO).[22]

We as theologians must look very carefully at all these efforts. We should be sensitive to the problems of culture, education, and popular religion. Even though they belong to the infrastructures of social formations and are influenced by the mode of production, they have some autonomy and are in a dialectical relationship with the economic basis of a given society. At that level, conscientization, political involvement, and Christian commitment can play an important role in changes within that society.

Transfer of Technology. Science and technology have had a fantastic development in modern times. The scientific community of the rich countries is discovering more and more what God has hidden in nature and history.

The World Council of Churches and the Academy of Sciences of the Vatican follow the development of scientific discoveries and try to evaluate the progress and the ambiguities of science.[23]

Technology, however, has become another weapon against the countries of the Third World. The second industrial revolution has accumulated in the hands of the rich countries the fruits of one and a half centuries of technical progress.[24]

Today it is impossible to upgrade a national economy without technology. And there is no open market where the needed technology can be bought. The Third World countries find themselves dependent on the developed countries for progress and development. "Since the industrialized countries hold the monopoly of technology, they give access to it on one condition only, which is that their own capital must be the agent of the transfer of this technology."[25]

These are some of the issues that we have to take into consideration when we study the Third World as the context of our theological reflection.

The poor constitute the majority of the world's population and should become the active subjects—not the passive objects—of history. We have to insert ourselves in the movement of the poor for a more just society and keep in mind that "the whole of the biblical record reveals that the struggles of the poor for their liberation are signs of God's action in history, and as such are experienced as imperfect and provisional seeds of the definitive Kingdom."[26]

A New International Economic Order

The growing gap between rich and poor countries and the deteriorating conditions of the disadvantaged masses have forced Third World governments to demand a New International Economic Order (NIEO).[27]

This process started with the sixth special session of the United Nations, in 1974. It was considered a diplomatic victory for the poor of the world and has been followed through at many international conferences since then.[28]

The demands of the Third World have been elaborated at the UN, UNCTAD, FAO, North-South Dialogue, and elsewhere. Some of their demands are: more money through another monetary system; open access to the markets of the developed countries for their exports; higher and more stable prices for raw materials; unconditioned transfer of technology; a code of ethics for transnational corporations; cooperation among Third World countries; formation of a "solidarity fund."[29]

Despite a long succession of international conferences and the hopes pinned to numerical strength, progress toward NIEO has been almost nil. The proposals of the North incorporated in the "Brandt Report" represent a program that would not alter the basic structures of injustice in the international economic order.[30]

We need to be very lucid and to have a prophetic vision about the efforts for NIEO. We reject and condemn the attitude of the rich countries that do not want to make any concessions and do not want to give up their lifestyle made possible by the plundering of our riches and resources.[31]

Most of the NIEO conferences are an effort to convince the rich and the powerful to alleviate the suffering of the poor and to work toward the transformation of the prevailing international structures. But, "it is a vain attempt to ask the wealthy and the powerful of the existing societies to dispose of much of their resources and abdicate their positions of power. There are very few instances in history when the powerful have abrogated their power willingly and changed the system that protected their interests."[32]

As Christians and Third World theologians, we should emphasize the political power of the people and put our confidence in the masses. We should encourage the Third World political movements that seek a negotiated breakthrough supported by the power of our poverty, of our natural resources, and of our cultural richness, and the hopes of youth, women, and urban and rural workers. That is our vocation. The hope for real liberation points in that direction.

THE IRRUPTION OF THE POOR: A CHALLENGE TO THEOLOGY

The Poor Challenge the Churches and Theology

The poor call into question the mission and the identity of the church. "The poor are challenging the Church to rethink its mission and reorder its priorities in the light of its redemptive role in human history as proclaimed in the Gospel."[33]

It is still true that ecclesiastical institutions, by and large, reflect the worldview and the values of the middle classes of society. Despite the progress of many Christian communities, the poor do not feel at home in this church.

The church needs to be converted. History shows that when Christian leaders identify themselves with the powerful of the world, the church fails to fulfill its responsibility that "the poor [hear] the good news" (Luke 7:23).

And the poor will be at the center of the life of the church, but not because the rich and the middle classes favor the idea. The poor will have to turn to the help of the Spirit: "The church of the poor is also a result of the work of the Holy Spirit through a process in which the people themselves are taking a leading role."[34]

In Dar es Salaam we said: "Theology is not neutral."[35] Nor can the church be neutral:

> The church can never be neutral in society, it is either for or against. Its silence in vital issues of poverty and human anguish is a clear indication of its preoccupation with the oppressive system which impoverishes over three-fourths of the world's population. Silence is acquiescence and acceptance is collaboration.[36]

We have to respond to some questions that the poor are asking: Is Jesus still in the church? Should the poor look outside the church for help in their struggle? Does the church find Christ in the poor? These are hard and challenging questions. But they are relevant and cannot be dismissed.

It has always been our assumption that the poor also challenge traditional theology. EATWOT justifies itself as an attempt to develop a new theological reflection based on this assumption. We find a clear description of this kind of theology in the declaration of an Asian group: "Theological thinking is truly historical when it deals with the historical transformation of the structures of dehumanization and injustice."[37]

Change and conversion take time. Theology, not only in the North, but also in seminaries and divinity schools of Third World countries, is ahistorical. "This is due in part to the priority given to the systemization and conceptualization of Christian symbols without constant reference to the historical life of the Christian community."[38] Because theology is ahistorical it can become part of oppressive systems and structures.

There are at the same time efforts being made toward a contextual and historical theology that starts with the poor and the oppressed. Especially interesting is the rediscovery of the Bible by the poor themselves. "When they open the Bible the poor want to find there the things of life, and in life they want to find the things of the Bible. Understanding the Bible as a critical mirror of reality awakens a sense of inquiry in the people."[39]

Salvation in the Context of Religions and Cultures

It was in Wennappuwa, Sri Lanka, in 1979, at the Asian Theological Conference of EATWOT, that we became more conscious of the relationship between Christianity and other religions.

This is another crucial issue. It is wrong for Christians to ignore the existence of other world faiths that provide spiritual homes for hundreds of millions of persons. Islam, Buddhism, Hinduism, in Asia; traditional religions in Africa; Indian beliefs and the popular practice of religion in Latin America; black Christianity in the U.S.A.—all of these challenge the institutional churches of the Christian tradition with very important questions.

Christianity has traditionally considered itself the universal faith and the exclusive way of salvation. Christians believe that "Jesus Christ is Lord of all." He is the only Savior. "There is no salvation in anyone else at all, for there is no other name under heaven granted to men by which we may receive salvation" (Acts 4:12).

This claim clashes with the existence of many other solid and well-established faiths and religions. It is at this point that the theological basis of the relationship between Christianity and the other religions has to be reformulated. This process has already begun and has been entered into by the institutional churches.[40]

But we need to recognize that we are not yet prepared for this dialogue:

It must be said that Christianity—both its theologians and its missionaries—is far from equipped for such an encounter. Despite the growing number of words written and spoken concerning a "theology of the religions" over the past fifteen years, Christian thinkers are still not agreed on how to fit the religions into the economy of salvation, nor on how far we can go in dialoguing with and accepting them.[41]

Despite this difficulty, there is a history of theological development on such dialogue, by both Protestant and Catholic theologians. It ranges from Christian absolutism, such as that of Karl Barth,[42] to religious popularism, such as that of Ernest Troeltsch.[43] Somewhere between are Wolfhart Pannenberg,[44] Paul Tillich,[45] Piet Schoonenberg,[46] and Karl Rahner.[47]

On the Catholic side, one of the most important developments was the Vatican II "Declaration on the Relation of the Church to Non-Christian Religion." It showed a significant change in the rigid position of the Catholic Church.[48]

Some issues have been clarified; others still remain unresolved. There are two that belong to the core of this discussion: revelation and salvation. Today most Protestant and Catholic theologians would agree that there is divine revelation in the non-Christian religions.

There is less agreement on the issue of salvation. Many Protestants, with the exception of those working in the Commission on Dialogue with People of Living Faiths and Secular Ideologies of the World Council of Churches, tend to deny the possibility of salvation outside the Christian faith. Catholic theologians affirm the possibility of salvation apart from explicit recognition of Christ, though Christ is the privileged way.

Theologians from countries of the Third World have taken up the discussion. Dr. Choan-Seng Song says that it has been a mistake to reflect "on Asian or African cultures and histories from the vantage-point of the messianic hope which is believed to be lodged in the history of the Christian Church . . . and redemption loses its intrinsic meaning for cultures and histories outside the history of Christianity."[49]

Raymond Panikkar thinks that Christianity and Hinduism are very compatible: "Hinduism and Christianity as two God-believing religions undoubtedly meet in God. We do not say that they meet in their conception of

God, but in God, in the Absolute, in the Ultimate."[50] He goes beyond that point of encounter: "Christ is already at work in any Hindu prayer as far as it is really prayer; Christ is behind any form of worship in as much as it is adoration made to God."[51]

We must study this crucial relationship between Christianity and the other religions from a Third World perspective. And we must search for a common approach that takes into consideration both our likenesses and our differences.

It will be well to remember what we have said in Wennappuwa, Sri Lanka, and to discuss religions and popular culture in relation to poverty. This could be an original contribution from our perspective.

We have to react against the tendency of the dominant classes that disdain popular culture and its religious expressions. Popular religions have a tremendous survival capacity; it surprises theologians and social scientists. It seems that "there exists undoubtedly a significant reserve of resistance and hope, which can never be destroyed by colonial domination, by the process of secularization of the enlightened elites, or by the consumer culture of world capitalism."[52]

Even in the socialist countries, including Russia and China, popular culture and the religious traditions of racial minorities survive the assaults of scientific socialism.

The value, strength, and characteristics of the religion and culture of the people must be essential components of Third World theology.

Reformulation of Traditional Themes

EATWOT has helped to develop a different method for theological discourse. We emphasize the role of the praxis of the poor as the starting point for reflection on the Christian faith. We read the Bible from the underside of history.[53]

I believe that we still have to devote some time to this methodology. We have to find a critical formulation that can be applied to similar situations, yet make allowance for diverse real-life contexts and cultures.

I also believe that it is time for us to start a reformulation of some traditional themes of theology from a Third World perspective. Some of these themes refer to God, Jesus, and the mission of the church. We have been criticized because in the final statements of our past conferences we did not speak enough about God and Jesus Christ. But those final statements did indeed highlight themes that express the foundational realities of our faith.

(1) With non-Christian religions we share a common faith in the Ultimate. But we need to understand God in a different way. We have been deeply influenced by the speculations of Greek philosophy about God. It will be necessary that we pool our experiences and find the mediations through which God can be recognized as the source of life and meaning for all of us.

The God of the Bible, revealed in Jesus Christ, is a liberating God. We proclaim God as the God of love, savior and deliverer of all peoples. But we want also to dialogue with the God of African traditional religions and with the God of Hinduism and Islam. Maybe a theology based on the covenant established with Adam and with Noah could be the common ground for a recognition of the same God.

(2) In the Third World there has been a rediscovery of the historical Jesus. This is not the Jesus of the liberal tradition in Protestantism. The Third World has sought an understanding of Jesus according to the historical circumstances in which he lived.

The praxis of Jesus, his way of life, serves as inspiration and source of commitment and obedience for thousands of Christians of the Third World. We need to explore that way of life. But we also need to listen to the other religions and understand how they look at Jesus. We have to be open to their questions and to their challenges.

(3) In São Paulo in 1980, we discussed the role of the church in relationship to the kingdom of God. We said that, "In the Third World context we must recall that the church does not exist for itself, but to serve human beings in the building of the Kingdom of God, revealing to them the power of the Kingdom present in history, witnessing to the presence of Christ the Liberator and to his Spirit in the events and in the signs of the life in the peoples' march.''[54] But even this affirmation has to be tested and verified in the reality of the concrete existence of the local churches. For the peoples of the Third World, Christianity has been more a hindrance than a liberating force. How can we define the mission of the church on our continents?

It seems to me that these are some of the theological themes that we need to explore very carefully. We are faced with a heavy but exciting challenge. I ask God's guidance for our journey. I am confident that we will give the best of ourselves to respond to this challenge.

We also need to find time for discussion about the future of EATWOT. This is a different kind of challenge. During the past five years, the association became more alive at the time of the annual conferences. After our dialogues with First World theologians, we will not hold annual conferences. We will need creativity, imagination, and commitment if we want to stay together. Otherwise EATWOT will die and disappear. We cannot, however, keep the organization going for superficial reasons. EATWOT will stay alive only if it has clear goals and something to contribute.

In the past five years, I have devoted a great deal of my energies to EATWOT. I have seen it grow and develop. Seeds have been watered by tears of sorrow and exile.

We are grateful to all those who have made a contribution to the growth of EATWOT—Russell Chandran, the president, and all the other members, as also Orbis Books, agencies and donors, friends and institutions in the U.S.A., in Canada, in Europe, in the Third World. Virginia Fabella, our program coordinator, deserves a special word of gratitude. EATWOT has been the beneficiary of her religious commitment and dedication. She deserves our thanks for this and the help she has given in coordinating the preparations for the present conference.

We are in the beginning of a new stage. What is our task for the next five years? That is for us to discern and to risk together, with the Spirit guiding us.

NOTES

1. A. G. Frank, *Crisis: In the World Economy* (London: Heinemann, 1980), p. 1.

2. See ibid., p. 34.

3. See ibid., pp. 32–73.

4. See ibid., p. 102.

5. See ibid., p. 263.

6. See ibid., p. 182.

7. See the four opinions about the role of the socialist countries in A. G. Frank, ibid., p. 182.

8. See Kwan Ha Yim, ed., *China Since Mao* (London: Macmillan, 1980).

9. See MIEC-JECI, *Iglesia de Nicaragua: Tiempo de crisis, tiempo de discernimiento y de gracia* (Lima: Centro de Documentación, 1981).

10. See Robert L. Rothstein, *Global Bargaining: UNCTAD and the Quest for a New Economic Order* (Princeton, N.J.: Princeton University Press, 1979).

11. See Robert A. Mortimer, *The Third World Coalition in International Politics* (New York: Praeger, 1980).

12. See A. G. Frank, *Crisis*, pp. 12–15.

13. Julio de Santa Ana, ed., *Towards a Church of the Poor* (Geneva: World Council of Churches, 1979), p. 25. The Commission on the Churches' Participation in Development (CCPD), of the World Council of Churches, has made an important contribution to the new understanding of the church of the poor through a special program that published, besides the one just mentioned, two other books on the subject, edited by Julio de Santa Ana: *Good News to the Poor: The Challenge of the Poor in the History of the Church* (1977) and *Separation Without Hope?* (1978); U.S. editions have been published by Orbis Books.

14. Julio de Santa Ana, ed., *Towards a Church of the Poor*, p. 27.

15. Ibid.

16. The World Council of Churches held a World Consultation on Racism in Noord-wijkerhout, Netherlands, June 16–21, 1980, "Churches Responding to Racism in the 1980s." The Central Committee of the WCC, meeting in Geneva, August 14–22, 1980, reaffirmed the controversial Program to Combat Racism.

17. See Cora Ferro, "The Latin American Woman: The Praxis and Theology of Liberation," in Sergio Torres and John Eagleson, eds., *The Challenge of Basic Christian Communities* (Maryknoll, Orbis, 1981), pp. 24–37.

18. See Ibid., pp. 34–35.

19. See Sergio Torres and Virginia Fabella, eds., *The Emergent Gospel* (Maryknoll, N.Y.: Orbis, 1977), p. 262.

20. See Karl P. Sanvant, "From Economic to Socio-Cultural Emancipation: The Historical Context of the New International Economic Order and "The New International Socio-Cultural Order," *Third World Quarterly,* 3/1 (1981): 57–58.

21. Odette Sankowitsch and Karl P. Sanvant, ed., *The Third World Without Superpowers: The Collected Documents of the Non-Aligned Countries* (Dobbs Ferry, N.Y.: Oceana, 1978), pp. 1554–55.

22. See Karl P. Sanvant, "New International Order," p. 48.

23. See *Anticipation,* No. 19, *Science and Technology for Human Development: Report of the 1974 Conference on Church and Society, Bucharest* (Geneva: WCC, 1975).

24. See Celso Furtado, *Prefacio a Nova Económica Política* (Rio de Janeiro: Ed. Paz e Terra), p. 135.

25. Julio de Santa Ana, *Towards a Church of the Poor,* p. 39.

26. Final Statement (São Paulo Conference), in Sergio Torres and John Eagleson, eds., *The Challenge of Basic Christian Communities* (Maryknoll, N.Y.: Orbis, 1981), p. 235.

27. See note 10, above.

28. See Robert A. Mortimer, *Third World Coalition,* p. 48.

29. See Robert L. Rothstein, *Global Bargaining,* p. 135.

30. The Brandt Report was published under the title *North-South: A Programme for Survivial* (London: Pan, 1980). This report received wide publicity. It has been criticized by Third World economists and political leaders.

31. See A. G. Frank, *Crisis,* p. 255.

32. Julio de Santa Ana, *Towards a Church of the Poor,* p. xviii.

33. Ibid., p. 97.

34. Ibid., p. 68.

35. Torres and Fabella, eds., *The Emergent Gospel,* p. 270.

36. Julio de Santa Ana, *Towards a Church of the Poor,* p. 98.

37. *Towards a Theology of People,* vol. 1 (Tokyo: CCA-URM, 1977), p. 174.

38. Julio de Santa Ana, *Towards a Church of the Poor,* p. 121.

39. Ibid., p. 72.

40. The Catholic Church, after Vatican II, established the Secretariat for Non-Christian Religions, and the World Council of Churches has initiated a program called "Dialogue with People of Living Faiths and Ideologies."

41. Paul Knitter, "European Protestant and Catholic Approaches to the World Religions: Complements and Contrast," *Journal of Ecumenical Studies,* 12/1 (1975): 14–28.

42. Karl Barth, *Church Dogmatics,* vols. 1 and 2, section 17 (Edinburgh: Clark, 1956).

43. Ernst Troeltsch, *The Absoluteness of Christianity* (1901) (Atlanta: John Knox Press, 1971).

44. Wolfhart Pannenberg, *Towards a Theology of the History of Religions* (Philadelphia, 1971).

45. Paul Tillich, *The Philosophy of Religion* (New York, 1969).

46. P. Schoonenberg, "The Church and the Non-Christian Religions," in D. Flanagan, ed., *The Meaning of the Church* (Dublin, 1966).

47. Karl Rahner, *Christianity and Non-Christian Religions* (*Theological Investigations,* 5), pp. 115–34; idem, *The Anonymous Christians* (*Theological Investigations,* 6) (New York: Seabury, 1966), pp. 390–98.

48. *The Conciliar and Post-Conciliar Documents,* Austin Flannery, ed. (Northport, N.Y.: Costello), pp. 738–42.

49. Choan-Seng Song, "From Israel to Asia, A Theological Leap," *Mission Trends,* no. 3, p. 211.

50. Raymond Panikkar, *The Unknown Christ of Hinduism* (London: Darton, Longman and Todd, 1964), p. 138.

51. Ibid.

52. Julio de Santa Ana, *Towards a Church of the Poor,* p. 57.

53. Torres and Fabella, eds., *The Emergent Gospel.*

54. Torres and Eagleson, eds., *The Challenge of Basic Christian Communities,* p. 237.

PART II

EMERGING THEOLOGIES
IN THIRD WORLD CONTEXTS

2

Emerging Theological Perspectives in South Africa

Bonganjalo Goba

It is not just a privilege to be here but a great challenge to me personally, for I am aware how inadequate our role has been as members of the black Christian community to challenge and eradicate the structures of bondage devouring our people. For as you all must be aware, our situation in South Africa with its policy of apartheid poses one of the most formidable challenges to the future of Christianity in the entire subcontinent.

SOUTH AFRICA: THE REALITY

Our situation, with its sophisticated, racist socio-political structures, raises serious fundamental questions about the role of Christians in a society gone mad because a white minority believes it has a divine right to dominate the black majority, and in doing so solicits the support of the Western international community. This has broadened the dimension of the struggle of blacks, for they confront the monster of oppression both at home and abroad. This dimension of the struggle must be taken into consideration when we look at developing trends in theology in the South African context.

The victims in South Africa—the black community—are victimized by a syndicate of Western powers working closely with the white South African regime, and this is something we share with many of our brothers and sisters in other parts of the Third World. But we all also have a common destiny, and that destiny is to realize our liberation here and now. This has very serious theological implications for all of us as members of the Body of Christ.

South Africa continues to dominate the agendas of many world bodies. This suggests that the problems we confront as members of an oppressed community are very complex and will demand a sacrifice from many of our communities brutalized by the unrestrained force of a police state. As we see more and more of our young leaders being banned or silenced, we are more and more aware of the conspiracy of Western powers.

As we groan under the yoke of a massive and well-coordinated system of oppression, we can no longer look outside for help. Instead, we are challenged to discover within ourselves the power to liberate ourselves. That power is our faith and commitment to respond to the call of liberation embodied in the Christian vision. This vision we share with you as we engage in the struggle for liberation and as we confront the same monster of oppression together. Your struggle and ours invites each one of us to a realization of how much we need each other and how important it is to understand our respective situations critically.

Looking at the Reality

Those of us who are involved in theological reflection in South Africa have become aware that we cannot theologize without looking at the South African reality. To attempt to do so is to misunderstand the challenge of faith in Jesus Christ.

We are also aware that it is no longer tolerable to perpetuate the theologies of death that have dominated our church traditions and our lack of involvement in the struggle of our people. Our theological agenda is no longer to be dictated by a foreign theological community somewhere in Europe. South Africa itself has become the first item on our theological agenda. It is for this reason that theological conflict has emerged in the Christian community in South Africa. This is a source of polarization in the churches, for those of us who belong to the oppressed community are committed to a new theological perspective, one that confronts the socio-political dynamics of South African society. On the other hand, those who belong to the dominant Christian community, with few exceptions, are committed to a theology of establishment or what is sometimes called apartheid theology.

Let me share with you some of the key issues that confront us in the South African situation. There is no doubt in my mind that one of the current problems in the South African situation is the prevalence of what I call a colonial type of Christianity. Let me explain what I mean.

Christianity in South Africa has played a major role in supporting and defending the ideology of apartheid. From its inception it worked hand in hand with the colonial administration. It played a major role in destroying the cultural values of our traditional communities. This is why many of our traditional peoples continue to reject Christianity as a force of oppression. This attitude is maintained especially by young blacks who equate Christianity with apartheid and the existing capitalistic structures of the economy. In many ways this continues to be at the center of the problem confronting the churches in South Africa. The oppressive socio-political structures of our divided society are painfully reflected in church structures. I hope to show later how this continues to be reflected in the theology of the dominant white

Christian group. Christianity, if it is to play an important role, will have to be liberated from the structures of bondage embodied in the policy of apartheid.

The other issue that I believe constitutes one of the key problem areas in our conflict is the question of land. Today we blacks occupy 13 percent of the land; the rest belongs to the white minority. The land issue has been the source of many challenges in our struggle. One cannot take on the prevailing socio-economic problems without addressing the land issue. The exploitative loss of our land has created a frightening state of dependency in our people in terms of labor and means of livelihood. The original owners, deprived of their means of production, had no alternative but to work for the new owners simply in order to survive. The land issue has also brought it about that our movements are closely monitored by the dominant group.

As blacks we have lost virtually all our land. Most of our people live in unwanted areas or resettlement camps—areas infested with disease and all kinds of socio-economic problems. I need not give you much detail about this, for Cosmos Desmond has documented it very well in his book *The Discarded People* and those of you who have seen the film "The Last Grave at Dimbaza" understand what I am talking about. The issue of land will have to be examined in our theological reflections, and it is being done by those who are closely involved in the struggle. We are also becoming aware as an oppressed people that this subject must be given very high priority in our theology especially because land to us black Africans has a sacred character. It is closely associated with deep religious ties that we have with our ancestors.

There is yet another key issue, that of racism. The ideology of apartheid ensures that at all levels of South African society whites dominate. This means that we, as blacks, cannot participate fully in the institutions of our society, nor can we make even a minimal contribution to establishing a society of which we could be proud. Because of racial conflict we do not share the values of the white dominant group, nor do they share our values. Our communities are ideologically opposed, and as a consequence our country is heading for a serious confrontation that could result in a bloody revolution. Racism is like cancer in our society; it destroys all attempts being made to work toward a common society. The churches are just as racist in their general outlook and organizational structures as is our society. This racism has long been justified theologically in what we call the theology of apartheid.

No one should underestimate the racial character of our struggle in South Africa. To understand the dynamics of the South African conflict one will have to confront the problem of racism, particularly as it is reflected in the socio-political structures of our society. The struggle against white domination is also at the center of our concern in theological reflection. As we struggle to reassert our God-given dignity we shall continue to fight the monster of racism. This is a challenge not only for South Africans but for all who are committed to the struggle for integral human liberation—everywhere.

Political Developments

Many, especially in the West, are under an illusion that things are changing for the better in South Africa. Some have even gone to the extent of consolidating their old relationships with the white South African regime, as in the case of the Washington administration. At the same time, through a very sophisticated network of friends, the South African regime is trying to convince the world that it is moving away from the policy of apartheid. There is a lot of talk about constitutional changes in South Africa under the guise of the President's Council.

What *we* see in these so-called constitutional changes is titivation of the oppressive structures of apartheid; nothing has changed. The structures of apartheid are intact. Our society is going through a very cunning process of giving apartheid respectability. The motive is very clear—to get the support of dominant Western capitalistic societies. To win these countries over, a new gospel is being preached—that of the free-enterprise system, supported in the mass media by its well-known disciples, eager to promote its cause. This is why Milton Friedman's economic ideas are popular among the economic theorists of the white ruling elite in South Africa.

The major political *parties* in the country are exclusively white. They have one thing in common: to maintain the federal political system. There is a playing down of the ethnic pluralism in our society, especially by white politicians and some of the black Bantustan—"homeland"—leaders. This has led many of them to reject the concept of democratic majoritarianism. On the other hand, most of the significant political *movements* in the country and abroad are committed to a unitary state adhering to the main ideas reflected in the Freedom Charter.[1] The "changes" that are envisaged by white politicians are there to ensure that whites will continue to dominate the political decision-making process. This is part of the mockery of the so-called consociational democracy. At the ideological level this way of thinking is shared by the white Christian community. It is at this point that we question whether we can expect any radical theological reorientation from the white Christian community in South Africa.

One conclusion we must draw is that the present white political thinking, even among the so-called opposition parties, supports the status quo.

In black political thinking, there is a clear commitment to the struggle for liberation especially among our young people. The explosive events of 1976, in which many young persons were killed by the South African police, continue to inspire our people to confront the monster of oppression. At the wellspring of black political thinking, black consciousness continues to be a dominant force. What Steve Biko and other leaders succeeded in doing was to promote a new revolutionary consciousness by inculcating in the minds of our young blacks a sense of pride and a clear commitment to values that arise from our experience. This has had a tremendous influence in the way we do theology. Although many of the young leaders of this movement have been banned or are now outside the country, the impact of this movement continues to be a critical force in our struggle. This has given our struggle an important dimension in that it has managed to create political solidarity among our people at a time when the present white regime is trying to divide us by creating bogus political institutions at the tribal level.

The other important dimension emerging in the black struggle in the South African situation is the challenge of black trade unions. This is not at all a new feature in our struggle, but more and more our peoples are realizing that economic issues must be confronted and that one of the ways of challenging the existing political structures is through strikes. This is why we have had numerous strikes in the past three years, throughout the country. This is a crucial matter, for many multinational corporations continue to dominate the economy of the country.

The Present Dilemma of the Churches

Political development in South Africa serves as a thought-provoking context for examining the role of the Christian churches. I mentioned earlier that the churches reflect the same oppressive patterns as does South African society. The majority of white Christians support the status quo and their political vision is no different from that of white politicians. Over the years there are those within the Dutch Reformed churches who have given theological support to the ideology of apartheid. Although there has been a shift among some of the younger white theologians in the Dutch Reformed churches and Afrikaans-speaking churches, the leadership of these churches is still committed to the ideology of apartheid. The struggle of the church in the South African situation must be to free itself from this ideological captivity to apartheid. Unfortunately, owing to the socio-political dynamics of our situation, more and more white Christians at the grassroots level are committing themselves to the status quo.

On the other hand, members of the black Christian community have reached a turning point in their relationship with white ecclesiastical structures, particularly as they question the commitment of white Christians in the issues that confront South African society. There is a strong conviction emerging within the black Christian community that black churches should go it alone and participate in the ongoing struggle without appealing for any support from the white Christian community. Recently, as in the past, we have heard voices calling for polarization, inviting blacks to establish their own church within the mainline Protestant tradition. Such developments reflect a deep ideological rift in the thinking of black and white Christians. This further explains why our theological perspectives will never be the same. [This article was written prior to the historical decision of the Dutch Reformed Church meeting in Ottawa. —Ed.]

With this rather brief background it should be clearer to those who have

read John de Gruchy's book *The Church Struggle in South Africa* why his
analysis of the political dynamics of the South African situation is inadequate, particularly as they relate to the struggle for liberation.[2] Our political
commitment as Christians in South Africa very much reflects the socio-
political dynamics and the side we take in the struggle.

It is my hope that this rather sketchy background will enable others to
appreciate what we are doing in our theological pursuits in South Africa and
to understand as well some of the serious challenges that still lie ahead in
developing a theology that will emerge from the struggle of the people against
international and local political structures of bondage.

CONTEMPORARY THEOLOGICAL TRENDS

Theologies of the Status Quo

In this brief report I cannot cover all aspects of South African theology.
One important aspect to mention is that white theology is very much rooted in
the theological traditions of white mainline Protestant and Catholic
churches. With few exceptions, it tends to be very apolitical in its orientation
keeping its gaze averted from the South African reality. And there is another
characteristic of this theology to be mentioned here, although without going
into any detail in analyzing the various writings of white South African
theologians. It is enmeshed with a Western liberal tradition and therefore
tends to be uncritical in projecting alternative ways of doing theology. This
theology unfortunately dominates the thinking of the church in South
Africa. At the ideological level it represents what one may call a theology of
the status quo. To understand this let me recommend Charles Villavicencio's
book *The Theology of Apartheid,* particularly the section concerning the
white Dutch Reformed churches (published by the Methodist Church of
South Africa).

It is significant that even those white theologians who come from the white
liberal tradition support, in their theological reflection, certain elements of
the status quo as they project a political vision of the so-called white opposition in South Africa. In many ways their theology is that of the establishment, even if some aspects of it are opposed to the policy of apartheid. This is
a criticism that has also come from some younger white theologians who are
trying to develop a critical theology. White status quo theology is a victim of
the ideology of survival. Unfortunately, many of our leading white theologians reflect this tendency—a tendency dominated by fear, not by a critical,
rational spirit.

One thing is clear: as long as white theologians are still committed to the
prevailing liberal political vision especially prevalent in English-speaking
churches, their theology will continue to be irrelevant to the ongoing struggle
for liberation. The challenge before the theologians who belong to the Afri-
kaner churches is to reject the prevailing ideology of apartheid and become

part of the process of liberation. Beyers Naudé, one of the leading white theologians has made a clear commitment to the struggle for liberation. Those who are concerned with the struggle have no choice but to follow Naudé's example. There is no doubt that this kind of decision comes only at great cost. White theology in the South African context will become relevant to the extent that it makes a clear commitment to the struggle of the people. It is encouraging that there is already a small group of white theologians beginning to respond to this challenge.

Black Theology—Ideological Divergencies

The emergence of the black consciousness movement, at the end of the 1960s, represented a turning point in black theological thinking in South Africa. Before this period, theological thinking reflected traditional white theological thinking. But young theologians working with leaders of the black consciousness movement began to ask critical questions about the South African situation. One of the fundamental questions we tried to address was on the role the church should play in the struggle for liberation, taking the black experience of oppression as the starting point.[3]

This was the beginning of the black theology movement in South Africa. One of the important influences of this development was James Cone's works. However, it must be emphasized that, although inspired by Cone, African traditional values became pertinent in our work. One of the things we tried to do was to destroy the distorted image that Christianity had acquired in our situation. To many young blacks, Christianity is the religion of the oppressor: for a long time it had supported the prevailing ideology of apartheid—and still does. This, unfortunately, is part of the dilemma of the church in the South African situation. And Christianity continues to be rejected by our traditional peoples because it has more than challenged African values. What black theology has succeeded in doing is to challenge this distorted image of Christianity and to state categorically that our faith is an expression of our commitment to the struggle for liberation. Apart from that, we have emphasized the significance of African values as a basis for theologizing. This is why black theology in the South African context has had a close affinity to the development of African theology with emphasis on traditional African religious values.

One of the ongoing challenges confronting black theology in South Africa is the diversity of emerging methodologies. This represents an ongoing conflict in our work. There are, for instance, those who are committed to an ethnographical method, emphasizing traditional values in the working out of a theology. This approach has emphasized the importance of traditional African religious values and their relevance in developing an African theology. This continues to be a very popular way of doing theology in South Africa because of the challenge of the process of Africanization.

The problem some of us have had with this approach is that it does not deal with the present South African reality precisely as it concerns the oppressed. However, there have been variations in this approach. There are those who have appealed to African values in order to develop a theology of liberation. But what one generally finds in this approach is a lack of critical analysis of the socio-political structures of apartheid. The other danger in this approach is that it can easily be associated with the government policy of separate development, emphasizing the importance of ethnic and tribal pluralism in the South African situation. This, I believe, can be avoided if those who use this approach enter into critical dialogue on contemporary African values and their importance in the process of liberation. There are thinkers—Nyerere and others—who have explored the possibilities of African socialism.

On the other hand, there are also critical perspectives in black theology in South Africa. These perspectives focus attention on contemporary issues within the black oppressed community as expressed in the works of theologians such as Manas Buthelezi, Allan Boesak, Buti Tlagale, and, more recently, Simon Maimela. Their work continues to take African values seriously but within the context of the liberation struggle. Among us there are those who come from an existentialist background and others more open to certain perspectives of critical theory.

Our approach, because of its clear commitment to the aspirations of many blacks, has drawn criticism not only from white theologians but also from the white Christian community. We have openly challenged the association of our churches with the prevailing status quo. We have also openly supported groups that challenge the South African political establishment. This approach has prompted many young blacks to rethink their Christian faith. The issues that we believe should be at the center of our theological enterprise are those shared by the masses as they struggle for liberation.

We have to emphasize that the black Christian community has to play a significant role in the process of liberation. This is why at the moment attempts are being made to examine critically the socio-political structures of our society from the perspective of a black theology. There is also an attempt to reassess the role that black theology has played in the black Christian community.

The other emerging concern in black theological reflection is that of being involved in a people's theology, the oral theology emerging from people's struggle. Many of us believe this is where we have to put our energies by being part of a grassroots theological movement. This is why there is an interest in us to work closely with black youth movements and workers, who constitute a majority of the members of our churches.

In our attempt to contextualize theology, we are inspired by the vision of our peoples as they confront the terror of apartheid. This has given us a new perspective of what it means to be followers of Jesus Christ in South Africa. Besides that, we are aware that we have before us a formidable task in challenging our Christian community to participate concretely in the de facto struggle for liberation. One thing clear is that the church will have to be part of the radical process of change or be destroyed with the powers of darkness and oppression. We believe that the theological vision that has emerged and has promoted critical consciousness among us will bear fruit in the new Azanian Society.

GROUPS INVOLVED IN LIBERATION THEOLOGY

Black theological reflection in South Africa at the moment is taking place at many levels. Some of it reflects a continuing church affiliation; in other cases it reflects the interests of particularized groups. But they all share a common theological objective—that of doing theology within the South African context. My concern here is not with theological institutions, because most of them are still trapped in the traditional way of doing theology. This would be true of our seminaries and universities. These institutions tend to be dominated by the white theological establishment.

The Broederkring

One of the most exciting groups to emerge in the South African situation is the Broederkring of the black Dutch Reformed churches. The significance of this group is that it has emerged from the black division of the Dutch Reformed Churches—churches closely associated with the white Dutch Reformed Church, one of the denominations that have openly supported apartheid. As a significant black voice, this group has challenged the position of the white Dutch Reformed Church in supporting the racist policies of the present South African regime. The Broederkring has also taken a clear stand on the struggle for liberation within the black community. One of its better-known members is Allan Boesak. On a number of issues related to the national political situation, the Broederkring has sided with the South African Council of Churches, whose secretary general is (Anglican) Bishop Desmond Tutu. Theologically the Broederkring is committed to a critical theology of liberation and plays an important role as a theological catalyst within the South African context.

The Black Methodist Consultation

Like the Broederkring, this body of black ministers has emerged within a specific church identity—that of the Methodist Church. Theologically it is a body committed to a theology of liberation, but emphasizing the process of Africanization within the structures of the Methodist Church. This group represents a turning point especially among the mainline English Protestant churches in South Africa. Although a number of its prominent members are inclined to an ethnographic method in theology, their approach is significant in that it is clearly committed to the struggle for liberation. Its influence has been particularly strong among lay members of the Methodist church, because of its emphasis on African values and the struggle for liberation.

The Black Theological Reflection Group

A few theologians who believe that there is a need for us to evaluate the whole process of black theological reflection in South Africa have formed a group in the Pretoria-Johannesburg area. It consists of myself and some colleagues of mine. At the moment we are all involved in particular spheres of research—for example, the present role of the black church in South Africa, an evaluation of black theology since its inception in the late sixties, a theology of the land. There is also a focus on labor issues and the development of a black African social ethic. When our individual papers are written, we hope to put them together and publish them as a book. But this will depend on whether it will be considered publishable in South Africa. As soon as we finish this project we hope to invite other interested persons to become involved in our work. One of our limitations at the moment is that we have no funds. This whole enterprise depends on our individual contributions.

The Institute of Contextual Theology

This institute has just been established. It will focus on critical issues confronting South Africa—employment, for example—critical analysis of socio-political structures, and exploration of different types of contextual theology. The institute will become a forum for critical theological reflections in South Africa.

It will try to cover different regions of the country. At the moment we are looking for a director, and already members of the Black Reflection Group serve on the steering committee. The importance of this institute is that it will bring together all those—both black and white—who are involved in contextual theology in the South African context. And we hope that this institute will not be just another theological group but will be involved concretely in the praxis of liberation.

CONCLUSION

What I have tried to do in this report is to give a bird's-eye view of the developing trends in theological reflection in the South African situation, without attempting a full critique of everything that is coming out of South Africa. What must be clear is that there are many challenges and risks ahead. These challenges are an invitation to the whole South African Christian community to be involved concretely in the praxis of liberation before it is too late. I believe that critical theological reflection in solidarity with other theological groups in the Third World will make an important contribution to the liberation of all humankind. One thing is beyond dispute: as long as there is oppression and dehumanization in the Third World, the challenge of doing theology and of siding with the oppressed will continue. It will continue until the kingdom of God breaks through in our respective situations.

Let me end this report with a poem written by a young black South African, Rahab S. Potje, in 1942:

> Sing songs, ye children of Africa
> Songs of freedom and songs of love,
> Song of praise for your native land;
> For the Lord with his merciful right hand
> Hath blest us with freedom and love.
> Forget, ye sons of slavery!
> Ye daughters, forget your orphanage!
> Arise and show your bravery!
> For lost are the days of strife with age,
> And liberty is at hand.
> How long have we longed, O Africa,
> Have we longed for joys in our land!
> How long have we struggled with thee, O Fate—
> With thee, O Fate, thou cruel Fate—
> Gainst struggle, hate, and strife!
> Let us with our banner unfurled
> March to the graves of our dead,
> With hands overflowing with offering
> With hearts full of Mirth and Joy,
> Then, O then
> Let us with one voice our prayers raise.[4]

NOTES

1. See Marjorie Hope and James Young, *The South African Churches in a Revolutionary Situation* (Maryknoll, N.Y.: Orbis Books, 1981), pp. 41, 216.

2. Grand Rapids: Eerdmans, 1979.

3. Some of the early essays on this movement are in *The Challenge of Black Theology,* Basil Moore, ed. (Atlanta: John Knox Press, 1974).

4. From *Reconstruction: Ninety Years of Black South African Literature,* Mothobi Mutloatse, ed. (Johannesburg: Ravan Press, 1981).

3

Theological Priorities in India Today

Samuel Rayan

We want Indian Christian theology to be of service to the Indian people in our common search for full humanity in an open fellowship. Indian theology seeks to discern, illumine, and support the people's struggle for human wholeness in freedom and dignity. Its endeavor is to make a meaningful contribution to the march of our people toward human fullness in a just society.

We are convinced that an academic type of theology divorced from action for change is irrelevant. With our oppressed brothers and sisters elsewhere, we are prepared for a radical break in theological methodology, in order that commitment to the oppressed and to their struggle for freedom, justice, and fellowship be the first act of theology. This commitment is, we hold, implied in and demanded by our faith-commitment to God in Jesus Christ.

We understand that this means serious critical reflection on the reality of our country, which includes the praxis of secular and religious movements as well as our own lifestyle, ideology, and alignment. It demands solidarity with the poor and the oppressed; the bending of all our resources to serve the cause of their *mukti*—liberation from all that shackles—hunger and social bondage no less than alienation from God and neighbor; the sharing of the joys and risks of involvement in action with them; and the celebration of our common hope.

In preparation for the fifth EATWOT dialogue, scheduled for August 1981 in New Delhi, eleven Indian Roman Catholic and Protestant theologians held two meetings at the Ecumenical Christian Center in Bangalore to consider Indian priorities in the emergence of a Third World theology.

The first meeting, held on November 21-24, 1980, centered around the main issues of the Indian situation as well as approaches for theological reflection. After discussion a tentative statement was made and circulated among other theologians, action groups, and secular thinkers, for their critique and comments. At the second meeting, held on April 8-10, 1981, the group worked together to incorporate the various concerns expressed in the responses.

Samuel Rayan then put all this material in written form. Entitled "Theological Priorities of India Today: Statement of the Indian Preparatory Group," it was read at the New Delhi conference. It appears here as edited for inclusion in the present cumulative volume.

Our theology will therefore take local, grassroots action, experience, and thought into account. It will concern itself with questions that the people and the theologians with them ask, and the questions implicit in our day-to-day existence. It is to come to birth and grow where the masses are, in their suffering and their struggle. It will be our faith-reflection on our own history; it will be a theological history, the story of our struggle for the freedom that beckons to us from the future—a future that God offers and that takes shape within the history God is making with us. We shall therefore avoid a sectarian interpretation of our history and of the gospel of Jesus, for all who work for justice are God's co-workers. With them we are in solidarity. Christian theologians in India have to fulfill a function vis-à-vis the Christian community as well as the entire national community. Our own search for a theology must take into account all other searches and movements for liberation. This we do in conversation with historically relevant reinterpretations and fresh insights of Hindu, Muslim, Buddhist, and Christian theologies while safeguarding the uniqueness of each.

THE INDIAN CONTEXT

We recognize the crucial character of our times and realize that what is at stake is the very life of our people, even the physical life of the masses—to say nothing of the quality of their life, or of their participation in culture, or of space for that creativity. The situation is complex, but in our discussion we found the problem of poverty and of caste particularly urgent and deserving of emphasis. Clearly related to these are questions concerning women's status and rights, the orientation and organization of youth, and the restructuring of our educational system. These problems cannot be addressed, however, without a due consideration of the people's movements and stirrings from below, as well as the situation of religious plurality and the social role played by religious symbols.

Poverty

Among the most shocking features of our country is the poverty of the masses, often nothing less than total destitution and misery, side by side with enormous wealth and affluence enjoyed by the few who form a thin stratum at the summit of our social hierarchy. Our economic policies are not designed to deal with this gruesome reality; they cater to the consumerist tastes and the profits and power of the privileged elitist class. Almost all the means of production (land, capital, technology) are owned and controlled by this small group. It therefore also has a grip on political power and manipulates the state apparatus, preventing it from taking effective steps to reform land-ownership, to create jobs, to restructure the educational and legal systems of colonial legacy, to free bonded labor, or to improve the buying power of the lowest income groups.

The result has been that, although the country is rich in natural, technical, and labor potential and the national income has grown considerably through the several Five Year Plans, the condition of the masses has deteriorated. Around 87 percent of the population lives below, at, or just above the poverty line. This has given rise to widespread embitterment and restlessness, which the ruling class meets by stepping up repression.

Political Setting

The economic situation has structural links with the political situation. Our independence movement terminated in a transfer of power without a social revolution. A Westernized elite with economic interests integrated into the interests of the outgoing colonial power became the successor to the British. It has been to their advantage to keep practically everything unchanged. This new bourgeoisie—together with the industrial magnates, the landlords, the plantation owners, and the professional politicians—monopolizes political power and controls political and economic policies and processes. Local self-governing bodies —panchayats and municipalities—either do not function at all or are manipulated by the wealthy class. The masses are fast becoming cynical and losing faith in the political system that has proved incapable of meeting the real problems. Within a global neoimperialist framework, our political decisions are controlled by those who control our economic processes—namely, the super powers and their multinational corporations.

Our parliamentary democracy was devised by our ruling class as a system where all the symbols of social democracy were preserved and elevated to the highest level of principle, but which also provided the formal groundwork for every form of repression and exploitation. Its strains and contradictions were too severe for it to continue wearing its mask of double-think and double-talk indefinitely. By 1975 the mask had to be dropped, and emergency rule was imposed on the nation. But that was "only a formalisation of what had been a fact of life for a large number of Indian people. Nevertheless, the fact that the rulers had to take recourse . . . to that extraordinary measure was an eloquent confession of the failure of a whole set of institutions."[1]

This structural impasse is now giving birth to the distortions of an opportunist philosophy cultivated by power structures centered around privileged individuals. The competence of persons and institutions is carefully avoided or immobilized in favor of subservience. But even the bourgeois, who think that the system, though now in deep crisis, could still be made to work, finally admit that only the people can find a lasting solution to our real problems.[2]

Culture

Our complex cultural reality is at once unified and multiform. The linguistic, religious, and ethnic pluralism of India is borne by an underlying unity of perspective and outlook brought about forcibly or spontaneously by spiritual, historical, literacy, and geographical factors at work for centuries. There exists a sense of community with the cosmos, a keen awareness of the oneness in multiplicity, and a search for the "within" of reality.

But feudal social patterns of patronage and dependence still persist. Cultural institutions such as the educational system and mass media are made to serve the interests of capitalism and big business. Just as colonialism reinforced the caste system, consolidated the feudal mentality, and spawned a hybrid elitist culture, so now neocolonialism, the subtle but forceful impact of the multinationals and their indigenous agents and brokers are the bearers of capitalist culture and consumerism. Middle-class values and ambitions to climb the ladder of privilege and power inspire and govern much of the organized chaos in our country.

In the process the rhythm of national life and growth has been deeply disturbed, the people's self-image distorted, and creativity shelved or destroyed. A pressing need of the hour therefore is to rebuild the pride of the people, and restore its confidence in its creative ability to come to grips with life and shape its own future.

Tribal Patterns

Tribal traditions are of particular significance in this context. The various ethnic tribes all over India are struggling to liberate themselves from social and economic oppression and maintain their identity in the face of threats from the values of the dominant groups and militant Hinduism as well as capitalism. Tribal societies are in general based on a nobler conception of human nature than are feudal and capitalist societies. Production in tribal societies is organized for the service and holistic development of human beings in community, whereas in capitalism human beings are treated as means for profit. The tribal conception of human nature and its relationship to physical nature is what we need for building a better future.

Caste

Caste is a powerful, divisive, and oppressive institution, deeply entrenched in the very flesh of the people and infecting all the limbs and movements of the nation. Indian caste has its peculiar features; it also has elements in common with racist and classist structures elsewhere. Used for long as a tool and technique for dividing and conquering, caste still acts as the main obstacle to the unity and organization of all the exploited for an effective struggle against oppression.

Is the irruption of the poor in India as much in opposition to caste as it is to class, or is it a bid to climb the social ladder within the caste hierarchy? Is the Marxist analysis of caste and its support of outcasts adequate? Upper-caste leadership has often withdrawn and betrayed the struggles of the downtrodden at critical moments. What is needed is a profound political and spiritual education that will enable the people to overcome caste and class and to ready itself against possible betrayals.

What is needed is a basic cultural struggle in which the economic will be a key component. Here we meet with and recognize the paradox of a situation in which caste must overcome caste. As things are, the solidarity provided by caste identity seems to be necessary to initiate the struggle. Different castes and tribes as well as the Harijans have developed their own customs and recognizable cultures. The lower castes and the oppressed classes have an identity of their own.

Can we distinguish between a negative identity or self-depreciation and fear and the positive identity of courage and cohesion? Should we not be careful about making such artificial distinctions? Contaminated values are often survival values that will be made whole only as the involvement of a group in the work of its own liberation deepens. A historical criticism of values is, however, necessary. Equality and participation could be held as normative values. And we must also ask ourselves: Is it realistic to think that caste will disappear from the existing socio-economic system within the fore-seeable future?

Religion

Traditionally, religions in India, notwithstanding notable exceptions at various points in our history, have acted as bastions of legitimation for the power, privileges, and exploitive practices of upper caste and upper class. The caste system too—born of conquest, enslavement, an imposed vertical division of labor, and racial prejudices—received religious legitimation at the hands of priestly groups. In societies at the mythical stage, myth was part of the means of production.

The claim was that there was no wealth without sacrifice and that such sacrifice has had an impact on the cosmos. But it was only the priestly group that had knowledge and control of sacrificial technology. Through its use this group grew rich and powerful. Ritual technology defined ritual untouchability and pollution, by which the enslaved were disqualified and excluded not only from cult but from ownership of land as well.

The Christian religion was no exception. In Christianity too legitimators of exploitation have become rich. Some Indian churches have accommodated caste within themselves, making a mockery of the gospel. All this points to the need for radical questioning and a thorough sifting of the whole world of religious symbolism. This symbol system cannot be touched at its root without effective land reform; the interlinkage of agriculture, culture, and cult are stronger and deeper than was realized in the past.

Movements for liberation have also to reckon with sidetracking pieties and gurus; with domesticative charismatic and evangelical trends that seek to capture radical student organizations; and with the gap between the church's radical words and stance on the one hand and its feeble, ineffectual deeds on the other. The Indian church—not the 85 percent of Indian Christians who are poor, passive, and alienated, but the bishops and the organizational institutions—has not yet made a clear option for the poor. Often decisions are made in the light of a theology and spirituality that is colonial and anesthetic. We are now seeing persons seek charismatic renewal without questioning capitalism and unconcerned about the quality of social life and the shape of tomorrow.

We need to repent of and seek corporate forgiveness for privatizing the gospel of Jesus and distorting its message by relegating its thrust to other-worldly concerns. Could a spirituality whose main function is to provide private satisfaction be truly Christian? But then by what criterion can authentic gospel spirituality be distinguished from what is inauthentic?

Seeds of Hope

But not everything around us is gloomy and stagnant. There are movements that, though ambivalent, could develop into springboards of change, of hope, of liberation and human growth. Such are the crises within capitalism, the growing popular disillusionment with bourgeois institutions and promises, and the struggle of the trade unions, the rural poor, and the landless laborers for freedom and participation and a due share in the wealth of the nation. Such are also the presence and activities of leftist parties (communist, socialist, Naxalite,[3] independent) and the social pressure they exert. Political ideologies for decentralization are developing, as well as demands for more autonomy for the states, and statehood for tribals and Daliths. There are attempts to clarify the vision of a new India and to organize the people for its realization.

The search is on for new forms of education to serve the awakening and organizing of the masses, to serve their quest for self-rule, and their socialist aspirations. Radical publications are helping to sensitize and link up grassroots movements and action groups, and the committed among the intelligentsia. New liberative interpretations of religious tenets and symbols are beginning to appear in all the great spiritual traditions of our country, bearing the promise of a living theology at the service of the people.

There is a growing perception that Hinduism without caste is as possible and desirable as Christianity without hierarchy, even if what emerges in the process will be different from the Hinduism and the Christianity we have known, provided they are in touch with the people whom God loves and liberates. There are attempts to go to the roots and origins of religious heritages to draw inspiration for the struggle for the humanization of our history. These sources may be Hindu, Christian, Muslim, or Buddhist. They are not in conflict as long as they are for human wholeness. It is with all these new stirrings of life that we identify ourselves.

THEOLOGY

Such, in outline, is our present reality. To theologize is to interpret this reality in the light of the tradition of God's liberating action in our history in order to lead to a renewed humankind. But who is to do this? It is the community that theologizes; the professional theologian speaks for the community. The theologian's presence within the community saves theology from the danger of becoming academic on the one hand and the danger of becoming overpopulist on the other. It must be rigorous but not divorced from life; it must be a people's theology but not uncritical. This obviously calls for a restructuring of theological studies and of theological institutions.

Approaches

All theological expressions remain barren unless they arise out of and shape the ongoing life and active involvement of the whole people of God. It is to facilitate such participation by the whole community that we attempt what follows.

In the act of theologizing there are two moments—namely, awareness and articulation. Awareness is the experience of total reality at the personal psychological level, at the broader socio-cosmic level, and at the mystical level, which the other two point to and in some measure reveal. Value and meaningfulness are part of depth-awareness, and it is depth–awareness (and not any empirical awareness) that forms the predicate of theology. It is the people with liberated consciousness that articulates the Jesus-values.

Articulation first develops a worldview that is both empirical (scientific) and in depth (absolute), and then expresses it in existential, social language, interpreting it in terms of values and meaningfulness accepted from tradition. Tradition includes the Judeo-Christian, Hindu, Islamic, and Buddhist, and their scriptures. All traditions and scriptures have to be critiqued.

God's liberating action in history is the norm for doing it. In Christian tradition the key symbol for this is the life, death, and resurrection of Jesus. This implies:

(1) Wholeness, in contradistinction with all dualism (of word and action, history and eschatology, people and authority, secular and sacred, human and divine, and so forth);

(2) Historicity, meaning that it is in our encounters with other persons and in interhuman relationships that the divine is met;

(3) The power of the powerlessness of love that says no to every form of domination and serves to enable others even at the cost of one's own life. The essential task and goal of such a theological project is not some private piety but the building of a new, truly human future—God's promise for all, which we proclaim, celebrate, and anticipate in our worship and sacraments.

As we face this theological task in the context of our wider Indian heritage, we wish to pose to ourselves the following questions: Does not the Hindu or Buddhist tradition have its specific role to play, just as the Christian has its own, in the common task of building the future? It there not then a need for mutual criticism? If so how could Jesus be the ultimate norm of critique for all scriptures and realities? Will Jesus also be subject to a critique in the light of Indian experience past and present? And what is Indian reality when I know that I have more in common with a socialist Chinese or New Yorker than with a capitalist of New Delhi or Bombay? In all these we wish to emphasize again the truth that the foundational, essential articulation is life itself—our corporate social life, not verbal formulations.

It is possible to move on from here to another conception of theology on the common grounds that the locus of our encounter with God is present history and the persons making it. Jesus's own way of doing theology is illustrated in his reply to the followers of John the Baptist in Matthew 11:1–4. There is here no narration of the past, no framing of definitions, no recourse to philosophical concepts, no search for logical structures. There is rather the engaging invitation to see and hear and touch what is present, and to understand and interpret it. We have the same approach in the Johannine writings and Hebrews and in Indian traditions. India's desire is to see. Seeing implies that what God is doing is taking place in the arena of human struggle. Seeing is an involved, engaged process, ongoing, open-ended, holistic, with continuous refocusing as scenes change in an unfolding history.

Seeing has three components: memory, hope, and involvement. These are related because we see properly only what we do and what we are committed to. We see as well with the hands that break down and build up as we do with the eyes. Theology, then, is the interpretation of seen events—the blind recovering their sight, the lame walking, the dead rising to life, and the poor hearing good news that is hope-giving. Theology is the interpretation of events in a people's struggle, in the light of an enduring pattern of meaning provided by the creative, redemptive, and constitutive events in Jesus' ambient for the purpose of transformation of individuals and society.

The Christ-event provides a way of seeing, and we call it faith. It familiarizes us with the voice of God and the sound of his footsteps that we can then distinguish with a sure sense amid the confusion of crises and claims that resound on the highway of history. Our quest in India is for a just, participatory, inclusive, sustainable society. History is the struggle between this God-initiated process for renovation and the forces that are hostile to it. Only the God who appears in this history today can be the norm for critiquing ideology, society, church, and Jesus.

There is yet another way of viewing our theological task in India today. Theology is an articulate discourse on the ultimate, unconditional dimension of reality. We may distinguish three ways of experiencing this dimension and three corresponding styles of discourse present in the Indian tradition. These are the cosmic, the gnostic, and the totalizing. We need to recapture the authentically Indian and positive dimension of all three and hold them in living unity, liberated from every kind of alienation and misuse.

COSMIC EXPERIENCE OF THE ULTIMATE

The context for this experience was a primitive stage of technical production, dependence on nature, and relationships of kith and kin. Human continuity and unity with the cosmos stand out in relief. In such a context the divine was seen in nature and its cyclic processes. Immersion in the mystery of nature brought healing and renewal. There is here something deep and authentic, but in the course of time it became alienated through the identification of the small human world with the vast universe of matter; through an attempt to control the cosmos by means of the protoscience of magical rites; and through the emergence of experts in ritual on whom the rest of the village came to depend. Another source and process of alienation was extreme asceticism and extreme self-indulgence, both resting on the idea that death gave birth to new life. Ruling classes could use this as a law of nature in order to exploit and restrain the lower classes.

For many sages in India this unity vision provided a sense of wholeness and enabled their meaningful participation in life. Later, however, this mystical vision lost its original dynamism because of an overemphasis on metaphysical identification.

GNOSTIC EXPERIENCE OF THE ULTIMATE

In the classical philosophy and theology of India the Brahma is the supreme reality. The atman is the self—absolute and universal, or relative and individual. In the gnostic experience of the ultimate, Brahma and atman are perceived as one. The consequences were (a) a view of the world as an illusion, which one should therefore flee, ignoring the human situation; (b) use of this maya[4] theory to legitimate institutionalized injustice and the mechanisms of oppression; and (c) the assumption of a superior pose, as having reached the highest jnana marga,[5] whence one could complacently look down upon others.

But the mystical experience of unity has a validity and significance that can be recovered and relived. We would then discover that it is the ultimate reality that grounds and frames us, and that the historical process is a process of our ever freer, fuller, and more self-awakening participation in its jnana—light, liberty, and mystery.

TOTALIZING EXPERIENCE OF THE ULTIMATE

The third way of experiencing the ultimate—the way of Buddha—combines what is positive in the other two and develops a humanizing discourse. The historical context was the fragmentation of tribal unity through the rise of independent peasants and householders with private property, the emergence of individualism, new forms of suffering affecting an ever larger segment of the population, and the deepening alienation of life.

Buddha, emerging from a profound experience of the ultimate, with a sense of vocation and challenge, proposed the transcending of the fragmented self through knowledge ripening to love. He saw reality in a new way. The experience of the ultimate led him to the discovery of universal fellowship, to the rejection of everything that came in the way of this vision, and to commitment to this loving, limitless inclusiveness. The Buddha's love issues from his light.

As Indian Christians, all these elements are part of our heritage and we have been made aware of their misuse in history. Our question is: How do we let these various traditions mutually criticize and enrich each other? Also, how do we relate these modes of experience of the ultimate to the concrete struggles of our people for liberation?

It is in addressing these and related questions that we shall evolve a theology appropriate to our context.

The Church

Our communion in Christ, which we call church, must have the character of the fellowship that Jesus had with the marginalized and defenseless of his time. Theology must help the church see and live the dialectic between commitment to Jesus and the option for the poor; between faith in his cross and insertion in the people's struggle against forces of oppression and alienation; between the ritual celebration of his death and the historical combat for human wholeness, freedom, and dignity. Christ's presence in the church's rituals corresponds to and depends upon his presence in the ecclesial community itself as his Body given for the life of the world wherever action is taken for justice and freedom, and where authentic fellowship is sought and built.

To enable the church to be the sign of God's liberating presence, theology will have to engage in a sustained critique of the church. We need to become aware of the ambiguity of the church's role in history: its close and long association with the ruling classes and colonialism; its colonialist and imperialist approach to mission and to the Christian communities in Asia, Afriea, and Latin America; its efforts to alleviate misery while legitimizing the structures that cause misery and aligning itself with antiproletarian power groups.

Its traditional involvement has given the church a middle-class image and mentality that makes it difficult for it to work for positive social change or to establish solidarity with the oppressed masses—the majority of the Indian people. Ours is a church that keeps silent on most issues of justice and injustice, and seems to be uncomfortable with programs of land reform and with any suggestions or movements that are not feudal or capitalist.

The Indian church, though it is a small minority, has enormous institutional power and influence with the bourgeois classes, which its institutions mainly serve. To preserve this advantage and to maintain its institutions, the church carefully avoids every radical option in word and deed on behalf of the masses. The result is that the church, clutching its institutional influence, is marginal to the life of the nation and to the struggle of the poor and oppressed. Its eschewal of politics usually amounts to support for the status quo and the powers that be. And its opposition to leftist movements is based more on capitalist ideology and ignorance of socialism than on informed judgment and gospel principles. It is the task of theology to aid the church to let itself be critiqued and challenged by the radicalism and historical realism of the gospel.

Additional reasons for the church's marginalization and limited credibility are the caste division it has accepted and the denominational divisions it has inherited from the West. But the road to unity and reconciliation is not preoccupation with institutional elements, doctrinal formulations, and balance of power. Nor is unity served by standing aloof from the struggling masses. The path to unity leads through joint effort for justice and freedom, through concerted effort to overcome caste and class hierarchies within the church, and through entrance into the mainstream of the people's struggles. Our participation in the cross of Christ includes commitment to the abolition of the mechanisms of injustice; it includes sharing in the *vedana*—pain—of the people.

We wish to see the church in real rather than purely ritual terms; to understand it as constituted by commitment to liberation and justice, and by participation in the baptism of blood that Jesus is undergoing now in the defenseless people with whom he is one. Our ecclesial solidarity can only be a solidarity in justice and freedom. We see the church taking shape where Jesus-reality is being actualized in history by defense of human dignity and human rights in a struggle even unto death.

We need therefore to scrutinize the structures of fellowship and freedom in the church as well as in human society at large and work to eliminate the cleavage that now exists between people and power, so that the people can have *swaraj*—self-rule, independence—and be its own master, free with the freedom of God's children in the power of God's Spirit. The task of theology is to assist in the birth of a new church and a new humanity.

A New Language

The birth of a new humanity will go hand in hand with the emergence of a new language in which differences of experience will lead to a comprehensive vision of harmony, not to a division of hearts. The new language will integrate the music of the different dialects into a rich symphonic composition. It will be a concrete language, a historical and committed idiom. It will refuse to be merely rational, in the service of abstraction, speculation, and metaphysics. It will be the language of the people, not an esoteric, academic jargon.

The new language will not reduce human beings and their world to mere objects and commodities. It will proclaim the human being a "poet"—that is, a shaper and singer of our destiny. It will at the same time stress and evoke the mystery that has appeared in flesh, flower, and fruit; the mystery that is at work in the heart of every man and woman and is experienced as the urge to seek and realize what is loving and loveable, what unites and liberates.

The new language will be an ever growing reality, assimilating every genuine search for freedom and fellowship but refusing to absolutize any one sign or set of symbols. The new language will enable the people to sing a new song, a song as ancient as their own quest for communion with the cosmos and its inhabitants. "And the lion and the lamb shall lie down together and every man shall sit under his own vine and fig tree and none shall be afraid."

We are convinced that our theology will and must remain an unfinished endeavor, open-ended and hopeful of correction, improvement, and growth. Because historical reality keeps evolving and changing, and because we are all conditioned by our situation and class position, we recognize the need of ongoing criticism and relativization of our approaches to theology. The norms of criticism are themselves judged by their capacity for humanization. The values, methods, and symbols used must be such as to promote the cause of liberty and the emergence of a participative society. Concretely, the direction for us as Indians is the human person on the way to completion. The norm for us as Christians is Jesus (and we are not unaware of his own social and historical conditioning).

We stress that our Indianness must be free of provincialism. We recognize the need to maintain open dialogue with theological trends, concerns, and insights in other countries and in different socio-cultural contexts. We should always keep in mind that contacts and conversations can provide mutual enrichment, challenge, and stimulation.

NOTES

1. *EPW,* Special Number, Oct. 1980, p. 1689.
2. See ibid., p. 1697.
3. An extreme leftist movement advocating violent revolution; it originated in Naxalbari, West Bengal.
4. Maya: the creative, self-expressive power and creativity of the absolute; creation as self-expression of the absolute through its incomprehensible power; the incomprehensible, transitory, relative, or illusory character of the created universe.
5. The path of knowledge, considered by some to be the best of three paths to the liberation and realization of self. The other two paths are *bhakti marga* (the path of devotion) and *karma marga* (the path of [religious] action).

4

Peruvian Reality and Theological Challenges

Jorge Alvarez Calderón

In view of the extreme complexity of Peruvian reality, we selected a method of preparation for the New Delhi conference that consisted in participation in meetings of landworkers, urban laborers, and pastoral ministers in the several regions of the country. Thus we were able to engage in the problematic to be addressed by the fifth conference of EATWOT at the level of the life and experience of the communities themselves. Then, working at the Bartolomé de Las Casas Research Center, we used the material gathered in these meetings to prepare the following presentation.

PERUVIAN REALITY

Socio-Cultural Characteristics

Peru, together with South Ecuador and Bolivia, is situated in the Andean region of South America. The ancient autochthonous cultures that developed here had been absorbed and centralized by the Inca Empire scarcely a hundred years before the arrival of the Spaniards in the sixteenth century.

As a result, there is an important native Andean component in our population. The complex process of racial and cultural mélange that began with European colonization is far from having attained homogeneity even today. The shades and degrees are many. By and large, we can say that the Andean zones farther removed from the centers of economic development continue to maintain their own language and customs. It is estimated that 18 percent of the population of Peru has preserved the Quechua and Aymara languages. Other, smaller, ethnic minorities live in the Amazon region. The rest of the population is constituted by Spanish-speaking *mestizos*, spanning a broad spectrum of greater or lesser Andean admixture, and containing an African component (derived from slaves introduced into Peru from the colony's very inception) and an Asiatic element ("imported" from China under conditions of extreme exploitation, practically as slaves, in the middle of the last century).

The whole social mixture is still far from forming a cohesive whole. So long subjected to so many types of economic, political, and ideological oppression, including strong racial discrimination, it has not yet managed to shape a clear consciousness of its identity, although important advances in this respect have been noted in recent years.

The greatest cementing factor in this process is, without any doubt, the situation of extreme poverty to which these Peruvians are subjected, due to different systems of exploitation that have been in effect since colonial times, conditions aggravated today by the special character of imperialist penetration into Latin America. The imperialist penetration implants a certain type of "modernization" and "development" that is of no real benefit to the popular classes. On the contrary, it prioritizes a particular type of development and industrialization that abandons the so-called *atrasados*—the "retarded sectors" of the farm population—with the result that rural inhabitants, especially since the 1950s, have been swept up in a powerful migratory movement from the countryside to the city. Indeed, somewhere in the course of the 1970s, *campesinos* ceased to constitute the majority of the Peruvian population. But the city, too, fails to provide sufficient jobs, basic services, or hope for the future of our youth.

The popular masses of our country—the *mestizos* and Amerindians (Quechuas, Aymaras, and Amazonian minorities)—are all subjected to the raw reality of extreme, and ever increasing, poverty. By way of illustration, Peru now holds third place, after Haiti and Bolivia, in infant mortality, according to the *Anuario Estadístico de América Latina 1979*, published by the Comisión Económica para América Latina in December 1980. This dramatic situation spurs the discovery of common interests: the struggle for land, for work, for health services. Racial and cultural demands are beginning to crystalize, along with the defense of women's rights, as an integral part of the task of liberation. From within this situation of exploitation and oppression, the country's poor are discovering, slowly but surely, that they are a majority, that they are a people—that they are a potential force for liberation.

But there is another factor binding the people together, as well: the majority of them are Christian. It is true that the gospel arrived on these shores under Spanish auspices. Still, it cannot be said that it today represents nothing more than "the religion of the dominator." Over the course of the centuries, this mixed mass of poverty-stricken human beings has gradually made the gospel message its own. Many times, to be sure, the gospel has functioned as a factor of submission and resignation. But in the last decades, with ever increasing force and power, the good news of the God of the Bible has struck roots in this soil in an original way, absorbing authentic cultural elements in such a way as to provide a potential dynamic factor for self-affirmation and identity in a profoundly religious people, which has begun to lift up its head.

Political Situation and Popular Process

In the course of the last decades, especially since World War II, Peruvian society has entered upon a stage of accelerating intensification of the contradictions. The objective process of capitalistic modernization, in all its dimensions, not only creates new social sectors that battle for common interests, but very strongly affects the situation of the masses as well. Their impoverishment has become most acute in terms of visible social inequality, and it is due to this inequality that powerful movements and struggles developed among the rural population during the 1950s—such as the mass migration to the cities, mentioned above. This new phenomenon has taken only a few years to change the urban situation and render it potentially explosive. This is the context of the radicalization of the student movement as well; the Cuban revolution had a strong impact on the university milieu. It is on this terrain that new leftist nuclei sprang up and set out in quest of alternative solutions. Traditional power groups, faced with the growing social complexity and its increasing tensions, demonstrated their inability to resolve new difficulties. Their timid efforts at reform had the effect only of pointing up the urgent need for radical change. What was really happening was the dissolution of the old socio-economic order, preponderantly agrarian and semifeudal, and the development of a penetration by a modernizing industrial capitalism, involving the demand for an across-the-board reorganization of the whole social order.

This is the moment when, in 1968, the armed forces, with a new concept of "national defense," determined to take up the reins of state for the purpose of implementing a structural change that by then, with different content in different sectors demanding it, was seen as a matter of urgency. This so-called Peruvian Revolution took steps to satisfy long-standing demands on the part of many sectors of the country. It held itself forth as an "anti-imperialist and anti-oligarchical" government, which now proposed a "social democracy with full participation." Measures were undertaken of a style and scope never before seen—nationalization of the petroleum industry, agrarian reform, business reform, and so on. The radical indoctrination accompanying these reforms clearly contributed to the conscientization of the masses. Even in its first phase, however (1968 to 1975), the character of this process was one of radical reformism, and not of revolution properly so called.

The second phase became one of total conciliation with investors, both foreign and national, representing huge sums of money. It never succeeded in breaking with the overwhelmingly capitalistic character of the economy and soon became enmeshed in its own ambiguities. The stark economic crisis to which the reform process led was intensified at the same time by the international crisis. This general crisis now caused the military government to take measures that evoked general popular rejection. Finally, politically isolated, the armed forces began in 1977 to seek an electoral solution, along the strategy lines of the Carter administration. In 1978 elections for the Constituent Assembly were held. In 1980, presidential, parliamentary, and municipal elections were held.

The outcome of the elections may serve as a kind of balance sheet for this agitated and important period in our political life. We find a strongly polarized country. On the right, those elements linked to a transnational capitalism are modernized, very aggressive, and determined to consolidate their domination in the long run. The popular masses, who have undergone so much political conscientization during all these years, now tend significantly toward positions of the left (with 25 percent of the vote, as compared with 6 percent in the 1962 elections). In the center is a popular party of hoary vintage, the APRA, which had been evolving toward a strategy of conciliation with the modernized middle class since the 1950s.

This brief sketch will furnish the necessary elements for understanding what occurred with the popular classes during these years.

The first phase of the so-called Peruvian Revolution (1968 to 1975), along with initiating important reforms, attempted to set up, through the state, a network of grassroots social organizations linked to government. It was a moment of respite for leftist organizations, and they took the occasion to multiply their activities among the *campesinos*, in the unions, and in the barrios. Never had so many persons been working to organize the people at once. Popular organization was thus the common basis for both reformism and leftists tendencies; their quarrel was over the objectives and forms that popular organization should be taking.

It is altogether understandable, then, that in a moment of increased impoverishment resulting from mismanagement of crisis, the popular response should be so massive and uncontrollable. Economic betterment was over and done, in reality and in expectation. To boot, popular organization was acquiring ever more autonomous characteristics and becoming ever more hostile toward the state. Mass movements of various hues occurred between 1975 and 1980, and the government lost control over the popular movement. It is in this context, the product of several years of gestation, that we can understand the sudden shift to the left on the part of the masses. This reorientation, to which we have alluded, is much more the reflection of a rejection of the status quo than it is of any clear political consciousness armed with an alternative program. But it is an important phenomenon, and it will leave its traces. It challenges us to mold it into an efficacious force for change.

At present, our regime is a liberal democratic one without effective social democratization. Various groups on a new right, with ties to transnational capitalism, have managed to take power, and proclaim that they maintain it in the light of "lessons learned" from the period just past. Their response to the acute economic crisis is to opt for a frank liberalization of the economy by opening it up to foreign capital. The cost in social terms is very high: inflation, unemployment, acute impoverishment, and no room for measures of any breadth that would benefit the people. The absence of real alternatives to offer the people is this government's greatest weakness. Hence it feels it has no choice but to work for a carefully calculated weakening of popular organizations, by means of a mixture of disparagement, distortion, and isolation of the popular struggles, as also job dismissals and other forms of repression—including torture and murder—as circumstances may seem to require.

Accordingly, the popular movement has been greatly weakened during this period, in spite of having achieved a certain presence in the national and municipal administrations. And yet the years have not passed in vain. The results of the elections show that an objective process of maturation is underway among the people. There is now a considerable sector of the masses, the lower middle class, and labor and political leaders, who perceive this state of affairs as globally unjust, and who place less and less confidence in the state and the minorities controlling it. They seek to launch forms of autonomous popular power, however local or sectoral their purview, for the purpose of fighting for their own rights, in opposition to minorities more or less clearly perceived as dominant classes. The fact that this association is such a loose one—indeed, not even centrally organized—does not appear to militate against its consideration as a historical process in a stage of formation. The challenge at this stage is to consolidate this nascent social bloc and to discover, from within the increasing suffering of the masses, the appropriate organizational forms that will permit it to develop into an alternative force.

THEOLOGICAL CHALLENGES

Thus far, this has been a description and analysis of the context in which the life of our popular Christian communities is developing. These communities are a part of a poor *mestizo* people that grows by suffering. They are also a particularly vital and alive part of a church that, all during the course of these years, has been discovering—in spite of tensions—pathways of fidelity to the gospel in the concrete conditions in which the popular masses find themselves. Out of the practice of these communities, a faith reflection has gradually arisen. Its first formulations were achieved in 1968, with what is called theology of liberation. This reflection, this theology, marks a break with the stage that had gone before, in which theological reflection was presented in terms of a European problematic.

The theological interrelationship between practice and reflection has been, and continues to be, most intense. It is a response to the continual challenges that have to be faced by our communities at each hairpin curve in the zigzag road along which our people is careening. Our presentation here will seek to make a brief clarification of two points that in our context constitute key sets of theological questions: (1) the relationship between theology and the life of the people, and (2) the relationship between Christian faith and popular identity.

Theology and the Life of the People

The poverty of the great majority of the people in our land has been, and continues to be, a mighty challenge to our life in faith and to theological reflection.

There are many reasons for this. But there is one special reason, which not only expresses the cruelty of a human situation, but has acquired renewed urgency in our time, as we have shown above. We refer to the relationship between poverty and death.

This is the nub of the whole matter. A people has been thrust down into a condition of death, death by hunger, unemployment, abandonment in sickness, repression, and brutal murder. A people has been thrust down into a situation of death by racial and cultural disparagement and contempt, which tend to loosen one's roots. It has been thrust down into a situation of death due to political positions and procedures with scant qualms indeed about sacrificing the life of the oppressed to the interests of national and foreign capital. Death has been a daily reality for our poor for a long time now. The situation has not changed in recent years, but our consciousness of it has. Gradually our awareness has become more acute. Slowly but surely, we are coming to fathom the injustice of death beyond its individual dimension. The injustice of the death around us is coming to acquire a collective scope. Little by little, unjust death is no longer something that must be fatalistically accepted by the poor, something almost "natural." And ever increasingly, popular forces are massing for a struggle for liberation and life.

This death/life relationship, anchored in the daily reality of an exploited Christian people, functions on a most profound human level and touches, without mediations, the very nerve of faith. It is not a matter, then, of a challenge arising from a "social situation," almost as if the demands of this state of affairs were something beyond the bounds of the basic demands of the gospel message. No, here we are face to face with concrete historical conditions for approaching the God of life the Bible speaks of, the concrete historical conditions for living the dialectic of death and life that the Risen One reveals to us.

The Johannine logion, "I have come so that they may have life and have it to the full" (John 10:10), expresses the depth of the mystery of the Father—the Father of Jesus, who, precisely because he is the God of life, makes himself *Go'el*: Rescuer—the Redeemer, the Ever Near, the Defender of those marginalized from the banquet of life. His transcendence resides in the gratuity of this love. His covenant, his alliance, itself transcending the infidelities of his people, manifests the persistent determination of his life-bestowing intention. His manifestation as a "jealous God" is but a reflection of his own being, unyielding before any attempt at reductionism. And now he will brook no murder of the life he has bestowed on us. Jesus, the revealer of the Father, incarnates this divine trait in his practice. This is why he lives among persons condemned to nonlife, and from there proclaims the kingdom, inaugurates the banquet for the desperate ones of the earth—discloses to them the meaning of life eternal and the way in which one is born to it: by surrendering it.

Our peoples, inasmuch as they are under sentence of death, have all the more need of forcefully asserting their God as the God of life. This places us under the obligation of discovering the theological meaning of the liberating option of the struggle against the idolatries that generate death and the theological meaning of the self-abandonment in martyrdom of so many authentic witnesses of the resurrection. This is the great theological challenge: to find a language about God that, grafted onto the stalk of the biblical experience, will strike root in the profound suffering of the masses of our people and draw sustenance from the hope that has begun to make them live again.

Christian Faith and Popular Identity

Closely related with the foregoing, but with a specificity of its own, is the need to work out, with greater precision and depth, the role of the faith residing in a people that is poor, *mestizo*, of mainly Andean stock, but whose consciousness of its identity is still confused.

The question is: In what way can the Christian message, present and alive among the popular masses, become—or rather, develop as—a factor in a liberating popular identity? This is a question with obvious political implications, but the political is not the whole. This is also a question about the quality of a people who, in its own specificity, must find a way of affirming themselves in history with all its virtualities.

Here, then, at the theological level, we have not only the question of the relationship between God and the poor, but of the relationship of the God of the poor, the God of life, with the racial and cultural particularities of these concrete oppressed peoples. The multifaceted epiphany of the God of life must be synthesized, examined in depth, and asserted wherever he makes his appearance. This God appears in the ancient Andean and minority Amazon cultures—both so admirably resistant to the continual harassments of the invader—as well as in the complex world of the poor *mestizo* majority, who predominate in numbers, it is true, but who are still only in the process of shaping their own identity.

Part of the dislocation of our people's identity is owing to a social order to crush the values that unite that people, in order to weaken it, atomize it, and thereby more easily subject it to an oppressive machinery. And yet the very weight of the oppressive situation of poverty and subjugation functions as a unifying factor of resistance and struggle. In the very act of discovering itself as a poor class, this people sinks deeper and deeper roots—and identifies with the roots it progressively and creatively accepts and assumes. Thus the cruel phenomenon itself becomes a potential factor for renovation and renewal.

The Christian faith accompanies—forms a part of—the life of our people. Many times, as we have admitted, it functions as consolation, yes, and resignation, in their situation. But it likewise constitutes a reference to the mystery that gives meaning to human existence, and partially re-orders a crushed, confused universe. It is not difficult, if one but enter profoundly into the religious world of our people, to perceive that religion as an element of identity for them—an element of rejection and refusal of the destruction that constitutes the dominator's sole wall of defense. This process has been clearly present from the first moment of the raising of popular consciousness to the fact that we stand at the start of a long journey of liberation. The episodes of the struggle have close, spontaneous bonds with faith—indeed, the poor discover motivation in their faith to fight for their right to live with dignity. In this way religion develops its potentiality as a factor in the identity of a poor people.

These considerations must lead us to deepen our theology of covenant— that which makes a people to be a people of God. Israel's identity arose out of a consciousness of its election, which was at once gift and demand. And the demand is ever this: concrete, ongoing fidelity to the originative experience. Israel would not be God's people if it did not bear witness in its practice, before all other peoples, that God is the God who delivers the poor and the oppressed.

If the popular classes of Peru interiorize this intrinsic dimension of faith, if this faith is called upon to have an effect on history, then its verification will necessarily begin to include, as a vital element in the people's identity, their relationship with the Father. It will therefore also include their ongoing solidarity with the cause of the very poorest and most despised, their commitment to every deed of justice rising up from among the oppressed. And this solidarity will involve the obligation to gather up, reinforce, and project in new directions the ethnic, historical, and cultural origins proper to our *mestizo* peoples, as they are integrated into the long struggle for liberation. What is really at stake is the transformation of a self-achieved identity of the people of God into a basic element of the self-achieved identity of our people—a people exploited, poor, *mestizo* . . . and believing.

—Translated by Robert R. Barr

5

Toward an American-Hispanic Theology of Liberation in the U.S.A.

Virgil Elizondo

There are today in the United States approximately 17 million American Hispanics. In addition, there are 5 to 7 million "undocumented" Latin Americans living in the United States. The two principal groups are those of Puerto Rican origin and those of Mexican origin. Most of these persons are poor, brown-skinned, and continue to use Spanish as their ordinary language.

It is important to keep in mind that the two principal groups did not emigrate to the United States to become Americans: they became Americans when the U.S.A. expanded its territorial boundaries to include Puerto Rico and what had been the northern half of Mexico. We can say that in the last five hundred years these peoples have been twice conquered, twice colonized, and twice oppressed—first by Spain in the sixteenth century, and then by the United States, beginning in the nineteenth century.

From the beginning the conquered and colonized peoples have been stereotyped as inferior, lazy and, generally speaking, immature. This has "justified" the massive exploitation of these peoples, with the result that most of them have remained quite poor. Beyond economic poverty, they have also been locked into poverty of spirit, which comes when a people is looked down upon and continually told by all the media of communication that it belongs to an inferior stratum of humanity. Oppression is justified by those in power on the grounds that they were the ones who ascertained that it was an incompetent, undeserving, and inferior people. And it is assumed that the needs of the oppressed are not the same as the needs of the "civilized and superior" peoples who "by God's will" are destined ("manifest destiny") to govern.

ECCLESIAL ENTERPRISE

Even though the vast majority of Hispanics are Roman Catholic, and many continue to be cultural Catholics even when they turn to Protestantism,

50

a number of Protestant denominations are growing among the Hispanics. A very dynamic and active proselytism is being conducted by Protestant churches. Wherever there are Hispanic communities there is evidence that Protestant communities are growing and spreading rapidly. It is estimated that 85 percent of American Hispanics still identify as Roman Catholics, but this figure is declining rapidly.

Among Catholic Hispanics the phenomenon of basic Christian communities has burst into life. This movement originated in Latin America and is having a very positive effect in helping the people to realize that "we are the church." It has also given rise to a style of theological reflection that begins within the small community of believers. Much of the work that is being carried out in work-centers such as the Mexican-American Cultural Center in San Antonio, Texas, is precisely the result and the response of small believing communities.

Within the institutional church in the United States, especially in some areas where there is a heavy Hispanic concentration, there is an awakened and socially active church body. The official church in some areas, such as San Antonio, Houston, El Paso, and Los Angeles, is acting as an animator informing and forming lay Hispanics in their mission to transform the marketplace. The official church itself, as church, is not getting involved in political issues, but an informed and awakened laity is gathering in parishes to analyze social, economic, and political situations and take concrete action to bring about needed changes. This movement has had many results, all of which can be traced to the rise of a social conscience in committed Hispanic Christians.

We are also beginning to see the first stages of a native leadership within the Hispanic church. By "native" I mean born in the United States. Often in the past native-born American Hispanics have been oppressed and dictated to by U.S. taskmasters *and* by Latin Americans, who also took it for granted that we could not do our own thing. Today leadership is beginning to grow out of the Hispanic communities. We have learned much from Latin America but we have also learned much from our own U.S. experience. Today we are blending aspects of both to put together new models of thought and action.

There are two major underlying problems facing our Hispanic church communities. One comes from the unquestioned acceptance of capitalism as the only or the best economic system. Many of our people come to the United States seeking a higher standard of living and to them it is unquestionably what the U.S. free-enterprise system has made possible.

The other problem arose in the classical nineteenth-century Latin American liberal school of thought that believes it has to reject everything religious if a people is to be set free. This thought is very strong among our Chicano intellectuals, university students, and the militants in liberation movements. Because in the past the church was almost always in league with the oppressor, they feel that they have to eliminate the church and everything religious for their people ever to find integral human liberation.

THEOLOGICAL ENTERPRISE

In April 1981 we held at the Mexican-American Cultural Center a meeting of Hispanic doctoral candidates and those who had recently received their doctorate. The financial resources for the meeting came from the Fund for Theological Education and the inspiration came from the Ecumenical Association of Third World Theologians. It was the first such gathering of native-born American Hispanics who are preparing themselves to be able to conceptualize, analyze, and propound the feelings, struggles, and dreams of their people.

It was also thought to be the first such experience of authentic fellowship among Hispanics of various ethnic subgroups and of diverse religious communities. There were Roman Catholics, Disciples of Christ, Baptists, Methodists, Episcopalians, Presbyterians, and others. They came from all over the United States and Puerto Rico.

All the participants came from the people and identified very closely with the struggles and aspirations, the problems and developments, of Hispanics in the United States. They were preparing themselves to be leaders, but they were very definitely of the people. It was a group searching critically and intellectually from the point of departure of the heart of their people. A twofold common bond was evident: solidarity with our Hispanic poor and acceptance of liberation theology as basic to our ministry.

They took the first steps toward formulating and proclaiming the voice of the Hispanic Christian in the U.S.A. Following are the themes that emerged from that meeting.

Religion and Mental Health

The first theological theme that surfaced was the interrelationship between religion and mental health. It must be remembered that a major problem of the Hispanic in the United States is that of total cultural disintegration. Our Latin culture is radically different from the culture of the United States: Nordic-European in origin, heavily technical, very competitive, very individualistic, and very materialistic. Persons coming from a Latin American culture find themselves in a totally strange world. They undergo a dissolution of their Latin culture and feel a need to integrate themselves into the U.S. culture.

The intense desire to live and work in the United States but not lose their fundamental Latin identity causes serious identity problems. Many immigrant Hispanics become quickly aware that they are no longer just Latin Americans from Latin America, but neither are they accepted as North Americans. They are in a limbo of nonidentity. They know who they are not, but they cannot say who they are. This brings serious problems at every level of life: personal, familial, work-related, and religious. Thus one of the key topics that is beginning to be explored by a good number of Hispanic leaders is the interrelationship and role of religion and mental health.

Secular Structures

Hispanics are aware that traditionally they have been bypassed and ignored and exploited by the structures of society in the United States. Today they are making strenuous efforts to become involved in the structures that shape and determine our life. Thus another emergent theological theme is that of the need for a liberation theology that arises from the uniqueness of Latin experience in the United States.

In the United States the oppressed are not the masses of the people but the minorities. This conditions the type of critical involvement of which we are capable. We know that we cannot be authentic Christians and *not* be involved in the "secular" structures that shape and determine the lives of our people. We have become aware that the structures of society can be either the incarnation of sin or the incarnation of grace. It is our duty to become involved in them so that they may serve the people and not continue to be a vehicle for the exploitation of the people.

Cultural Assimilation

We are aware that our cultural questions probe a level deeper than that of social structures and touch on the very soul of the innermost earthly identity of a people. Culture is that which gives us the ultimate root of our collective earthly identity. It is at this level that the deepest questioning is now beginning. Just what does it mean to be a Hispanic Christian living in the U.S.A.? To what degree do we assume the cultural ways of this country so as to be able to participate in them critically and intelligently? To what degree do we allow ourselves to be remade by the structures of this country so that in belonging to them we cease being who we are as a people and become someone else? This is a burning question that we feel has to be studied theologically for we are convinced that it is of the essence of the gospel to work for unity and harmony within a functional diversity of peoples.

We feel we can be a prophetic minority that poses critical and radical questions within the flow of U.S. church life. We do not want, then, simply to be absorbed into the U.S. way of life, but to participate critically in its purification and evolution. Simply to succeed in becoming "good Americans" would be to fail as Hispanic Christians.

We are convinced that if we are going to make a unique contribution to our country we cannot give up the greatest treasure that God has given us, which is precisely our ancestral identities and the ancient ways of our people that have come to us from countless generations. To give up such ways entirely would be an offense to God the Creator and an insult to the very people that have given us life and sustenance.

We are beginning to explore the whole question of the interrelationship of biblical faith and culture. Furthermore, in order to do this adequately, we are having to study the whole phenomenon of culture in a thoroughly scientific way, which moves far beyond culture merely as folklore. We explore culture as that which is natural to the group, and therefore appears to be the law of nature itself.

Ecumenism in Action

In the past the question of ecumenism never arose among Hispanics, for we were convinced that to be Hispanic was to be Catholic, and in the West, until recently, ecumenical dialogue usually centered around doctrinal questions. Today ecumenism among Hispanics opens some very interesting and challenging questions.

It is generally agreed that Catholicism is part of Hispanic culture. The question is raised by many Protestants, whether Hispanics could be culturally Catholic and denominationally Protestant—in other words, Catholic but not *Roman* Catholic.

On the other hand, there is also the rise of the spirit to work together on the social problems that afflict our people. There is a tremendous unity among the members of various Christian denominations who are committed to working for the well-being of Hispanics. There is great unity in working for the rights of farmworkers, for the betterment of the lot of migrant workers, and for proper treatment of those resident in the U.S.A. without legal documentation. In this, denominational labels peel off and we catch sight of a profoundly Christian and unified people. This is a beautiful experience of a unity that is already in effect. It is a unity in action, which, we hope, will be followed by other forms of unity in Hispanic and other Christian communities.

Beginnings of Systematic Theology

We are also witnessing the beginnings of properly Hispanic theological productivity. Christology and ecclesiology, biblical studies and interpretations, indigenous liturgical reworkings, and spirituality are all beginning to emerge from Hispanic communities, bearing the signs of their distinctive provenance.

We are more and more convinced that *all* theological reflection is socially and historically conditioned. Thus we do not consider our thought to be any less authentic than that of any other theological tradition. It is just that we are very clearly aware of the point of departure of our own reflection. And we feel that this type of conditioned theological reflection is not only more honest but even more universal. For at the core of the Judeo-Christian tradition is the fact that through the particular, determinate actions of a people and a person, God wrought salvation for all humankind. In the Scriptures it is precisely through the particular medium that the universal message is broadcast. We are convinced that the more universal one tries to be, the less one has to offer to others. Conversely, the more particular a thought is, the more its universal implications become evident. Hence, when we reflect out of our own unique experience, we are certainly doing it for our own people but we are aware that it will have something to offer to all others. We have been greatly enriched by theological movements in Latin America; they have helped us to discover our own uniqueness, identity, and mission within the universal Christian community.

Role and Function of Popular Expressions of Faith

For an oppressed minority, popular expressions of faith are not an opium but the language of ultimate resistance to the gods of a threatening empire. It is the unique expression of our faith that keeps us alive as a people no matter how strong the external threats to our existence might be. Popular religious expressions (not dogmatic or doctrinal formulations or church laws) are the ultimate justification of the way of life of a people. They are fundamental to the existence of those who belong to the group, and incomprehensible to outsiders. To the dominant, they appear as mere folklore, something that can be used as tourist attractions. It is through the ongoing dialogue of the Scriptures with the expressions of faith of the masses that a liberating evangelization takes place—an evangelization that does not destroy the soul of a people, but purifies it of its enslavements.

Theologizing out of the living expressions of the people is one of the most exciting developments taking place within the Hispanic Catholic community in the United States. It is just beginning, but we are already aware of the very positive response that it is receiving from the people. It is a way of affirming the people, yet helping them to grow and develop as a people.

Small group dialogues will continue and efforts are already beginning to start dialogues with American blacks. We have not yet started to dialogue with the Native Americans of the United States but in due time we will begin. The process of doing our own theological reflection according to our own specific genius as Hispanics of the U.S.A. is just beginning. We want to learn from others, but we do not want to be a mere copy or imitation of someone else. The uniqueness of our geographico-cultural situation demands that we come up with our own methods of work that will in time produce a new knowledge that is truly expressive of our situation and our mission.

6

In Search of an African Theology

African Report Group

The African Group, which had prepared for its part in this international conference on the basis of regional meetings in Southern, East, Central, and West Africa, conducted a trio of work sessions on August 21, 1981. The work method we selected consisted in listening to the four regional reports, then commenting on them by filling out a questionnaire that the steering committee had sent to the regional groups.

The questionnaire listed four points. The members of the regional groups were invited to analyze (1) their socio-economic reality and political situation, (2) their regions' cultural, ethnic, and religious worldviews, (3) the involvement and commitment of Christians in their regions, and (4) the influence of Western theology and local efforts at indigenization, inculturation, and contextualization.

The four regional reports were presented by, respectively, the Reverend Bonganjalo Goba for Southern Africa; Professor Kibicho, of Nairobi, for East Africa; Professor Ngindu Mushete, of Kinshasa, for Central Africa; and Professor Appiah-Kubi, of Ghana, for West Africa. Father Engelbert Mveng, S.J., secretary general of the Ecumenical Association of African Theologians, served as coordinator.

SOCIO-ECONOMIC REALITY AND THE POLITICAL SITUATION

In the area of socio-economic realities and the political situation, in spite of the diversity of regional situations, there are a number of constants for the continent as a whole. Among them are:

(1) Western capitalism's domination of Africa through the multinationals, with the complicity of the local dominant classes.

(2) Neocolonialism, in its political, economic, and cultural forms.

(3) The breakdown of North-South dialogue, and deterioration of the terms of international trade between North and South.

56

(4) General breakdown of technical assistance and of the system of technological exchange.

So much for certain common factors. It will also be useful to underscore local divergencies.

(1) In Southern Africa, the agrarian dilemma, with the usurpation of the land by the white minority, seems to form the basis of the whole system of apartheid, racism, and institutionalized violence. The immediate consequence is the stiffening of the political regime, which is becoming more intransigent by the day, all mass media propaganda to the contrary notwithstanding. This intransigence is aggravated by military alliances with Western powers.

(2) Of special note in East Africa is the collapse of the East African Community. Today we have three heterogeneous countries, whose attitude toward one another is, if not antagonistic, at least indifferent. Kenya, politically stable, wealthier than its neighbors, is also under the sway of Western capitalism. Uganda, in spite of the fall of its military regime, is writhing in economic catastrophe. Tanzania, which is not very wealthy, is enjoying a certain degree of stability thanks to Ujamaa socialism, which is attempting to promote a greater sense of cultural identity in that country.

Other East African nations—Somalia and Ethiopia—like Uganda and Tanzania, live in a tension that invites the intervention of foreign powers. The Asian presence is an additional factor in the tension and instability there, especially in the economy.

(3) In Central Africa the postcolonial crisis is bringing on a "generalized debilitation" of the very bases of existence.

It is generating social debilitation by reason of the collapse of the foundations of traditional society, together with the instability caused by an elite class educated abroad and often a stranger to its own people.

It is generating a debilitation of political and economic institutions—hand-me-down copies of the West without any meaning for the people.

It is generating cultural debilitation in the wake of cultural neocolonialism in the schools and mass media, the absence of a committed, "rooted," elite, and the absence of leaders and thinkers capable of original and independent thinking. The result is internal economic catastrophe and ideological disarray, coupled with political instability, both in countries under capitalist domination, such as Zaire, and in those under socialist domination, such as the Congo.

(4) West Africa enjoyed a period of euphoria with the disappearance of the military regimes in a number of countries—Nigeria and Ghana, for example—and the return to civil government, but the economic situation is still a concern. Nigeria's oil boom is occasioning mass abandonment of the countryside and food production, and the influx of the multinationals. The economic debacle in Ghana, with its galloping inflation, is marked by an unemployment crisis, together with the siphoning-off of that country's food production by export interest.

In spite of the creation of an economic community among the nations of West Africa—and thus horizons filled with promise—its countries still turn to their old colonizers. The presence of Lebanese and Greeks in West Africa is another factor in the destabilization of their region's economy.

ETHNIC AND RELIGIOUS WORLDVIEWS

As to worldviews, the situation across the African continent is rather more uniform. Everywhere, traditional religions manifest a vitality that seems to have suffered very little at the hands of colonialism and Christianity. Everywhere they are a leaven of cultural and spiritual renewal, through the independent churches as well as through movements under way within the official churches.

At the same time, one must keep in mind the destructive blows dealt African society by cultural colonialism, with its negation of the concept of a distinctive African personality or of an African anthropology—entailing the collapse of the very foundations of our society and institutions, as well as the cultural depersonalization of the elite. It is in reaction to this situation that movements fostering blackness, black consciousness, African presence, and the like, have arisen.

Traditional medicine has played an important role as well, not only within the churches—via charismatic movements stressing healing, and because of the importance accorded the care of the sick in ministry—but also in medical research, with its profound influence on modern Western medicine.

The African cultural renewal of the last thirty years, with its literature, its art, its music, its modern films, and so on, is a challenge to theology and religion, and to Christianity in particular, which is continually being called to account by the new generation of writers and artists.

CHRISTIAN INVOLVEMENT AND COMMITMENT

It is especially in the area of Christian presence and commitment that our situations clearly differ from region to region. Still one must be aware of a number of constants. On the African continent as a whole, several churches are forthrightly engaged in the struggles for political, economic, and cultural liberation. Several are in the forefront of the promotion of African languages, art, music, and so on. But there are serious shortcomings as well. The first is in the absence of any coordination of efforts, not only on the continental level, but even on the regional one. It is to these, and like deficiencies, that the Ecumenical Association of African Theologians, as well as the Movement of African Christian Intellectuals, which has arisen and is developing in Central Africa, are attempting to respond today.

On the regional level, there are several things to be noticed. In Southern Africa, the churches in large part reflect the image of the populations themselves: white churches espouse the white racist cause, and black churches are plunged in the misery of the oppressed. Still, some churches have accepted their prophetic role courageously. The South African Council of Churches illustrates this very well.

In East Africa, the commitment of the churches is on the timid side, as they prudently tiptoe past the real issues in a way that, although short of out-and-out complicity with the established powers, is nevertheless an obstacle to the prophetic role of the church. And yet on the level of grassroots Christian communities, the breath of fresh air that wafted from Vatican Council II is stimulating sincere commitment and a genuine spiritual and cultural renewal, and the racist situation in Southern Africa is arousing the solidarity of the people for integral human liberation in Africa. Here is where the need is felt for coordinating and dynamizing movements such as the Ecumenical Association of African Theologians and the Movement of African Christian Intellectuals.

In Central Africa, the commitment of the churches seems to be enhanced by the fact that, in the economic and political crisis shaking certain countries, the churches are the only real force the people have to rely on. The grassroots communities play a fundamental role here—to the point of undertaking services of *diakonia* that should actually be the duty of the absent established powers. Thus the need for leadership is felt here as well, and the Movement of African Christian Intellectuals and the Ecumenical Association of African Theologians are beginning to play a role. The contribution of the churches to cultural renewal is remarkable in a number of countries—Cameroon and Zaire, for example, to name but two.

In West Africa, the churches' contribution to cultural renewal is equally remarkable. The African languages are enjoying a true renaissance, thanks to translations of the Bible and their use in the liturgy and religious education. The vitality of Christian movements, especially women's movements, deserves special mention. In September 1980, an especially important event took place—the birth of the Association of Women Theologians of West Africa. Finally, Christians have played an important part in the revamping of the Volta Dam project, as well as in the overthrow of certain military regimes.

WESTERN THEOLOGY AND LOCAL EFFORTS
AT INDIGENIZATION, INCULTURATION,
AND CONTEXTUALIZATION

The influence of Western theology throughout the continent is a fact of its colonial heritage and cultural domination by the West. All, or nearly all, African theologians have been trained in Western schools of theology. The development of a living theology outside the traditional molds now appears on the scene as a great adventure to be undertaken.

On the other hand, the official churches exercise a perduring, albeit uneasy, control over the thought and work of African theologians. African churches are often faithful copies of their missionary mother churches, and so they refuse to admit any theological thought, any ecclesiology, or any church law but that developed in and sent here from the West.

Hence the development within the churches of a reactionary movement opposed to any and all efforts at inculturation. It will stop at nothing to reverse our efforts toward an African theology by undermining their base. Thus we must stay very much on our guard.

We have all these tendencies pretty much everywhere in Africa, under different forms and with different nuances. But we Africans are resolutely committed to take historical destiny, and the future of Christianity on our continent, in hand. This is our sacred task, and no intimidation can deter us from it. This is why African-type liturgies are developing, slowly but surely. This is why an African Christian literature is being born. This is why a properly African spirituality is beginning to nourish the devotion of searching souls. This is why an African ecclesiology is drawing more and more scientific theological attention. This is why African religious orders are springing up, to enrich the tradition of a consecrated life at the heart of the universal church. This is why a catechesis, and a pastoral ministry addressed to all the social classes of God's people are beginning to bear fruit. We are beginning to see a new African theology, and that theology is relentlessly on the march—shoulder to shoulder with the great movement for the total liberation of Africa.

CONCLUSION

The African delegates to this fifth general assembly of the Ecumenical Association of Third World Theologians are happy to greet their brothers and sisters from the other continents and to share with them the concerns and the hopes of Africa. This we do with faith and modesty, in full consciousness of our feeble means and the humble measure of things human. We likewise address an urgent appeal to the assembly at large that the hopes placed in EATWOT not be in vain—that the efforts of us all may open up a constructive, liberating future to the peoples we have come here to represent.

—Translated by Robert R. Barr

7

Toward a Relevant Theology in Asia

Asian Report Group

Although we call ours the Asian Group Report, we are aware that we do not represent all the countries of Asia. The seventeen Asians who participated in our intracontinental dialogue at the Delhi conference represented only seven countries. Of the group, only those from India, Sri Lanka, and the Philippines came with preparatory documents, which were used as the basis of our discussion and joint report. The participants from Hong Kong, Indonesia, and Vietnam were invited as observers and therefore had not participated in any national preparation for the conference.

Conscious of this limitation, we looked at our similarities and differences, and attempted to determine which aspects of Asian reality particularly challenge our task of doing theology in our continent today. We saw most similarities in the realm of the socio-economic and political, whereas differences lay mainly in the area of culture and religious worldviews. The variety and complexity of our background and situations have provoked varied theological outlooks, approaches, and emphases. Despite our differences, we also recognized common threads in our efforts to contextualize our theology. We shall present a synthesis of these common elements at the conclusion of our report.

CHALLENGES POSED BY ASIAN SOCIO-ECONOMIC AND POLITICAL REALITIES

We identified five common socio-economic and political realities in our different Asian countries: (1) colonial experience and debilitating structures of domination; (2) poverty of the many and opulence of the few; (3) increasing marginalization of sections of our national communities; (4) the inferior and oppressed status of Asian women; (5) growing international militarism and repressive regimes in Asia.

Colonial Experience and Debilitating Structures of Domination

The socio-economic and political history of the peoples of the Asian countries that we represent is blemished by the scar tissue of centuries of colonial experience. In addition to the psychological dependence and its effects upon the attitudes, thought-forms, and lifestyles of our peoples, such experience has left behind a network of dominative structures created by our colonial past and maintained by neocolonial economic relationships with First World economic communities. These structures—external and internal—constrict the process of socio-economic revolution in our countries.

EXTERNAL STRUCTURES

During the colonial period, our basic economic structures as well as our educational and social systems were made to support colonial interests. After independence, these structures of domination were maintained by the new economic relationship with the North Atlantic economic communities and with Japan. Therefore, a radical detachment of our economic and other structures of life from the affluent First World economic structures is an immediate imperative.

But because the scientific and technological know-how and instrumentation that our countries need are also controlled by First World nations, detachment is not easy or feasible without an adequate transfer of technology or the development of a viable alternate economic structure relevant for our context. Are there any lessons that our countries can learn from the China experiment?

Our quest for an alternate economic structure leads us to a careful examination of the state of both capitalistic and socialistic societies since the EATWOT meeting in 1976. This examination must take seriously the phenomenon of North-South dialogue, the rather fruitless quest for a New International Economic Order, the present role of international bodies such as the World Bank, the International Monetary Fund (IMF), and the like.

Various factors are causing an ongoing and almost irreversible crisis of capitalism in the industrial and advanced countries. Recession, chronic large-scale unemployment, bankruptcies, and inflation are leading to widespread discontent especially among youth. Migrant laborers in these countries are most vulnerable to the consequences of these trends.

The crisis of capitalism strikes the free-enterprise countries of the dependent Third World with particular vehemence. The capitalistic world powers impose upon our countries a pattern of development that leads to further underdevelopment.

The technological advances have enormously increased the power of capital over productive processes. Capital can now rapidly move productive bases or factories to different parts of the world purely for reasons of profit or cheap labor. The development of electronics, micro-processing, and silicone-chip technology is making labor more and more redundant and more dependent upon capital.

Out of this matrix, various forms of debilitating consumerism are now rampant in our countries. Our national priorities are lopsided. For example, even the promotion of exports is dictated by the priorities of transnational economic concerns. Asian countries are being used for cheap labor, leading to many forms of violation of fundamental human dignity in all countries.

It is in this context that we are led to recognize the increasing influence of socialist concerns and Marxist insights upon the Asian masses. While we welcome these socialist trends, we are also aware of recent developments in the socialist world that have led to a crisis of socialism. Socialism is no longer critiqued simply on the basis of what the communist states have done with human rights. The inroads of market economy and consumerism in socialist countries; their growing indebtedness to the World Bank and the IMF; recovery in China, with its critical evaluation of Marxism and cultural revolution, and yet seeking Western aid for modernization; the Vietnam-Kampuchea conflict—all these developments raise serious questions as to whether we have any clearly defined model of socialism as an alternative to capitalism.

An additional difficulty for such a formulation derives from the political use of religion, including the Christian evangelistic enterprise, for anticommunist propaganda. Subtle persuasion as well as overt propaganda have the effect of turning populations against socialism and leading them to a naive acceptance of capitalism as the more suitable ideology.

We are called upon to clearly affirm the viability of a socialist option for our countries while critically discerning the self-interest expressed in the socialist world and the consequent watering-down of the socialist cause in history. By "socialist option" we do not mean any particular historical manifestation of the socialist system, but rather the political process that brings about liberation and justice for all and involves all persons as free agents of their own history, and guarantees them freedom and dignity as a fundamental right.

INTERNAL STRUCTURES

When the colonial imperialists withdrew from our part of the world, power was not transferred to the people of our Asian countries but rather to small, powerful elites. The feudal structures of Asian societies were conducive to such transfer of power. As the Indian Preparatory Statement puts it:

Our independence movement terminated in a transfer of power without a social revolution. A Westernized elite with economic interests integrated into the interests of the outgoing colonial power became the successor. . . . It has been to their advantage to keep practically everything unchanged.

In all our countries, these elites not only benefit themselves at the expense of the masses but also continue to serve as effective instruments in the transfer of profit to Japan and the North Atlantic economic communities. The self-interest of these elites has constricted the zone of self-reliance in many Asian countries, keeping millions at the lowest level of subsistence.

Poverty of the Many and Opulence of the Few

In all our countries, widespread abject poverty alongside one of the most evident and shocking features is that of segregated affluence. Inasmuch as all the means of production are owned or controlled by a few who also control political power and can therefore manipulate the government, the economic policies of our countries are not designed to deal adequately with this gruesome reality.

We do take note, however, of the growing restlessness, positive movements, and even organized struggle of the poor masses for liberation. It is lamentable that in many countries these popular movements are suppressed by the rich and powerful. Moreover, they often are discouraged or condemned by our Christian churches.

Increasing Marginalization of Sections of our National Communities

We also critique our countries for a failure to integrate all groups within a nation into a single people and to provide a sense of identity. Often, in the name of national security and integration, minority groupings have been marginalized. It is in view of this context that the whole concept of "nation" and its integrity must be redefined.

Inferior and Oppressed Status of Asian Women

Although women constitute more than 50 percent of Asian populations and have contributed to the social, economic, and political development of Asian countries, they have been accorded a "minority" and inferior status both in society and in the churches. In our male-dominated societies, there still exist oppressive customs and practices stemming from feudal times and systems. The dowry system practiced in many of our countries makes women the object of bargaining and has led to tragic and inhuman consequences. "Wife-burning" still occurs in parts of India.

With the coming of capitalism and the modernization of our societies, the oppression of women has become all the more evident by their absence in decision-making positions even in issues and events that radically affect their lives. A lower pay scale for women and their vulnerability to sexual exploitation to boost the nation's economy are only two of the degrading ways in which women are oppressed. In more recent times, consumerism and tourism have pressured women into a cheap labor market with inhuman working conditions and late hours, exposing them to the harassment of unscrupulous employers. This situation has led many women and even young girls to prostitution. This is especially true where there has been a mushrooming of free trade zones—for example, in the Philippines, Sri Lanka, and Taiwan. Asian women working in the Middle East have been subjected to abusive treatment and discrimination as "house maids."

Society at large has failed to recognize the economic value represented by women who willingly work full time in keeping their home and rearing their children.

Growing International Militarism and Repressive Regimes in Asia

International militarism and the arms race have become a threat to the Asian countries, in at least three ways. First, it has led many of our nations to be increasingly dependent upon the superpowers for security. Secondly, many of our countries, caught up in the arms race against the national will, have been forced to give a disastrously low priority to social and economic planning. Thirdly, the competition of the superpowers for military and economic dominance has kept many of the Asian nations divided among themselves.

In the name of national security and integration, repressive regimes in several of our Asian nations suppress various forms of freedom, such as the press, the right to protest and strike, the right to organize for liberation. The preparatory statements of various regions of the continent for this conference testify amply to this fact.

CHALLENGES POSED BY OUR CULTURES, RELIGION AND WORLDVIEWS

Because of the great diversity in the cultural and religious traditions of the people of Asia—even just among the seven countries represented at the conference—and because of the limitations of time, we did not attempt to synthesize our similarities. Rather, we looked at the diverse positive and negative aspects of the worldviews, religions, and cultures in our various regions that need to be addressed in doing theology in Asia.

Hong Kong

Though tempered by modern capitalistic and scientific outlooks, the worldview of the people is predominantly Confucian-animist. Within the feudalistic context, Confucianism concentrates authority in the head of the family. Importance is attached to family relationships expressed in filial piety as well as ancestor worship or veneration. However, filial piety is increasingly influenced by the self-seeking individualism of capitalism.

The Buddhist influence in Hong Kong is Taoist, expressed in the desire and search for "quiet" amid the tense, busy, and noisy day-to-day life in the crown colony.

Christianity is also an element in the religious milieu. Although for the majority of the faithful, Christianity provides a sort of stabilizing influence that promotes a sense of complacency and a middle-class mentality, for a few it challenges the status quo.

Due to the continued colonial experience, the majority have no clear sense of identity, though this is slowly changing. There is a search for meaning among youth.

A special characteristic of the recent past is a steadily growing interest in the history of the Chinese people, expressed in a nostalgic celebration of the past in novels, stories, movies, and so forth. There is some attempt to bring about change through "social" films.

In spite of the maxim, "All men of the four seas are brothers," the people of Hong Kong are still narrowly "inner-centered."

India

Despite the predominance of Hinduism in this country of 680 million persons, pluralism is the striking feature of India's complex cultural reality—a reality marked by great ethnic, linguistic, and religious diversity, and the rigid and religiously-sanctioned social stratification of the caste system. Underlying this pluralism is a unity of perspective and outlook shaped by centuries of literary and religious tradition. There is a sense of community with the cosmos, a keen awareness of the oneness of the many, and a search for the "within" of reality.

However, this vision of oneness is often blurred and its humanizing potentialities unrealized. For example, an overemphasis on the metaphysical identity between *atman* (self) and *Brahma* (absolute) led to a view of the world as illusion and the historical process as relatively insignificant. It was also easy for the upper castes to create a symbolic system based on the unity of agriculture, culture, and cult and to make use of it for reinforcing its control over the masses. Thus, in India, we see religions providing legitimation of the power, privilege, and exploitive practice of upper castes and classes.

In cultural and religious areas there are movements that, though ambivalent, could help in the liberation of the masses. New liberative interpretations of religious tenets are beginning to appear in all the great spiritual traditions of India. There are attempts to go to the roots of Indian religious and cultural heritage and draw from them inspiration for the struggle for humanization.

The tribal awakening that is going on in India today is of particular significance in this context. The various tribes all over the country are struggling to liberate themselves from social and economic oppression and maintain their identity in the face of threats from the values championed by dominant groups and militant Hinduism as well as capitalism. Tribal conceptions of human nature and its relationship to physical nature should be preserved for building a more human future.

Indonesia

In Indonesia, where 90 percent of the total population of 147 million are Muslims, the Islamic tradition has long been a vital part of the fabric of national life.

Society is looked upon as a huge family. This, on the one hand, may tend to reinforce the authoritative father-figure; on the other hand, mother is respected as "the source of all blessings," as expressed, for example, in the Koranic saying: Paradise is under the sole of mother's feet.

Because society is seen as a family, relationships are more important than achievements. Consensus and cooperation are essential elements of this "family spirit" *(kekeluargaam)*.

In this context, "religious conviviality" is more easily understandable and practicable. Hence, a triumphalistic approach is neither feasible nor realistic in Christian theology in the Indonesian context. Instead, theology should adopt an attitude of openness and humility in interfaith dialogue in Indonesia.

Korea

The strands that make up the Korean religious and cultural ethos are many. Among the most significant are (1) the moral code of Confucianism, (2) shamanism among the poor, and (3) the Dong Hak indigenous movement.

The moral code of Confucianism was accepted as the political methodology by the ruling elite and the upper strata of society, and Buddhism was adopted for religious practice. The prevailing social values were founded upon these two major traditions. The lower strata of society found their consolation in shamanism. Thus, for many centuries, the authoritarian humanism of Confucianism and the other-worldly emphasis of internal harmony of the Buddhist teaching were influential among the elite, and shamanism provided a temporal healing function for the poor but without offering any possibility of social transformation.

The Dong Hak (Eastern Teaching) movement, the only systematized indigenous religion, arose and spread in the nineteenth century. It taught an anti-Western ideology and projected some liberation motifs for the poor. This movement, as well as the current attempts to reinterpret shamanism, Confucianism, and Buddhism, must be included by Christian theologians in their theological reflections and reformulations.

The involvement of Korean Christians in the struggle for justice and human rights, in dialogue with members of indigenous religions, principally shamanism and Dong Hak, as well as with social scientists and literary figures, brought about the emergence of *minjung* theology in Korea in the 1970s (see pp. 70–71 below).

The Philippines

Plurality of worldviews and sets of values is a striking feature of the Philippines today, marked by a mixture of the original Malay-Asian, the Westernized Malay, and the emerging Filipino culture.

The Malay-Asian culture is preserved by the Muslims and the non-Christian tribes who have resisted outside domination and maintained their cultural and political autonomy. In spite of their animistic worldview with its tendency to superstition and fatalism, the tribal peoples have developed a viable and meaningful culture that centered around the land and the community. Their present struggle against the imposition of Western forms of development is a sign of their determination to maintain a vital tradition that values life and land, self and others, responsibility and sacrifice, freedom and honor, common goals and the future.

The westernized Malay-Asian culture in its varied forms is adhered to by the large majority of lowland Christians in rural and urban areas. The dualistic worldview that they imbibed from the West reinforced the negative elements in their cultural values. Their experience of Spanish colonial rule and American domination left them with a colonized consciousness, a split-level Christianity, and a fragmented culture. Neither fully Malaysian, Christian, or American, nor a synthesis of the three, today they are suffering an identity crisis. Nevertheless, Western social science in the 1960s portrayed the lowland Christian Filipinos as a smiling, peace-loving people, obedient and patient, grateful and hospitable, happy with family and friends with whom they share whatever economic and social blessings they have.

Reaction to the domesticated image sketched by others and a serious search for national identity have given birth to a new breed of Filipinos. The emerging Filipinos want to recover the Malay-Asian tradition of freedom, participation, and concern for a common goal and future. They want to find true Christianity, without Western trappings. They want to extend personal Filipino values to the social realm, expanding self-esteem to self-reliance, clan-centeredness to mutual cooperation, familial closeness to national consensus, regionalism to patriotism, and smooth interpersonal relations to solidarity with humankind in viewing the world and social structures with a liberated consciousness.

Sri Lanka

Sri Lankan Christianity has increasingly shown its concern for a change of the social order in terms of the realization of human freedom, though more by noninstitutional Christian action groups than by ecclesiastical representatives. More recently, under pressure from such groups and in the face of increasing repression, even the official churches have responded to this need, going beyond the purely welfare policies previously followed.

The liberating thrust of other religions has not yet been so marked, but the establishment of a multireligion Liberation Doctrine Circle (Vimukthi Dharma Kendraya) has enabled representatives of all religions with this orientation to work together for liberation. Buddhism, the majority religion, would prove itself a valuable motivating force for all who pursue liberation; the core of Buddhist doctrine contains such a potential. Islam, in the context of the Islamic revolutionary movement in the Middle East, and Hinduism could also become heralds of liberation.

However, all these four religions in their institutional forms have a dangerous tendency to support the status quo and even act as a deterrent on progressive movements. It is only insofar as believers make common cause with those who can ideologically motivate others that they will spur their religions to promote integral human liberation.

In this sphere, the work of the Christian Workers' Fellowship and the Centre for Society and Action, both of which are open to adherents of diverse religions, as well as specialized agencies, such as the Justice and Peace Commission of the Catholic Church and the Council of Church and Nation of the Methodist Church, should be mentioned. In the case of the other world religions, the All-Ceylon Buddhist Congress and the Young Men's Muslim Association may be mentioned as having some potential though they are inclined to be inward-looking and sectarian.

Vietnam

The religious heritage of Vietnam derives mainly from Buddhism (Malayan), Confucianism, and Christianity. These three traditions, separately and together, contributed positive and negative elements to the spirit of the Vietnamese people.

Among negative elements, the following can be identified: evasion of worldly and historical realities; a dogmatic and legalistic spirit; an individualistic and authoritarian inclination.

The principal positive elements are: the Confucian incentive for social involvement; the Buddhist respect for life and nature, its spirit of tolerance, love, and compassion, its emphasis on endurance and spirituality; the Christian communitarian tradition and spirit of service in love, the affirmation of human dignity and justice.

In addition to the three major religions, with their worldviews, we may add the Marxist ideology. This revolutionary and atheistic element brings positive influence inasmuch as it entails a corrective to theistic superstitions, idolatry, and complacency. It is also positive in its influence by challenging Christians to be concretely involved in history and society.

REGIONAL THEOLOGICAL BEARINGS

It was in formulating our understanding of theology that the sharpest differences appeared in the discussion of our Asian report group. Because the question was seen to be both crucial and complex, we decided to present a summary of our theological understanding taken from our regional reports and to follow this up with a synthesis of our discussion. We recognized that our different contexts, values, and experiences had led us to different theological perspectives and priorities.

Theology in Korea

In general, both Catholic and Protestant theology in Korea reflects the traditions and modern trends of the West. This is largely due to the training— past and present—given in seminaries and the resources available.

The question of indigenous Korean theology is provoked by the question of the relevancy of Western theological traditions for the Korean people. Korean Christian theology cannot be a mere clothing of Western theology in the language of traditional Confucian thought, as was done in the initial attempts of Protestant theologians to indigenize theology in the mid-1960s. In those attempts, the historical and political situation of the Korean people was not taken into consideration.

In the 1970s, the churches began their involvement in the struggle for justice and freedom against the repressive policies of the Park regime. Praxis of Christian faith became an important part of Korean theology. The active response to, and through, suffering for the sake of the kingdom of God was manifest in Christian movements—Christian in the sense that Christians as individuals and as groups integrated themselves into the people's struggles for human rights and justice.

It was in this context that *minjung* theology was developed. It is a theological attempt to clarify a witness to the gospel in response to the Korean situation in the 70s. Koreans have not reached a definitive definition of the term *minjung,* but there is a consensus that it designates a people politically oppressed, economically poor, and socially and culturally alienated, yet seeking to be the artisan of its own destiny in an active way.

Minjung theology developed in the course of serious reflection upon the experiences of Christian movements such as the rural and urban industrial missions, movements of farmers, workers, and students, and human rights struggles. In this process, theologians in the movements gained new historical perceptions and new theological perspectives. The major discovery was that of the *minjung* in relation to suffering—in socio-biographical, socio-cultural, socio-economic, and political terms as well as in religious and spiritual terms. The *minjung* reveals its own reality by telling its own stories in its own language and expressions. *Minjung* theologians seek to understand that historical reality through an analysis of these stories. This analysis is multidimensional; it does not use one approach only, such as the Marxist or Maoist. There is at present a theological community working on *minjung* theology.

There are, however, some Protestant theologians who find *minjung* too hazy and narrow in its meaning. The concept has undergone change, with the result that, although it is used widely (not only by theologians but by social scientists and writers as well), it is ambivalent, sometimes carrying a revolutionary sense (though with reservations), but more often the sense of liberal democracy. These other Protestant theologians therefore prefer a theological exploration of the notion of "people," because it seems more pertinent to the actual socio-historical problems of Korea.

The core problem of the Korean people lies in the division of Korea into south and north. Many have come to realize that the truly democratic and egalitarian society they desire cannot be realized without the unification of Korea.

Unfortunately, the churches of South Korea have greatly contributed to the prolongation of the division by their strong anticommunism and rejection of North Korea. Since 1945 South Korean Christianity has provided the spiritual undergirding for division in the name of the Christian faith. The intense anticommunism made it inevitable for Christians to line themselves up blindly with the capitalist world, thus relinquishing their Christian freedom to venture out in search of a new future, the freedom to move from an unjust to a just world order. Given this situation, Korean theology today must include among its tasks a critique of Christian anticommunism, not in the light of communism but in the light of biblical faith in God's justice for the world. Without this seemingly negative task, theology in Korea cannot open up to the possibility of a positive attitude toward unification.

In view of the desired unification of Korea, the term "people" instead of *minjung* becomes more appropriate and needs to be explored in Korean theology; however, in view of needed social changes, it should include the theme of *minjung* liberation.

The more universal meaning of the word "people" is eschatological, pointing to the people of God. The people of Yahweh in the Old Testament sense is to be reinterpreted in the light of the new reconciled humanity of the future.

Christianity in Korea must engage in a ministry of reconciliation that anticipates the coming kingdom of God. Because of its eschatological and transcendent character, a ministry of reconciliation can retain its freedom to exercise a negative critique of any socio-political order. But this ministry must have some bearing upon the divided land, opening up a way toward the realization of a society of equals, where causes or elements of social inequalities have been eliminated. So that the universal reconciliation of humankind does not remain in the abstract, Korean theology must confront the present plight of the divided Korean people and be at the service of its reconciliation and unification.

Theology in India

With few exceptions, theology in India has been and continues largely to be academic, focusing on Western concerns and using Western noetic models. It is only in recent years—since the late 1960s—that serious and sustained efforts have been made to break away from this mainstream pattern and elaborate a theology more in touch with Indian reality.

The reality of India is extraordinarily complex. Its most conspicuous characteristic is the poverty of the masses side by side with the luxurious affluence of a very few. This shocking contrast is principally the inheritance of colonial exploitation, which ended with a "transfer of power without a social revolution." It left behind a small elite, which, operating in close conjunction with the erstwhile colonial powers, continues to exploit and dominate the masses.

Poverty is accentuated by caste, which acts as a great divisive force deeply entrenched in the flesh of the nation and infecting every institution in it.

The existence of minority groups such as the tribal peoples, with a culture differing from and in many respects socially healthier than the prevailing Indian (Hindu) culture, adds to the complexity of the cultural maze.

The most remarkable feature of this complex cultural reality is the prominent part that religion plays in it. Traditional religions are very much alive, exerting a powerful influence on the masses. Although they have largely acted as legitimizers of the exploitive upper classes and castes, they have also on occasion given rise to great movements of social protest, utilizing a storehouse of stirring religious and national symbols, without which no movement can really grip the masses.

Given this context, it is not surprising that attempts to break away from the dominant Westernized theology in India have sought relevance along two lines. An attempt to express the Christian faith in traditional Indian symbols, generally Brahmanic, with strong emphasis on contemplation and great indifference to social change, is paralleled by a liberation theology that, prompted by its concern for the poor, strives to articulate the experience of the people's struggle for liberation without looking for an Indian "language" to achieve it. These two trends, which surface in every theological meeting in India, have as yet failed to meet. Yet it is only at their meeting point that a genuinely Indian theology of liberation will emerge.

Thus to theologize in India would mean to understand and experience both the economic and cultural realities of India in the light not only of Judeo-Christian biblical tradition, which powerfully affirms that God is at work in the world bringing about a new liberated humanity, but also of the Indian religious traditions, which affirm the unity of the human with the cosmos (hence nature is not to be plundered for human greed) and the ultimate unity of the self with the absolute. Theologizing in India would indeed begin with commitment to the oppressed and to their struggle for freedom, justice, and fellowship, for this is implied and demanded by our faith commitment to God in Jesus, and by the authentic *advaita* traditions. But it would not stop here. For theology has two moments: awareness and articulation, each a complex reality. Awareness means the experience of reality at diverse levels—the personal-psychological, the socio-economic, and the mystical-depth level. Articulation, the spelling out of the significance of this experience at its diverse levels, also takes place at various depths, progressively disclosing the layers of meaning in a given event or situation. Both awareness and articulation are essential to the task of Indian theology.

Theology in the Philippines

In the Philippines today, academic theology, both Catholic and Protestant, is still deeply influenced by European and North American patterns. However, some initial efforts have been made toward a local theology. There are attempts at inculturation (from the anthropologico-cultural perspective) by a few professional theologians, and also toward contextualization by some committed pastors, religious, and lay persons done mostly in the non-academic setting of informal group reflections, collective study sessions, and short, intensive workshops and seminars.

The group that made preparations for the Delhi conference understands theology as an interpretation of contemporary life in the light of faith. In the attempt to develop a more relevant theology for Filipinos, it reaffirms the basic position taken by the Philippine delegation at the Asian Theological Conference in Sri Lanka—namely, that commitment to and solidarity with the people's struggle for full humanity is an important prerequisite. Another vital part of the theological task is a serious analysis of all the dimensions of human society: the economic, political, cultural, religious, psycho-spiritual. Theology must face up to the central problem of today, which is the injustice and oppression of the social order. The group also asserts that for theology to be meaningful, it must be effective—that is, it must lead to transforming action.

To speak of theology as an interpretation (or reinterpretation) of contemporary life from a faith perspective is to speak of a new set of religious meanings, insights, and outlooks regarding life, the world, God, and salvation, as well as the struggle for justice. It involves the search for a religious counter-culture.

If this is so, then the most appropriate interpreters of contemporary life in the Philippines are clearly those who experience the typical life of the majority of the people—the poor, the oppressed, the marginated, the deprived, who constitute 85 percent of the population. The grass roots have begun to express their faith-based life interpretations in their prayer sessions, liturgy, storytelling, drama, songs, and poems. These expressions constitute real theology.

The question has arisen about the contribution to Filipino theology by middle-class theologians. They generally are not poor themselves but are in solidarity with the poor and oppressed and are attempting to change the mentality typical of their class. As an art and science, theology is a discipline that requires study and technical competence, so the contribution of these trained middle-class theologians is valid and needed. However, theology in the Philippines will be meaningful to the people only if it stems from a liberated consciousness, whether of the grass roots or the middle class. Neither a bourgeois nor a domesticated mind-set shaped by a culture of silence will be capable of producing a truly Filipino theology. A remolding of consciousness is taking place in some dioceses, parishes, and religious groupings where grassroots and middle-class believers reflect on their reality and life situation together. It is also in this setting of action/reflection that many Christians find integration of their faith and their political calling.

Among these groups there is a continued biblico-historical effort to interpret life, God, and the world. This reeducation process is bringing about a new understanding of theological issues: human life is no longer just a period of trial to be rewarded or punished in an afterlife; it has value in its own terms and opposes whatever is dehumanizing in *this* life. Salvation is no longer simply eternal bliss and beatific vision for the disembodied soul in heaven above, but a new world of justice, resurrection, and life in a future that challenges us to make something of that future actual today. God is no longer someone who watches us from "up there" but someone involved in our history of struggle for justice and the life of abundance that Jesus spoke of. Faith and religion are not a collection of ahistorical truths but have to do with a saving history that continues in our day. In this effort for biblical renewal, middle-class theologians may facilitate the theological process of grassroots communities or even accompany them in their rediscovery of the Bible, but not influence the hermeneutical moment. That must be authentically theirs.

The new theology developing in the Philippines is a *lived* rather than a written, systematized theology. There is no ready-made blueprint for it. It is in the process of struggle for full humanity that a truly relevant theology for the Filipino people will emerge.

Theology in Sri Lanka

The Sri Lankan report centers mostly on Catholic theology, though there are similarities with Protestant efforts as well. Since Sri Lanka's independence in 1948, theology has gone through a period of increasing polarization. The combination of internal pressures from nationalistic, socialist, and Buddhist groups on the one hand, and the thrust from Vatican II and the Faith and Order Commission of the World Council of Churches on the other, led to much questioning within the Catholic Church. This led to the two polarities within the Catholic Church: theologians involved with worker or student groups or engaged in dialogue with other religions and secular ideologies tended to move ahead, whereas the official church took up a decidedly conservative stance, maintaining traditional theological positions borrowed from the West with some grafting from Vatican II.

Because of this rigidly conservative posture of the official church, progressive theology was increasingly localized in small groups more or less peripheral to the institutional church. Such groups have moved toward a stronger option in favor of joining the struggle against oppression and a wider opening to dialogue with other religions and ideologies. They are fashioning a new theological trajectory oriented toward a truer realization of the values of the kingdom of God—that is, of justice, equality, freedom, and peace.

Such a theology will be nourished by a rereading of Scripture focused on a renewed understanding of the historical Jesus and his proclamation of the kingdom. Concern for the kingdom is spelled out as respect for the dignity of all human beings, the acknowledgment of other living faiths as paths to holiness and salvation, and a sharing in the struggle of oppressed groups for their integral liberation as persons in a given society. This presupposes a serious analysis of society and leads to a theology that is open to self criticism and conscious of its limitations as a form of knowledge that, like all other forms, is socially conditioned. Through this rereading of Scripture and analysis of society, this new theology attempts to rethink the history of our times from the point of view of the marginalized masses, and tries to evolve a theological method (inductive and action-oriented in some groups, philosophical and psycho-analytical in others) that can cultivate theological engagement in both a popular and a professional way.

SYNTHESIS OF SHARED CONVICTIONS

Synthesizing the common elements from the regional reports and the discussion that followed, we arrive at six general conclusions.

(1) The official mainstream theology of the Christian churches everywhere in Asia continues to be a Western theology, focusing on Western concerns, with little relevance to the Asian reality. Such a theology is alienated and alienating. Asian theology needs to be liberated from the colonial bondage in which it finds itself.

(2) As the need for such liberation is increasingly felt, attempts are being made, generally in groups more or less peripheral to the official structure of the churches, to elaborate a theology more in touch with the Asian reality.

(3) Because the feature of Asian reality that is most urgently and immediately experienced is the oppression that dehumanizes and threatens the very existence of the people, and because the message of the Bible is primarily a proclamation of the integral liberation of men and women from every sort of oppression and alienation, Asian theology must make the oppression of Asian peoples struggling for liberation its primary concern.

(4) Such a theology will emerge from the liberated consciousness of Asian peoples themselves. The new perception of reality brought about by the experience of struggle for liberation is the point of departure for Asian theology.

Asian theology is a lived theology, expressed in the lives of the people before it is articulated in thought and word—by the people in a popular idiom, or by professional theologians in a more systematic way.

(5) Christians in Asian countries—except the Philippines—are a small minority surrounded by persons inspired by other living traditions. Asian Christian theology must view the rich and multifaceted religious heritage of Asia in a new light. It will have to integrate—not reject or ignore—this plenitude. It should enter into dialogue with other faiths in order to discover and activate the liberating factors they contain, and to discover new insights into its own biblical tradition that may come from encounters with these other age-old religions.

(6) The degradation of women is particularly acute in Asia. Although God created man and woman in God's own image—and hence equal—the divine plan has been distorted and violated not only by secular society but by churches, theologians, and even biblical scholars. The reality of this oppression must be taken seriously. It must be part and parcel of our study and reflection without subsuming it into the framework of a broader oppression. Our commitment must make us seek to correct this injustice to women and include their perspective in all theological reflection. Otherwise, there can be no truly relevant theology, no genuine social transformation, no holistic human liberation in Asia.

PART III

COMMON ELEMENTS OF
THIRD WORLD THEOLOGIES

8

A Methodological Approach to Third World Theology

J. Russell Chandran

EATWOT

Let me begin by giving a brief overview of the Ecumenical Association of Third World Theologians (EATWOT) for the benefit of those for whom it is something new. The present meeting in New Delhi is the fifth international conference of EATWOT. The first conference, held at Dar es Salaam, Tanzania, in August 1976, brought together representatives from Africa, Asia, and Latin America for the purpose of ecumenical dialogue on Third World theology. It was at the end of that first meeting that the decision was taken to form EATWOT.

The next three conferences were also ecumenical in character but continental in focus, inviting theological reflection on the de facto situation in Africa, Asia, and Latin America, respectively. The first continental meeting was held in Accra, Ghana, in December 1977. The next one was held in Wennappuwa, Sri Lanka, in January 1979. The Latin American conference was held in São Paulo, Brazil, in February-March 1980.

For these continental meetings participants were mainly drawn from countries of the continent under study, but there were also a few delegates from other continents. The reports of all the previous four conferences have been published by Orbis Books, Maryknoll, New York. The Dar es Salaam papers were edited by Sergio Torres and Virginia Fabella and published under the title *The Emergent Gospel: Theology from the Underside of History* (1978). The Accra papers, edited by Kofi Appiah-Kubi and Sergio Torres, were published under the title *African Theology En Route* (1979). The papers from the Wennappuwa meeting, edited by Virginia Fabella, were published under the title *Asia's Struggle for Full Humanity: Towards a Relevant Theology* (1980). The São Paulo papers, edited by Sergio Torres and John Eagleson, were published under the title *The Challenge of Basic Christian Communities* (1981).

These books have had quite a powerful impact on theological circles throughout the world. In addition the publication of a bulletin edited by Sergio Torres and Virginia Fabella, *Voices of the Third World,* since changed to *Voices from the Third World,* has also helped to promote interest in EATWOT concerns.

EATWOT is not the huge global organization its name might suggest. It is an informal group of about forty-five theologians. The question has been raised about the EATWOT emphasis, whether it should be on *theologians* or on *theology.* Are we concerned about Third World theologians or Third World theology? A further question asks: Who is a Third World theologian? What is Third World theology? Is not theology universal?

The term "Third World theology" did not originate at the Dar es Salaam meeting. In 1972 I was invited to give a course at the Episcopal Theological School in Cambridge, Massachusetts, on Third World theology. I was regarded as a Third World theologian simply because as an Indian I was supposed to belong to the Third World, and not because of any particular type of theology I was associated with. But EATWOT does not regard everyone doing theology in a Third World region a Third World theologian.

I have to ask myself what my credentials are to be recognized as a Third World theologian. My being an Indian does not by itself qualify me. In order to be Third World theologian one must have an orientation to do theological reflection on the gospel of Jesus Christ as it comes alive in the totality of the struggle of an oppressed people to be fully human.

Another point to be borne in mind is that for EATWOT theologians are not exclusively professional academic theologians. Academic theologians have an important role in formulating precise and systematic interpretations of different dimensions of the Christian faith. But in order that such definitions and the conceptualizing process itself not be divorced from the concrete reality of human struggle, other responses to the gospel, such as those of socio-political activists, pastors, social workers, educators, artists, and social scientists, are also considered to fall within the scope of theology. They too are included among Third World theologians.

Third World Theology and the Pursuit of Justice

Let me quote from the final statements of the earlier four EATWOT meetings to give you some idea of the directions of Third World theology. All the final statements call for an *understanding* of the situation of the people through appropriate historical, socio-political, and cultural analysis, a definite *commitment* to justice, and *solidarity* with the poor and the victims of oppression and exploitation.

The Dar es Salaam statement affirms:

A theology of the Third World has to take into account this historical situation. It has to ask: What role has the church been playing throughout these developments at each stage and in every situation? How did

Christians react to this phenomenon of the western invasion of other peoples? What was the prevailing theology? How does Christian theology relate in today's continued exploitation in the world? What is its contribution to the building of a just world society? What contribution will the church make to the liberation of the oppressed peoples who have long suffered due to sexist, racial, and class domination?[1]

We call for an active commitment to the promotion of justice and the prevention of exploitation, the accumulation of wealth in the hands of a few, racism, sexism, and all other forms of oppression, discrimination, and dehumanization. Our conviction is that the theologian should have a fuller understanding of living in the Holy Spirit, for this also means being committed to a lifestyle of solidarity with the poor and the oppressed and involvement in action with them.[2]

The Accra statement adds:

We must recognize the persistence of the domination that resulted from colonialism. This domination also exists in the churches. The organizational model imported from the West is still proposed and accepted. . . .

We believe that African theology must be understood in the context of African life and culture and the creative attempt of African peoples to shape a new future that is different from the colonial past and the neo-colonial present.[3]

The Wennappuwa statement adds:

In the context of the poverty of the teeming millions of Asia and their situation of domination and exploitation, our theology must have a very definite liberational thrust. . . .

To be truly liberating, this theology must arise from the Asian poor with a liberated consciousness. It is articulated and expressed by the oppressed community using the technical skills of biblical scholars, social scientists, psychologists, anthropologists, and others. . . .

In this context, we question the academic preoccupation to work toward the so-called "indigenization" or "inculturation" of theology divorced from participation in the liberational struggle in history. In our countries today, there can be no truly indigenized theology that is not liberational. Involvement in the history and struggle of the oppressed is the guarantee that our theology is both liberating and indigenous.[4]

The Latin American conference in São Paulo concentrated on the theological significance of basic ecclesial communities. Its final statement reads in part:

The basic ecclesial communities, or popular Christian communities, form an integral part of the people's march, but do not constitute a movement or political power parallel to the popular organizations, nor do they seek to legitimate them. The Christian communities—through consciousness-raising, popular education, and the development of ethical and cultural values—exercise among the poor a liberating ministry that is an integral part of their specific mission of evangelization, prophecy, pastoral care, and ministering the sacraments.

The church redeems the people's symbols of hope, manipulated for centuries by the system of domination. The church celebrates the presence of the God of life in the people's struggles for a more just and human life.[5]

The liberation of the poor is a journey full of grief, marked by both the passion of Christ and by the signs of resurrection. The liberation of the poor is a vast history that embraces all of human history and gives it true meaning. The Gospel proclaims the history of total liberation as it is present in today's events. . . . Evangelization of the masses is carried out within the perspective of the preferential option for the poor.[6]

We affirm with joy that through solidarity with the cause of the poor, through participation in their just struggles, in their sufferings, and in their persecution, the first great barrier that for so long has divided our different churches is being broken down.[7]

In this option for the poor and in the practice of justice, we have deepened the roots of our faith in the one Lord, the one church, the one God and Father.[8]

Shift in Methodology

The EATWOT final statements have also explicitly opted for a new methodology for doing theology. The Dar es Salaam statement affirms:

We reject as irrelevant an academic type of theology that is divorced from action. We are prepared for a radical break in epistemology which makes commitment the first act of theology and engages in critical reflection on the praxis of the reality of the Third World.[9]

What is implied is a movement away from the deductive to the inductive approach. The Accra statement resumes the same argument:

The African situation requires a new theological methodology that is different from the approaches of the dominant theologies of the West. African theology must reject, therefore, the prefabricated ideas of North Atlantic theology by defining itself according to the struggles of the people in their resistance against the structures of domination. Our task as theologians is to create a theology that arises from and is accountable to African people.[10]

We find the same stress on methodology in the Asian and Latin American final statements.

A New Reformation

We need to ask whether the concern for justice and liberation and the shift to contextual methodology in theology are peculiar to EATWOT. The answer is no. EATWOT does not have a theology or theological approach peculiar to itself. For the last two decades, particularly through the impact of the ecumenical movement on theological reflection, concern for a praxis-oriented theology and a justice- or liberation-oriented interpretation of the gospel has emerged in all parts of the world. Involvement in the struggles of the people to overthrow unjust economic and political structures is recognized as an essential dimension of participation in the gospel mission in many of the statements of the World Council of Churches, including the document issued by the Commission on World Mission and Evangelism at its Melbourne meeting in 1980. The action/reflection dialectic has been stressed in many consultations on theology and theological education. The principle proposed again and again for theological education has been *to do theology in context.*

Even though traditional forms of theology, theological education, and church life continue to dominate, the new thrust for a praxis-oriented theology committed to the people's struggle for justice is widespread. Liberation theology in Latin America and black theology in the U.S.A. are also evidence of this new movement in the interpretation of the Christian mission.

This global and ecumenical movement of concern for justice, commitment, and solidarity can be interpreted as a "new reformation." The task of theology today is to discern the needs of and promote this new reformation. EATWOT seeks to follow and foster the spirit of this new reformation and to mobilize theological reflection related to the struggle of the peoples of the Third World to overcome their Third-Worldness.

THIRD-WORLDNESS: THE BITTER FRUIT OF OPPRESSION

The term "Third World" has been applied in general, geographically, to Africa, Asia, and Latin America. But when we speak of Third World theologians or Third World theology, the geographical connotation is not the main point. Its full significance has to be understood in terms of the historical facts of colonial, imperialistic domination and economic exploitation of those regions by the North Atlantic and other First World powers and the consequent creation of Third-Worldness. The regions known as the Third World today are eloquent monuments of humankind's selfish, greed-driven aggressiveness and inhumanity. Our concern, however, is not about past inhumanity, but about the even more complex forms of inhumanity rampant today.

Wrongly, we sometimes imagine that we belong to a civilized global community, having progressed from the days when the "law of the jungle" characterized human relations. But we need to ask whether the stockpiling of modern weapons—including the latest neutron bombs that destroy life but leave property intact—and the consolidation of political and economic power structures that condemn vast sections of the global community to a perennial state of dependence or virtual enslavement make us more civilized than our ancestors who settled disputes by fistfights or bows and arrows. Corresponding to and even linked with the global structures of domination and exploitation there are regional, national, and local structures.

During our sharing of experiences and reflections, our attention was drawn to the exploitation of African peoples by Indians in East Africa. The challenge was formulated that Christians in India do something to change the policies and attitudes of Indians in East Africa. The fact is that the exploitive Indians in East Africa are linked with the exploitive classes in India also, against whom the masses of the Indian people have to struggle.

Even though no part of the world is free from the struggle of the oppressed against dominant oppressive classes, the struggle of the peoples of the Third World is much more complex and is both quantitatively and qualitatively different. What it entails is not a natural phenomenon, but a socio-political and economic phenomenon brought about by deliberate acts of exploitation and oppression that have to be condemned as sinful. Proclaiming the gospel of Jesus Christ as the "power of God unto salvation" will be meaningful only if that salvation includes the uprooting of the injustices that produce and perpetuate Third-Worldness. This context makes EATWOT and its commitment to promote a Third World theology or theologies particularly relevant and even mandatory.

BEYOND IDEOLOGIES AND SLOGANS

In humility we have to acknowledge that concern for promoting struggle against oppression and injustice is by no means an exclusively Christian concern. Many political, religious, and cultural movements are involved in the struggle. This raises the question of exactly what role a Third World Christian theology will have.

Two points must be borne in mind. The first is that we do not first develop a theology and then participate in the struggle. Our commitment to the gospel of Jesus Christ and our faith that he is our risen Lord continuing the ministry he began in Galilee challenge us to discern the reality of his presence in the struggles of the people and to participate in the struggle. We are to cooperate with others who are in the struggle, regardless of their religious, ideological, or political affiliations. Theological reflection follows upon participation.

Secondly, our commitment to the risen Lord who mediates to us the sovereignty of God's love as the ultimate reality will guard us from absolutizing any particular theological formulation, ideology, slogan, or program. Without the love of God, we are in danger of sacrificing what is best for the people for the sake of doctrines, ideologies, or programs. Our theology should keep us sensitive to this danger and enable us always to be committed to what God in his love has willed for the people.

This does not mean that we ignore the role of ideologies. Ideological commitment and even the adoption of slogans are helpful for the sharpening of our objectives in socio-political transformation. In the broad polarization separating the capitalist and socialist approaches to socio-political and economic policies, our stand has to be with the leftist, socialist approach. In his Niles Lecture presented for the CCA Assembly in Bangalore in May 1980, Bishop Lakshman Wikramasingle said categorically that in Asia the Christian commitment today has to be for a socialism influenced, but not dominated, by Marxism.

In the global situation also we cannot ignore the fact that unity in the socialist bloc is important for the minimizing of exploitation by the capitalist bloc with the almost totalitarian power of the multinationals and transnationals. But the present situation has become too complex for a simple, Marxist analysis. Nor is it possible simply to opt for any of the existing socialist systems.

A Third World theology sensitive to the gospel of Jesus Christ will enable us to be aware of the dangers of absolutizing Marxist or any other ideology. Even though Marxism has contributed more than any other ideology to contemporary struggles for justice, we must be aware of the possibility that a Marxist fundamentalism could betray the cause of liberation of the oppressed. What is happening today in Poland is a warning that the absolutization of any particular form of communism can betray the cause of the working class. Along with the task of helping the churches to overcome the dangers of biblical fundamentalism, theology has to come to grips with the dangers of Marxist fundamentalism also and find ways of reinterpreting Marx, on the basis of his original concerns and our present realities.

Equally important is the concern of Third World Christian theology to keep the Christian churches of the Third World vigilant as to the subtle ways in which some powerfully organized evangelistic movements use the gospel to support the status quo and keep Christians insensitive or blind to the injustices of political and economic structures. The gospel is used to make them nonpolitical by individualistic, interioristic, and other-wordly interpretations of salvation. By the same token, the gospel is put to political use by making it an instrument of anticommunist propaganda. This has to be boldly and systematically exposed so that the gospel will really be good news to the poor and the oppressed. Bringing ideologies, slogans, and action programs under the judgment of the gospel so as to prevent them from betraying the authentic struggles of Third World peoples is an important task for EATWOT theology.

Depending upon the variety of cultural, religious, and socio-political factors of different situations, many Third World theologies may emerge. But one common feature of the theologies within EATWOT will be the recognition that the God we confess and proclaim is the God who saves and brings about reconciliation by the offer of forgiveness to the sinner and solidarity with the victims of oppression and injustice.

Third World theologians and Third World theologies will enable Third world peoples to make the Magnificat their own song of liberation and praise:

> He has brought down monarchs from their thrones,
>   but the humble have been lifted high.
> The hungry he has satisfied with good things,
>   the rich sent empty away [Luke 1:52–53].

NOTES

1. Sergio Torres and Virginia Fabella, eds., *The Emergent Gospel* (Maryknoll, N.Y.: Orbis Books, 1978), p. 264.

2. Ibid., p. 270.

3. Kofi Appiah-Kubi and Sergio Torres, eds., *African Theology en Route* (Maryknoll, N.Y.: Orbis Books, 1979), pp. 192–93.

4. Virginia Fabella, ed., *Asia's Struggle for Full Humanity* (Maryknoll, N.Y.: Orbis Books, 1980), pp. 156–57.

5. Sergio Torres and John Eagleson, eds., *The Challenge of Basic Christian Communities* (Maryknoll, N.Y.: Orbis Books, 1981), p. 235.

6. Ibid., p. 238.

7. Ibid., p. 243.

8. Ibid., pp. 243–44.

9. Torres and Fabella, eds., *The Emergent Gospel,* p. 269.

10. Appiah-Kubi and Torres, eds., *African Theology en Route,* p. 193.

9

The Socio-Economic and Political Context of Third World Theology

Ajit Roy

Accumulated pressures, accentuated contradictions, aggravated tensions —in short, unresolved problems of historical evolution—are challenging humankind today and demanding conscious intervention for intelligent resolution. The multiplicity of issues and their particularity notwithstanding, all these basic questions are closely interrelated and they have to be grasped and grappled with within a worldwide framework. This is the challenge of history at this hour.

First, humankind is today faced with a dire choice between survival and annihilation—that is, between effective control and gradual elimination of nuclear weapons on the one hand, and nuclear cataclysm that would obliterate all traces of civilization from this planet on the other.

Secondly, society is fast entering into a period when the need for the establishment of a proper balance between humankind and nature will reach a point of no return. Imbalance will then entail humankind's massive capitulation to physical and mental disease and deformity and the destruction of its natural habitat by toxic accumulations, its vital resources having first been pillaged and then squandered away in mindless wastage.

Thirdly, and most importantly, the two foregoing sets of global alternatives are organically interrelated with the four sets of interdependent sectoral alternatives:

(1) *Either* the fast accelerating maldistribution of wealth and resources between the developed and underdeveloped parts of the world is halted and a more equitable redistribution effected, *or* hunger, disease, and civil convulsions of unprecedented dimensions will embroil the nearly two-thirds of the world population living in the so-called Third World and then backlash upon the population of the wealthier regions.

(2) *Either* the masses of the Third World are able to unite nationally and internationally on the platform of a more just, more egalitarian share in socio-economic development and corresponding cultural regeneration, *or* they will fall total victim to economic exploitation by local exploiters and their foreign patrons, subjected to yet more severe political repression and reduced to yet lower levels of subhuman existence.

(3) *Either* the highly developed capitalist countries change from an acquisitive, consumerist to an egalitarian, sharing mentality conducive to reconciliation between individuals as well as between humankind and nature, *or* fast accentuation of social, economic, and ecological crises arising from contradictions between long-term interests of the masses and shortsighted demands for high profits by multinational corporations will lead to utter chaos.

(4) And finally *either* the postcapitalist societies in the so-called Second World consciously and consistently embark on a path for recapturing liberative and humanistic dimensions of essential Marxism and are thereby able to appear to the peoples of the First World as an alternative civilization of a higher order, *or* they themselves will be corrupted by the penetrating culture of decadent, consumerist society, riven by national conflicts, and suffer from the consequences of the disaffection of the alienated workers in their own society.

All these crises and contradictions are closely interrelated and interacting. Impulses in one sphere will stimulate impulses in other spheres. It will be extremely difficult, if not impossible, to solve the crises and contradictions in one sphere in total isolation from all others. Specifically, for instance, the threat of nuclear holocaust cannot be fully eliminated as long as the crisis-ridden capitalist order remains dependent on armament sales for its survival, and as long as the present image of the Warsaw Pact as a mirror reflection of the NATO persists in the mind of the Western world.

Similarly, as long as hawkish politicians and militarists remain in control of NATO institutions, it will be difficult for Warsaw Pact countries not to put a premium on the advice of their own military experts.

On the other hand, just as the final victory of Vietnam against the U.S. interventionists could not have come about without the massive rebellion of American youth against the Johnson and Nixon administrations, similarly the radicalization of American public opinion in the late 1960s and the early 1970s would not have occurred without the heroic resistance of the Vietnamese people.

In other words, vast differences and divergences notwithstanding, the world today has really become one world. We of the Third World can neither develop any deep insights into our basic problems nor hope to solve them without viewing them in global contexts and without linking ourselves with global, epochal processes.

We of the Third World who are perturbed by the human degradation in our part of the world have to understand our own problems in relation to the global problems of war, problems of poverty or maldistribution arising from property ownership, technology and culture, and those arising from social divisions. We can advance toward the solution of our urgent problems only in solidarity with world forces—through our involvement in common struggles.

We may get a clearer view of all these interconnections if we take a closer look at the problems briefly stated above.

THREAT OF NUCLEAR HOLOCAUST

According to a UN study, the stockpile of nuclear weapons is today estimated to have reached forty thousand to fifty thousand in number, equivalent to some thirteen billion tons of TNT or more than three tons for every man, woman, and child in the world. This involves an annual expenditure of over $500 billion or about $1 million per minute.[1]

The following was reported during a session of the UN Disarmament Committee in Geneva (February 4, 1981):

> Mrs. Inga Thorsson of Sweden and Mexico's Mr. Alfonso Garcia Robles spoke of the recent US disclosures that there had been 147 false alarms in 18 months about a possible nuclear attack. They said that on four occasions the crews of B-52 bombers and the controllers of intercontinental missiles were put on increased alerts.
>
> "Sooner or later one of these incidents may produce unforeseeable consequences," the Mexican delegate said. Mrs. Thorsson said thunderstorms and lightning caused 3,703 lesser alarms in the USA and there seemed little doubt there were similar false alarms and accidents in the Soviet Union.
>
> "Should human survival be dependent on natural phenomena, technological, or human failures of this kind?," she asked.
>
> Mrs. Thorsson said one accident was reported to have left only one of six control mechanisms preventing the explosion of a 24 megaton bomb, 1,800 times stronger than the 1945 atom bomb dropped on Hiroshima.[2]

Reuter reported from Washington on February 15, 1981, that an undetected asteroid hitting the earth might be mistaken for a nuclear attack and might set off a nuclear war, according to a U.S. space program advisor.

According to geneticists, even without war, if the bomb tests of various nations continue on the present scale, each year of testing will lead to 230,000 defective births and 420,000 embryonic and neonatal deaths.

From the end of World War II to 1981, according to the Stockholm International Peace Research Institute (SIPRI), 1,272 nuclear tests were recorded, more than 1,100 of them accounted for by the U.S.A. and the U.S.S.R. In 1980 alone, forty-nine underground explosions were registered.

A new laser weapon, AFP reported from Washington on May 31, 1981, whose "death ray" moves at 186,000 miles per second, enabling it to hit a target almost instantly, was soon to be tested. The U.S. army has spent more than $1,200 million on the weapon and the Soviet Union has been trying to develop something similar for twenty years, the Pentagon said.

Military rivalry, SIPRI reported, is being carried into outer space: 103 military satellites were launched in 1980 alone: 89 by the U.S.S.R. and 14 by the U.S.A. This, however, does not mean that the Soviet Union is superior in this sphere. Its satellites have a much shorter life than those of the U.S.A.

The U.S. Congress endorsed the Reagan administration's defense build-up program by authorizing a record expenditure of $136 billion for fiscal 1982, which was $26.4 billion more than the 1981 defense expenditure level. This enlarged volume of "defense" expenditure covered stepped-up militarization in different parts of the world, most importantly Asia and Africa. Its own bases at Diego Garcia in the Indian Ocean and Ras Banas in Egypt apart, the 1982 authorization included large amounts of "military aid" to South Korea ($167.5 million), the Philippines ($50 million), Indonesia ($45 million), Malaysia ($12.5 million), and Thailand ($80 million).

The step-up in military expenditure by the U.S.A. has been reciprocated by the Soviet Union. The Soviet defense minister Marshal Dmitry Ustinov made that very clear in an article in *Pravda* on June 22, 1981, when he said: "The U.S.S.R. has never advocated nor will ever advocate the arms race. But if we are forced to do so, we will match any challenge and match it effectively."[3]

The dynamics of the arms race was earlier elaborated on by another high-ranking Soviet military figure, General Fyodor Tonkih, on May 17, 1981. He said in Moscow:

We built our nuclear submarines only after we faced the threat of aggression from the other side in this field. It was the Pentagon which first built missiles with multiple warheads, forcing us to change our strategic missile systems. The Pentagon's Trident forced us to create our Typhoon systems. In other words, our country has been forced to take countermeasures.[4]

Commenting on escalation in the nuclear arms race, a New York Times News Service despatch stated:

Unless the two superpowers act quicky to renew negotiations on limiting their nuclear weapons, it soon may be impossible in a practical sense to stop the accelerating arms race.

The reason for making that gloomy statement is the volume of new nuclear weapons coming out of Soviet and U.S. research and development all the time. Not only are both countries planning more warheads and more delivery vehicles, but also the balance of weaponry is becoming less stable. And perhaps most ominous, the newest weapons promise to be a good deal less verifiable: less subject to the checking process that is essential to any arms limitation agreement.[5]

Unless our work in other spheres is linked up with the struggle to eliminate the overhanging threat of a global holocaust, advances toward a more just and better society in any part of the world would be comparable with work on refurbishing a stateroom on the *Titanic* during its fateful voyage.

Besides, a cut-back on the huge expenditure for developing the most efficient means of destroying the world would yield large resources for alleviating the suffering now heaped on wide segments of humanity—hunger, disease, illiteracy, and so on. For instance, according to the calculations of the Willy Brandt Commission:

(1) The military expenditure of only half a day would suffice to finance the whole malaria eradication program of the World Health Organization; less would be needed to conquer river-blindness, which is still the scourge of millions.

(2) A modern tank costs about $1 million; that amount could provide storage facilities for 100,000 tons of rice and thus save 4,000 tons or more annually—and one person can live on just over a pound of rice a day. The same sum of money could provide 1,000 classrooms for 30,000 children.

(3) For the price of one jet fighter ($20 million), some 40,000 village pharmacies could be set up.

(4) One-half of 1 percent of one year's world military expenditure could pay for all the farm equipment needed to increase food production and approach food sufficiency in food-deficit low-income countries by 1990.[6]

THE DYNAMICS OF POVERTY

Although the danger of total annihilation as a result of nuclear holocaust is still only a threat, slow death from hunger and malnutrition, mass mortality from epidemics and other preventable diseases, and a subhuman existence for millions in the underdeveloped Third World is a present reality:

Whichever data are used to define the less developed countries—Gross National Product (GNP) per head, the net *per capita* income, amount of energy per head of population, the literacy rate—a similar pattern emerges and the startling imbalance in the distribution of the world's wealth is revealed. The range between the richest and the poorest nations is dreadfully wide; the income per head in the United Kingdom, which is now well down the list of "rich nations," is fifteen to twenty times that of the world's poorest countries. . . . Such poverty is utter and absolute and is endured today by hundreds of millions of human beings. With this poverty goes hunger and undernourishment. The current United Nations estimate is that up to 500 million people are now suffering from malnutrition. This is almost one-fifth of the total population of the Third World, but in many developing countries from one-quarter to one-third suffer from protein-calorie malnutrition.

If an arbitrary upper limit of $600 annual *per capita* income is set, the Third World embraces about one hundred nations. It comprises 60 percent of the earth's surface and is the home of about 70 percent of the human race, some 2,800 million people. By AD 2000, the population of the Third World could be as many as 5,000 million. Their spread on the map should remind us of the diversity among the less developed countries of climate, terrain, geographical position, culture, traditions, institutions, and demographic situations.[7]

Is this mass poverty in the less developed parts of the world ordained by fate? Is it because Third World countries are denied the bounties of nature? Hardly so. All this misery is the product of historical evolution and socioeconomic developments. As the Brandt Commission says in terms of North (developed) and South (underdeveloped) duality:

Behind these differences lies the fundamental inequality of economic strength. It is not just that the North is so much richer than the South. Over 90 percent of the world's manufacturing industry is in the North. Most patents and new technology are the property of the multinational corporations of the North, which conduct a large share of world investment and world trade in raw materials and manufactures. Because of their economic power, northern countries dominate the international economic system—its rules and regulations, and its international institutions of trade, money, and finance.[8]

The predominant position occupied by the North on the economic map of the world today is the culmination of a long historical process. Referring to its early beginnning, Karl Marx wrote:

The discovery of gold and silver in America, the extirpation, enslavement, and entombment in mines of the aboriginal population, the beginning of the conquest and looting of the East Indies, the turning of Africa into a warren for commercial hunting of black-skins, signaled the rosy dawn of the era of capitalist production.[9]

Referring to the advance of capitalism in Western Europe, Marx wrote:

A new and international division of labor, a division suited to the requirements of the chief centers of modern industry, springs up, and converts one part of the globe into a chiefly agricultural field of production, for supplying the other part, which remains a chiefly industrial field.[10]

Economic analyst Ernest Mandel has written:

> From the conquest and pillage by the Spaniards to the sacking of Indonesia by the Portuguese and the Dutch, and the ferocious exploitation of India by the British, the history of the sixteenth and eighteenth centuries is an unbroken chain of deeds of brigandage which were so many *acts of international concentration of values and capital in Western Europe,* the enrichment of which was paid for, in the literal sense of the word, by the impoverishment of the plundered areas.[11]

By the end of the eighteenth century, European nations had spread their control to 35 percent of the globe's land surface; this proportion increased to 67 percent in 1878, and 84.4 percent in 1914.

Due to the emergence and strengthening of a number of world historical developments, which we need not go into now, the old style of direct domination became untenable. The essence of domination and exploitation in the current phase is being sustained, and indeed intensified, through various so-called aid programs and controlled through international mechanisms, backed up by:

> (1) the direct and indirect interference by the United States and other powers in the politics and class conflicts in the ex-colonies, including (a) strengthening those sections of the ruling class which are most sympathetic and reliable, and (b) military assistance and military alliance; and (2) the chain of military bases around the globe, the mobile air force and navy, and the more-or-less frequent use of these instruments of power.[12]

Role of the Multinational Corporations (MNCs)

Within this overall framework of neocolonial domination, strategic industries and multinational corporations play the key role, as Harry Madoff has written:

> In contrast to the past when the [processings] of military goods were pretty much a distinct industrial group, the new military technology and the growth of conglomerates have resulted in the integration of military production with the dominant industrial sectors.
>
> The rising importance of the multinational corporation . . . drives towards worldwide control of the most profitable and new industry in both the periphery and advanced countries. The structure and strategy

of the multinational corporation generate further penetration of the ex-colonies and strongly influence the course of development—or, more accurately, of underdevelopment—in these countries.[13]

As a result of these organic, structural constraints represented by the domination of the advanced countries, the Third World nations rot in their deepening underdevelopment, despite their reserves of natural resources. The underdeveloped countries account for 97 percent of the capitalist world's manganese, 91.4 percent of its tin, 89.5 percent of its oil, 74 percent of its antimony, 67 percent of its nickel, and so on. Yet:

> The 1970s showed a marked slowdown in the economic growth of the developing countries. Their share in world trade dropped from 30 percent in the mid-1960s to 15 percent at present [mid-1970s] and that in the export of manufactured goods to only 2 percent. The foreign debts of the developing countries reached $300 billion and annual payment on this account reached to $40 billion, taking up 20 percent of their export earnings. . . . All the developing countries, whose population constitutes 65 percent of the world's total, account for only 8 percent of the world's industrial output.
>
> In the ESCAP [Economic and Social Council for Asia and the Pacific] region (with more than half the world population) the decade of the 1970s commenced with the numbers of unemployed and those living in the conditions of socially unacceptable squalor at record levels in absolute terms. . . . This situation will have further deteriorated by the end of the decade. In [terms of] what the IBRD defines as absolute poverty, this ESCAP region contains approximately two-thirds of the global total.[14]

The intensification of stagflationary crisis in the advanced capitalist countries has indeed led to a faster deterioration in the economic position of Third World countries in recent years than was visualized in the ESCAP prognosis quoted above. For instance, it is estimated that by the end of 1979, the less developed countries had already accumulated $360 billion in foreign debts. Excluding OPEC nations, their foreign debts, which stood at $64.1 billion in 1971, reached $108 billion in 1974, $201 billion in 1977, and were projected at $275 billion for 1979. The total debt of less developed countries grew at an average annual rate of 16.8 percent from 1967 to 1972, and 21 percent from 1973 to 1976.[15]

Other forms of drainage from Third World countries are also growing in volume. According to data compiled by the UNCTAD secretariat, payments for technology transfer (patents, licenses, technical documentation, and so on) increased from an annual rate of $1.5 billion in the late 1960s to $5 billion in the mid-1970s, and $9 billion in 1980. The cost of technology imports is estimated to rise to over $100 billion by the turn of the century.

The burden of the world capitalist crisis is shifted to the Third World: It is transmitted from the center to the Third World through growing balance of payment deficits. As demand in the industrialized countries declined or grew more slowly, prices for exported raw materials other than petroleum declined or grew more slowly. At the same time, the vast world inflation in the industrialized economies increased prices of manufactured commodities imported by the Third World. Therefore, the terms of trade have been shifting against underdeveloped countries during the crisis (despite a temporary raw materials price boom in 1973–74 which was completely reversed after 1974) and the non-petroleum-exporting underdeveloped Third World countries have faced increasingly serious balance of payments problems and a mushrooming foreign debt. Moreover, it is not accidental or incidental that the OPEC [income] is more or less equivalent to the increase in the balance of payments deficit of the Third World, suggesting that most of the increases in the prices of petroleum since 1973 have been ultimately borne by the Third World.[16]

Apart from manipulation of the terms of trade, the multinationals of the developed capitalist countries, through the mediation of international institutions, have contrived to foist on the Third World what passes for "the strategy of export-oriented industrialization." As the levels of technology and wages rise in the developed capitalist countries, there is a need and drive for shifting low-technology and labor-intensive manufacturing processes to the Third World with its abundant supply of cheap labor. A study by the Japanese-dominated Asian Development Bank frankly calls this method "international subcontracting" and admits its pitfalls. It says:

A few DMCs [Developing Member Countries] improved their market shares in the developed countries . . . through their participation in the international division of production processes by manufacturing parts, components, and accessories for large firms in the developed countries . . .

Since the mid-1960s, international subcontracting has grown rapidly. . . . One of the main drawbacks of international subcontracting is that principals (in the metropolitan countries) may utilize subcontracting as a means of countering the effects of business fluctuations and the LDCs' [Less Developed Countries] subcontractors may bear the larger part of severe business fluctuations in developed countries.[17]

A more refined and logical form of export-oriented industrialization is the setting up of free trade zones in Third World countries. These enclaves are devised to provide the multinationals not only with cheap labor, but also cheap supplies of infrastructural services such as transportation and power. These zones are utilized by metropolitan capital for sending raw material and technical and managerial skills from the developed capitalist countries and getting processing or assembly work done at greatly reduced cost, without incurring any liability to the host countries, apart from some taxation.

One very important result of the involvement of multinational corporations is the maintenance of a "proper political climate" in the host countries, by which is meant the assurance of a continued supply of cheap labor and the prevention of any threat of a radical trade-union or political movement. This invariably leads to interventions in the political processes of the host countries, stepped-up "aid" to army and police, and patronage of reactionary politicians.

The indigenous counterpart of this process of neocolonialist consolidation is a new ruling alliance in Third World countries—an alliance of the comprador bourgeoisie, semifeudal landed aristocracy, upper strata of the rural, military, and civil bureaucracy, and the rising class of technocrats.

Due to world factors as well as its own limitations, this ruling alliance is unable to relieve the age-old misery of the masses, which on the contrary deepens. The ruling elite in these countries has been compelled from the very beginning of its "independent" career to lean increasingly on the repressive apparatus of the state and ultimately in many cases to opt for military dictatorship—openly or under some disguise.

This repressive power structure in most cases is sustained by metropolitan powers—directly through state-to-state financial, technical, and military "aid" and indirectly by massive bribery and undercover activity of the CIA variety.

Within this global framework, the situation of southern Africa is particularly tragic because of naked racial discrimination, sustained and safeguarded by U.S. patronage. Africa is extremely important to U.S. multinationals. According to one account, at the end of 1975, direct U.S. investment in oil refining amounted to 54.5 percent of the total investments on the African continent. In ore mining the figure was 20.3 percent; in manufacturing industries 9.6 percent; in trade and other branches of the economy 15.5 percent.

Africa supplies the U.S.A. with 72 percent of the cobalt it imports, 51 percent of the manganese, 43 percent of the antimony, 14 percent of the copper, almost its entire import of diamonds, columbite, and palm oil, more than 50 percent of the cocoa, mahogany, long-stable cotton, and considerable amounts of gold, rubber, and graphite.[18] No wonder the U.S.A. stands foursquare on the side of the racist regime of South Africa! As an AP dispatch from the United Nations on May 23, 1981, related:

> The United States has refused to endorse a passage in a United Nations Security Council message to the conference on apartheid in Paris, which calls for recognizing the "legitimacy of the South African people's demand for the elimination of apartheid."

President Reagan has spoken in defense of South Africa, describing
it as "a country that has stood beside us in every war we have fought. A
country that strategically is essential to the free world."

Reagan apparently missed the irony in his statement—a "free" world strategically linked with racist slavery of black Africans!

Technology Invasion

Within this framework of neocolonialist, comprador rule, the invasion of
technologies evolved in the West with a view to maximizing capitalist profit
has created many acute problems in Third World countries. "The process,"
says a well-known Western economist, "of diffusion or transfer of technology to poor countries is of relatively little overall consequence to most developed country technology owners."[19]

Another well-known Western economist has said of the multinational enterprise:

[Its] capacity to make profits derives essentially from its possession of
productive knowledge, which includes management methods and
marketing skills, as well as production technology. It has no commercial interest in diffusing its knowledge to potential native competitors.
Nor has it any interest in investing more than it has to in acquiring
knowledge of local conditions and investigating ways of adapting its
own productive knowledge to local factor/price ratios and market conditions. Its purpose is not to transform the economy by exploiting its
potentialities (especially its human potentialities) for development, but
to exploit the existing situation to its own profit by utilization of the
knowledge it already possesses at minimum cost to itself of adaptation
and adjustment.[20]

Evolved in the developed capitalist countries and consequently labor-
saving as they are, the introduction of imported technologies to the heavily
labor-surplus underdeveloped countries is not what they need. Another serious fallout is, as an Asian Development Bank study notes, widespread pollution:

With growth of various economic activities, environmental pollution is
increasing in many DMSs [Developing Member Countries]. Emphasis
on raising agricultural productivity has led to increased use of chemicals such as fertilizers, pesticides, and herbicides. Such chemicals, together with other industrial chemicals and heavy metals, have infil-
trated into surface and ground water.
Although the consequences of water pollution are generally more

localized and specific, the increasing uncontrolled discharges of such pollutants can lead to contamination of food chains, both on land and in the sea. In most of the large urban areas, the increasing concentration of people and industrial activities has resulted in severe air pollution which is also threatening human health.

According to the FAO, in many Asian countries the growth of water pollutants is exceeding the expansion of sewage and other water pollution treatment facilities. . . . Indonesian inshore waters are heavily contaminated with sewage bacteria. . . . In Malaysia, the wastes discharged from palm oil mills into rivers cause the river pollution level to be about 20,000 parts per million (ppm) BOC [Biochemical Oxygen Demand] which far exceeds the safety pollution level of 500 ppm. In the Philippines, mining operations discharge about 100,000 tons of mine tailing per day in eight major river systems. . . . In the Republic of Korea and the Republic of China (Taiwan), industrial wastes discharged into inshore waters are causing heavy damage to marine products. . . .

Malaria . . . was believed to have nearly disappeared in Asian countries, but now it has returned. . . . In India, the number of reported malaria cases increased more than a hundred times during 1966–1976 from about 40,000 to 6 million. In Pakistan, every fifth person is estimated to be suffering from the disease. In Sri Lanka, the number of reported cases had reduced to about 300 in 1965 but is now over 2 million per year. Serious outbreaks have also been reported in Thailand, Laos, Burma, Afghanistan, and other Asian countries. . . .

The main reason for the malaria resurgence is the mosquito's growing resistance to insecticides. Also the malaria parasite, which is injected into human blood by a mosquito bite, is becoming resistant to known drugs. There is enough evidence that insecticide resistance in mosquitos has resulted from the large-scale use of insecticides in agriculture.[21]

Another lamentable result of technology transfer is cultural distortion—creation of an urban elite modeled on Western consumerism and fed on the products of multinational enterprises. An Indian writer gives a graphic description of this cultural milieu:

The moment he [an average urban middle-class individual] gets up in the morning, he takes out his Colgate toothbrush over which he spreads Colgate toothpaste (both products of Colgate-Palmolive-India, Ltd., a subsidiary of the U.S. company of the same name) . . . [it] is preceded or followed by a cup of tea packaged and distributed by Lipton (Unilever controlled) or Brooke Bonds (a subsidiary of a U.K. company). After this, for his morning shave, he uses Palmolive lather shaving cream and aftershave lotion of the same company. The blade he uses is

Erasmic (of Hindustan Lever, a Unilever affiliate). . . . Proceeding to his bath, he uses Lux or Rexona (Hindustan Lever) soap. He uses for his hair Vaseline Hair Tonic (product of Cheeseborough Ponds). For his breakfast, he takes toasted Brittania bread (U.K.) . . . , which is washed down with his favored Nescafé cup of coffee from Nestlé of Switzerland. To go to his factory or office, he dresses himself in a Terylene suit or a mixed fabric dress consisting certainly of Terene manufactured by Chemicals and Fibres India, Ltd., a subsidiary of ICI. He has to catch a Leyland bus or in the alternative a Tata-Mercedes Benz fitted with tires manufactured by Goodyear, Dunlop, or Firestone. In the office he does a good deal of writing with Parker Quink or its variant Chelpark, and refreshes himself with Coca Cola. In the office, he gets his facts and figures through machines hired from IBM or ICL, and he gets his material typed on a Remington typewriter. In the evening, when he returns home, he has a cup of Pournvita (a Cadbury product). He takes his children for a walk and they demand Cadbury's chocolate. . . . He smokes cigarettes manufactured by the India Tobacco Company (subsidiary of British American Tobacco Company). . . . On important occasions he goes for a lunch arranged by his friends in one of the India Tobacco Company's hotels (Chola or Maurya) or to Oberoi-Sheraton. At night his wife spreads a table for dinner with cutlery manufactured under foreign collaboration and serves him . . . [food] fried in Dalda (hydrogenated vegetable oil) of Hindustan Lever. He retires to a bed with a Dunlopillow (product of Dunlop) after taking, if he is on the wrong side of forty-five, Digene or Boots, or in the alternative Gelucil of Warner Hindustan. If he does not get his sleep, he takes Valium of Roche. . . . When tired or bored [his wife] tunes on the radio/TV manufactured by Philips/Murphy/GEC. . . . If she has a headache (often), Roche's Saridon is the answer or, if the doctor advises differently, Crocin of British Celluloids.[22]

The maldistribution of assets and property that constantly sharpens polarization serves also to increase these cultural distortions. As the poor become poorer and the market for mass consumption goods continues to shrink, the accumulated profits of indigenous and foreign enterprise seek investment outlay in luxury and semiluxury products, the demand for which continues to rise because of the ever higher lifestyle of the elite.

The Indian Planning Commission candidly admits this distortion in the growth pattern:

The pattern of industrial development that has emerged obviously reflects the structure of effective demand, which is determined by the distribution of incomes. An unduly large share of resources is thus absorbed in production which relates directly or indirectly to maintaining or improving the living standards of higher income groups. The demand of this relatively small class, not only for a few visible items of conspicuous consumption but [also] for the outlay on high quality housing and urban amenities, aviation and superior travel facilities, telephone services, and so on, sustains a large part of the existing industrial structure.[23]

A crude example of this distortion in the investment/outlay pattern is the plan of the government of India to introduce color television to a country where about a quarter of the villages do not yet have access to a supply of clean drinking water. These neocolonial propensities drew this rueful comment from a Gandhian economist in India: "Whatever is done, whatever is set up, is quickly converted into just another establishment to create a mini New York in this poorest land on earth."[24]

It is hardly surprising that the social milieu in the Third World is pregnant with revolt and revolution. The neocolonial antidote for this developing situation is authoritarian regimes, military dictatorships, fascist suppression by local governments, backed by U.S. Green Berets and Rapid Deployment Forces.

There is, however, another dimension of the developing situation—an attempt at articulation of the demands for reform and some realignment of forces within the developed and underdeveloped countries as well as in their interrelationships without seriously disturbing the existing infrastructures. These developments are taking place in response to the call for the New International Economic Order (NIEO) and North-South dialogue.

NIEO AND NORTH-SOUTH DIALOGUE

One of the important issues that dominate contemporary world politics is the proposal for the NIEO along with continuing North-South dialogue related to it. The process started with the Non-Aligned Nations summit meeting held at Algiers in 1973. The issue was taken up and endorsed by the so-called Group of Seventy-Seven (underdeveloped nations) during the UNCTAD session later in the same year. The campaign was carried forward in the form of a resolution adopted by the UN General Assembly the next year. Since then a number of international conferences have been held to thrash out and elaborate concrete steps necessary for the implementation of the main objectives of this proposal. The main demands raised by the underdeveloped countries in these conferences are:

(1) Tariff liberalization for facilitating exports of goods and commodities from underdeveloped countries to developed countries;

(2) Price stabilization of commodities exported by Third World countries;

(3) Increase in the quantum of official aid from the developed countries to Third World countries;

(4) Formulation of codes for the regulation of the operations of MNCs in Third World countries;

(5) Reforms of the international monetary system for according a greater share of control to Third World countries.

The campaign for NIEO is both historically and organically associated with the rise of OPEC. On the one hand, the distress caused by the sudden increase in oil prices spurred Third World countries to action in demand for its amelioration. On the other hand, the success of the collective bargaining by OPEC encouraged Third World countries to attempt collective bargaining for better prices for their exports and more favorable terms in economic relationships with the developed countries in general. But, for objective reasons—such as the much wider dispersal of the participants as compared with OPEC, much less strategic importance of their exports as compared with oil, and so on—besides the fact that the developed countries had in the meantime prepared themselves effectively for resisting further pressures from the Third World, the NIEO movement failed to achieve as spectacular a success as had OPEC.

Along with the NIEO discussions, though initiated somewhat earlier, another contentious problem—the Law of the Sea—has been dominating the international diplomatic scene. The oceans have been found to be a rich source of petroleum, manganese, copper, cobalt, nickel, and so on. In 1970 the UN General Assembly adopted a resolution, with the U.S.A. and about a dozen other countries abstaining, declaring the ocean floor to be "the common heritage of humankind." Discussions have since been going on about the proposal of extending the limits of territorial waters, which should be the exclusive preserves of the adjoining littoral state, and about the procedures for exploiting resources beyond territorial limits.

Neither the NIEO nor the Law of the Sea negotiations have reached their objectives.

In relation to the first, the developed capitalist countries have adopted different tactics at different times. At times they tried to draw OPEC into an alliance against the non-oil-producing countries; at other times they sought some understanding with the latter against OPEC. So far, however, OPEC has succeeded in preserving its alliance with the rest of the Third World countries, by making some concessional gestures to them, thus foiling the maneuvers of the developed capitalist countries.

At another level, the tactics of the developed capitalist countries have varied from the reformist confrontationism of the Trilateral Commission to the reformist conciliationism of the Brandt Commission. The Trilateral Commission, founded in 1973 at the initiative of David Rockefeller, president of the Chase Manhattan Bank, was composed of leading businessmen, bankers, and politicians of the three most important segments of the developed capitalist world—the U.S.A., Western Europe, and Japan—as an "organization oriented toward the formulation of political decisions." Its major thrust was toward: (1) working out a unified strategy for the entire bloc of the developed capitalist countries by sharing out the leadership among the three geographical segments mentioned above, and (2) making some minor tactical shifts in their approach and offering some nominal concessions to the underdeveloped countries, while seeking to consolidate the hold of the developed capitalist countries on the world economy.

The Trilateral Commission counterposed its own conception of a "new economic system" to the demand for NIEO voiced by Third World countries.

An analyst says of the commission:

[It has defined] its policy for the establishment of a new international economic system, which is opposed . . . to the claims for a new world economic order put forth by the Group of 77. To the claim of structural reorganization, ensuring the economic development of the dominated countries, formation of a really pluralist system respecting the options of each country, the Trilateral opposes its reaffirmation of the excellence of the liberal system, the priority given to the development of the industrialized countries, the refusal of any structural reform in the direction indicated by the Group of 77. Rejecting any idea of pluralism, it proposes, to the countries who can do so, to join its economic order, existing on the basis of exchange and mutual interests. Recognizing the importance of the movement for a new world economic order, the commission has decided to divide it and to make it deviate from its objective by providing its core and infiltrating it ideologically.[25]

Though the suggestion for its formation originally came from World Bank President Robert McNamara, the Willy Brandt Commission, in contrast to the Trilateral, which was an exclusive "club of the rich," had ten members from Third World countries and eleven, including the chairman, from the developed capitalist countries. The Commission completed its work with expedition—within two years, from December 1977 to December 1979.

A passionate plea for disarmament apart, the Brandt Commission emphasizes the objectives:

To diminish the distance between "rich" and "poor" nations, to do away with discriminations, to approach equality of opportunities step by step, . . . not only a matter of striving for justice. . . . It is also sound self-interest, not only for the poor and very poor nations, but for the better-off as well.[26]

The commission strongly supports the essential elements of the Third World's demands, encompassed in the program of the NIEO. In one of its concluding sections, the report of the commission reads:

The large-scale transfer of resources we call for should be organized in partnership between developed and developing countries. Our proposal for a new financial institution should be examined by the international community. Those on the use of IMF gold, international taxation, and power-sharing in the existing institutions must also be examined, and joint efforts must be made to restore international monetary stability. . . .

The industrialized nations must give greater access to processed products from developing nations and take serious steps jointly with the developing nations to stabilize prices for commodities. The industrialized countries should also introduce measures to liberalize the international trading system, with a greater determination to restructure their industries toward higher levels of productivity, and allowing developing countries in the process of industrialization to expand their markets.[27]

Among a number of other important recommendations, the commission proposed: "Effective national laws and international codes of conduct . . . to govern the sharing of technology, to control restrictive business practices, and to provide a framework for the activities of transnational corporations."[28]

With regard to the Law of the Sea, although the international conference under the aegis of the UN arrived at a broad consensus that leaves a wide area—including marketing, processing, and distribution of sea resources—free for the operations of MNCs, the U.S.A. has announced its dissociation from the proposed agreement.

Preparations for a world summit meeting, recommended by the Brandt Commission, for arriving at North-South agreement on NIEO are afoot, but without any particular prospects of success. The foreign ministers' conference, preparatory to the summit, held in Cancún, Mexico, in October 1981, apparently failed to arrive at an agreement about the agenda for the summit:

The ministers agreed, after extensive discussions, that the [summit] meeting would not work on the basis of a formal agenda, but rather within a "discussion framework." According to a press report, observers are skeptical about chances of the forthcoming summit removing bitter differences in North-South relations.

The consensus among the developed countries has been an unwillingness to commit on anything. The trend in official thinking in Washington in the matter has been evident in the last several months and the Ottawa summit [of the leading industrial countries] made it official.[29]

Thus, there is nothing to indicate that anything approaching a new international economic order—an order that could really help solve the problem of burgeoning mass poverty in the Third World—is in the offing.

The advocates of the North's position sometimes raise a plausible moral objection against any demand for appreciable resource transfer from the North to the South. Why, they ask, should the workers of Detroit be taxed in order to subsidize the ruling elite of Zaire? Why is the French government to be congratulated for forcing the dockworkers of Marseilles to help subsidize the petty bourgeoisie of the Ivory Coast? In short, why should the poor of the industrialized North transfer resources to the seemingly self-indulgent rulers of the Third World? This moral mask has been effectively disposed of by a noted African political scientist, Ali Mazrui:

> Those who claim that the workers of Detroit should not be forced to subsidize the ruling elite of Kenya or Zaire are, unfortunately, the same ones who would be alarmed by the ruling elites' of Kenya and Zaire going socialist. Salvador Allende paid with his life not because he was getting too elitist but because he was trying to transcend economic elitism in Chile.
>
> When Third World leaders are elitist and corrupt, we are told that no dockworker of Marseilles should be forced to subsidize them. When Third World leaders are earnest and socialistic, and seek to end elitism and corruption, we are told that they are recklessly interfering with the market—and the dockworker of Marseilles must not subsidize them either.
>
> It looks as if Third World leaders get it either way. They are either guilty of elitism or of socialism. They are either condemned as corrupt or as interfering with the market.[30]

Though forceful in his exposure, Mazrui has, however, failed to unveil the deeper reality—namely, that the corrupt elite of Third World countries have in most cases been installed in power by the affluent West, which is also sustaining them with massive financial and military aid, including the protective umbrella of the upcoming Rapid Deployment Force.

In reality, however, the massive poverty of the Third World is rooted in politico-economic structures, jointly created and dominated by the metropolitan capitalist countries and their collaborators in the Third World. The process of the eradication of this colossal poverty cannot be initiated, and a genuinely new international economic order introduced, without the replacement of this neocolonial substructure.

These basic structural factors apart, any tinkering with Third World problems by the affluent countries has become extremely difficult because of the economic crisis the developed capitalist countries have been passing through. Demand recession and sharply rising unemployment have combined to make these countries resort to protectionism, while inflation and budgetary deficit continue to plague their economies. Moreover, weighed down by the heavy burden of military expenditure, most of these countries, particularly the U.S.A. and the U.K., are resorting to heavy cutbacks on social security and welfare programs. Hence, the prevailing climate in the developed capitalist countries is extremely unfavorable for easing the market restrictions on the import of Third World manufactures, or for offering better terms of trade for agricultural commodities from the Third World, or for transfer of resources in the form of "aid" on liberal terms.

As regards the demand for codes of conduct for the MNCs, the whole thing is an exercise in naiveté. The MNCs as corporate bodies can never voluntarily subject themselves to any chivalrous codes that go against the laws of their own inner dynamics: the highest possible profits and domination to ensure it. The enormous economic powers of the MNCs in absolute terms as well as in relation to the commodity economy of Third World countries can be seen from the data in Table 1 on page 106.

In view of the enormous powers of the MNCs, any talk about control over them by means of codes of conduct is pure moonshine. Even a top executive of an MNC has candidly discounted the efficacy of such codes. Irwin J. Miller, president of the Cummings Engine Company, said some years ago:

> I doubt whether codes of conduct will serve, in the near future, as a means to accomplish a worldwide homogenization of national policy governing multinationals. Rather codes of conduct are most usefully perceived as descriptions of perceptions, intentions, plans, expectations, and, to some extent, promises which a nation-state gives to multinationals and multinationals give to nation-states. Their function, therefore, is to set the parameters of negotiations and relationship.[31]

On the other hand, some observers of the present-day world scene describe the MNCs as a new superpower:

> Suddenly, it seems, the sovereign states are feeling naked. Concepts such as national sovereignty and national economic strength appear curiously drained of meaning. . . . Though the sense of nakedness and dependence has produced only inhibited responses so far, it has focused the world's interest on the institutions that are thought to be the main agents of change. One of these is the multinational enterprise.[32]

According to Jean-Jacques Servan-Schreiber, in a few years the third major power in the world, after the U.S.A. and the U.S.S.R., will be the American corporations in Europe.[33] However, he is somewhat wide of the mark inasmuch as he regards the U.S. state and the U.S. MNCs as two separate powers; they are in fact a composite entity representing the U.S. military-industrial complex.

Indeed, George Ball, a former undersecretary in the U.S. State Department, has made a straightforward demand for MNCs to have a controlling role in world affairs:

> The multinational corporation not only promises the most efficient use of world resources but, as an institution, it poses the greatest challenge

Table 1

CORPORATE CONTROL OF GLOBAL COMMODITY TRADE, 1977

Commodity	Total exports ($ million)	% marketed by the 15 largest MNCs[a]
Food		
Cocoa	4,588	85
Bananas	1,250	70–75
Tea	1,290	85
Coffee	9,821	85–90
Sugar	7,500	60
Rice	3,274	70
Wheat	11,285	85–90
Raw materials		
Hides, skins	1,788	25
Tobacco	3,809	85–90
Natural rubber	2,800	70–75
Cotton	5,958	85–90
Jute	182	85–90
Forest products	37,185	90
Ores, minerals, metals		
Crude petroleum	306,000[b]	75
Copper	6,304	85–90
Iron ore	5,099	90–95
Bauxite	701	90–95
Tin	2,406	75–80
Phosphates	1,389	50–60

Source: UNCTAD Secretariat, quoted in *Economic and Political Weekly,* Bombay, Annual Number, 1981, p. 531.

a: 1980 estimates.
b: In most cases, it is only three to six transactional traders who account for the bulk of the market.

to the power of the nation-states since the temporal power of the Roman Catholic Church began its decline in the fifteenth century.[34]

The author of a recent study on MNCs comments on Ball's viewpoint:

> Ball believes that if nation-states were to give up their sovereignty over economic and political decisions, and let the multinational decide for them, this would be indeed the "harbinger of a true world economy." In this fantasy world of Ball's, the centers of decision-making for the solution of world problems would be the home offices of multinational corporations . . . New York, Chicago, Los Angeles, San Francisco, Paris, Frankfurt, London, Zurich, Milan, Tokyo. Capitals of many nation-states, such as New Delhi, Cairo, Tel Aviv, Brasilia, Lima, Mexico City, and others, would turn into sleepy backwaters, as there would not be much to do for their governmental and other elites. . . . To promote the development of this techno-economic world, various self-serving organizations such as the International Chamber of Commerce, the United Chamber of Commerce, the Federation of Industries, and others, have already begun to formulate codes of conduct which, in effect, limit the role of the nation-states in intervening in the functioning of multinational corporations.[35]

The truth of the matter is that all this is no longer in the realm of fantasy, but a growingly assertive reality. Indeed, there is a new urgency felt by the MNCs for such a development. Faced with the increasingly acute crisis of the capitalist world economy—a crisis in the deepening of which MNCs play no small role—these supranational entities have opted for a course of action that is further intensifying the crisis.

CRISIS OF THE CAPITALIST WORLD ECONOMY

According to the report on the world economy in 1981 released by the IMF:

> With respect to economic activity, a development of central importance is that the average growth of real GNP in the industrial countries slowed from an annual rate of 4 percent in the 1976–79 period to 1.5 percent in 1981. Recovery in 1982 is expected to be modest, with the rise in real GNP in the industrial world from 1981 projected at only a little over 2 percent. The overall rate of unemployment in the industrial world, already as high in 1980 as it was during the international recession of 1974–75, would rise further in 1981–82.[36]

The IMF report stresses that monetary and fiscal policies in the major industrial countries turned increasingly restrictive during 1979 and 1980, in response to mounting inflationary pressures. Despite low or negative growth rates, accompanied by worsening unemployment, this stance was generally maintained in 1981. Growth in the volume of world trade slumped to 1.5 percent in 1980 and was projected to remain at a very low rate in 1981. Interest rates in the large industrial countries have been high and volatile, and have been accompanied by rapid movements in the exchange rates for major currencies: repercussions have been felt not only in those countries but also in smaller industrial countries and in developing countries.

The increase in wages in major industrial countries, the IMF report says, has been more restrained than after 1974. Wage restraints have been accompanied by savage cuts in social security provisions in Britain and some other countries. The Reagan administration in the U.S.A. has plans to effect a cutback of $82 billion in this sector over the next five years.

The impact of the crisis in general and the cut in social security in particular affect most heavily the poorest stratum of the population, but the high life-style of the upper echelons remains undisturbed. The British newspaper *The Mirror* recently featured the response of a "white young kid" in Liverpool to this situation in a graphic manner:

We are eating our dinner—a bowl of cornflakes and a bit of bread and jam. Ascot [horse race] is on the telly and mom says, "Oh, look at them all, don't they look lovely?" I went mad. I flung my spoon against the wall. . . . What a sick country it was when people like that can spend thousands of pounds in a day going to the races when we are struggling just to get enough to eat.[37]

Newsweek magazine reported a similar predicament faced by a divorcee at the prospect of the heavy cuts in social welfare proposed by Reagan: "I know they have to make some cuts somewhere," she said, "But why pick on the lowest income group to cut back on?"[38]

The depth of the world capitalist crisis today can be guessed from the fact that the noted U.S. economist Paul A. Samuelson compares it to terminal cancer:

If, in the present state of medical knowledge, certain types of cancer cannot be cured or even checked, it is the duty of the good physician to face up to this fact, to profess the limits of scientific knowledge and therapy.

So it is the duty of modern political economy to record a simple truth. In the current state of knowledge . . . no jury of competent economists can reach broad agreement on how to recommend a feasible and optimal incomes policy, which can tackle the present affliction of stagflation.[39]

The continuing, and in fact deepening, crisis of the developed capitalist economies has seriously eroded the "legitimacy" of the system. The post-World War II miracles in the economic sphere had given rise to an image of crisis-free and continuously expanding capitalist economy—at least in the developed capitalist countries. Though certain negative features in this growth—such as the disturbance of ecological balance—were leading to questionings in some sensitive segments of the population in those countries, confidence in the overall capitalist system was untouched until the mid-1970s. Lingering stagflation, attended by growing unemployment and increasing deterioration of living standards of the masses, further accompanied by direct cutbacks on social security and welfare programs has since rudely shaken this confidence. All this is leading to significant shifts in the political position of the working people in many of the developed capitalist countries.

In Britain, which had a classic example of consensus politics based on collaboration between the Tories and the Labour politicians, not only has this consensus been shattered, but a sharp polarization between the right and left wings of the Labour Party has developed, resulting finally in a split, as also a certain differentiation even among the Tories.

In Sweden, another theater classic of social-democratic class collaboration, the Social Democrats suffered a setback some years ago. There are now signs of a regrouping of forces in their favor, after an interlude of billing and cooing between the conservatives and a segment of the working people.

In Italy, for the first time in the entire post-World War II period, the corrupt and conservative Christian Democratic leadership was forced to cede the leadership of a coalition government to another party. It seems inevitable that a new coalition will one day include the Italian Communist Party which has for years attracted the loyalty of about one-third of the nation.

Recent elections in France have served to demonstrate clearly a leftward thrust in French politics.

All this reflects not only the accumulation of tremendous stress and strain in the developed capitalist countries, but also ripeness for transcending the existing social order, for passing over to a rational, humanizing, and egalitarian social order, in the wake of a socialist transformation.

A major factor retarding such a historic transition is the somewhat negative impact of certain aspects of developments in what is now called "actually existing socialism" in the U.S.S.R., Eastern Europe, and China.

"ACTUALLY EXISTING SOCIALISM"

In 1981 the *Marxist Review* elaborated on the negative aspects of de facto socialism and their impact on the world outside:

The absence of systematic and consistent attention to the work for authentic cultural revolution in the socialist countries, indeed, the promotion and absolutization of some bourgeois values . . . in the course of the actual development of the economy of the U.S.S.R. and other socialist countries, created conditions for the penetration of the consumerist and other distorted elements of the bourgeois culture in the socialist countries.

Instead of the socialist culture emerging as an alternative of a higher order, the fact that in some areas the socialist countries were trying to imitate the bourgeois culture, the obvious decadence of which had in the meantime started repelling the healthier elements in the bourgeois countries themselves, led to a serious devaluation of socialism among a section of the population of the advanced capitalist countries.

The sorry spectacle of petty bickerings, conflicts, and even armed skirmishes among some of the socialist countries, authentic exposures of the brutality of the Stalin regime, and repeated rebellions by wide sections of the working people in a number of socialist countries severely undermined the appeal of scientific socialism to large masses of the working people in, at least, the advanced capitalist countries.

The world has thus reached a twilight period when on the one hand the economic, political, social, and moral crises of the capitalist system are fast deepening, but, instead of a growing surge for the socialist alternative, a skepticism and even contempt for the existing socialism are growing.

The situation has to be tackled radically and energetically if humanity is to pass from moribund and crisis-ridden capitalism over to the high road of human emancipation, through socialism. For this, the historical evolution of the socialist society has to be critically examined, the negative features sharply intensified and a broad-based struggle unleashed in these countries for structural, cultural, and ideological renewal. Otherwise, ideological-political conflicts within and between them, blended with national chauvinist conduct and disaffection and/or apathy among sections of their population, would further weaken the socialist system, more and more distort their development, and inevitably dilute the attraction of socialism itself to the exploited and oppressed masses in the capitalist countries. All this would serve to embolden and encourage the desperate imperialist forces to embark upon provocative gambles.[40]

CONCLUSION

The foregoing survey of the contemporary world situation points to the following tasks:

(1) Humanity is facing an unprecedented danger of total annihilation, which has to be averted by a universal mobilization of humanist forces.

(2) The massive poverty of Third World populations can and must be removed through a basic restructuring of the politico-economic system in those

parts of the world—a restructuring that will not only establish a new equation between the Third World and developed capitalist counties but also change the internal social situation by overthrowing the domination of subservient, privileged, and oppressive local elites.

(3) The struggles for the elimination of the threat of a global holocaust and for the reestablishment of ecological balance, as well as for the emancipation of the peoples of the Third World, are organically linked with the struggles of workers in the developed capitalist countries against the crisis-inducing domination of military-industrial complexes, based on the foundation of the powerful MNCs.

(4) All these struggles are directly related with the struggles for the improvement of the quality of "actually existing socialism."

The world today has become more a single organic entity than ever before. Advance in any sector of the world is, to some extent, premised on advances in other sectors. We who want to carry forward the struggle for human liberation in our own spheres can do so more effectively if we view our own tasks in this global, epochal perspective.

NOTES

1. *The Times of India,* New Delhi, Jan. 5, 1981.

2. *The Statesman,* Calcutta, Feb. 5, 1981.

3. Ibid., June 23, 1981.

4. *The Times of India,* May 18, 1981.

5. Printed in *The Times of India,* Aug. 4, 1981.

6. *North-South, A Programme for Survival: The Report of the Independent Commission on International Development Issues under the Chairmanship of Willy Brandt* (London: Pan, 1980), p. 14.

7. Alan B. Mountjoy, ed., *The Third World—Problems and Perspectives* (London: Macmillan, 1980), pp. 13–14.

8. *North-South,* p. 32.

9. Karl Marx, *Capital* (London: Allen & Unwin, 1949), vol. 1, p. 32.

10. Ibid., pp. 453–54.

11. Ernest Mandel, *Marxist Economic Theory* (Calcutta: Rupa, 1971), p. 443; italics in the original.

12. Harry Magdoff, in *Imperialism in the Modern Phase* (New Delhi: PPH, 1974), p. 15.

13. Ibid., pp. 17–18.

14. *Economic and Social Survey of Asia and the Pacific* (Bangkok: ESCAP, 1975), p. 3.

15. R.L. Chawla, "Third World Debt," in *The Economic Times,* Calcutta, Aug. 28, 1980.

16. André Gunder Frank, "Development of Crisis and Crisis of Development," in *Economic and Political Weekly,* Bombay, Annual Number, 1980, p. 238.

17. *Export Expansion and Economic Growth in Developing Member Countries of ADB* (Manila: Asian Development Bank), Occasional Papers, no. 10, pp. 16, 18.

18. Vladimir Simonov, *Seething Continent* (Moscow: Novosti Press Agency, 1980), pp. 10–11.

19. G. K. Helleiner, "International Technology Issues: Southern Needs and Northern Responses," in J. N. Bhagwati, ed., *New International Economic Order: The North-South Debate* (Cambridge, Mass.: MIT Press, 1977), pp. 295–96.

20. Harry Johnson, *Technology and Economic Independence* (London: Macmillan, 1975), pp. 79–80.

21. Occasional Papers, no. 12 (Manila: ADB, 1978), pp. 20–22.

22. V. Gauri Shankar, "The Performance of Transnational Corporations in India," in *Mainstream,* New Delhi, July 23, 1977.

23. Planning Commission, Government of India, *Draft Five-Year Plan, 1978–83,* vol. 1, p. 3.

24. Vladilal Dagli, *Growth for Whom?,* Commerce Pamphlet, no. 62, 1973, pp. 6–7.

25. Gustave Massiah, "Imperialist Crisis and Strategies, The Trilateral Commission," paper presented at the International Conference on Alternative Development Strategy and the Future of Asia, New Delhi, March 11–17, 1980; p. 14.

26. *North-South,* p. 17.

27. Ibid., p. 280.

28. Ibid.

29. *The Economic Times,* Calcutta, Aug. 6, 1981, editorial.

30. J. N. Bhagwati, ed., *New International Economic Order,* p. 374.

31. Quoted in A. R. Negandhi and B. R. Baliga, *Quest for Survival and Growth: A Comparative Study of American, European, and Japanese Multinationals* (New York: Praeger, 1979), p. 5.

32. Ibid,. p. 10, quoting R. Vernon, *Sovereignty at Bay* (New York: Basic Books), p. 3.

33. Negandhi and Baliga, *Quest for Survival,* quoting Jean-Jacques Servan-Schreiber, *The American Challenge* (New York: Athenaeum).

34. Negandhi and Baliga, *Quest for Survival,* p. 97.

35. Ibid., pp. 97–98.

36. Excerpts printed in *The Economic Times,* Calcutta, Aug. 8, 1981.

37. Reprinted in *The Statesman,* Calcutta, July 21, 1981.

38. *Newsweek,* May 18, 1981.

39. Paul A. Samuelson, *Economics* (McGraw Hill/Kogakusha: Tokyo, 1973), 9th ed., p. 825.

40. *The Marxist Review,* Calcutta, April-May 1981.

10

The Place of Non-Christian Religions and Cultures in the Evolution of Third World Theology

Aloysius Pieris

THEOLOGY OF RELIGIONS: CURRENT BOUNDARIES OF ORTHODOXY

Basis and Background:
The Third World as a Theological Perspective

The phrase "Third World" is a theological neologism for God's own people. It stands for the starving sons of Jacob—of all places and all times—who go in search of bread to a rich country, only to become its slaves. In other words, the Third World is not merely the story of the South in relation to the North or of the East in relation to the West. It is something that happens wherever and whenever socio-economic dependence in terms of race, class, or sex generates political and cultural slavery, fermenting thereby a new peoplehood. Because, however, there is no people unless summoned by God, and no God worth talking about except the God who speaks through a people, all theology is about a people's God—that is, about God's people. The major focus of all "God-talk" or theology, then, must be the Third World's irruption as a new peoplehood announcing the liberating presence of a God who claims to humanize this cruel world.

But the irruption of the Third World is also the irruption of the non-Christian world. The vast majority of God's poor perceive their ultimate concern and symbolize their struggle for liberation in the idiom of non-Christian religions and cultures. Therefore, a theology that does not speak to or speak through this non-Christian peoplehood is an esoteric luxury of a

Christian minority. Hence we need a theology of religions that will expand the existing boundaries of orthodoxy as we enter into the liberative streams of other religions and cultures.

One regrets, therefore, that the only Third World theology presently being given substance is circumscribed by the exclusively Latin and Christian context of its origin. This remark is not leveled against the Latin American model but against the antithetical attitudes it has evoked in the Afro-Asian churches, in that some "liberationists" want to duplicate a Latin, Christian model in their non-Latin and non-Christian environments, thus driving the "inculturationists" to a defensive extreme.

In fact, at the EATWOT Asian consultation in 1979,[1] I tried to forestall this futile debate by avoiding the liberation/inculturation schema and by defining theology as a discovery rather than an invention—that is, as a Christian participation in and a Christic explicitation of all that happens at the deepest zone of a concrete ethos wherein religiosity and poverty, each in its liberative dimension, coalesce to forge a common front against mammon, the anti-God.[2] Nevertheless, the subsequent controversy fell back upon the old paradigm and reduced religiosity and poverty to the categories of inculturation and liberation respectively,[3] though efforts were made to restore the original framework where the *cultural* context of theology was equated with the *liberative* dimension of religiousness and poverty.[4]

The polarization continues to this day. The reason, presumably, is that in both the First and the Third Worlds there still lurks a crypto-colonialist theology of religions (and cultures) that keeps our revolutionary rhetoric from resonating in the hearts of the Third World non-Christian majorities. Is this not the appropriate time and place to discuss it frankly?

Our analysis of this question presumes that every religion, Christianity included, is at once a sign and countersign of the kingdom; that the revolutionary impetus launching a religion into existence is both fettered and fostered by the need for an ideological formulation; that its institutionalization both constrains and conserves its liberative force; that religion, therefore, is a potential means of either emancipation or enslavement.

But, theologically speaking—which is to say, "from a Third World perspective"—the test case that reveals the twin aspect of sin and grace in religion is its response to the phenomenon of poverty. Poverty is itself ambivalent. It can mean dispossession forced upon the masses by the hedonism and the acquisitiveness of the greedy. But it can also mean the virtue of poverty, which, according to Albert Tevoedjré's thesis, is "the status of someone having what is necessary and not the surplus," a *conditio sine qua non* for the elimination of what we have defined here as enforced poverty.[5] A religion fails in its salvific mission even if it only connives at the sinful dimension of poverty. It is salutary if it zealously promotes the liberating virtue of voluntary poverty both as a personal choice (the monastic praxis) and as a political system (the socialist praxis). For, depending on its bearing on the problem of poverty, religion either serves or starves humankind not only in the micro-ethical sphere of the individual soul, but in the macro-ethical world of politics and economics.

We grant that this criterion is not universally accepted, nor is the ambivalence of the religious phenomenon comprehensively spelled out in theological circles. Thus, a certain unilateral view of religions still prevails and accounts for the polarization of the church into a Christ-*against*-religions theology and a Christ-*of*-religions theology. The rift between liberationists and inculturationists is only a recent manifestation of it; there have been other versions earlier, as indicated in Table 2 on page 116.

The Liberation Thesis on Religion:
Its Western and Colonialist Character

The contrast between these two perspectives (Christ-*against*-religions and Christ-*of*-religions) is quite evident even in the Latin American theologies. But on the whole the perceptive pioneers, such as Gustavo Gutiérrez and nuanced systematizers, such as Juan Luis Segundo, have always viewed religion as an ambivalent phenomenon. At the EATWOT São Paulo Conference, both the enslaving and the liberating dimensions of religion (i.e., Christianity) were recognized.[6] Gutiérrez contrasted "popular religiosity" with "liberative faith."[7] Enrique Dussel therefore called for a new theory of religion.[8]

However, there still prevails a species of Christ-against-religions theology in Latin America, which is uncritically accepted in small but vocal circles of Asian activists. That there are two major trends in liberation theology—one with a Marxist mood and method, and the other with a pastoral rootage in popular cultures—is perhaps not sufficiently appreciated here in Asia.[9] Although I personally assess both these theologies to be basically valid, I feel compelled to question the unilateral theory of religion presupposed in the former.

The best exponent of this theory is José Miranda, a Latin American biblicist avidly read in Asia. For him religion is an evil to be destroyed, because it is an escapist objectification of the Absolute, a projection of one's own self, a justification of the status quo, a total alienation of the human person, an alibi for interpersonal justice, a cyclic view of life that stifles the voice of the Absolute in suffering humanity—and, therefore, something that negates Christian commitment.[10] Even the more sober Sobrino speaks in the same strain, taking religion to be a degradation of faith.[11]

This theory is certainly not of Latin American creation. As we shall indicate later, it is a blend of two European patterns of thought dating back to an era when the West was less informed than now about the complex structure and history of non-Christian cultures. How ironic that liberation-conscious Asians should subscribe to a thesis that is as colonialist as it is Western![12]

Table 2

CHRIST AND THE RELIGIONS
HISTORICAL PANORAMA OF A POLARIZATION

Christ-AGAINST-Religions	Christ-OF-Religions
SIXTEENTH CENTURY ONWARD The **COLONIALIST CHRIST** of early Western missionaries conquers non-Christian religions, which are linked with the **moral poverty** of "colonized" nations. The medium of his action is the **Western** form of **civilization**.	**NINETEENTH CENTURY ONWARD** The **GNOSTIC CHRIST** of Indian theologians; beginning of the fulfillment theory of religions. The link between religion and material poverty is ignored.
LATE 1960s The **NEO-COLONIALIST CHRIST** of the developmentalists conquers non-Christian religions, which are linked with the **material poverty** of "developing" nations. The medium of his action is the **Western** model of **development**.	**LATE 1960s** The **ASHRAMIC CHRIST** of monks and mystics, incarnated through traditional practice of religious poverty —i.e., voluntary acceptance of material poverty (Renunciation, monasticism). The link between religion and structural poverty is ignored.
LATE 1970s The **CRYPTO-COLONIALIST CHRIST** of the liberationists conquers non-Christian religions, which are linked with the **structural poverty** of Third World nations. The medium of his action is the **structural liberation** based on Marxist occidentalism and **Western Biblicism**.	**LATE 1970s** The **UNIVERSAL CHRIST** of the inculturationists, particularized in cultures through the appropriation of religious structures (idioms, symbols, moods, etc.). The link between religion and liberation struggles is ignored.

Why is it Western, why colonialist?

It is Western, first, because of the implied notion of "religion." None of the Asian soteriologies, not excluding the biblical ones, have offered us a comprehensive word for, or a clear concept of, religion in the current Western sense. Some vernacular words have no doubt acquired that meaning through usage under Western impact. Earlier we had words only for the various facets of what could be designated as religion. For, in our context, religion is life itself rather than a function of it, being the all-pervasive ethos of human existence. This is even more true of tribal religion, which often overlaps with "culture."

In the West, the word "religion" crept into the English language and, perhaps, into other modern languages as well, from the Vulgate, which rendered the Greek *threskeia* the Latin *religio*. In James 1:26 ff., one hears of "pure religion" and in Acts 26:5 the word clearly refers to Judaism. The Latin apologists, unlike their Greek counterparts, spoke of a *vera religio* (meaning Christianity) in contrast with *falsa religio*, a conviction that grew aggressive due to conflicts with Judaism and Islam. Thus the classic Roman missiology (phases 1 and 2 in Table 2) had set Christ against *other* (i.e., false) *religions*, unlike some contemporary liberationists who have gone further and put Christ against *religion as such* (phase 3). In this lies both the continuity and the contrast between the early and the modern versions of this conservative evangelism!

The narrow concept of religion as advocated by the liberationists seems more Greek than Roman. Most Greek apologists were inclined to churn "paganism" theologically and extract only its philosophy, leaving aside its religion as incompatible with Christianity. The tendency to squeeze religion out of human existence (by way of sacralization and secularization, which are two sides of the same coin) is not alien to the Western tradition. Schillebeeckx has cogently argued that even the modern phenomenon of secularization took form under the sacred shadow of medieval cathedrals.[13]

But the two forms in which this tendency influenced liberationist interpretation of religion appeared only within the last hundred years. For the philosophical rejection of (the Christian) religion characteristic of certain intellectual movements in Europe (Enlightenment, scientific revolution, rationalism) found an ideological as well as theological formulation in the two Karls of "dialectical" fame. Marx's dialectical materialism set religion against *revolution;* Barth's dialectical theology opposed it to *revelation.* In their systems, religion was a major obstacle to liberation and salvation, respectively.

In dismissing the immanentist thesis coming down from Schleiermacher to Otto, a thesis that postulated a "religious *a priori*" in the human person, Barth initiated an evangelistic theology that reduced the notion of religion to a blasphemous manipulation of God, or at least an attempt at it. The pioneering Protestant exegetical tradition—anterior to and stimulative of later Catholic biblical scholarship—was seriously infected by this bias. Kittel, for instance, referring to the conspicuous infrequency of such words as *threskeia, deisidaimonia, eusebeia,* and *theosebeia* in the New Testament, reaches the conclusion that the whole concept of "religion" (obviously, as understood in that particular theological tradition) is alien to the Bible and that in the mother tongue of the New Testament authors there was no linguistic equivalent for these Greek terms.[14] This last remark, as we already observed, is true of *all* oriental religions, and should have thrown doubt on the very concept of religion employed here!

It is, therefore, hardly surprising that many good dictionaries of biblical theology (e.g., that of Dufour or Bauer) would have no column on "religion." From "redemption" they pass on to "remnant"—indeed a symbolic *saltus,* suggesting another possible concept of religion that could be extracted from the Bible! Regrettably, it is under the aforesaid category of "religion" that all non-Christian soteriologies are subsumed and dismissed in favor of biblical faith.

In the militant stream of liberation theology, this Barthian view of religion dovetails neatly with Marx's equally evangelistic and Eurocentric evaluation of religions and cultures. Though many a Latin American critic has succeeded in pushing the Marxian analysis to the opposite conclusion—namely, that religion could be a "leaven of liberation rather than an opiate"—it still requires an Asian sensitivity to monitor its occidentalist bias.[15] Marx, whose contribution to the liberation of Third World nations dare never be underestimated, does not, for that reason, cease to be a man of his own time and clime: a nineteenth-century European. A recent writer who revels in revealing the racial and class prejudices of Marx and Engels concludes:

> Their attitudes were typical attitudes of the nineteenth-century Europeans who, regardless of their ideology, thought in terms of a hierarchy of cultures with their own at the top and who occasionally used biology to provide a scientific basis for their categorization of societies into higher and lower forms.[16]

The late Lelio Basso, the Italian Marxist theoretician, acknowledged this deficiency with laudable frankness.[17] Let me cite a few of his well-documented observations.

In Marx's *Manifesto,* the whole idea of "progress" and "civilization" is simply equated with the westernization of the East, the urbanization of the countryside, and the proletarianization of the peasantry—all in the name of socialism! And in *Capital* the European form of capitalist industrialization is envisaged as the model for the rest of the world, an indispensable prelude to the proletarian revolution. For this reason, Engels rejoiced at the American aggression in Mexico and the subsequent annexation of rich provinces such as California. He also hailed the French acquisition of Algeria—though he did have second thoughts about it. Similarly, Marx welcomed the British conquest of India because the breakdown of the ancient Indian civilization followed preferably by europeanization seemed an indispensable condition for the building up of a modern industrial culture. That there could, in fact, be a non-Western non-European way to socialism culturally based on the peasant communes of the *obscina* was of course proposed and debated at length even before the October Revolution; but Marx and especially Engels did not really shed their Western chauvinism in this regard.

Lenin's postrevolutionary policies seem to have further entrenched this occidentalism in the orthodox stream of classic Marxism. After gaining power he not only tried to expedite the industrialization of Russia (supposedly on a state basis rather then on a capitalist basis) but tried also to bring about socialism *from the top*, vertically, with little faith in the process of allowing it to emerge from the people below. In "accelerating the historical process," as it is called, many extraneous elements had to forget that Lenin (perhaps influenced by Černyševskij's ideal of destroying the Asian character of the Russian people—the *Aziatična* as it was called) introduced a steamroller socialism that ruthlessly sought to level down the religious and cultural identities of a people. The cry for proletarian *internationalism*—valid in itself—was in practice a zeal for *occidentalism*. In this he excelled the Western missionaries of his time who preached a "universal gospel," which in reality was their own narrow European version of it! The Brezhnev principle is a variation of this intransigent verticalism.

It is true that Lenin made many theoretical concessions to other ways of socialism as verified, for instance, in the case of Mongolia, as modern Marxist apologists observe with pride.[18] But denying to the founders of Marxism the right to be men of their own times does not help. Would that a massive effort to be made to purge Marxism of its Eurocentrism and cultural colonialism! It should revise its notion of Afro-Asian religions and cultures in terms of their liberative potentialities and discover indigenous ways to socialism—the kind of aggiornamento inaugurated by Markov, Ernst, and other Marxist intellectuals of the Leipzig School—vis-à-vis the precapitalist societies of Africa.[19] Such a corrective measure, moreover, has already been anticipated in the political praxis of Africans themselves. Amilcar Cabral's Marxism is a case in point.[20] One could also cite with some reservation Lumumba and Nkrumah. Asia has Ho Chi Minh. They wrote little and transmitted much to posterity through their praxis, which therefore serves as a *locus theologicus* for those groping for a liberation theology of religions and cultures.

This Afro-Asian critique of Marxist occidentalism is also an implicit judgment on the militant stream of Latin American theology, which maintains a methodological continuity with Western Marxism and a cultural continuity with European theology. Their Latin and Marxist idiom does not permit the ethnic identity of racial minorities to be reflected in their theology. The Amerindians, he blacks, and the Asiatics—almost one-fifth of the South American population—are also absolute majorities in certain provinces.[21] Has their unique community sense (e.g., the Indian *cofradías*, which are alleged to be a rich cultural alternative to Latin *hermandades*)[22] made a visible impact on the ecclesiological revolution of basic communities?[23] I agree with the Marxists that a conflict between ethnic struggles and class struggles could jeopardize the total liberation of a people. But this fear—if it is coupled with the Marxist tendency to confuse internationalism with occidentalism—could be an excuse for reinforcing Latinism. As a matter of fact, racism remains a contemporary problem, not a mere thing of the colonial past.[24] Not surprisingly, even the Marxist Lipschütz, who conceded that these non-Latin ethnic groups could form self-governing "linguistic" republics, would not think of a hypothetically socialist nation of Latin America except in Hispano-American terms, always having the Soviet model before him,[25] a model not entirely free of Russian cultural and linguistic colonialism.[26] It is, therefore, heartening to note that the participants of the São Paulo conference did touch on this delicate question, though in the Final Document they skirted the subject, giving it only a passing nod.[27]

Liberation and Inculturation: The History of a Tension

Some theologians display an exaggerated solicitude for inculturation, which calls for an equally severe judgment especially when the historical context of the liberation/inculturation tension is brought into focus. Table 2 does precisely this by tabulating the three successive versions of the two christological perspectives: the Christ-*against*-religions theology and Christ-*of*-religions theology. The table is self-explanatory, and we shall here only skim over the three phases, touching down only on salient points.

Phase 1 covers the era of Euro-ecclesiastical expansionism when the colonialist Christ was set on a warring spree against false religions in the lands now called the Third World. Not even De Nobili and Ricci contested this Christ-*against*-religions theology! They only questioned the policy of imposing Western civilization as a means of conversion, a policy that prevailed despite their protest, and persists to this day in subtle ways (phases 2 and 3). The theological breakthrough began perhaps in the nineteenth century with the epiphany of the Gnostic Christ. He appeared in the works of both Hindu and Christian theologians.[28]

Some Christian theologians anticipated the later official doctrine of the Lambeth Conference (1930) and the Second Vatican Council—namely, that Christ works in other religions as the final consummation of all human aspiration for redemption. Obviously this "fulfillment theory of religions," even in its post-Vatican II versions, is fraught with intrinsic theological difficulties that need not be discussed here. Suffice it to note that it is an abstract theory that excludes from religious disclosure the basic theme of any genuine theology: the poor. After all, is not the story of Jesus preeminently the story of a God *of* the poor, a God *with* the poor, a God *for* the poor? No wonder that in the 1960s, with the sharpening of Third World consciousness, the nexus between the religions and the poor began to receive articulate attention.

Thus begins phase 2, with its own version of the two theological perspectives. Enter first the neo-colonialist Christ in the person of the missionary with the jeep. Western "civilization" now yields place to Western "development" as the medium of Christ's saving presence. I even remember its being called preevangelization! How could other religions relieve the poor in their plight if those religions themselves are the partial cause of their underdevelopment, and if technology and progress are unique Christian achievements destined to free the non-Christian masses from their superstitious traditions?[29] That the non-Christian worldview could provide a saner philosophy of development,[30] as illustrated, for instance, by the Sarvodaya movement in its earlier phase, or that, in the process of "modernization," the evangelical values of other religions and cultures were being immolated on the altar of mammon, were still the opinions of a dissenting minority.[31]

A counterthesis to developmentalism, however, did come from the Christ-of-religions theology. It found an anchor in the numerous ashrams and their equivalents already in existence for decades. They embodied the spirit of renunciation central to many cultures, thus expressing their solidarity with both the poor and their religions. Material progress need not necessarily mean human development, nor is material poverty in itself human impoverishment. The ashramic Christ fought neither of these. His sole attack was on that which caused such polarity: greed, the demon *within*, an enemy of all authentic spirituality.

And there was the rub. The organized character of greed passed unnoticed. While the war was waged and even won *within* the walls of ashrams, the poor—the waste product of the earth's capital-accumulating plutocracy—continue to grow in number and misery. Could their struggle for sheer survival succeed if that sinful system is not its target? Unless stained by the stigma of solidarity with that struggle, monastic poverty will always remain a shallow status symbol of a client-gathering guru. The claim to have renounced wealth is vanity of vanities if those who have no wealth to renounce cannot benefit from it. There is a precedent in Jesus, in his precursor John, and in Gandhi, his Hindu admirer, for whom voluntary poverty was not only a renunciation of mammon in the micro-ethical sphere of one's soul, but a denunciation of its stooges in the macro-ethical order of politico-religious institutions.

It is sad that whereas yesterday's feudalism turned some monasteries into oases of plenty amid deserts of poverty, pushing them into the hands of today's revolutionaries who *force* monks to practice *voluntary* poverty for the benefit of the masses (as has happened in Tibet and Mongolia), today's capitalism has entrenched some ashrams, zendos, and prayer centers in the grip of wealth-accumulating patrons who frequent them for spells of tranquility and return unconverted and unrepentant, awaiting another revolution to disrupt that unholy alliance with mammon. Have we not also heard of mystics spinning dollars by exporting meditation to the West? Like rubber, coffee, and copper, our spirituality too gets processed in the West and returns with expensive price tags and sophisticated labels ("Transcendental Meditation") to be consumed locally! Who is the beneficiary? And what of the horror of caste and sexist discrimination that thrives on religious sanction? How many prayer centers have cared or dared to go against the grain? The ashramic Christ seemed no more sensitive than the neocolonialist Christ to the demands of justice.

It is, therefore, worth noting that phase 3 dawned during a period when the pendulum of politics poised for a brief passing moment on the left extremity before it began its present rightward swing with the massive crisis in the socialist states and the rise of Reaganism. Disappointment with doctrinaire theologies and disillusionment with both the developmentalism and "mysticism" of the previous era added fuel to the fire of mounting liberation fever in the expanding circles of Christian activists in our part of the world. It was at this time that the Latin American theology (equated here with liberation theology), with ten years of maturity behind it, began to awaken the Afro-Asian "indigenizers" from their ethnocentric stupor, just as it had earlier shocked the Euro-American theoreticians from their dogmatic slumber. It is understandable that some Asian theologians with leftist leanings began to sing the liberation song out of beat with the non-Latin rhythm of their own cultures. The "lord of the dance" was the liberator Christ who redeemed the poor not only from their poverty but also from their traditional religions, which sustained the sinful systems. It is therefore equally understandable that the incarnate Christ of the inculturationists stood aghast on the opposite pole!

Just as one particular stream of liberation theology pursues, even today, the colonial evangelism of the past—as was shown in "The Liberation Thesis," above—so also the bulk of literature churned out in today's ever proliferating seminars on inculturation does not show any significant departure from the previous era's narrow focus on religion and culture. It pays scant attention to the colossal scandal of institutionalized misery that poses a challenge to every religion.

A defensive posture adopted against the liberationist thesis may partly explain such blindness. The implications of this limitation are serious and I have spelled them out clearly elsewhere.[32] Nevertheless, I shall resume this discussion in the second half of this paper, after dealing with the liberative and revolutionary potentials of non-Christian religions—something that both the liberationists (the school that we are criticizing here) and the inculturationists have failed to discern, but which is the very texture of a Third World theology of religions.

TOWARD A THIRD WORLD THEOLOGY OF RELIGIONS

The Anatomy of the Religious Phenomenon in the Third World

Every theologian should be alerted to the fact that a substantial amount of information regarding religions and cultures in the Third World is gathered, processed, and distributed by Euro-American research centers. The First World still has a monopoly on the resources required for such studies— money and media, academic prestige and personnel. Even the highly acclaimed "participatory observation method" in anthropology has been unmasked as another arm of Western dominance.[33]

The occidentalist bias that liberation theology was shown (above) to have absorbed from a tradition traceable to Marx and Barth is only the tip of the iceberg. There are deeper predispositions acquired by all of us—the present writer included—in the course of our intellectual training: we are all dependent on these same sources for our understanding of the relgious phenomenon in its global magnitude.

As Evans-Pritchard has noted, generations of writers on religion (Taylor, Frazer, Malinowski, Durkheim, Freud, and their followers), in their sincere search for truth, were only reacting against the religion of their upbringing.[34] In the face of their attempts to explain religion by explaining it away, theologians such as Barth tried to save Christianity by lifting it above the realm of religion, indirectly offering a biblico-theological prop to their anti-religion theories.

C. E. Stipe has diagnosed the malaise of Western anthropologists as "functionalism," which tends to gloss over religion as something redundant in the cultures they study.[35] Taking the focal aspect of religion to be something outside natural, human experience, they perceive the rite and not the system of meaning and beliefs. They study the social relations without due regard to the worldview that religions provide.

An interesting case cited is that of Sierksma accusing Lanternari of leaving anthropology in favor of theology[36] because the latter merely observed Christianity to be transcendent, unlike the messianic movements, which are more interested in human salvation on earth.[37] Marxist interpretation of Mau Mau as purely Kenyan nationalism or Melanesian cargo cults as purely economic phenomena shares in this Western reductionism. According to Stipe, this is precisely what hinders Western anthropologists from assessing the role of religion in relation to cultural change.[38]

Is not the same bias keeping the theologian (liberationist or inculturationist) from perceiving religion in positive terms of liberation struggles and revolutionary change? I recommend that a critical discernment be exercised in perusing available studies on religions and that fieldwork on this subject be undertaken afresh from within the Third World perspective of peoples struggling for integral human liberation. It is with this forewarning that I wish to begin describing the anatomy of the religious phenomenon in the Third World.

The intricate network of religions and cultures that spreads across the Third World baffles the theologian as much as it does the anthropologist. To do more than trace its major contours would, therefore, be unpragmatic within the space allotted to me. Nor should we spend time on definitions of religion and culture—an academic pastime that has bred confusion in the West. We who breathe religion as our normal atmosphere would rather go by the first intuitive and experiential grasp of what it means in life. Therefore, without formulating definitions for ourselves, we can still detect the ones that are wrong!

The first observation is that religion and culture coincide fully in tribal societies practically everywhere in the Third World. Culture is the variegated expression of religion. But as religions meet each other always in and through their respective cultural self-manifestations, there result subtle differentiations between the religions and cultures. Thus, one might speak about several cultures within one religion and, conversely, about many religions within one culture. The former case is exemplified in the three missionary religions: Buddhism, Islam, and Christianity (listed here in descending order of cultural differentiation). As for cultures that accommodate several religions, we can cite a whole series—for example, Buddhism and Hinduism in Nepal, Taoism and Confucianism in China, Buddhism and Shintoism in Japan, Hinduism and Islam in Java.

In some instances the culture of one religion relates to the other as host to guest. Hence these terms possess the conceptual elasticity that the complexity of reality has bequeathed to them. For reasons that are implicit in our prefatory remarks above, we are here primarily speaking about religions as the pivotal point of reference, and obliquely about culture. This premised, let me attempt to sort out the various strands of religiosity that have been woven into the exquisite cultural fabric of the Third World. Actually one can pick up about three of them; the crisscrossing of racio-linguistic contours within the so-called scriptural religions must be mentioned first.

The so-called scriptural or book religions of the world have all taken their origin from three reservoirs of Asian spirituality, each having its own racio-linguistic idiom: the Semitic (Judaism, Islam, and Christianity), the Indian (Hinduism, Jainism, and Buddhism), and the Chinese (Taoism, Confucianism). These streams of religiousness have not confined themselves to the neighborhood of their sources, but have been meandering beyond their linguistic boundaries, even across the continents, thus flooding the world—Asia in particular—with a plethora of hybrid cultures.

For instance, Islam's Semitic religiosity pervades both the Malayo-Polynesian and the Indo-Aryan cultures of Indonesia and Pakistan, respectively, and it also permeates many African tribes. Hinduism has a firm grip on the lives of both Dravidian and Indo-Aryan peoples of India, besides serving as the subterranean foundation of many South East Asian civilizations. Buddhism, which preserves its original Indian format only in Sri Lanka, has shaped several cultures by allowing itself to be shaped by them, with the result that one hears of Ural-Altaic, Malayo-Polynesian, Sino-Tibetan, Japanese, and Indo-Aryan versions of Buddhist culture. Christianity too can make a few modest claims in this regard.

The second type of cross-fertilization takes place between these religions and tribal religions. As a matter of fact it coincides with the process by which, as described above, a scriptural religion acquires citizenship in another linguistic zone. Regrettably, our theological manuals that deal with non-Christian religions focus mostly on these scriptural religions, or what sociologists call "the great traditions." But the peasantry and the proletariat of the Third World are, for the most part, bearers of a nonscriptural or regionalized traditional religiosity either *within* the framework of a major religion (so-called popular Buddhism, popular Taoism, popular Hinduism, and, as in Latin America, popular religiosity) or *totally outside* any scriptural religion (e.g., tribal religions not yet proselytized by the former). This is why I urged at the Asian Theological Consultation that due attention be paid to these religions.[39] Their beliefs and practices have not frozen into written formulas but flow with time, thus exhibiting the *flexibility essential for social change*. This is the first corollary I wish to underline here, for future reference.

Inasmuch as all scriptural religions began as oral traditions, and traditional religions of today are bound, sooner or later, to transfer their sacred heritage, too, into a written form, I prefer to fall back on two other terms that I coined to describe them on an earlier occasion: metacosmic (not to be confused with acosmic) and cosmic, respectively.[40] The former type of religion defines its soteriology in terms of a metacosmic "beyond" capable of being internalized as the salvific "within" of the human person, either through the agapeic path of redeeming love or through the Gnostic way of liberative knowledge—this being the major difference between the biblical religions and most nonbiblical ones. The cosmic religions, on the other hand, as the word indicates, revolve round cosmic powers—normally rendered as "gods," "deities," or "spirits" in English. They refer to natural phenomena (often personified) as well as the spirits of past heroes and one's own ancestors, not excluding "departed souls" and "saints" in popular Christianity. For this reason Confucianism is to be classed as a cosmic religion despite its scriptural base.

Further, wherever the two species of religiosity have merged, the common people's genius has created a synthesis that a superficial observer mistakes for syncretism. That is why Richard Gombrich has suggested the word "accretism" to describe it. For, in the hybrid cultures that issue from this symbiosis, *homo religiosus* learns to align locally determined cosmic concerns (food, harvest, rain and sunshine, floods and drought, health and sickness, life and death, marriage and politics) with the soteriological orientation of his or her life toward a metacosmic Beyond.[41] One welcomes, therefore, the bi-disciplinary approach of scripturists who take to anthropology (Dumont, Bechert, Gombrich, and others) in order to respect the hermeneutical reciprocity between the book and the beliefs, scripture and tradition, the written text and the living context. For the popular hermeneusis of ancient lore reveals the people's ongoing creative response to contemporary reality. This is the second corollary I wish to put on record.

This phenomenon of accretism points also to a third corollary. No major religion could have traveled beyond its seat of origin and become incarnate in the lives of the masses had it not sent its roots deep into the popular religiosity of each tribe and race.[42] In other words, historically and phenomenologically speaking, there cannot be a metacosmic religiosity having an institutional grip on the people save on the basis of a popular religiosity! The converse, however, is not true. For there can and in fact there do exist tribal religions independent of, though open to, scriptural religions.

The patterns of mass conversion offer us another valuable corollary, the fourth in the series. As stated elsewhere, mass conversions from one soteriology to another are rare, if not impossible, except under military pressure.[43] But a changeover from a tribal religion to a metacosmic soteriology is a spontaneous process in which the former, without sacrificing its own character, provides a popular base for the latter. Being cosmic religions, they are this-worldly in every sense of the term, and are often drawn by some "community advantages" to accept the institutional framework of a scriptural religion.[44] (The latter, which generally shuns change, tends, paradoxically, to use its other-worldly teachings to consolidate its this-worldly institutions!)

The stratified castes and tribes in India that have accepted Christianity, or more particularly Buddhism and Islam, on a mass scale substantiate this thesis. A better illustration is provided by the missionary conflicts between Christianity and Islam. After three and a half centuries of concerted proselytism, colonial Christianity in Indonesia pocketed a little over two million converts from Islam and even those came mostly from Northern Sumatra, Moluccas, Ambonia, and other outer islands where tribal culture prevailed; Christian "successess" among the tribals of the Atlantic coast of Africa— compared with the miserable failure in Muslim Africa, except for a minor conquest among the mountain tribes in Kabyles,[45]point in the same direction.

Let me end with the fifth and final corollary. Tribal and clan societies, given their strong religio-cultural cohesion, are never immune to the danger of intertribal conflicts. Tribalism—often equated with divisive provincialism —can be exploited ideologically by the enemies of social change. The strategy of "divide and rule" can thwart liberation movements, as will be discussed in the next section.

To sum up, we have described the anatomy of the religious phenomenon first in terms of the crisscrossing of racio-linguistic contours within scriptural religions, and, secondly, in terms of the five consequences issuing from the accretion of cosmic into metacosmic religions.

There is another interaction that deserves attention if our picture is to be complete: interaction between these religions and various socio-political ideologies. And this brings us to the core of our inquiry: religion and revolution.

The Revolutionary Urge in Religions and the Role of Ideologies

Luna Charsky, the first Soviet minister of culture, had this confession to make about religion: "It is like a nail," he declared. "The harder you hit it, the deeper it goes into the wood."[46] By persecuting religion, revolutionaries would hardly kill it but only make it more reactionary. Conversely, when challenged by an oppressive system, religion might unleash its potential for radical change.

A true revolution cannot go against religion in its totality. If a revolution succeeds, it does so normally as a cathartic renewal of religion itself. Seven decades of Marxism make us say this. Che Guevara sensed it when he said: "Only when Christians have the courage to give a wholehearted revolutionary testimony will the Latin American revolution become invincible."[47] With this prophecy he seems to have suggested the theme for a new chapter in the history of both the Marxist ideology and the Christian religion—a chapter that Nicaragua is struggling at death point to write for posterity!

This is even more true of the other religions that have a more extensive hold on the Third World than does Christianity. No *true* liberation is possible unless persons are "religiously motivated" toward it. To be religiously motivated is to be drawn from the depths of one's being. This motivation, we concede, could be occasioned by alien ideologies, as history has often attested. But the peoples of the Third World will not spontaneously embark on a costly adventure unless their lives are touched and their depths stirred by its prospects *along the "cultural" patterns of their own "religious" histories—* which, of course, differ widely from place to place, as was demonstrated in the previous section.

Take, for instance, the Chinese peasant culture, which is marked by a history of revolts, in contrast with, say, the culture of the Guinean peasantry, which has had no such tradition—a fact explicitly noted by Amilcar Cabral, who laid great emphasis on the local cultural variants of every socialist revolution.[48] This did not imply for Cabral that Guinea was incapable of radical change but that he had to consult his own culture rather than merely copy an alien model. Let us therefore linger first on the African situation; it offers many lessons to Third World theologians.

ISLAM AND CHRISTIANITY IN AFRICA

The tribal communities of Africa, if Marx is rightly interpreted, can be classed as "precapitalist socialist societies" in that they can reach full-fledged socialism without passing through the crucible of capitalism.[49] Jean Ziegler, with World Bank statistics, tries to vindicate the Tanzanian experiment of Julius Nyerere in favor of this theory.[50] But this is no easy task: both colonial and indigenous elements have left *ideological* dents in these societies. I refer to the local bourgeoisie and the feudal barons (not to mention the white settlers in Rhodesia and South Africa!) who inherited power from colonial rulers so that even progressive patriots such as Lumumba and Nkrumah could not radically change the basic character of the *nationalist* liberation movements.

Mozambique gives us the other alternative—if we may agree with Sergio Vieira, himself a member of FRELIOM (National Liberation Front of Mozambique) and a government minister.[51] Portugal, unlike Britain, Belgium, and France, had good reasons not to give even "flag independence" to its colonies but to cling to a fascist rule, thus inviting armed struggle.[52] Mozambique responded. The arbitrary demarcation of the future frontiers of African "nations" by the colonialists, which increased racial and tribal fragmentation, and the local exploitation of tribal loyalties (corollary 5, above) were attacked simultaneously, to bring patriotism in line with intertribal proletarianism as shown in the Mozambique people's massive self-immolation for the liberation of Zimbabwe.[53] This is an African response to one ideology—in repudiation of another. This process is bound to be normative in the future, because Africa is, by far, the most exploited of continents.

This is the background against which the role of scriptural religions should be assessed. Of course there are only two candidates for the conversion contest in Africa: Islam and Christianity. Because the rule of the game is "first come, first served," a tribal society that has already given its allegiance to one will not normally withdraw it in favor of the other (corollary 4). Hence, by the turn of the century, with tribal Africa mostly shared between Islam and Christianity, we can expect one of three things, if not all of them: a disastrous confrontation, a defensive compromise, or a daring collaboration between the two religions. The first is *not* unlikely; the last is imperative—provided one knows wherein collaboration is desired. Let me comment on each alternative.

Why confrontation? The Christianity of the colonial masters, which still dominates the African church, is institutionally handicapped because of its history of hostilities with Islam in Europe and in the missions.[54] It is humbled before Islam's credibility in the movement for African unity. It is hampered by its reluctance to disengage its ecclesiastical loyalties from the ideological grip of the countries of its provenance. And it is pastorally inhibited by its dread for liberation struggles. Hence, unless thoroughly revolutionized— that is to say, substituted by an indigenous alternative—it is bound to turn overdefensive in the face of Islam. God forbid that it should summon every available external help to consolidate itself against its rival. Have not Rhodesia and South Africa given a precedent? The other alternative might be "dialogue"—the dubious type that is insidiously fostered and even financed by various ideological blocs, a dangerous compromise that blunts the liberative edge of both religions.

Common sense dictates, therefore, that the climate be created for harnessing the religious zeal of both traditions into a prophetic movement in the service of God's poor, through a socio-political collaboration in a common *theopraxis of liberation*. And this obviously presupposes an unbiased Christian acquaintance with Islam.

ISLAM IN IRAN

Let Christians, therefore, step back for a while and gauge Islam's gigantic stature as it stands with self-confidence at the portals of the Third World, where it remains the most widespread single religious force to reckon with.

Christians are made to believe by the media that it is also a generator of religious fanaticism and fundamentalism. Khomeini is the obvious symbol that springs up in their mind. Why not focus, then, precisely on Iran and see where the fanatics come from and how a revolution is born?

Scan the last hundred years of history, pleads Eqbal Ahmed, Pakistani scholar, and you will note that the Khomeini episode is the *eighth* major battle that the Muslim nation embarked on to defend its sovereignty against mercantile and military exploiters from the West![55] Religious clerics were in the thick of the struggle. Reuter's concession (1872) and the tobacco concession to Major Talbot (1895) were the first two Western maneuvers. The third uprising was in 1905 against D'Arcy's concession to open Iran's oil resources to the West, as before, with the monarch's collaboration. This revolt succeeded in bringing about a modern constitutional government in 1906, which was soon overthrown by Czarist Russia and Britain in 1911. The opposition gathered momentum by 1919 against Lord Curzon's Anglo-Persian Treaty, which would have turned Iran virtually into a British colony. This fourth national victory lasted only for two years. The British maneuvered a coup d'etat led by Reza Khan in 1921. Thus absolute monarchy was reestablished with Khan as dictator, the father of the notorious ex-shah!

Reza Khan was hailed in the Western press for ushering in "modernization and westernization under the aegis of foreign domination," adds Ahmed. The Nationalists did throw him out in 1941 but could not regain control of the administration, for the British maintained a regency while the future shah grew up under colonial tutelage. The Nationalists staged a return in 1950 and, after a struggle, forced new elections (under the 1906 Constitution) and established the Mossadegh government, which eventually nationalized the oil resources of Iran.

Then came Iran's nightmare: the CIA organized a coup d'etat against the Mossadegh government in 1953 and installed the shah, the tyrant who massacred nearly two hundred thousand Iranians—among them poets and writers. "Iran's wealth was looted, transferred, and spent in the West." Iran's Muslim masses did not simply fight the shah. They fought the super power that forced him to be its gendarme in the Persian Gulf, sold him $19 billion worth of weapons, and supported his repressions until the last murderous days of his reign.

Who were the fanatics? Who were the liberators? Is this also the future of the ASEAN countries with a restless Muslim majority, and of Pakistan, which are all in the hands of the same powers that provoked the wrath of Iran? And what of the Russian intervention in Afghanistan—understandable in the light of capitalist aggression, but not less abominable? Islam *is* a giant, and *not* a sleeping one.

HINDUISM IN INDIA

Our third sample is Hinduism—a great religion comprising many little religions, inscrutable even to the expert who can only concentrate on one little corner of the maze. However, given our particular focus—the revolutionary urge of religions—we can still make valid observations illustrative of principles enunciated above (especially corollaries 1, 2, and 3).

First, Hinduism can be taken as a metacosmic soteriology centered round the sacred texts of revealed and interpreted truths (*Śruti* and *Smṛti*). It is from within this orthodox tradition that the Indian renaissance took off as a reform movement, stimulated by the challenge of Western Christianity. Despite its social influences and theological adventures (including the discovery of the Gnostic Christ alluded to above), it did not cease to be elitist.

According to one sociological survey, the offshoots of this movement have now withered into devotionalist sects. Some in the north and west of India have succumbed to political rightism and xenophobic chauvinism. Even god-human cults seem an apolitical middle-class phenomenon, indeed a far cry from the medieval savior cults, which were "liberational." And perhaps in reaction to the onslaught of urbanization, these new cults show a marked shift from the classic concern with liberation to a mere quest for meaningfulness as in affluent societies elsewhere.[56] Besides, the most disturbing issue of caste-discrimination—a socio-economic slavery "religiously" enforced by Brahmanic orthodoxy—is not squarely faced in these reforms.

To watch the transition from reform to revolution, one must, therefore, move away from this orthodox center of Brahmanic Hinduism. The Bhakti movement, the *Dalit Sāhitya* ("Writings of the Oppressed"), and the Tribal revolts represent three grades in this centrifugal trend.

The Bhakti movement—initially a popular tendency on the fringes of Brahmanism—"is the most creative upsurge of the Indian mind," which has inspired "several social and political revolts . . . from Shivaji's rebellion in the seventeenth century to Mahatma Gandhi's in the twentieth."[57] A comparative study of two such movements in Maharashtra helps bring out the ingredients of a *religious* revolt against caste and sexist discrimination.[58] The first is the Mahanubhava movement inaugurated by Chakradhar (1194–1276) who, in his ruthless denunciation of Brahman orthodoxy, did not spare even the Vedic scriptures. The brotherhood it fostered offered equality of status to both the 'sudras and women. Chakradhar, of course, was killed for it. Yet the movement (revived even recently) could not muster popular enthusiasm, because it was conservative, monastic, and relatively removed from the grassroots struggles. Its message too suffered in that the mode of transmission was limited to the written word, a medium totally inaccessible to the illiterate masses.

Contrast this with the Warkari movement, which spread wider, grew deeper, and survived persecution by continuing underground. It was a lay initiative with a popular base and truly a movement of the oppressed: the untouchable castes. It produced a galaxy of revolutionary poet-saints, many of whom were martyred: indeed the counterpart of the Hebrew prophets! In India's religious ethos, a reformer, in order to arouse the masses, must also be a poet and a saint. The other secret of success, as clearly exemplified in the

Warkari movement, is the use of the oral medium for transmitting the message, because it necessitates a personal encounter between the mutually in-
spiring agents of social change: the suffering masses and the poet-saint. A
vast production of oral literature and the extensive use of song and dance
ensured an ongoing program of "conscientization." It has, therefore, never
petrified into a written text but ever remained fluid and flowing with the
passage of time. Even the sacred lore of the ancients, whenever cited or insin-
uated in their freedom songs, went through a creative popular hermeneusis.
And in their later encounters with Islam and Christianity, too, they displayed
a spirit of humane ecumenicity.

On the other hand the *Dalit Sahitya* ("Writings of the Poor"), circulating
for two decades now, make an ideological departure from the aforemen-
tioned Bhakti movement of which it still is a historical continuation.[59] A
greater openness to other revolutionary ideologies has given teeth to this
movement, which had been a mere consciousness-raising exercise within popular religiosity. Marx, Lenin, Mao, Che, Ho Chi Minh, and Martin Luther
King figure prominently in these writings: the Dalits see themselves associated with the liberation struggles of all the world's oppressed. From openness to all that is liberative in other religions, there has grown a new openness
to other secular ideologies. Hence the Bhakti movement has lent itself to be
used ideologically to destroy the oppressive religious system in which it still
has its roots![60]

As we come to tribal India, we have not merely moved to the fringe of
Brahmanic religiosity, but to *another* religious system *outside* it. The student
of indology is not often introduced to this reality. It is, no doubt, the precapitalist socialism that we meet again, in contrast with the feudalism of monastic
religions (e.g., Buddhism) and of theocratic religions (e.g., Brahmanism).
Yet, as in Africa, so even more in India, feudalistic tendencies are gradually
seeping into tribal societies.[61] It is said that though the tribal and the untouchable caste woman often enjoys equality with the male, because of her relative
economic independence, it is the adoption of Hindu values that tends to
diminish the status of the harijan woman.[62]

Tribal society, wherever it is found, is egalitarian, free of caste and class,
based as it is on a *religious socialism* and uninhibited by puritanical mores
characteristic of scriptural religions, but prone to counter-violence if defense
of the community requires it. No wonder, as Gail Omvedt documents, the
tribals as a whole can boast of a history of nationalist and class struggles all
over Asia including India, not to speak of the bandit tradition of "Robin
Hoods" robbing wealthy landowners with the poor Indian villagers applaud-
ing as spectators.[63]

BUDDHISM IN CHINA

Let me terminate this survey with an extensive note on Buddhism, for it is a
pan-Asian religion occupying a position analogous to that of Islam in the
Third World.

It is common knowledge that the Buddhist scriptures demand radical social change but lend no support to violent struggles, even though naive theories about "righteous killing" have been advanced in the course of Buddhist history.[64] But tradition makes up for scripture, and it does so extravagantly! Here even orthodox Buddhism has to its credit a theory and praxis of rebellion. Some scholars warn that it is only when Buddhism as a religion is challenged in the midst of political chaos that monks come to the forefront with lay support, as in Thailand.[65]

But what about Burma's Buddhist resurgence, which was messianically political? Initially aimed at Burmese kings, it was later directed toward their British successors. There must have been about twenty revolts from 1838 to 1928—all inspired by the Maitreya cult: the eschatological expectation of a just social order to be ushered in with the appearance of the future Buddha. It is a belief that has scriptural foundation. Note also that it was this wave of Buddhist rebellions that brought to the surface the later independence movement with which U Nu, a philo-Marxist initially, tried his abortive experiment with "Buddhist socialism."[66] Sri Lanka and Indochina have followed similar patterns. Vietnam's history of the Li dynasty and the concept of emperor-monk reflect a militantly political Buddhism, which is not less virulent today.

Not surprisingly, revolutionary praxis on the fringes of the Buddhist institution shows greater radicalism. China offers us a series of persuasive examples, of which I make here a random selection.[67] From about A.D. 402 there were about ten armed rebellions organized by monks, climaxing in A.D. 515 with that of Fa-K'ing, a revolutionary monk who, like many of his kind, married a nun. These monastic rebellions were directed against both the state and the official religious establishment. Since then there have been many messianic sects that had a popular base, clearly indicating the influence of cosmic religiosity over the metacosmic. One such was the Maithreya Sect founded in A.D. 610 by a Buddhist monk who declared himself emperor. This sect had incorporated into its belief system the cult of Buddha Amitābha and the desire for rebirth in his heaven known as the Western Paradise. The adherents of this sect maintained that this paradise should be created on earth, here and now, rather than in a remote future. They wished to bring about a Buddha land, a state of peace and equity in this existence. This sect left its traces in the whole period from the seventh to the sixteenth centuries.

The White Cloud Sect (between 1108 and 1300) and the Lo Sect (1505–1956) were two others of the same kind. The most significant, perhaps, is the White Lotus Sect (Pai-Lien Ts'ai, 1133–1813), a branch of which continued under the name I-Kuam-Tao as late as 1956 and was hunted out by the Maoist regime. The founder was a Buddhist monk called Mao-tzu-Yuan (1086–1166), who was assisted by women and married monks—something that provoked the wrath of the orthodox *samgha*. But these movements continued to enjoy a certain amount of popular support. Mao-tzu-Yuan was exiled and the movement proscribed several times; then it was once more recognized by Emperor Jen T'sing (1312–1321). Among its many revolutions, the most successful was that of 1351 under the leadership of Han-Shan-T'ung, who also called himself Buddha Maitreya. This revolution succeeded in destroying the Mongol rule and established a new dynasty—the Ming Dynasty. Its first emperor was Chu-Yuang-Chang, ex-Buddhist novice and a former officer of the White Lotus army. The irony was that he later turned anti-Buddhist. This movement was crushed again in 1813. The ban was removed in 1911, and a branch of it, as mentioned earlier, was active as late as 1956.

By Marxist standards these were not real revolutions; they could at best be classed as rebellions. But they show how Buddhists could respond to the revolutionary moods and creeds of the time. In these instances, the Buddhist messisanic interpretation of the scripture and the scriptural justification of "revolution" had come as a response to a contemporary ideology springing from the Taoist secret societies that awaited the true ruler who was to give great peace to those awaiting him, and the Confucianist expectation of the enlightened emperor. What I wish to underscore here is that Buddhists living in a particular historical situation may, under the influence of non-Buddhist ideologies and movements, reinterpret their scriptural sources in order to respond creatively to a contemporary need—even if it means a costly revolution. This tradition continues to this day in Chinese Buddhism.

Religion and Revolution in a Third World Theology

In scanning the wide expanse of non-Christian cultures in the Third World, we beamed our searchlight on only four areas: African religiosity (which resembles that of Oceania), West Asian Islam, South Asian Hinduism, and East Asian Buddhism. Though by no means exhaustive, these four samples are illustrative of some of the major features of religiousness in the Third World and warrant the following three conclusions.

(1) Outside the pale of Semitic monotheism, there is perhaps only one stream of religiosity (and that is one form of Hinduism) that regards the one ultimate reality as a personal being who summons the cosmos into existence and into a personal redeeming encounter with himself/herself. A God who is one personal absolute creator-redeemer of the world and of humankind is neither universally affirmed nor universally denied. Religiousness—especially in Asia—is for a greater part metatheistic, or at least nontheistic, if not, at times, explicitly atheistic. The common thrust, however, remains *soteriological,* the concern of most religions being *liberation* (vimukti, moksa, nirvana) rather than speculation about a hypothetical liberator. Many metacosmic religions point to a future that is attainable as the present moment of total human emancipation, putting the accent on a metapersonal Beyond, if not on an "impersonal" but transphenomena "It": Tao, dharma, tathata, Brahma, nirvana. The cosmic religions, on the other hand, look up to many gods and spiritual forces, which constitute the spectrum of a complex unity of

being enveloping the whole of human and cosmic existence. Even where the two forms of religion—the cosmic and metacosmic—merge, the net result is not a simple equivalent of biblical monotheism.

Hence, theology as God-talk or God's talk is not necessarily the universally valid starting point, or the direct object, or the only basis of interreligious collaboration in the Third World. But liberation is. Soteriology is the foundation of theology. Regrettably, the contemporary theologies of religions (with Christ pitted *against* religions or niched within them) are devoid of any Third World perspective: they take off from textual accounts of non-Christian religiosity and ignore the historical fact that a religion's micro-ethical concern for self-purification of individuals ("cultural revolution") is often projected onto the macro-ethical level of socio-political catharsis ("structural revolution"). This is true even with those religions that are academically dismissed as "world-denying" or "escapist." Equally glossed over are the many explosive liberation myths that, in their symbolic enactments—such as dance and drama, song and ritual, parable and poetry—store the seeds of revolution in the heart of a people. Should not, then, a Third World theology of religions necessarily have a unitary perception of religion and revolution?

I submit that the religious instinct be defined as a revolutionary urge, a psycho-social impulse, to generate a new humanity. It is none other than the piercing thrust of evolution in its self-conscious state, the human version of nature's thirst for higher forms of life. The religious quest, in other words, is an irresistable drive to *humanize* what has merely been *hominized.* As in the biosphere, where it can end up in blind alleys, so also in the *noosphere,* this evolutionary upsurge can be sidetracked to regressive states of inertia. Revolution could turn reactionary, religion irreligious. But the foundation of a Third World theology of religions remains unshaken—namely, that it is this revolutionary impulse that constitutes, and therefore defines, the essence of *homo religiosus.*

This unified view of revolution, religion, and cosmic evolution imparts a Third World dimension to the understanding of technology and the allied concepts of "progress" and "modernization," and consequently lifts the whole debate on inculturation to another plane.

(2) Technology is the immediate and inevitable consequence of noogenesis or hominization. The human mind, as it emerges from the biosphere, demands more sensitive organs of perception (senses) and more effective means of movement (limbs), which the body does not provide physiologically. For the mind is capable of extending the brain, the senses, and the limbs of the body by organizing external matter into sensitized and mechanized tools of knowledge and action. Technology, to be sure, is the art *(techne)* of expanding the human presence and activity into space and time cognitively and conatively in order to further humankind's psycho-social evolution. Being, however, the natural accompaniment of hominization, it too can accept or escape the impact of humanization that issues from the revolutionary upsurge of

religiosity. Let me therefore recall, with parenthetical explicitations, the concept of technology I proposed to EATWOT earlier:

> Technology is an [humanly] induced cosmic process, which is a conscious [i.e., self reflective] continuation of the [infrahuman] biological evolution and, like the latter (i.e., like biological evolution), becomes humanized [i.e., liberative] only by its metacosmic orientation [i.e., by the revolutionary thrust of religion toward ever nobler levels of human existence].[68]

If, then, the law of evolution has prescribed in the book of nature the revolutionary imperative to humanize technology through religion, then a dehumanized technocracy is indeed a reversal of the evolutionary trajectory, a cosmological disaster, an irreligious undevelopment, though boorishly advertised in our countries as "international culture," modernization, and progress—if not also as preevangelization!

What dehumanizes technology is the sin of acquisitiveness organized into a socio-economic order of human relationships, a distorted cosmology that invariably fosters what Marx calls "the antagonism between man and nature." In that system, technology alienates its inseparable human partner, of whom it was meant to be the cosmic extension; it desecrates the *cosmic religiosity* of the peasant masses with the transfer of biospheric pollution from industrialized countries to the Third World, and with its acquired (not inbuilt) propensity to pillage nature in order to produce the weapons of cosmic holocaust.[69] It deflects the metacosmic orientation of nature and culture with a secularism that eclipses the "beyond" from the "now," and consequently engenders in the human heart a pathological obsession with cosmic needs—or "consumerism," as it is known in the cultures that first produced it. Then "modernization" and "progress" *must* imply the overthrow of this regressive but all-persuasive system in favor of a new order of human relationships wherein technology is not so much "in control of" nature as "in harmony with" its innate thirst for humanization—that is to say, with the revolutionary dictates of religion itself.[70]

Sexism, a sensitive issue in most religions, cannot be divorced from our discourse on technology and civilization, for there is an intimate correspondence between the anthropo-cosmic harmony advocated here and the androgynous mutuality that it presumes. If nature is an exclusively feminine symbol and if the metacosmic beyond, which is the redemptive consummation of the cosmic processes, is made to wear a masculine mask, then of course the religious enterprise of humanizing nature, civilizing technology, and divinizing the human amounts to a masculine absorption of the feminine. Woman will be the last thing to be civilized by man, says George Meredith scornfully; and also the other way about, corrects Theldore Reik.[71]

The task of humanizing nature, which is both masculine and feminine, is founded on the reciprocal activity of men and women civilizing each other. In this, the revolutionary impulse of all religions—save that of *some* tribal societies and *one* tiny vein in Hinduism—is ruthlessly curbed. Sexism points to an uncivilized area in religion. The new cosmological order that the Third World clamors for includes unhampered feminine participation in religion and revolution.

(3) Inculturation, that infelicitous word coined in the West and reminiscent of the reductionist notion of religion running through theology, anthropology, and Marxist ideology, has, fortunately, come to mean, in actual usage, the Christian search for meaningfulness within the *religious* ethos of non-Christian cultures. This is what compelled us to place it in the Christ-of-religions column. In this case, however, the relevant question to be asked is: Into which stream of non-Christian religiosity does Christianity hope to enter—the reactionary or the revolutionary? Or again, at what level—the micro-ethical level of liturgy and mysticism only, or *also* at the macro-ethical level of sociopolitical righteousness? To allay the liberationist's misgivings about inculturation, one more crucial question has to be raised: Which brand of Christianity seeks to be inculturated, the one framed within a cosmology that is repudiated in the Third World, or the one derived from a Third World hermeneusis of the gospel?

A Third World hermeneusis vivifies the Christian kerygma by recharging the three key words round which it revolves, words now worn out by ideological misuse: *basileia* (the new order), *metanoia* (interior conversion to that order), and *martyrion* (overt commitment to it.)

True to our non-Christian religious traditions, we can neither describe nor define the new order but boldly strive toward it by the *via negativa*—namely, by negating the present order not only in theory and analysis, but also in the actual commitment to overthrow it! The future that calls in question the present ever remains the "unnamable" or at least the "unmentioned presupposition" of every true revolution. For the intimate encounter with the ultimate reality—the core of mysticism—almost overlaps with a profoundly transforming experience of present unreality. The salvific truth dawns as the unknowing of delusion. Being shines in the darkest depths of nonbeing. Brahma/atman is reached by piercing through Maya. Nirvana culminates the pilgrimage of samsara. Life is the passage through death. Grace overwhelms where sin abounds. Revolution is born of bondage. Yahweh abides in the anawim. God's saving power erupts from the earth's slaving poor.

Can we touch the one without being touched by the other? Only the victim of the present order is qualified to be its judge and authorized to "proclaim the imminent future"—which is what the kerygma means. *Metanoia,* then, is the disturbance of heart and change of life that such mysticism evokes. It is a religiously motivated desire and decision to move toward the new humanity—a "cultural revolution" in the vocabulary of those who are allergic to the term "religious conversion." *Martyrion* is the concomitant growth of a collective testimony in the communities of converts, who are a personalized anticipation and a visible guarantee of the new order. Like the supreme martyr, Jesus, they too are the victim-judge of the existing system and the paradigm of the future they announce. This incipient "structural revolution" is known as the church—which is good news to the poor, because the poor by birth and the poor by option constitute it.

Such basic communities are now mushrooming all over the Third World. They are not subservient to the "international culture" of the ministerial church but are shaped by the local religiosity of the poor. As I have argued elsewhere, genuine inculturation is the fruit of this ecclesiological revolution, not its seed.[72]

Hence the embarrassing question: Is not the Third World theologian exposed to the same temptation that the Western and westernized anthropologists have succumbed to in their studies on "primitive" cultures? These anthropologists are accused of apocalyptic megalomania in that they claim to possess a secret power of knowing these cultures "empathetically" by means of "participatory observation" and to have the authority to interpret them to the ignorant West![73]

Inculturationists' enthusiasm for a culture from which they are estranged and liberationists' defense of the poor against those whose culture they happily share point to a dangerous trend to Third World theology. Should not theology be the explicitation of the theopraxis of these *ecclesiolae* that have appropriated the revolutionary religiosity of the Third World? And should not the writing of this theology be relegated to later redactors? Did not all the Sacred Scriptures originate in this manner? Is this not the Third World's way of doing theology?

NOTES

1. Virginia Fabella, ed., *Asia's Struggle for Full Humanity* (Maryknoll, N.Y.: Orbis, 1980).

2. See Aloysius Pieris, "Towards an Asian Theology of Liberation," in Fabella, ed., *Asia's Struggle,* pp. 75-95, passim.

3. Some aspects of the controversy can be gleaned from *Voices from the Third World,* 2/1 (June 1979); see also Fabella, ed., *Asia's Struggle,* pp. 10, 11, 165, 186.

4. See Pieris, "The Dynamics of the ATC. A Reply to Paul Caspersz," *Voices from the Third World,* 2/1 (June 1979): 23-28.

5. Albert Tevoedjre, *Poverty, Wealth of Nations* (Oxford, 1978)—a rejoinder to Adam Smith's *Wealth of Nations.*

6. See, e.g., Luis A. Gomez de Souza, "Structures and Mechanisms of Domination in Capitalism," in Sergio Torres and John Eagleson, eds. *The Challenge of Basic Christian Communities* (Maryknoll, N.Y.: Orbis, 1981), p. 16.

7. Gustavo Gutiérrez, "Irruption of the Poor in Latin America and the Christian Communities of the Common People," in Torres and Eagleson, eds., *The Challenge,* pp. 113-14.

8. Enrique Dussel, "Current Events in Latin America (1972-1980)," in Torres and Eagleson, eds., *The Challenge,* pp. 100-101.

9. See J.C. Scannone, "Theology, Popular Culture and Discernment," in *Frontiers of Theology in Latin America,* R. Gibellini, ed. (Maryknoll, N.Y.: Orbis, 1979), p. 221.

10. See José Miranda, *Being and the Messiah: The Message of St. John* (Maryknoll, N.Y.: Orbis, 1977), pp. 39-42 and passim.

11. Jon Sobrino, *Christology at the Crossroads* (Maryknoll, N.Y.: Orbis, 1978), pp. 275 ff.

12. This trend is not restricted to the Philippines. In the Indian group that discussed my (Wennappuwa EATWOT Conference) paper in Bangalore immediately after the conference, many of the participants shared this conviction.

13. Edward Schillebeeckx, *God, The Future of Man* (New York: Sheed & Ward, 1968), pp. 57–58.

14. G. Kittel, *Theological Dictionary of the New Testament* (Grand Rapids, Mich.: Eerdmans, 1971), vol. 2, p. 20; vol. 3, pp. 123–28; vol. 3, pp. 155 ff., 175, 181.

15. See esp. A. Pérez-Esclarín, *Atheism and Liberation* (Maryknoll, N.Y.: Orbis, 1978), pp. 160–61.

16. Diane Paul, " 'In the Interest of Civilization': Marxist Views of Race and Culture in the Nineteenth Century," *Journal of the History of Ideas,* 62/1 (1981): 138–39.

17. Lelio Basso, "La Via non-Capitalistica al Socialismo," in S. Amin et al., *Imperialismo e Rivoluzione Socialista nel Terzo Mondo* (Milan: Franco Angeli, 1979), pp. 9–31.

18. See "A Leap across Centuries" (team report on Mongolia on the sixtieth anniversary of the Revolution), *World Marxist Review,* 24/1 (1981): 49–54.

19. See Jean Ziegler, "Elementi di una teoria sulle società socialiste precapitaliste," in *Imperialismo e Rivoluzione,* p. 42.

20. See Patric Chabal, "The Social and Political Thought of Amilcar Cabral: A Reassessment," *Journal of Modern African Studies,* 19/1 (1981): 31–56.

21. See P. G. Casanova, "Le minoranze etniche in America Latina: dal sottosviluppo al socialismo," in *Imperialismo e Rivoluzione,* p. 96.

22. See John Swetman, "Class-based and Community-based Ritual Organization in Latin America," *Ethnology,* 17/4 (1978): 425–38.

23. At the Cartagena CELAM meeting (July 1980) the church was invited to study, defend, and foster Afro-American cultural values; see *Misiones Extranjeras,* 62 (1981): 217.

24. See R. R. Burgoa, "Clase y Raza en los Andes," *Misiones Extranjeras,* 62 (1981): 269 ff.

25. See Casanova, "Le minoranze etniche," p. 118.

26. The Soviets are accused of russifying and westernizing Asians in the U.S.S.R., and Soviet apologetics does not fully answer these charges; see Z. S. Chertina, "The Bourgeois Theory of Modernization and the Real Development of the Peoples of Soviet Central Asia," *The Soviet Review* 22/2 (1981): 77–78.

27. *The Challenge,* pp. 5, 15–16, 42–45, 234.

28. For an extensive treatment of these Indian christologies, see M. M. Thomas, *The Acknowledged Christ of the Indian Renaissance* (London: SCM, 1969), and S. J. Samartha, *The Hindu Response to the Unbound Christ* (Madras: CLS, 1974).

29. The most popular statement of this thesis at the time was that of A. T. Van Leeuwen, *Christianity in World History: The Meeting of Faiths of East and West* (London: Edinburgh House, 1964). It is taken up also by P. Gheddo, *Why is the Third World Poor?* (Maryknoll, N.Y.: Orbis, 1973), esp. pp. 30–37 and passim.

30. See the chapter on "Buddhist Economics" in E. F. Schumacher, *Small is Beautiful: Economics as if People Mattered* (London-New York: Harper & Row, 1973); see also K. Ishwaran, *"Bhakti* Tradition and Modernization: The Case for *Lingayatism,"* The Journal of Asian and African Studies,* 15/1–2 (1980): 72–82.

31. A delicate and comprehensive critique, representative of this period, is that of Denis Goulet, "On the Goals of Development," *Cross Currents,* 18 (1968): 387–405.

32. Namely, in my paper "The Mission of the Local Church and the Major Religious Traditions," presented at the SEDOS seminar, Rome, March 1981, included in *Mission in Dialogue* (Maryknoll, N.Y.: Orbis Books, 1982).

33. For a forceful exposition of this thesis, see E. T. Jacob-Pandian, "Anthropological Fieldwork, Empathy and the Crisis of the Apocalyptic Man," *Man in India* 55/4 (1975): 281–97; see also Epeli Han'ofa, "Anthropology and Pacific Islanders," *Man in India,* 55/1 (1975): 57–66.

34. See Evans Pritchard, "Religion and the Anthropologists," *Practical Anthropology,* 19 (1972): 193, 205, quoted in Claud E. Stipe, "The Role of Religion in Cultural Change," *Christian Scholar's Review,* 10/2 (1965): 455.

35. Stipe, "The Role of Religion," pp. 117 ff.

36. F. Sierksma in *Current Anthropology,* 6 (1965): 455.

37. See Vittorro Lanternari, *The Religion of the Oppressed: A Study of Modern Messianic Cults* (New York: Mentor, 1963), p. 312.

38. See Stipe, "The Role of Religion," p. 121; for concrete examples, see pp. 124–28. See also Ishwaran, *"Bhakti* Tradition," pp. 80–82.

39. Pieris, "Towards an Asian Theology of Liberation," in Fabella, ed., *Asia's Struggle,* p. 77.

40. Ibid., p. 78.

41. Ibid., p. 83.

42. Ibid., p. 78.

43. Ibid., p. 79.

44. For some case studies, see Stipe, "The Role of Religion," p. 124–28.

45. See G.H. Jansen, *Militant Islam* (New York: Harper & Row, 1979), pp. 54–56. Though tendentious, these pages are an eye-opener.

46. Quoted in James H. Billington, "Christianity in USSR," *Theology Today,* 36/2 (1980): 207.

47. Quoted in *CALA News Letter,* 8/4 (1981): 1.

48. Chabal, "The Social and Political Thought of Amilcar Cabral," pp. 42–54.

49. Ziegler, "Elementi di una teoria," pp. 38–39.

50. Ibid., p. 36.

51. Sergio Vieira, "Stages of Fundamental Changes," *World Marxist Review,* Jan. 1981, pp. 15–20.

52. Ibid., p. 15. Unlike Belgium, France, and Britain, Portugal did not accumulate capital but wasted it on aristocratic pageantry, except during the last hundred years, so that it could not have maintained the metropolis and Portuguese settlers in colonial territories had it not given them independence.

53. Ibid., p. 17.

54. Jansen, *Militant Islam,* chap. 3 and 4.

55. From a manuscript version made available to me of a lecture by Dr. Eqbal Ahmed given at the Riverside Church in New York on Jan. 20, 1980.

56. See Margaret Chatterjee, "The Concept of Multiple Allegiance: A Hypothesis concerning the Contemporary Indian Spectrum," *Man in India,* 56/2 (1976): 123–33.

57. Balachandra Nemade, "The Revolt of the Underprivileged," *Journal of Asian and African Studies,* 15/1–2 (1980): 113.

58. Ibid., pp. 113–23.

59. See Jayashree Gokhale-Turner, "Bhakti or Vidroha: Continuity and Change in Dalit Sahitya," *Journal of Asian and African Studies,* 15/1–2 (1980): 29–42.

60. Ibid., pp. 37–39.

61. For a case study on feudalization of tribal societies, see Jaganath Pathy, "Political Economy of Kandha Land," *Man in India,* 55/1 (1975): 10–58.

62. See K. D. Gangrade, "Social Mobility in India: A Study in Depressed Classes," *Man in India,* 55/3 (1975): 258 and 278 n. 19.

63. See Gail Omvedt, "Adivasis and Modes of Production in India," *Bulletin of Concerned Asian Scholars,* 12/1 (1980): 15–22. See also Gautama Bhadra, "The Kuki Uprising (1917–1919): Its Causes and Nature," *Man in India,* 55/1 (1975): 10–58.

64. See Paul Demiéville, "Le bouddhism et la guerre," in *Mélange* (Paris, 1957), vol. 1, pp. 375–84.

65. See Charles F. Keyes, "Political Crisis and Militant Buddhism in Contemporary Thailand," in *Religion and Legitimation of Power in Thailand,* Bardwel Smith, ed. (Chambersburg, Pa.: Anima, 1978), p. 160.

66. For an excellent treatment of this history, see E. Sarkisyanz, *The Buddhist Backgrounds of the Burmese Revolutions* (The Hague: Nijhoff, 1965).

67. See Demiéville, "Le bouddhism," pp. 357–68; see also Daniel L. Overmyer, "Folk-Buddhist Religion: Creation and Eschatology in Medieval China," *History of Religions,* 12/1 (1972): 42–70.

68. Pieris, in *Asia's Struggle,* p. 87.

69. See K. Zaradov, "The Environmental Movement and the Communists: The Political Class Approach," *World Marxist Review,* 24/3 (1981): 50–53.

70. See Chertina, "The Bourgeois Theory of Modernization," p. 69.

71. Theodore Reik, *Of Love and Lust* (New York-Toronto: Bantam, 1967), p. 470.

72. See Pieris, "The Mission of the Local Church."

73. See Jacob-Pandian, "Anthropological Fieldwork."

11

Biblical Hermeneutics
in the Theologies of Liberation

J. Severino Croatto

Every theology has a point of departure. No theology is a "deposit," even in the most dogmatic and fundamentalist traditions. A theology is always a "production"—something in continuous process. Hence it has to be "motivated." It has to have starting points. It has to have criteria of legitimation. For the theological act is a convergence of the theologian's praxis (or the praxis of his or her concrete historical context) and the font, or fonts, of revelation.

But how is this convergence actually produced? One of the fonts of revelation is the Bible. All Christian theologians have to cite and base their assertions on it. But to what end? How? With what methodology? Why might there not be as many variations as there are theologies?

Any attempt to rethink theology in the light of socio-historical situations or processes so utterly different from those presiding at the birth of traditional theological discourse will find the use of the Bible to be a new and distinct problem. The Bible seems quite distant from our new problems. Yet at the same time one discovers new possibilities for reading it.

This is what faces the oppressed countries of the Third World that are in the process of liberation. In the Latin American theology of liberation, the tension is altogether explicit. The reading of the signs of the times as signs of liberation, the analysis of social and political reality, the interpretation one makes of traditional academic theology, a new scientific criticism of the Bible wielding all the refinements of exegetical method—all this converges to formulate a question of paramount importance: What is the Bible in the building of a theology of and for the oppressed peoples of the Third World?

There are four different ways in which one might approach this problem.

(1) One might relegate the Bible to a secondary role, as a text of the past—

140

unable to hold its own with "test" of present reality as our primary *locus theologicus*. For this reality is so charged with meaning that any other theological index becomes secondary. When the options are clear, one need not go to the Bible at all.

(2) Or one might take the Bible as it is, and look for a correspondence between our situations and the events reported there. When the two coincide, we take it that God is speaking to us through an archetypical event. Obviously, this is a concordist approach to the Bible.

But biblical concordism—that most common of exegetical phenomena in our day, especially in fundamentalist circles—is beset with two great drawbacks. First, it reduces the applicability of the biblical message to situations equivalent to those in which the ancient Israelites or the primitive Christian community found themselves. Secondly, it makes a basically superficial reading of this message—a reading at the level of externals.

The same danger threatens if we look for a *continuity* between the ideas of the Old or New Testament and those of a given Asian, African, or Latin American culture. What happens when the two cultures fail to coincide—as happened with the ancient Hebrew and Greek anthropologies? We are not suggesting that a search for similarities between the Bible and the social or, especially, cultural, reality of today cannot be the point of departure for an investigation of the relevancy of the Bible for people today. What is so impoverishing is only out-and-out "historical concordism"—the attempt to prove the truth of the Bible with certain data of the natural or historical sciences. There is no such proof. On the contrary, any such concordistic attempt deprives the sacred text of its kerygmatic content.

(3) The critical methodology of modern biblical research has opened up a new path. A rediscovery of the historical and cultural horizon against which the Bible was first formed enables us better to "contextualize" the original sense of each passage. Critical exegesis has not only broken with the naive readings of biblical historicism and concordism; it has significantly broadened the exploration of the meaning of the texts. Criticism by form, literary genre, manuscript lineage, tradition, and redaction have all contributed to the revolutionizing of biblical studies over the course of the last decades. They have healed a good many of the defects of Christian theology and have indirectly generated a renewal of theological endeavor at all levels.

To be sure, critical exegesis has it pitfalls. For example, it is easy to become lost in the dead and gone—in "archaeology," where the attention of the exegete or reader is misplaced in the "precanonical." For example, the Pentateuch can be interpreted according to the Yahwist, elohist, and other theologies. At the opposite end of the spectrum, a concern to safeguard the truth of the spiritual sciences has so preoccupied the Western world over these last centuries that the West has concentrated its attention on the literal meaning as the "historical" one (as the expression "historical-critical method" betrays). This is a form of reductionism and exaggerates the importance of "the intention of the sacred writer" in the analysis of such or such a passage. Ultimately the danger is that we can turn to the Bible as a "deposit," with a closed meaning coinciding with the thought of the redactor, or even of the preredactors of the actual text. For purposes of a Third World theology this approach is incomplete—although, as we have said, it has its importance in other areas.

(4) The fourth way of approaching the biblical kerygma is the *hermeneutic* one—and this is the subject of this paper. First, some preliminary observations.

In spite of its etymology, and its older meaning, "hermeneutics," in the sense in which we shall be using the term, is not a synonym for "interpretation." The latter is a very general concept, and one that fails to convey the specific content of the former. Nor is the Bultmannian sense of hermeneutics or the "new hermeneutics" of Fuchs, Ebeling, or their followers, sufficient for our purposes. To be sure, in the reading of the Bible there is a *pre*understanding. This is a received datum, and altogether valid in our own approach. And of course there is a "speech event" (*Sprachereignis*), or a "word event" (*Wortereignis*), in all the richness of the current denotation of these terms. But this is not sufficient either. None of this does justice to the objective conditions of the Bible as *language*. The original referent of the text is undervalued, and the result is an individualistic reading.

In order to grasp the meaning of "hermeneutics" in all its richness—and in its methodological value for the theology of liberation—it will be appropriate to say something here about the sciences of language. Inasmuch as hermeneutics deals with the interpretation of a text, or of the events reported in a text, it is to be situated in the general area of semiotics, or the science of signs, of which language in the narrow sense is the most comprehensive expression.

At first view, we seem to be presented with a paradox here. Hermeneutics may seem to be bound up with diachrony, or the becoming of meaning, or semantics, or the tranformation of the meaning of words or texts. In fact, however, although semiotics does accord a special place to synchrony—to the structural laws that regulate the performance of language—semiotics and synchrony are not the same thing. They are parts of a circle. Upon our return from semiotics to hermeneutics, in a circular journey that has respected the individuality of each, our hermeneutics will appear solidly founded.

Let us undertake this long journey. At its end, biblical hermeneutics will appear in all its fruitfulness.

LANGUAGE AS EVENT AND LANGUAGE AS TEXT

I shall be very brief in this section, saying only what will be necessary for understanding what transpires in the hermeneutic reading of the text.

In linguistics there is a primary distinction between *language* and *speech*. Speech is the system of signs and laws regulating grammar and syntax. It is a kind of "canon." It sets up "meaning grids." Its basis is the distinctness and the structure or organization that we find within each language. In any given language, the repertoire of linguistic signs is finite. There is a limited number of ways in which these signs may be combined. But at the same time, any given language hosts an underlaying potential polysemy: the word "volume," for example, can mean a book, or it can mean a geometrical capacity. Every language has a great number of polysemious words. Further, even within a phrase or sentence with an unambiguous linguistic meaning—a single relationship between signifier and significants or thing signified—there can be an ambiguity with respect to its extralinguistic referent: "Jesus Christ saves us" is a correct sentence—it has meaning—but it is ambiguous in its reference.

So far, all this is a matter of the "competency" of language—to use linguistic jargon. But this system of signs is actualized only when it is *used to say something about something*. This is "speech" as language-event. The abstract system is now concretized in the form of a message, thanks to the intervention of three new elements: (1) a *transmitter*, or speaker who selects the signs; and (2) a *receiver*, or interlocutor to whom the speaker addresses the signs; and (3) a common *context*, or horizon of comprehension, which permits "coincidence in reference." In the act of discourse, there must be actual *closure* of the potential polysemy in the words or phrases. Otherwise speech is impossible—except where polysemy is deliberately maintained, as in poetry or symbolic language. Even here the context, or at least the dialogue between the interlocutors, facilitates the "closure" of meaning of a word or proposition. Otherwise discourse is no longer "saying something to someone about something"—which of course is the intention of one who is speaking, writing a letter to a friend, or telling a story to an audience.

In the speech act, the receiver is active as well: he or she is engaged in a process of assimilation or grasping of the linguistic code selected by the transmitter for conveying the message. As with music, so with language, the message comes in a given "key," or "code," which the hearer grasps at once. Otherwise there is no intellection. Language is communication in code. Speech *uses* a determinate code (another form of meaning-closure) to send the message. Confusing one code with another—as so often happens in a biblical exegesis—is the worst possible mistake and completely distorts the message. We shall return to this question below, in dealing with the hermeneutical process properly so-called.

Thus, from language to speech, from competency to performance, from system to use, a first *distantiation* occurs. Its framework is the "meaning-closure." But this is not the only step language must take. A new distantiation is produced when discourse is crystalized in a transmitted "text." We understand the word "text" here in the broad sense, to include oral texts as well as written ones. A myth, for example, or a song, can be passed from generation to generation orally before finding fixed expression in the written word. Nearly all the biblical narratives passed through some stage of oral tradition, and yet they always had a "text." *Text*, etymologically, means "texture"—the warp and woof of the elements of language (words, sentences, whole works)—all woven together according to structural functions, which, as such, produce a meaning.

The same laws of linguistics that govern a sentence are also applied and broadened at the level of narration. For there is a grammar and a syntax of narration as well. Here again structure, with its distinctiveness, its relationships, and its nature as an organized whole, is a key factor. This characteristic of the text has important consequences, the first of which is that it bestows meaning in its capacity to encode a message.

More concretely, this second distantiation—the distantiation between speech and text—occurs in the same three areas mentioned above:

(1) The original *transmitter* disappears. The author of a written text "dies" in the very act of coding his or her message. The "inscription" of meaning in the form of a text is a creative act in which, symbolically speaking, the writer ceases to live.

(2) Nor is the original *receiver*, the first interlocutor, present. The one who reads a written text, or hears a traditional narrative, is not that narrative's first addressee (is not the "narratary," in semiotic parlance). This switch of addressees is much more evident in the case of meaning over the course of generations and centuries.

(3) Likewise the original *horizon of discourse* vanishes. The cultural and historical context is no longer the same. The current addressees of the message live in "another world" of interests, concerns, culture, and the like. The horizon of the first discourse disappears.

These three areas—much emphasized by Paul Ricoeur in his latest hermeneutical studies—taken in conjunction, are of great help in understanding the hermeneutical process. The "author" disappears as a speaker who could be questioned as to the meaning of what he or she is saying. Henceforth the narrator is not a person of flesh and blood but a linguistic supposit. Someone is narrator or writer indeed, but this person is to be found *only in text*.

This physical absence is semantic wealth. Now the meaning-closure imposed by the transmitter is converted into an openness. The narrator is now the text itself. This concentration of the quality of narrator within the text itself permits the exploration of its meaning possibilities *as text*.

Next, the appearance on the scene of a new receiver of the message, situated on a new horizon of meaning removes the text still further from its original situation and from contact with its author. When a person speaks, he or she transmits a message (locutional language)—but does so with a particular force or intensity (*il*locutional language, expressed by intonation, gestures, and the like), and causes an effect that is part and parcel of the message (*per*perlocutional language). When a text is merely read, the finest shades of meaning are lost, inasmuch as these are less consignable to writing in code. Even listening to a recording fails to recover the act of first enunciation—for even if the addressees are the same, the context has changed. When we "hear" a text, it is the *text itself* that is speaking—not the person who is reading it aloud. The reader is only one of the addressees! Once more we are faced with the autonomy of the text. What happens now?

The finite horizon is replaced by a textual infinitude. The narrative opens up to a new polysemy—not a potential polysemy, as happened at the level of "language," but a polysemy potentiated by the network of meanings that constitute a work. This openness of the text now allows the new addressee to enter, with his or her own "world."

It is easy to understand that the letter of Paul to the Colossians, in which the author and his auditors were dealing with a specific problem, changed perspective when it was universalized in the primitive church. The new addressees of the text were not delimited by the previous reading of the Christians of Colossae, nor could they ask Paul what he meant in such or such a phrase. This letter, like any other—and like any text at all, whether it be a biblical one or one from other literature, whether religious or profane—is now open to many readings.

Here we note that the polysemy of a text in proportion to the distance from (our forgetfulness of) its author. Hence sacred or mythical texts are usually anonymous. Their burden of meaning is in inverse proportion to what we know about their authors. We know nothing of the identity of the authors of the books of the Old Testament, nor most of those of the New. The "attribution" of a work to a determinate author, such as the Psalms to David, the Pentateuch to Moses, and so on, is itself a hermeneutical fact, which we shall take into account below.

READING AS PRODUCTION-OF-MEANING: THE HERMENEUTICAL ACT

In semiotics we say that meaning is not something "objective"—not something *in* text in a pure state, not something exegetes can "discover" by means of their technical ability or philological and historical resources. If this were the case, all interpretations would be erroneous but one. The decision as to which interpretation were the true one would be forthcomng from an extra-textual "authority." Ultimately, this conception presupposes that *the* meaning of a text coincides with the one intended by its author, and that the present reader must simply repeat the reading of its first addressees. And we fall into the trap of exegetical "historicism."

In reality, every reading is a production-of-discourse, and hence a production-of-meaning from a point of departure in a text. It is an operation that engages a text's *competency*—which semiotics studies, and which is open to distinct selective organizations of that text. The structural analysis of a report (or of a narrative program), and of the discourse or text—being the organization of one meaning among many meanings of the words or themes that may be possible within a determinate society or world view—does not give mathematical results. Such analysis differs according to the different combinations that may be arranged. As a result, language itself combines so many semic elements that no analysis can reveal them totally.

The plurality of readings suggested by a practical semiotics is not due to ambiguity in the text, but to a plethora of meanings that are objectvely present simultaneously. Further, there are "interpretative" readings of a text (phenomenological, historical, sociological, psychological, literary, theological, and so on). Each of these readings of one and the same text is the production of a discourse from this text. It is a text upon a text.

This is possible, first, because discourse engages a plurality of codes, which each reading selects and organizes. Secondly, because, as we know, the author "dies," is "erased," leaving only what he or she has written: henceforth it is the text that contains within itself not only the moment of reading, or interpretation, but the moment of production as well. In other words the text becomes polysemic, even from the purely semiotic viewpoint. It contains a surplus-of-meaning, which wells up and spills over when the text is read.

But there is another fact: any and every reading of a text is done *from and in a given situation*—from and in a context that is no longer that of the first addressees of the text. Now what happens? What happens is that the reader interrogates the text from and in the reader's own being and concerns—not in order to *impose* an *extraneous* meaning, but in order to interpret *the text itself*. To this end the reader mobilizes the semantic potential of the text by selecting codes that correspond to his or her own situation and context.

This calls for a fuller explanation.

(1) Every text has a "context-forward"—a world of meanings opened in virtue of its potentiated polysemy—both by its very nature as a linguistic structure, and because of the "death" of its author. This world of meanings is not in the author's mind, but in the text itself. Of course, as we have shown, it is not there as a separable entity. It is there as *coded meaning* in a system of signs constituting an account that "says something about something." It is there in virtue of its character and presentation as discourse. It is the text that "speaks"—but *what* it says, as well as what it says it about, changes from reading to reading.

Let us take an example. The songs of the "Servant of Yahweh" from Second Isaiah (Isa. 42:1–7, 49:1–9a, 50:4–11, 52:13–53:12), in their original redaction—before their insertion into Isaiah 40–55 (which in turn antedates the composition of Isaiah 1–66) as a new "account"—describe a personage with royal characteristics who has received a mission from God to liberate the people of Israel, persecuted and humiliated to death, but to be exalted in the end. This discourse is the bearer of a meaning resulting from the organization of deep-seated codes ("actuants" and functions) as well as surface codes (symbols, semic elements, stylistic resources, literary genres). The text has meaning in virtue of the positing of such or such linguistic *signifiers*, which refer to particular *significates* or things-meant, which abide within the discourse despite the fact that we have lost the identity of its extralinguistic referent (Joachim? Zorobabel? Israel itself?).

The critical methods of biblical exegesis come to our assistance here in suggesting a possible original referent of these poems. But this is not the key to the reading. This is only an attempt to recover the "context-backward" of the text, the context that originated it as a primary production of meaning.

Important as the "historical" reading of these texts may be, it is a two-edged sword. An attempt to reduce its meaning to its primary production will be an attempt to exhaust the text in the very moment in which it begins to demonstrate it polysemy. Worse still, it will mean tying ourselves to a form of "historicism," from which will then arise those exegetical concordisms that, on the naive pretext of attempting to isolate the relevance of the word of God for the present, immobilizes it instead in its primary reference.

Thus the "referent," the extralinguistic phenomenon, is ultimately given precedence over the actual significate of the text. The mere fact that the songs of the Servant of Yahweh do not indicate their referent in explicit terms (the gloss "Israel" in Isa. 49:3 contradicts verses 4–5) leaves the interpretation more open, and this favors the polysemy of the text. But it does not constitute it. These songs, these accounts, are polysemic in their very linguistic structure, as we have already made clear. They are "projected-forward," demanding the explicitation of their "surplus-of-meaning." Hence their rereading will be a production, not a repetition, of meaning. This is basic for an understanding of the hermeneutical process.

It is no wonder, then, that these songs have been "reread," by successive generations, in such different ways. In the Septuagint it is the collective interpretation that predominates, and the referent is Israel persecuted in the diaspora, and off on a salvific mission among the gentiles. The New Testament does an individual, christological rereading. The Targum of Jonathan takes up the collective exegesis again (the Servant is Israel) for Isaiah 49:7, applies the oracle of Isaiah 42 to the messiah, considers the referent of Isaiah 50 to be the Prophet Isaiah himself, and shuns any messianic allusion at all for the fourth song (Isa. 52:13–53:12).

The New Testament does an individual, christological rereading. The Targum of Jonathan takes up the collective exegesis again (the Servant is Israel) for Isaiah 49:7, applies the oracle of Isaiah 42 to the messiah, considers the referent of Isaiah 50 to be the Prophet Isaiah himself, and shuns any messianic allusion at all for the fourth song (Isa. 52:13–53:12).

What will be our own rereading, as peoples of the Third World? What is the "context-forward" of the text on the Servant of Yahweh for the theology of liberation? Our reading, like those we have just cited, will not be conditioned by a primary referent of the prophetic narrative, now lost beyond recovery. Our rereading will be made in virtue of the organization of the account itself, in its deep-seated structure (as account and as discourse) as well as in its surface structure (the positioning of symbols, expressions bearing a contextual significate, and the like).

(2) What is remarkable in the various readings of one and the same text is the fact that, in spite of their divergencies, they begin with the text. In other words, they are intended as readings of the text, and not as arbitrary, adventitious accretion. The risen Jesus rebukes the disciples on the road to Emmaus: "How dull you are! How slow to believe all that they said! Was the Messiah not bound to suffer thus before entering his glory?" (Luke 24:25–26). Jesus is

interpreting a text. But there is no text in the Old Testament with a messianic referent of this tenor. Of course, it is evident that Jesus is referring to the songs of the Servant of Yahweh of Second Isaiah. This "attachment" to the prophetic text is a good example of both the *linguistic* phenomenon of polysemy and the *textual* dependency of the hermeneutic act. The reading Jesus makes of Isaiah 53 is a production-of-meaning. It is a discourse upon another, previous, discourse.

The Septuagint reading Jesus has used is not a mechanical translation of the original Hebrew, but an adaptation of it. Now, there is no question of the Septuagint translator's not knowing Hebrew. Then why did he not translate it literally and relegate this particular interpretation to another "account"? Because, precisely, he did not consider it an interpretation! His reading originated with the *text of Isaiah* itself. Further, he was concerned to render precisely *this* text, consecrated by tradition as having this particular messianic content. This the Septuagint translation is a discourse (in the semiotic sense of the word) upon a discourse (the Isaian text), but presenting itself as a single discourse (presented precisely as the Isaian text itself). For indeed the interpretation placed by Luke in Jesus' mouth refers to the *text* of Isaiah 53—in the targumic version of this poem, which differs from the Hebrew reading in so many ways that it could appear more as a midrash. And yet the text presented is that of Isaiah in the rabbinical tradition. The point of departure is not the personage of the Prophet Isaiah, but the canonical *text* of Isaiah, transmitted by tradition and held to be the "word of God."

Hence the great importance of the fact that any reading is a *reading of a text*. This phenomenon—and now we are at the heart of hermeneutics—only serves to set in relief two things to which we have already called repeated attention: (a) the fact that any text concentrates within itself a polysemy, which opens it "forward" in virtue of its quality as structural "texture" of linguistic codes; and (b) the fact that any reading of a text is a production-of-meaning in new codes, which in turn generate other readings as productions-of-meanings. Interpretation is a chain process. The chain, however, is not simply repetitive, but ascendant.

(3) Considered from another angle, however, a reading as a production-of-meaning is necessarily also an *appropriation* of meaning. A certain dependency is established in respect to the text interpreted—all the more so when it is a text consecrated by tradition—and the need arises to possess its entire meaning. This claim on the meaning of the text is totalitarian and exclusive. There is nothing partial about it. Precisely because it is an appropriation, it can leave no room for an interpretation via another reading. In the very act of exploiting, and thereby implicitly asserting, the inexhaustibility of the text's "reservoir of meaning," the rereading pretends to exhaust that meaning, leaving nothing to any other reading.

This is the origin of the "conflict of interpretations." Let us return to our example of the songs of the Servant in Second Isaiah. The readings done by the Septuagint translators, the Essenes of the Dead Sea, the primitive church (the New Testament), and the authors of the targums, are not "possible" readings by these different groups; they are *the* meaning of the prophetic text in each case. This totalitarian exegesis is more visible in, for example, the targumic interpretation. Here one discerns an anti-Christian polemic—an express intent to block the christological meaning of this so important text. And the root of this phenomenon is not merely ideological. It is facilitated by the very condition of the text—which is polysemic, yes, but which produces only a single meaning in its quality as narrative structure oriented to "saying something about something." Multiple meanings do not exist in a single reading. The rabbinical interpretation of Isaiah 53 voids the one made by the first Christians. It does not allow for its remotest possibility. In other words, every reading is a "meanng closure." What a paradox, this interplay between polysemy and monosemy! (See the diagrams on pages 167 and 168 below.)

Thus the reading of the Bible done by the theology of liberation, too, will be conflictive with respect to other "appropriations" of the meaning of the message. This fact supposes other causes, which we shall take up below. One of the most important lies in the "closuring" character of every reading. This phenomenon is as basic as that of dependence on the text.

Together, dependence on the text and the "closuring" reading of the meaning, can lead to extreme situations vis-à-vis other readings. Again, let us look at the targumic reading of Isaiah 53. The interpretation it makes (*of Isaiah*) cannot originate from the Hebrew text. The Aramaic version's modification is a *structural* one. It converts the Hebrew account into a new account, and this new account is reproduced in the synagogal reading and the *text of the Prophet Isaiah*. The rereading (midrashic more than targumic) continues to be "closuring." It continues to the account that permitted other readings. Thus the conflict of interpretations is vigorously expressed, but not in words. When the use of the targum is dropped and the Hebrew text is resumed, as in Judaism today, the polysemy of the songs of the Servant of Yahweh yields up yet another reading, which in turn pretends to absorb the whole meaning—and again excludes a christological interpretation. We shall encounter this same phenomenon when we examine the hermeneutical act from the viewpoint of praxis.

But for the moment, the question arises: If the plurality of meanings is a function of the very linguistic condition of the text, what is it that concretely disengages and diversifies this meaning?

FROM THE EVENT TO TEXT

The relevancy attributed to the text of the Bible as God's revelation causes us to forget the process of its production. The theology of biblical "inspiration" has been very deficient; and its shortcomings lie along two lines. It locates the inspiration of the Bible in its authors, the sacred writers; and it short-circuits the production process, setting up a tight, closed circle between the God who speaks and the sacred writer. This is appropriate matter for a hermeneutical critique.

A text always has its point of departure in some form of experience. It may be a praxis, a meaningful event, a worldview, and so on. Let us call this experiential point of departure the "event." This event may be a state of oppression, a process of liberation, a salvific event, or one of so many other occurrences in the experience of a people, a community, or an individual. Out of the plurality of their experiences, there arise certain ones that are particularly *meaningful*—and that come to be resumed in *words*.

Here two phenomena must be kept in view. First, the word that wells up out of the event is *selective*. It chooses to express one experience, leaving many others out. It is a form of "closure." Second, this work is *interpretive* of the event. Never is it mere chronicle, however it may pretend to be! The reading of the event is made from a particular *locus,* and hence from a particular perspective. This we all know, of course, but it will serve our purpose here to isolate the implications of this selection, or closure, and this interpretation.

Notice that an event becomes meaningful for an existential reason that we can here call its "historical effect," meaning its influence on the practices of a determinate human group. We are not dealing here with a *cause/effect* relationship, in which the significance of an event disappears once the event has produced its effect, but with a *meaning* relationship. At this level, one event is understood as the expression of the meaning of another, which in turn comes to the fore as *foundational.* But it becomes foundational only "at a distance"—only in the light of its projection into new events. That is, this foundational event, resumed in "word" as meaningful fact, manifests a surplus-of-meaning that was not in evidence at the moment of the occurrence of the original event. Thereafter, this significance enriching lection of the original event lends new meaning to the event or practices in which it operates today.

This "hermeneutical circle" is present in the events before it is present in the texts. There is a first word that wells up and "says" the event—no matter what the code, which may be chronicle, epic, hymn, or other. Even a festival is a form of the "reading" of an event. In the Bible, the "memory" of the liberation from Egypt is resumed and expressed in all possible literary genres and in all ages. But it is never the repetition of the meaning of the original exodus. It is always the exploration of its reservoir-of-meaning.

The events that assist at the birth of a people are never exhausted in their first narration. They "grow" in meaning, by their projection into the life of the people. In order to express this surplus-of-meaning, the word of the event reworks the event and gives it new dimensions. The call of Moses, the plagues of Egypt, the hasty passover meal, the crossing of the sea, are *not* episodes in the liberation event: they are all expressions of the *meaning* of that event as God's undertaking, and, as memory, celebrated in festival at passover. This means that the people lived that liberation experience as a "projection," continuously in process of realization. The people felt the need to hark back to it to revitalize its hope when once more it found itself the victim of oppression, or to deepen the gratitude aspect of its faith when it celebrated new situations of liberation.

It is remarkable that, for most peoples, national festivals are, in the main, celebrations of events of *liberation*. These events are seen to be, and come to be foundational, archetypical events in an interpretive process, as these peoples gradually develop their history. The "memory" of an event charges that event with meaning. It is the meaning of the events that generates the events— either generating them concretely, or harmonizing them by way of interpretation.

One may not say that the return from the Babylonian captivity was generated by the exodus event. And yet in Hebrew tradition, the return from the exile is indeed interpreted as a new exodus (see Isa. 11:15–16, 19:16–25, 43:16–21, 51:9–11). The first exodus manifests a further dimension of meaning when the Israelites remember it as a liberative projection in new situations of oppression or captivity. The inexhaustibility of its inspiration and meaning is demonstrated in all its readings—by the Hebrew people, then by the Christian community, and today by our liberation theologians. This is the way all the peoples of the world celebrate their "foundational" events (their wars of liberation, for example)—as inspiration and meaning for their sociohistorical praxis.

Here again the "conflict of interpretations" appears. We referred to this conflict in our discussion of the reading of texts. The same conflict occurs in the reading of events. Events always contain a reservoir-of-meaning not exhausted in their first occurrence. Further, they are interpreted from different standpoints. Each interpretation is totalizing and exclusive—"appropriative." The struggles of a people for independence are read by one group for the purpose of dynamizing and motivating a liberation process, and by another for legitimating the repression of that very process. One reading excludes the other, and yet both hark back to a single originary, "significative" event. Each reading obeys the laws of a different praxis; likewise, each generates a different praxis.

The Reading of Events and Texts

Above, we considered the phenomenon of polysemy and monosemy, or reservoir-of-meaning and closure-of-meaning, with respect to language. Now we can speak indiscriminately of the reading of a text and the reading of an event.

Thus we have established that the event becomes "word" to the extent that its meaning is interpreted and expressed. In the case of the Bible, before it was "God's word" it was God's *event*. The salvific experience is interpreted in an account that sets in relief a presence of God that was not factually manifested as it is presented now. The account is not a filming. It is *an exploration of its significate as message.*

This report is then incorporated into a tradition, within a determinate group, and the hermeneutic process of polysemy and closure continues. Tradition is living interpretation, intimately bound up with praxis. This is why it branches out (in virtue of the polysemy of the originary event-report), and this is why it comes in conflict with another tradition (in virture of the tendency of any interpretation to appropriate and exhaust the meaning).

The very conflict of interpretations—and in this case, of the traditions that are the manifestation of these interpretations—leads to a new stage: the fixing of event-report-tradition in the form of a canon. The emergence of a canon of writings occurs in all traditions, whether historical, political, philosophical, religious, or the like. One must establish what are the authentic texts of Plato, Thomas Aquinas, and Marx, just as with the sacred books of religions (the Vedas, the Our'an, the Bible, or such and such a cycle of myths).

This is "closure" once more—the phenomenon that excludes other readings of a previous tradition and orientates the interpretation of new practices. Closure of a canon is part of the hermeneutic process. At a given moment in their development, oral or written texts come to a "cut-off point," a point of delimitation, which henceforth will represent *the* interpretation of the events that have given rise to this particular tradition. If the texts are many, they are grouped, thereby constituting, from the viewpoint of linguistics, a brand-new text. Thus we move from intertextuality to intratextuality, and the Bible becomes a single book. From Genesis to Revelation, we now have a single, global, kerygmatic meaning, despite the multiplicity of its internal variations and manifestations.

At this point you will have noticed that we have returned to the level of language, the point we started from. The *event*-meaning has now been gathered into the *text*-meaning. The salvific events experienced by the people of Israel become present again as they are read, heard, and interpreted by the mediation of previous readings, which now converge in a single new text. What began as a polysemic event is now a polysemic text as well.

Here another hermeneutic moment occurs. The canon is attempting to closure the meaning of a single event-account. At this same moment, then, it exerts pressure on the polysemy of the event, and even of the account. There is a surplus-of-meaning present, which overflows, and must be gathered up in new practices and new words. New events are now read in the light of these normative writings. And yet at the same time the events transcend the writings. Hence we now see a commentary (the Upanishads for the Vedas, the Talmud for the Torah, the writings of the church fathers for the Bible, and so on), as well as other types of writing (targum, midrash)—all actually representing new readings of a text that is claimed to be a closuring one. At times the re-creative force of an event-account—the New Testament, for instance, vis-à-vis the Old—is such that, due to the conflict of interpretations that necessarily accompany it, it is *incorporated into the canon itself.*

Thus it is clear that the history of a canon of writings is part of a hermeneutic process, which in turn is part of the history of particular traditions. A canon is neither the beginning of a tradition nor the end of one. It is a moment in its uninterrupted journey. The concept of the "inspiration" of a canon is the expression of a new hermeneutical act: an interpretation of that closure of meaning for which this community has made a historical option, seen as the determination of God himself. Henceforth it will be possible neither to add a book to this normative canon nor to subtract one.

But, as we have remarked, the interpretive process cannot be closed off. A long literary production is generated, from simple translation (such as the Septuagint) to targum, pesher, or midrash; or from an exegetical or homiletic commentary to the theological and philosophical systematizations that are inscribed in one tradition and exclude another.

What we wish to single out here is the fact that the rereading of the Bible is not carried out simply as a literary endeavor, as the work of specialists. We are not dealing with a "neutral task." The exegete's claim to have isolated the objective, *historical,* meaning of the biblical text is illusory. Indeed, the rediscovery of the "context backwards" of a text is a difficult matter. What a text actually offers are the possibilities *of that text* for ever novel interpretation.

Of course, exegetes are immersed in a tradition, in a historical context. They are the agents of determinate social practicers. All this conditions their reading of the Bible as a rereading. The same thing happens when the church interprets God's word. Its reading is "closuring," for it is done from a determinate *locus*—that is, from a given practice at once religious and political.

What happens to the people at this point? Its reading of the Bible is mediated by that of specialists (the theologians, the biblicist) or else by that of powerful (church authority). And yet whenever the people takes up this so oft-forbidden book, it discovers a wealth of unsuspected possibilities. This is what occurs in a process of liberation, or any other process in which the people or a community is the agent of both a history and a reading of the biblical kerygma. What is going on here?

Any and every reading is a production-of-meaning. And every meaning takes place from within a given *locus* or context. Consequently, what is relevant is not the "context backward"—the historical context—of the text, but the "context forward"—the context intimated by the text as a meaningful message for the life of the one who receives it.

The Bible suffers two disadvantages when it is read by the theology of liberation—or indeed by the people in general. It is a very long book, in which there is a little of everything, and in which one can find everything. And it is a book whose structure has been determined by a well-to-do class isolated from the masses. This originary situation is thereupon transmitted down the length of the centuries in the catechetical and theological process.

But the Bible has a priceless advantage, as well; its origin, in its own people, was in a *liberation process.* The Israelitic conception of Yahweh, the God of the Hebrew people, is indissolubly bound up with the experience of deliverance from slavery in Egypt. In this context, the God who *saves* is identified with the God who *frees:* "When Israel saw the great power which the Lord had put forth against Egypt, all the people feared the Lord, and they put their faith in him and in Moses his servant" (Exod. 14:31). This is a faith springing from the experience of liberation. From now on, it is liberation that will constitute the referent in the historico-salvific process at work in Israel. Israel's institutions, its festivals, its prophetic critique of its own breach of the covenant, its proclamation of a new order of justice, its messianic hope, will all hark back to the memory of the exodus event as an event of liberation. To reinforce its theology of a God of liberation, Israel will adopt the theologoumenon of the worldviews of its neighbors about God (and about God's vicar, the king) as distributor and guarantor of justice and the common welfare.

All this will constitute the "semantic axis" on the level of text—which is also the "Kerygmatic axis" on the level of message. This axis, central in the Old Testament, will be prolonged in the New Testament by the salvific message of Jesus—which is addressed by preference to the oppressed of whatever title—in his options for the poor, and in his death as a prophet who was rejected because of his word and his involvement with the people (read in this light the programatic scene recounted in Luke 4:16–30). The paschal mystery, hinge of the Christian kerygma, can be interpreted and evaluated along different lines by the various New Testament authors precisely in virtue of its reservoir-of-meaning—as event, and as account—of the tradition that culminates in the gospels.

Here, in the light of the development of our subject so far, I should like to make two precisions.

Totalization Readings

Semiotics teaches us that the message of a text is not in a fragment of its report, but in its totality, as structure that encodes a meaning. In the report of the sacrifice of Isaac, for example, in Genesis 22, it is not "the main sentence" that demonstrates the significance of the episode, but the whole sequence of narrative functions, which all intervene in the production of meaning by a subsequent reading. But one report "textured" with another produces a *new* report, and the meaning will not be in the sum of the literary units or their originary significations, but in this new, coded totality, which now constitutes one single text. The production-of-meaning is modified—again and again—whenever one text enters another.

Another example: in the book of Amos, we can see that there are really two texts. Their content is mutually opposed. First there is Amos 1:1–9:10, with its message of castigation for Israel. Then there is 9:11–15, which proclaims the restoration of the Davidic dynasty and great future prosperity. (Each of these two sections is in turn composed of shorter accounts, but this is unimportant for our present considerations.) Critical exegesis has good reasons for holding that the latter text (Amos 9:11–15) consists of oracles uttered after the time of the Prophet Amos. The images and content of this material are ample evidence.

So what are we to think? That a redactor juxtaposed oracles from distinct eras is evident, but banal. It is more meaningful to recognize here a linguistic fact, and hermeneutical phenomenon, of profound theological value. For in its current form, the book of Amos is a single text, and must be read as such in order to grasp its message. The salvation oracles at the end *modify* the narrative stance, and hence the significative stance, of the castigation oracles.

Regardless of what these oracles of castigation meant *before*—when they were pronounced by their original prophet, or even first written down in literary form, announcing the definitive judgment and destruction of the people of Israel—what they mean *now* is that the castigation of Israel is *not* definitive and total; that it represents a pivotal intention—namely, the continuation of the promise. God cannot tolerate the sin, infidelity, and injustice (the themes of Amos 1-9) that void the historical process recognized in the liberation of the exodus event (cf. the tenor of Amos 2:6-16). Israel, however, will not be converted by this prophetic denunciation, but by undergoing ruination—whereupon it will recover its fidelity to the God of liberation—and then he, once more, will save it from a new oppression.

Again, Amos 1:1-9:15 is a single text, to be read as a narrative and structural totality that modifies the message of each of the integrated parts. In other words, it would not have been the same thing for Amos 9:11-15 to have been a separate shortbook—or even one of the sequences within the long report of 1:1-9:15. As a hermeneutical phenomenon, the single text of Amos gives us to understand that the *event* of the exile, or the situation of the people of postexilic Judah, has led this book to reinterpret the old message of the prophet, to the extent that that message now finds its expression of condemnation deactualized by the new experience of liberation. Not that this rereading means an evacuation of the original meaning of the oracles of judgment and destruction. It is but an exploration of its polysemy—its superabundance of meaning. Amos 9:11-15 altogether clearly identifies the need for justice expressed in 1:1-9:10 as the kerygmatic nucleus of the projected new stage proclaimed in the final verses of the report.

The Bible, too, must be read as a single text. And not as the sum of its many literary units, but as the unification of a central, linguistically coded, kerygma. In this one great account, one may recognize those "semantic axes" that orient the production-of-meaning constituted by our reading of the Bible in Latin America. This too is one of the tasks of the theology of liberation in its exegetical component. It is a hermeneutical task and a function, in this particular case, of an understanding of the Bible as (semiotically) one great text, whose theme is God's salvific project, and whose key is the concept of liberation.

This is the intent that presided at the birth of the theology of liberation: to discover these codes of the language of the Bible and formulate them as a liberation discourse. But we lacked any methodological control of the conditions and potential of the mutually related semiotic and hermeneutic readings.

To boot, a reconsideration of the Bible as a single text will actually enrich the fragmentary reading of the pericopes or books in the manner to which we have been accustomed. (In passing, we may note that there is no use in those *lexicographical* studies of poverty or liberation that actually regress from the narrative as a total unit to the words in their semantic value, which is sometimes a return to the language stage—the dictionary stage!)

The primitive church, remember, found it possible to reread the entire Old Testament as a *total, single text* (on the semiotic level), with a single hermeneutical key (the paschal mystery). This rereading did not consist in depriving the Old Testament of its less suitable books or passages, such as those extolling the value of the law, and at times directly contradicting the Christian message (the custom of anathema, or *cherem,* for example, or the ideal dominion of Israel over other nations, as is Deut. 15:6; Isa. 60:12, and elsewhere). No, the Old Testament as a unit is the word of God, overflowing the contextualization of each passage, and orientating itself toward a kerygmatic *telos,* or finality, in Christ (Gal. 3:24; Rom. 10:4). Had the church abbreviated the Old Testament, it would have produced *another text,* whose reading could no longer be the appropriation of the meaning of the traditions of Israel. This was a turning point, and it has other implications as well, which we shall make explicit below. But for the moment, there is a second precision we should make.

Privileged Readers

We have remarked that the Bible gains an advantage when it is read from the point of view of the oppressed, or of liberation. Its own origin is marked by profound liberation experiences, in which the Israelitic faith recognizes its saving God as deliverer, as liberator—which message it thereupon resumes in "creeds" (Deut. 6:20–24, 26:5–9, and elsewhere), in long accounts, in the prophets, and in worship. The reason why the tradition of Israel extended this theme through so many centuries was that the people experienced so many processes of oppression/liberation. And it is a fact of special import that, in the last stage of its history—the postexilic period, just when the canon of scripture was crystalizing—the nation found itself politically dominated by foreign empires (the Persian, the Seleucid, the Roman), and economically oppressed, both internally and externally, by tributes and taxes. This sociological factor helps us contextualize the fixing of the old traditions of oppression/liberation in codes of history and promise.

Where do we discover a closer harmony with the kerygmatic nucleus of the Bible than among the oppressed peoples of our own day, especially in the Third World? Without attempting to present an idealized picture of these peoples (a disservice sometimes rendered them in the theology of liberation), we shall not be off the mark if we propose that both the proprietorship and the relevancy most adequate for a rereading of the message of the Bible are to be found among the poor and oppressed. The Bible is theirs more than it is anyone else's. And Luke 4:43, "That is what I was sent to do," is the echo of Jesus' self-proclamation in Luke 4:18: "He has sent me to announce good news to the poor, to proclaim release for prisoners and recovery of sight for the blind; to let the broken victims go free."

For the "broken," then, more than for anyone else, the biblical kerygma is relevant property. They more than anyone else are both its addressees in depth and the objects of its challenges.

Their concept of the Bible as both their own book (subjective concern, "ownership") and as a message that concerns them in a special way (objective concern, relevancy), is "inscribed" in their totalizing reading of it via the axes of meaning that the Bible offers when taken as a single text.

Recently a union organizer of solid Christian formation, a person involved in liberation praxis, told me, "We already have what we need from the Bible." He was not depreciating the Bible. Nor was he saying he had "had it up to here" with the Bible. As he himself explained, he meant that his reading of the Bible had already given him a clear enough understanding of its message for his class. Now all we have to do is put it into action," he said.

Our reading of the Bible in the course of our Christian education, in the liturgy, in the homilies we hear, in our seminaries and theology departments, is the Bible in "infinite divisibility." Here we handle it not as one text but as a multitude of texts. In its wake it leaves an accumulation of meanings, a plurality of meanings, which, no doubt, can be valid in themselves, but which sidetrack a totalizing comprehension of the meaning—sidetrack the "axis" of which we are speaking, and which is much more relevant for praxis and for the theology of liberation than might appear.

In the theology department in which I am a professor, some of us are attempting to read the Bible as a single text, paying special attention to its structural focus, with the aid of historico-critical methods, as a step in the direction of its own hermeneutics. Ours is only a beginning, but results are already forthcoming, in the area of the "recontextualization" of the Bible, which is the area we have been considering in this paper. But it is not easy in a seminary or a department of theology, owing to the sociological conditions prevalent there, to do a reading *from the viewpoint of the oppressed* as *locus* of relevancy—as *locus* of the Bible's objective concern.

EXEGESIS AND EISEGESIS

By now it should be abundantly clear that the exploration of a text is not reducible to a purely literary and academic endeavor. Critical readers, or at any rate their socio-historical context, are engaged in a praxis, and this praxis defines the parameters of their reading. One does not extract pure meaning "from" the text (which would be pure *ex*-egesis), as a diver might come up out of the sea with coral in his hand, or as you or I might pull an object out of a suitcase. First you have to "get into" the text yourself, with questions the sacred authors never heard of, questions gathered on a new horizon of experience. This is "*eis*-egesis," and it will have significant repercussions on the production-of-meaning of a reading. For, after all, a reading is indeed a true *production*. We have already seen why any and every reading is a rereading of the meaning of a text.

The *whole* Bible, remember, as we have it today, is the result—product— of a long hermeneutic process. This process, in turn, is produced on the two levels we have seen: (1) Israel's socio-historical praxis, experienced and reflected on by successive generations in continuity with the promise and the great salvific events; and (2) the recollection of the presence of God in the form of discourse (the linguistic aspect of revelation)—in historical accounts, creeds, and all the different literary genres that abound in the Bible—until the point when they became individual texts: the legal corpus, the prophetic corpus, the sapiential, the historical, the liturgical, and finally, *the* final— canonical text.

Neither God's revelation (more in events than in words), nor inspiration (more in texts than in authors), are phenomena to be taken in isolation. Rather they complement and re-create each other, dialectically. The "word of God" is generated in the salvific event. Then the event is interpreted and enriched by the word, which takes it up and retransmits it in the form (or in various forms) of a message. The correlation between "historical effect" (of the event) and "meaning effect" (of the text) is most intimate. It extends to the relationship between praxis and the reading of a tradition or text (in our case, the Bible).

Critical exegesis seeks an understanding of the production of texts. A theological reading concentrates on the text produced, tapping its reservoir-of-meaning and treating it as the "word of God." But exegesis occurs *from a locus,* a social or theological praxis. Hence *ex*egesis is necessarily *eis*egesis at the same time. Theological rereading, for its part, is conditioned by the structure, codes, and polysemy *of the text* (not polysemy in general!), which it must tirelessly explore—so that its *eis*egesis becomes *ex*egesis.

Thus we have two inseparable elements in the act of production-of-meaning that we call a reading. Every reading is a hermeneutical act. It makes no difference whether we are reading the Bible, or any other text, sacred or profane. This is important to recognize. When one criticizes a political reading of the Bible made by the theology of liberation (which is not the only reading made by that theology), one is making a political option (from a determinate praxis, with political implications), and hence a hermeneutic option. One is seeking to "closure" one reading because its place is occupied by another reading of the same sign but different content. Further, such criticism ignores the fact that the Bible is a text that is "produced" in hermeneutic correlation with the socio-historical praxis of a whole people, and that by that very fact it is saturated with "politics." It is the word of God for a people seeking to execute a *historical* project of peace and justice, loyalty and love, welfare and freedom.

Let us recall what we worked out in "From Event to Text," above. The event generates an interpreting "word," and, inversely, is converted into a "foundational" event by being charged with meaning by successive readings (see Diagram 2, p. 167). It is on the level of praxis, where these same readings are contextualized, that they seek to "enter" word-and-tradition (the text in its semiotic and hermeneutic meaning) and that they are therefore *eise*getical (see Diagram 3, p. 168). This phenomenon explains the formation of the Old Testament in the great faith-experience of Israel, and it explains the formation of the New Testament as a rereading of the Old (not as a parallel literary production) in the life of the first Christian community.

A Process Bible

This succession is *part of the very message of the Bible.* In other words, the Bible, taken as the "product" of a hermeneutic process, offers us an important key for its own reading: the fact that its kerygmatic meaning materializes only in the prolongation of the same hermeneutic process that constituted it in the first place—the event-and-word process. Thus to claim to "fix" definitively its meaning at the moment of its "production" is to deny its true nature as "open meaning." But when read from our socio-historical reality—our political, economic, cultural, religious situation—the Bible reveals dimensions previously unseen, rays of light not captured by previous readings. What is "unsaid" in what the text "says" is said in *contextual interpretation.* This is the very marrow of the act of hermeneutics and synthesizes what we have analyzed up to this point.

To return once more to the theology being done from the standpoint of the oppressed and poor of the Third World (or wherever they are): to "read," in the gospels, or in the Bible, as one long single text, a message of liberation and justice for oppressed peoples, is not to force its meaning, but merely to harmonize it with its deeper and more totalizing semantic axis. Such a reading is an altogether legitimate entry into the text—via an unraveling of its reservoir-of-meaning. It is but saying the unsaid in what was said in another age. It is a closuring, appropriating, conflictive reading. Of course there is nothing else it could be. From the perspective of the oppressed, this is the *only* kerygmatic, valid meaning.

Here we must fine-tune some of our notions. First, what we have been talking about is much more than an "updating" of the biblical message, just as it is much more than an attempt to use the biblical message to "shed light" on our socio-historical reality. In the first place, these two overused notions are, if we look well, mutually exclusive. But they are not at the heart of the hermeneutic phenomenon in any case. Or if they are, they do not cover it adequately. What can it mean to "update" the biblical meaning of liberation? Express it in new terms? Use popular language, change the Semitisms into contemporary colloquialisms, dilute the "concentrated" terms and expressions (too hard to understand because they are culturally contextualized) by explanatory glosses? None of this is any more than translation—and therefore, like translation, it hovers on the edge of hermeneutics—but does not take the plunge.

What, then? Are we talking about making the biblical kerygma *effective for our situations?* Evidently, this is exactly what we are talking about. But how does one "make effective" a message expressed in another age by a people of another cultural and social milieu?

We have to "do something" with the *text* in which this message is written. We must apply the laws of the linguistics of discourse and recall the process of event-becoming-word (above). We must keep in mind that a meaning is unraveled in the biblical text as it overflows its original referent, and that a message not discerned in its original actualization is thereby discovered. Thus our project issues in *novelty of meaning,* characteristic of any hermeneutical reading, especially when it is a reading at the heart of a religious tradition.

May we not venture to say that there was novelty in a christological reading of the Old Testament, as practiced in apostolic times and reflected in the books of the New Testament? Then why should our own interpretation of the Bible not be *new*—created in a context of oppression and poverty, or in a context of the liberation process? We should be re-creating the biblical message, not just updating it.

Nor are we proposing anything unheard-of before. We are but clarifying the implications and richness of a reading that is already being done among the oppressed today—from and by the basic, grassroots Christian communities, for example, and out of cultural or religious contexts that differ from those of the Semitic or Western world. And it is being done by theologians who hear and know of, and often are themselves immersed in, practices of liberation, conscientization, or cultural affirmation of the peoples of the Third World.

The same applies to the notion of "shedding light" on the history of our peoples by means of the Bible as the word of God. There is more than one road out of the biblical text. Indeed, hermeneutic circularity posits a two-way street, where the praxis of faith in a context of oppression/liberation has something to contribute to the actual "meaning" of the Bible, by opening it up precisely in its quality as "word of God."

For example, does a positive reevaluation of the religions of Asia, Africa, and Latin America have nothing to say about the abundance of biblical texts disparaging the religous symbols of Israel's neighbors? Or is the cry of oppressed peoples not also an outcry against a hyperspiritualistic and hypereschatological reading of the New Testament?

Unending Revelation

But perhaps you are wondering whether all this is not "adding to" or "subtracting from" the word of God. Here of course we are up against the theologoumenon of the closure of revelation with (as it is variously formulated) Christ, or the last Apostle, or the last book of the New Testament. The three formulations, notice, are not equivalent. The first "closure" would be qualitative, the second would be spacio-temporal, and the third would be textual. They are surely interrelated: *Christ* is the culmination of revelation; but his immediate paschal experience resides in the *Apostles,* the witnesses of his life, death, and resurrection; and hence revelation is prolonged during their lifetime in a canonical *text,* culminating in the book of Revelation, which gathers and records the postpaschal experience of the primitive Christian community over which these Apostles preside.

All this is correct enough, but it is simplistic. Christ is the point of culmination, the high point, of the manifestation of God in salvation history, yes. But has he not manifested himself before? (And before Israel!) And does he not manifest himself in later history? Of course he does, unless "revelation" means merely "to speak words." Here we have the crux of the problem, as well as its solution.

The solution is fully hermeneutical. What happens is that the event has been gathered up in the word-account, which thereupon begins its trajectory from original-event message or meaning, to *language* message or meaning. This is very important. In fact, it is the matrix of the hermeneutic process. The event has "meaning" precisely insofar as it is interpreted. So the vehicle of the meaning is a text—either oral or writtten at first, but in any case finally written. And the last step is that the text is taken up via a particular hermeneutic option as a "canon," thereby closuring other traditions. (This option, in a degenerate form, pretends to closure even the rereading of the text and the event, so that the text is considered to be part of a "deposit" of revelation.)

Thus just as an *event* can be transformed into a "foundational" one in the light of its "historical effects," so also a *text* can become normative and archetypical within a community that now lives in and breathes its atmosphere. The canon varies only when a conflict of interpretations has reached such a pitch that a division results, and the new groups need to recompose, or re-form, its "reference text" (in the area of religion), its canon of sacred scripture.

This lends tremendous significance to the fact that, as we affirm in faith, the Bible is our paradigmatic text as word of God. We have no need of adding new books to the Bible. Besides, Christian practices are already definitively orientated by those of Jesus, as well as by his teaching—interpreted, of course, in the canonical *text.*

One of the "semantic axes" of the Bible is precisely that God reveals himself primarily in the events of human history—in a presence grasped by faith (at the same time as it generates faith!) and expressed most fruitfully as cognition, or "re-cognition," of God.

Everything we have said about the event as gathered into the word—the key principle of biblical hermeneutics—bears upon this point. Before he reveals himself in word, God reveals himself as salvific event—with all the consequences, or "historical effects," of this event, which prolong his manifestation in them. Regardless of whether God's revelation is expressed in a word or in a text, it is always in an "after." The word of the promise itself is mediated to us by a text, which orientates that promise to the exodus event. *This supposes, and actually is, already a form of rereading.* When a prophet speaks in the name of God, he or she is "reading" or hearing God in the life of the people, in their unfaithfulness or in their suffering. God's presence is coded as judgment, or as promise of salvation.

And what about: "The Word became flesh" (John 1:14)? Does not this, too, gainsay the intent to closure the word of God in the Torah? The Torah is the reflection and multiple expression of the revelation of God in history—yet it came to deny its own origin by being totalized as autonomous word, impermeable to new manifestations of God that might modify its readings, now seemingly fixed by tradition. But Christ was the *new* God-event that imposed a *re*reading of the Torah. Unable to "re-cognize" God in Jesus' practices and doctrine, many of the Jews of his time became "nonknowers" of God (see John 8:19, 12:45, 14:7). Hermeneutical conflict yielded reductionism of revelation.

And now this circularity is being repeated in the history of the church. The "closed revelation" theologoumenon, for all its good intentions, sets up a short circuit in the revelation process: God→word, instead of God→event→word. Are we to be left, then, merely with a *word* that sheds light on human events? Is God saying nothing new in the struggles of oppressed peoples, in the processes of liberation, in the contribution of the social sciences to knowledge of human beings, their problems, and their real situations of structural oppression?

It is not a matter of revelation in the order of cognition. It is not even a matter of God's manifesting himself in new and unheard of modalities. It is above all a matter of his *revealing himself in events,* and as he does so, his epiphany ought to generate a hermeneutic process that will produce its word—the faith discourse, in all its modalities and variations, such as prayer, creeds, proclamation, theology, and so on. And this word will be new. It will not simply be "light shed on" present history from behind (from the biblical text). It will be a seeing of the face of God precisely as he enters the present history of men and women. The Bible orientates the reading of God *within* the events of the world and teaches us to recognize him as he manifests himself right now—not as a repetition of the past. Human history is constant novelty, and so is the presence of God accompanying it.

Christ, as the great central fact of history, is an unfinished event. Christian apocalyptic looks for him a second time: *then* he will "close" history. Christ, as Word of the Father (John 1:18 says that Jesus *exegesato* the Father—"did an exegesis" on him, or "made him known," as our translations run), has not told all. He has left his Spirit to teach us all things (John 14:26) and to lead *(hodegesei)* us to the full truth (John 16:13).

The Bible is the faith reading of paradigmatic events of salvation history, and the paradigmatic reading of an unfinished salvation history. The Bible, as paradigmatic and normative, does not exclude its own rereading in the light of new events. It is nonsense to think that there will be no more salvation events. This would contradict the very essence of the biblical message. There is no closure of God's revelation in history. It is likewise nonsense to pretend to transform the Bible into a closured "deposit," from which one need only "draw." As normative, canonical text of God's salvific message—precisely because it is normative—the Bible produces, by its rereading, *new* meaning in the new events of history. *Interpretation means accumulation of meaning.*

*Ex*egesis is *eis*egesis. Interpretation is an "entering into" the biblical text with a content of meaning—which meaning re-creates the first meaning precisely by coming into harmony with it (not by simply identifying with it), whether in virtue of the continuum of a faith praxis (on the level of "historical effect") or in virtue of the continuum of successive interpretations or rereadings (on the level of the hermeneutical tradition).

These considerations are eminent justification for a Third World theology that must stand in opposition to a theology constructed elsewhere (where too, by the way, it was and is by all means a theology from *a point of departure in praxis,* with all the political connotations of praxis). Translated into Third World terms, this means that theological praxis is obliged to transform itself into a "theology of the font(s)," like the primitive Christian theology of the Torah. Theology from the standpoint of the oppressed and the poor will be troublesome. It will be conflictual. It will invite repression. It will be disqualified as theology because it will stress human praxis (and therefore must be "anthropology"), or because it will be "worldly" and accord a value to human history. Then it will be accused of being subversive, because it will subvert traditional values. It will be called "Marxist," ideological.

Evidently, the theology of the Third World has burst upon the scene with a hermeneutic challenge. Like the theology that is arising in the world of the poor, all theolog*ies* of liberation (socio-political, religious, women's, black, "theologic," and so on) mean to decipher a liberating God's new manifestation in situations of injustice and alienation. For, in the suffering of the poor, we are assisting at a new God-event. The poor are raising their consciousness and fighting for liberation. It is they, first and foremost, who "re-cognize" God, and who pronounce the first "word"—the first interpretation—of the God-event.

It is important to notice that the revelation of God *within the event,* and not only in the transmitted word, helps us to grasp in depth the biblical tradition itself. The language of the Bible, like all religious language, works via literary symbols and narrative codes. This is how it expresses the "meaning" that *faith* discovers in human events—which at first sight seem to have nothing extraordinary about them. The event of the deliverance from Egyptian slavery was the same event for the Egyptians as it was for the Hebrews, and could have happened to Canaanite or Lybian slaves of the time. The "representation" of that event as the "passage through the sea," or in any of the other ways this event is "reported," forms part of the "word"-of-the-event, the word that "says" this presence of the God who acts in history—says it concretely, in this liberation process.

This reflection has three immediately evident consequences:

(1) The event is now better "centrated": it is the experience of *deliverance,* and not that of sea-crossing or plagues.

(2) The *text* or account interpreting and amplifying the kerygmatic and theological dimensions of that liberation-event now acquires an importance of its own: once the event is "read" in a "word," it is subsumed in that word. Its "historical effects" (the practices it generates) will be subsumed in that word in their own turn, in a dialectical sequence of creation-of-meaning.

(3) The processes of liberation that we are experiencing today are historical facts in which *faith* is able to "re-cognize" the presence of God. To think that God must manifest himself in miracles and extraordinary phenomena as in Egypt is to fall victim to the naiveté of one who does not know how religious discourse is initiated. Religious discourse is the "after" of the event it *reads.* Was the liberation of Nicaragua not a salvific event, and from the Christian viewpoint a manifestation *of God?* To assert—in a theological statement—that it was a purely human political event would be to lock ourselves into a "deposit" of revelation—reminiscent of the (altogether hermeneutical!) attitude of the Pharisees who represented the Jesus-event as the work of the devil.

Liberation Theologies and the Future

Here we are face to face with the challenge of liberation theology. One of the things that that theology must do is to discover, in an event, a richness of meaning that need not be simply that of something that happened long ago in Israel. The language of faith has two meaning-conditions, and it has them in virtue of its own fecundity. First, it begins with an experience or event that of itself is evanescent and irrecuperable: but thereupon the discourse of faith moves about continuously, contemplating that event in view of new experiences or practices. It engages the unraveling distantiation of the reservoir-of-meaning of that event or of the account that has already read that event.

Secondly, the language of faith is, of necessity, culturally conditioned and limited, as is any language. Any discourse purporting to "say something to someone about something" presupposes the contextual closure that renders it intelligible. Otherwise it is not a message. There are no universal languages. Not even the Bible was written in an ether wafting above all times and cultures. It was written for the Hebrew people, and (only via the profound re-readings of the New Testament) for Christians of a limited geographical ambient. This means that its message is contextualized. Hence in order to be understood in other historical situations, it must be *re*contextualized. If the Christian is able to read the "signs of the times," which for the poor and exploited peoples of the Third World must be signs of liberation, his or her reading will be in harmony with the kerygmatic axis of the Bible—coded in turn in a semantic axis at the level of text, as already explained.

In this hermeneutical perspective, reinforced by the semiotic circularity, the legitimacy of the theologies of liberation is guaranteed. That these theologies take their point of departure in a correct and "conscientizing" analysis of reality does not transform them into sociologies. After all, is it of no value to *know* the reality within which God "epiphanizes"? Are not the social sciences themselves part of God's contextualized message? Of course it is the focus of faith that thereupon recognizes in these situations of captivity, marginalization, or oppression, God's call to an exodus. It is faith that recognizes in the processes of liberation the salvific presence of the Lord. It is not necessary that it be Christians who initiate, or conclude, these processes. But Christians do have to be where the God of liberation is. Otherwise they will set up an idol-god—a god of the legitimation of oppression.

From its point of departure in the praxis of the faith in the liberation processes, however ambiguous, slow or quick, successful or repressed, theology rereads the Scriptures as a message propounding a new social order—proclaiming the advent of the new human person, free and creative, delivered from all manner of sin and death (for death is not first and foremost its physical reality, but its anticipation in various forms of misery).

There has been an effort to disqualify the theologies of liberation on grounds of their marked recontextualization of the Bible, which its adversaries characterize as "subjectivity." The Latin American theology of liberation, in particular, is criticized for weak biblical foundations. In our opinion the case is just the contrary. In the light of the narrative and kerygmatic axes we have examined, the allegation of subjectivity lodged against biblical hermeneutics would be valid for all theology. There is no "objective" theology. The semiotic circularity, as we have seen, demonstrates that the hermeneutics of the texts is conditioned *by the texts themselves*. It is the *text* that delimits, however broadly, the meaning. One cannot make the text say something. It says what it permits itself to say. Its polysemy arises from its previous closure. Hence it is indispensable to situate it in its original context by historico-critical methods, and explore its potentiality for the production-of-meaning by applying the laws of semiotics. This is done to occasion the appearance of a "context-forward" from a point of departure in the practices of liberation—which practices recontextualize the reading of the Bible in its quality as production-of-meaning.

Another frequent criticism, at least in the case of the Latin American theology of liberation, is that it uses the Old Testament more than it does the New. But the whole Bible, not just the New Testament, is the word of God. Secondly, the Bible is a single text, and it is precisely as such that it underscores the continuity between the liberating God celebrated in the life of the people of Israel and the Christ who delivered the poor and oppressed. This is its narrative and kerygmatic axis.

Thirdly, the Old Testament contains a more extensive theological narrative than does the New, furnishing more numerous examples of historical events seen in the light of the foundational exodus event.

Fourthly, no one can deny that the Bible is an eminently rich and varied book, where many different theological currents speak their piece. Hence the importance of taking the Bible as a single text on the level of meaning—recognizing within it the axes of which we have spoken. And it is the reading done by liberation theology that best harmonizes with these axes of meaning.

Finally, it should be reemphasized that the Old Testament message (for example, the exodus as a salvific event of political and social content experienced by a community or a people), resumed and reread in the New Testament, far from losing its meaning, gains more: it manifests its reservoir-of-meaning. Every reading of the Old Testament will now be christological. What has been gained cannot be lost. And if the theology of liberation rereads the exodus via Christ—reading it upon its central kerygmatic axis—then that rereading, executed from a point of departure in the oppressed, and in structures of dependency, and with the Bible as a single text, has nowhere else to go but to the foundational event.

Let us also recall that some readings of the Christic event gathered in the New Testament neglect certain important kerygmatic elements of the Old Testament. Individual sin, for example, is much more emphasized in the New Testament than is the sin residing in social structures (think of the prophets!). In the New Testament, the eschatologization of the kingdom of God (except in Luke!) seems to relativize the struggle for a just order in this world. Paul contemplates servitude from such a height that he does not see it as having an effect on the real situation of the actual slave (1 Cor. 7:20–24, 1 Tim. 6:1–2) and excludes women from the proclamation of the word in church assemblies (1 Cor. 14:33–35, 11:2–15).

Any text, in the intention of its author, entails a closure on its meaning. Further, the message of each text is contextual, occasional. But the author dies in the act of transmission, and a polysemy emerges. This comports both a risk and an advantage.

The *risk* is in the decontextualization carried out by any later rereading of the text. Let us take the case of 1 Corinthians 14:33b–35. Writing to a Greek church, Paul may not have considered it opportune to negate without further ado a cultural practice doubtless based on the Orphic-Platonic worldview that idealized maleness and disparaged femaleness. But then the text was universalized. What could have been purely circumstantial was now raised to the status of doctrine. This seems to save Paul. But it does not save the text. And we only read Paul as a *text* he wrote.

What, then, is the *advantage* of the transition from author to text? Let us recall that, on the linguistic level, this account is situated within another account: the Bible in its totality. In this single, longer text, we find another Pauline assertion: "There is no such thing as . . . male and female; for you all are one person in Christ Jesus" (Gal. 3:28), and this assertion establishes a more radical principle than does the other—subsuming the other and definitively returning to the Old Testament (Gen. 1:26; cf. Eph. 5:31–33). It is this recirculation, established in the intratextuality (if not indeed in the intertextuality) of the Bible, that plumbs the inexhaustibility of the meaning of the

Old Testament, precisely by rereading the Old Testament through the christological prism.

This is what happens in the theology of liberation. There is no abuse being committed upon the Old Testament. The gospels sketch the liberating and prophetic deeds of Jesus in capital letters: his death as suffering servant and persecuted prophet, his resurrection as the triumph of life and of divine justice over both sin and the powers that annihilate life and justice. The Christ-event expresses—as a new hermeneutic key—the central salvific message of the Old Testament, in which the center of gravity is the liberation of the poor and the oppressed.

The Old Testament is a journey toward Christ. The deed of the deliverance of our own peoples today, read from a point of departure in the praxis in faith, is a journey toward the plenitude of Christ in a new humankind.

—Translated by Robert R. Barr

APPENDIX

Diagram 1

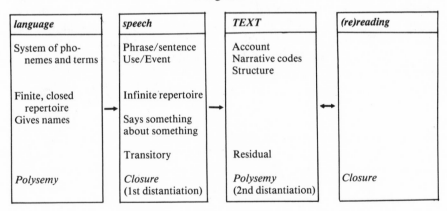

language	*speech*	*TEXT*	*(re)reading*
System of phonemes and terms	Phrase/sentence Use/Event	Account Narrative codes Structure	
Finite, closed repertoire Gives names	Infinite repertoire Says something about something		
	Transitory	Residual	
Polysemy	*Closure* (1st distantiation)	*Polysemy* (2nd distantiation)	*Closure*

Diagram 2

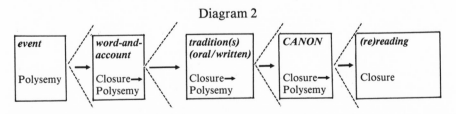

event	*word-and-account*	*tradition(s) (oral/written)*	*CANON*	*(re)reading*
Polysemy	Closure→ Polysemy	Closure→ Polysemy	Closure→ Polysemy	Closure

The event is open to many readings, each of which closes the meaning, only to have it open anew—and so on, indefinitely.

Diagram 3

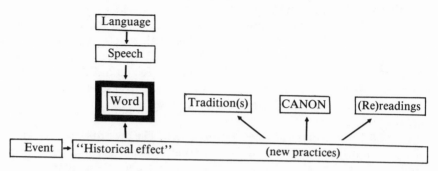

The word that interprets the event has one linguistic vector and one praxis one, which, once they have converged in the word, mutually develop and re-create each other. It is the word that marks the transition from semiotics to hermeneutics. The rereading leads to the event by way of the previous readings (text).

Could there be a shortcut to the event? Yes and no. The event is subsumed *in the text* and in its "historical effects," which in turn are mediated by its interpretations ("word"/text). From that point on, it will take a new praxis to open the meaning of the foundational event. (Is this not what is happening with the basic ecclesial communities?) The upward vertical arrows indicate that the rereading of the sacred texts is done *from within* a determinate praxis.

PART IV

PERSONAL EXPERIENCES AND LITURGY

12

Everyday Life in India:
Latin American Impressions

Ivone Gebara and Zwinglio Dias

These reflections are limited in scope. They result from two weeks of contact with the realities of India, on the occasion of the EATWOT Conference. The data we furnish was collected from personal contacts and the firsthand information we obtained. Therefore, we do not wish them to be either overestimated or underestimated. We simply share these reflections with the intention of contributing to an intercontinental theological dialogue in search of a theology for the Third World. Born in fact from the challenges to our different peoples who constitute this Third World, we hope it may serve the process of liberation long sought by them.

Some fifty persons representing different churches and countries from three continents, and ethnic mnorities from the U.S.A., and one person from the Caribbean, were in New Delhi for the conference. Before getting down to the specific tasks of the intercontinental group, the organizing committee, with the help of a local commission, planned a program of contacts with the realities of India that would permit the participants, as much as possible, a more direct view of the Indian national reality. This was aimed at enlarging and deepening the Third World vision of each participant, helping each to avoid being closed into their own particular national or regional experience.

In accordance with this program, the first day was dedicated to the rural situation, the second to the urban situation, and the third to an overview of the country's religious situation by way of a panel discussion with representatives from India's most prominent religions.

The participants were divided into four groups, each given a guide and interpreter, who besides facilitating contact with the population, pointed out to the participants different aspects and peculiarities in what they were observing. At the end of each day, there was a meeting to share impressions.

This was done in two parts: first the groups met to put together the different impressions by each member; the second part was a plenary sharing at which the observations of each group were presented and the problems that have most impressed them were discussed with the aid of Indian participants.

During the second part of the meeting on the second day, the group had the opportunity to attend a talk given by Doctor Swami, professor of economics at the University of Delhi, on current contradictions and impasses in the socio-economic and political reality of India. This helped us see how incomplete our statements and observations were, and how we were indeed foreigners in India.

SHARING WITH THE PEOPLE

Even though New Delhi is not the largest city in India, the first major impression that caused the greatest impact on the EATWOT participants (especially the non-Asiatics) was the great concentration of persons in the main streets of the city, the physical proximity that one could observe in whatever grouping of persons. The urban population was seen to be made up of, for the most part, poor persons, sellers of odds and ends, beggars and ragged children who ran after tourists, striking their own mouths and stomachs to make others understand how much they were suffering. On all, the same hungry faces, the same eyes at once hopeful and resigned. Certainly there was more than this, something deeper that our foreign eyes could not discern.

To this picture was added the deafening noise of car horns and buses, which sped through the streets in sharp contrast to the slow pace of tricycles, bicycles, and rickshaws pushed by humans in the boiling sun. The hundred-degree temperatures made the participants eager customers at the "refrigerated cold-water stands" and especially at stands that dispensed Campa-Cola, a kind of Indian Coca-Cola.

The group coordinators conducted the participants, both in the outlying parts of the city and in the downtown sections, on the normal means of transportation used by the people so that from the beginning we experienced as much as possible the difficulties and limitations the population faces every day. There were immense lines at bus stops and when one stopped the people began to push, just hoping to get on, deterred neither by the squeeze nor by the heat. All these difficulties can be easily imagined if one bears in mind that India is a country of seven hundred million inhabitants of which 65 percent live below the poverty line, as measured by World Bank criteria ($8 per month).

In Villages

We visited Hiranski, Sarna, and Dhurapur, rural villages about an hour and a half from downtown Delhi by bus. We were received by the heads of the three communities, who had been elected by members of their community. They are notable personages in the social and political world of rural India. They pointed out with pride and happiness the more important locales in their respective villages. They spoke to us of the forms of organization taken up by the small production units and community living. They stressed their own responsibilities in resolving vital problems of the people, such as water, electricity, distribution of employment, certain legal questions, and the like.

All the participants felt that the town leaders and interpreters were very helpful toward an understanding of some aspects of the Indian reality. However, the participants also felt profound limitations in that they were not able to communicate more directly with the inhabitants of the rural villages, not only by reason of language limitations, but because for the most part the local leaders took over when it came to responding to all the questions raised by visitors. We perceived that the linguistic and cultural barriers are enormous. It forced us to be more careful with our own interpretations of what we saw and heard.

Data and Reflections

(1) The number of inhabitants is more or less six hundred persons per village.

(2) The ordinary salary for workers is about three hundred rupees per month ($32).

(3) Social institutions: There are schools, temples, and local courts. We saw no local health clinics or hospitals.

(4) Production: The system of private landownership is in effect. Vegetables, rice, corn, and manioc (cassava) are cultivated.

(5) Social relations: We saw for ourselves the caste system. The villages we visited are dominated by the Brahmans. Some untouchables were observed to be living both physically and religiously segregated. Their material situation was the worst of the town. They were doing the simplest and the dirtiest tasks and remained at a distance from visitors.

It can be affirmed that the castes constitute a social structure deeply embedded in India. There are four basic groups: priests (Brahmans), warriors (Kahatrias), merchants (Vahishias), and servants or untouchables (Shutras). Besides these basic groups, there are further divisions and subdivisions. And it is important to keep in mind the existence of regional castes, which make the situation even more complex. No one ever leaves their caste. All marriages are between persons belonging to the same caste.

One's economic situation is not necessarily linked to caste membership, though the untouchables are in fact the poorest and the least respected. The caste tradition grew gradually and social activities solidified gradually, excluding the untouchables. This pattern of social behavior was interjected into and assumed by the majoriy of the untouchables as well. Such a situation makes structural changes even more difficult, especially because the caste system is legitimated by religion.

To penetrate this mysterious world is very difficult for us from the Western world, where we are so used to a scientific and rational spirit. We sense a need for a more profound comprehension of the castes and of the entire cultural horizon so strange to us. We need to perceive the real conditions and the real possibilities for change, starting with things as they are and working toward an overcoming of this kind of "destiny" or "will of God."

The visitors also observed the problem of the segregation of women. In rural villages, the women live segregated from the men. It was interesting to note that we were received only by men and we saw only a few women, from a distance. From what we gathered from our talks, we concluded that the most important task of the woman is to care for children and to cook for them and for herself.

There is an obvious submission of women to men and some of the leaders told us that women ought to treat men as their gods. The question of the emancipation of women has yet to be raised in rural areas. This situation is reinforced by the strong requirements of classic Hinduism, in which a woman's status is inferior, in view of the fact that she will reach salvation only after reincarnation as a man.

With the People in the City

The visit to the city had as one of its objectives to put the participants into physical contact, for the most part wordless contact, with the thousands of persons who go through or walk about in New Delhi every day. Besides this, the organizers wanted to introduce us as far as possible to the history of India. To this end, we visited temples of different religious creeds, historical monuments, and museums.

We could see the influence of the Islamic world in the formation of present India, especially in the north of the country. We were able to see the Red Fort, popular markets, temples (Hindu, Jainist, Sikh, and the Jasna Mosque, third largest in the Islam world), the central railroad station, the Catholic cathedral, and the city of Old Delhi with its narrow streets of ancient construction.

For everyone, there was shock at the widespread poverty in the city, a poverty terribly visible in the throngs who spend twenty-four hours a day on the sidewalks of the city, sleeping in the public parks and squares, and feeding themselves with miserable leftovers. A serious question remained: Can it be that this situation results from a tragic resignation to a "destiny" alloted to them? Or does their attitude reveal great wisdom expressed in a religious way in response to pain and misery? The age-old poverty of India and the age-old wisdom of India left us perplexed.

From the direct experience of poverty present in the great city, from the besieging children, beggars, and sellers of everything imaginable in their desperate search for a few rupees for daily survival, the EATWOT participants

felt profoundly challenged. There was a certain feeling of powerlessness before this challenge, a certain difficulty to balance all the impressions that
come from this subworld of poverty where the value of human life is calculated so very differently. After all, what is human life? What value does it
have? Why this frightening silence of the suffering masses? How do they face
this suffering? What do they hope for from life?

These and many other questions tormented our minds and hearts. They are
still with us to nourish in us the place of human mystery in our existence.
Where there are no immediate answers, where there are only questions, only a
profound act of faith brings us to hope against hope.

ECONOMY AND RELIGION IN INDIA TODAY

To bring to completion the initial contact with Indian reality, the organizers of the conference put us in touch with an economist and a group of
specialists on the religions in India, to furnish us with more data about the
reality we had begun to know.

Professor Swami, Economist

At the end of the second day, Dr. Swami gave us a critical view of the tragic
situation of the Indian people. He limited his reflections to the social and
economic area represented by the city of Delhi within the Indian context.
Here are some flashes from his contribution:

"New Delhi was built on the edges of Old Delhi by the English colonizers
when they decided to transfer the capital of the vice-regency from Calcutta to
the Delhi region. It became an elite area, a location for government administration buildings, international hotels, embassies, and residences for very
wealthy Indians and those in lofty government positions. It is a city which has
grown enormously in the last thirty years.

"Old Delhi, built by the kings of the Mogul dynasty in the sixteenth century, is inhabited by the poor of the city who overcrowd its dark and narrow
streets. They are confounded by the huge number of various means of transportation, starting from carts pulled by animals and rickshaws pulled by humans, to old cars, tricycles, bicycles, and buses. Misery is everywhere. During
the years 1975 and 1976, the city government tried to expel the poor in an
attempt to beautify the city, but to no avail.

"Many laborers who make it possible to sustain its life and contribute to
the overall wealth of the country have to live in small neighboring villages at
considerable distance from the downtown area where they work. Each day,
they spend about three hours on public transportation.

"Migration to the city because of serious agrarian problems has lessened
rural productivity and worsened the problems of the city."

Dr. Swami called our attention to the fact that the Indian economy faces
the problem of assimilating a growing number of workers—seven million

more each year. The system of landownership concentrates vast expanses in the hands of a privileged few. It is a situation that only compounds the problem of work for everyone. About 80 percent of the population lives in the countryside.

To complete the picture of present exploitation in India, he asserted that 10 percent of the population controls more than 50 percent of the arable land. This creates an even more complicated economic problem with social, political, and cultural consequences.

Finally, Dr. Swami emphasized the important fact that the process of liberation from the British colonial yoke did not bring to the country any fundamental change in its internal imbalance of socio-economic relationships. What happened, in truth, was a transfer of power from the colonial masters to the oligarchies that had been forming throughout the entire English domination period. It simply consolidated the islands of prosperity in the midst of an impoverished majority. Independence brought neither freedom nor prosperity to the great majority; the fundamental economic organization of the country remained what it had been.

Discussion with Representatives of Non-Christian Religions

Our contacts with the reality of India were brought full circle with a panel discussion on the principal religions and religious movements of the country. EATWOT participants were given the opportunity to hear five representatives from non-Christian religions speak on their efforts within their respective religious contexts to pursue social justice and search out solutions for the serious problems afflicting the nation.

The following religious specialists shared their ideas and points of view throughout an entire morning with the EATWOT participants: Dr. Suman Khana, a Hindu and specialist in philosophy; Dr. Wazire Singh, representing the Sikh religion; Dr. Mushlul Huq, representing the Moslem religion; Mr. Bhagwan Das, representing Buddhism; Mr. Bapurao Pakhiddey, representing a movement of the untouchables called the Dalit Panther Movement.

A valuable discussion ensued, enriching for all the participants, revealing the complexity of the religious problem projected within the socio-economic problem. We were impressed to note within the discussions the presence of a certain mobility in the religions, especially in relation to Hinduism. This mobility is of deep significance, for it relates to the departure of untouchables from Hinduism toward an integration with other religious bodies. It represents the beginning of a consciousness of their values as human persons. They are departing in search of religious groups in which they feel more respect. We know that many untouchables left Hinduism to adhere to either Buddhism or Sikhism (which has been in existence for about five hundred years), or to Islam, because duality is stressed in these religions as a principle.

It is important to keep in mind that in relation to the untouchables, Christianity has offered them some hope and treated them with respect by way of its institutions. Even so, its presence in India was for many years linked to English colonialism, which gave out many signals contradictory to the good news of the gospel of Jesus Christ.

The untouchables, euphemistically called "children of God" (Hara Jin), number approximately 20 million in India and little is ever said on an international level of the humiliations and exploitations they have suffered over the centuries. Today, in India, there are organized movements in favor of the emancipation of the untouchables, with leadership from among the untouchables themselves. They are small minority groups, but they reveal an awakening and growth in awareness in favor of fundamental equality of rights.

Through this discussion between panelists and participants, we were able to perceive that these small forces pertaining to different religious creeds are seeking a society that will respect the dignity of each person and consider all persons to be equal. For beyond the differences in formulations of faith, there seems to be a common starting point from which to begin dialogue respecting the diverse ways of living the Absolute in human life.

All these reflections, fruit of a lively and interesting debate, made the participants more aware that the "irruption of the Third World" entails an irruption of the non-Christian exploited masses of the world. The Third World fundamentally is exploited humankind, wherever it may be.

With regard to Latin America, limited, as we were, to an experience of poor, Christian masses, our horizons were greatly enlarged. In India we perceived a much wider world, with acute and enormously difficult problems to solve. The challenge was clear: as Christians, we must seek a way to a place common to all—in other words, a place where there is a committed struggle for justice, where humans will lead more human lives, where there is an irruption of the divine within the human.

TO INITIATE A DIALOGUE

After this general report, limited as it is from our foreign viewpoint, the language difficulty, and a lack of more complete information, we should still like to share with our brothers and sisters a few reflections. They are born of our Latin American contact with the Asiatic world. Obviously, these reflections will be no more than first-round observations and need to be deepened. Also, they must be understood as relative, for we speak from and take our position in relationship to our Latin American experience.

Toward the Plenary Truth

In Latin America, we live with a people for the most part Christian. Besides this, in spite of book-learning and our efforts to open ourselves to other cultural horizons, our view still remains limited by our life experience and our own world. Influenced by Western civilization, which built our institutions and lives within us, we are easily led to believe that we are the "owners of truth.'' It is so in all sectors of life and particularly so in the religious sector. We are inclined to think and act as though we possess the only true way to approach the mystery of God, and the unique, legitimate depository of his salvation. Almost without realizing it, we judge the rest of the world with ourselves as the starting point, and act as though it were possible to reduce everything to a monolithic uniformity of our creation, believing this to be the unity suitable for the whole human race. We make ourselves a sort of standard by which all things are judged good or evil, correct or incorrect.

In India, Christians are a minority. Of the 700 million inhabitants, only 2 percent are Christian. This number, along with our limited experience of sharing life with a secularly exploited people with a very impressive spirituality, upset our smug security.

We lived for a few days in what was for us a strange world. We were impressed by the number of Hindu, Sikh, and Buddhist temples and mosques. Their symbols are seen everywhere mingled into the life of the people. One sees a blend of devotion, faith, and commerce everywhere in the sale of tiny images of Krishna, Shiva, Buddha, and others, in the incense burning inside stores, and in the singing on the streets. The impressions and aromas were enough to remind us we were not in a Western world of rosary beads, crosses, or little statues of the Virgin Mary and the saints.

In India we saw another religious expression and it challenged us by its difference. These impressions, the cults, the sacred music so unlike any we had ever heard before, the prayer, the silences, the studied gestures, the color and flowers of religious ceremonies, awakened us. At one blow, we became aware that in the end ''our truth'' is only a part of the Truth, one profile, one aspect, and that the truth and love of God has many faces and infinite hues.

This contact with Asia brought us a profound religious experience of humility and attentive silence before the mystery of humanity and before the mystery of God.

If we agree that the Love of God manifests itself in different ways, we must believe in fact that this love invites us to build a society of brothers and sisters, to struggle against all forms of injustice that kill the human person within the real-life reality of each continent and each country. Every human group with its own history is invited to turn the present into the today of God's kingdom. No group or individual has the exact formula. Alas, no overall formula exists! We are all called, wherever we are, with all the historical, economic, and cultural conditioning that constitute our daily life, to roll up our sleeves so that we find love and justice and prove them to be the presence of God in the midst of humanity.

The Splendor of Differences

This small Asian experience warned us of the temptation to absolutize our analysis of reality. Even though today the world lives in an overall political and economic interdependence, and, in fact, our analyses cannot be isolated, frequently we forget other components of reality, components that provoke the differences and that are likely to be breakthroughs into new situations. We forget that human groups are more complex than the analyses of them. Analyses can be presented in theoretical form and then spread about even though they are quite unconnected with reality. The life of the different human groups of India and our contact with representatives of different cultures served as both a warning and a challenge. The warning is to be more conscious of differences, of the history of each people, its values and traditions, its customary ways of organization and religious expression. The challenge is to begin from these cultural differences and struggle toward a change in current international relationships—in other words, to truly change the face of the world.

India, with its age-old wisdom, invited us into silence, a silence in which to listen better, to let ourselves be penetrated by this overwhelming multitude of voices: to allow our ears, our eyes, and all our senses to accustom themselves to difference. This difference is revelatory of human riches and, once accepted as something constitutive of human experience, is a condition and a starting point for the building of a freer and more equal world.

Complementarity, not Exclusivity

This last point seeks to make explicit the experience lived on a religious level of complementarity. It was an experience that made us realize the need to seek out a real convergence within differing religious creeds. In spite of some interconfessional conflicts, such as exist in all places, we can state that in this immense country one religious creed does not necessarily exclude another. There does not seem to be religious proselytism as in the Western world. Things happen differently.

The logic of "either . . . or," extremely prevalent in the religious sphere in the different countries of the Western world, does not find much expression in India. For this world, wisdom seeks complementarity rather than exclusivity. Instead of "either . . . or," we find "both . . . and." This logic should not be understood in a simplistic way, as an eclectic grouping or a total relativism. Rather, it is respect for truth, which is no one's private property. To perceive this as a part of life, for such an immense population, constitutes for us a challenge to seek what is more fundamental in all things. This basis is well beyond explicit religious differences and appears to be the point of convergence for humanity.

These statements may be easy enough to accept relationally, but the great challenge for us Westerners is to let this statement take flesh in us. "Take flesh"—that is, live it from our heart, in our most profound attitudes and activities.

We call this dwelling together of different religious expressions complementary—that is, each religious expression, if there is in it nothing contrary to life and human dignity, is complementary to the others. We believe that acceptance of this complementarity is a basic step we all need to take and without which our experience of liberation runs the risk of turning into failure.

We believe that these three simple lessons learned in India are a preamble to the dialogue that EATWOT proposes on the level of a theology for the Third World. It is a dialogue for all men and women of good will, for all those who cannot bear to see the power of evil spreading over the earth, and who wish to offer their own "life for the salvation of the world."

13

Worship Service:
This Hour of History

Elsa Tamez, Sun Ai Park, and Others

INTRODUCTION

This hour of history is the hour of irrupting millions; having seen half their face, now they want full recognition. Where lies the hope of the countless nonpersons who have been dispossessed of what they own, despised for what they are, deprived of the fruit of their labor, bereft of their human dignity? Where lies the hope of the half-persons, because they are not male, not white?

Today the women invite you to join us in our moment of prayer, our hour of hope, for we are part of the irrupting millions seeking our rightful place in history.

We invite you to meditate on Sun Ai Park's poem written after a poignant experience of India's villages and Delhi's streets. We invite you to read with us the story of Hagar in Genesis 21:8–20 and listen to Elsa Tamez's reflections from a Third World woman's perspective. Together let us then sing Mary's song, which mirrors the longings not only of women but of all peoples, for total human liberation. And finally let us pray to Mother/Father God, the source of our hope, our Creator, Sustainer, and Liberator.

WORSHIP SERVICE

The Poor Shall Rise
by Sun Ai Park (Korea)

Doomed in poverty
millions of immobile creatures
clad in dust
barefooted
one facial expression
of destitution silenced.

As if devoid of all human marks
as if life were only a nightmare
they wander as in a sleepwalk
they lie still, crushed,
shrunk in size as if dead
under a broad daylight.
Oh, poor of India
poor of the Third World.

So young a child, many a child
too young to know
the hardships of life
made to inherit
not the wealth and milk of the earth
but possessed by hunger and cursed poverty.

Were they ever touched
by the warmth of home life?
Have they ever dreamt
a child's dream?

Driven by the need for survival
pushed out on the street
she stretches her little hands
begging, holding her little brother
on her side
begging for life
begging for her lost dignity.

In a nation
so rich in culture
where great sages and warriors reigned,
poets and artists fulfilled
their dreams of beauty,
where trail the echoes
of lute and chants in harmonious serenity,
What a scandal
What a violence.

Do you hear the curtains
in the holy of holies tear apart,
as Christ was killed on the cross,
crying: "Father, Father why have you forsaken me?"
It's your heart that's torn apart
it's your heart that's torn apart.

But the wretched of the earth shall rise.
Oh, the multitudes of the poor of India shall rise.
Oh, the poor of the Third World shall rise.
And you will rejoice
with the risen Christ.

Reading
Genesis 21:8–20

The boy [Isaac] grew and was weaned, and on the day of his weaning Abraham gave a feast. Sarah saw the son whom Hagar the Egyptian had borne to Abraham laughing at him, and she said to Abraham, "Drive out this slave-girl and her son; I will not have this slave-girl's son sharing the inheritance with my son Isaac." Abraham was vexed at this on his son Ismael's account, but God said to him, "Do not be vexed on account of the boy and the slave-girl. Do what Sarah says, because you shall have descendants through Isaac. I will make a great nation of the slave-girl's son too, because he is your own child."

Abraham rose early in the morning, took some food and a waterskin full of water and gave it to Hagar; he set the child on her shoulder and sent her away, and she went and wandered in the wilderness of Beersheba. When the water in the skin was finished, she thrust the child under a bush, and went and sat down some way off, about two bowshots away, for she said, "How can I watch the child die?" So she sat some way off, weeping bitterly. God heard the child crying, and the angel of God called from heaven to Hagar, "What is the matter, Hagar? Do not be afraid: God had heard the child crying where you laid him. Get to your feet, lift the child up and hold him in your arms, because I will make of him a great nation." Then God opened her eyes and she saw a well full of water; she went to it, filled her waterskin and gave the child a drink. God was with the child, and he grew up and lived in the wilderness of Paran. He became an archer.

Reflections by Elsa Tamez
(Costa Rica)

Let us read the Bible from a feminine and Third World perspective.

When we speak about women in the Bible, we think of the well-known women such as Deborah, Ruth, Sarah, Mary, and we soon come to the end of our story. These women are outstanding but isolated cases who have moved out of the traditional roles imposed on them by their male-dominated society, either because of their own exceptional lives or because of certain socio-political conditions at their moment of history.

It is very important that we learn to read the whole Bible from a liberating, feminine perspective, even when the text does not deal specifically with women.

I will not speak here of the great women of the Bible. I want instead to recall an unknown, forgotten woman who has been neglected in our traditional Bible reading. I refer to Hagar, the slave of the famous Sarah, the wife of Abraham.

Hagar is a woman who suffers a threefold oppression, like many women in the Third World. Hagar is thrice oppressed: because of her class (she is a slave); because of her race (she is an Egyptian, an impure race according to the Hebrews); and because of her sex (she is a woman). Who then is Hagar?

Hagar was a poor woman from Egypt who was sold as a slave. In Egypt, women were freer and had better social standing than in Israel, even though they still held an inferior position vis-à-vis men. Though this did not affect Hagar too much, because she was very poor, she at least knew a better world for women than the one she saw in Israel.

Hagar finds it very difficult to accept a society more male-oriented than her own. How can she go back to a better position such as was possible in Egypt? Hence Hagar refuses to submit to the will of her mistress Sarah. She prefers to be sent away from the house of Abraham than to live oppressed in it. She does not want to "butter up" Sarah her mistress to obtain her favor.

Sarah in turn does not want to have a rebellious slave in her home. As owner of Hagar, Sarah finally sends her away from her house. Thus both women prevail in their will.

Hagar does not know where to go with her son. The way is a desert. Hagar knows full well this means her death. Sarah also knows that this means Hagar will die.

When she and her son are about to die in the desert, Hagar does not call upon her Egyptian gods. Unable to watch her son die, she cries to the God of Israel, not because this God belongs to Israel, the nation that oppressed her, but because this God was the liberator who freed a whole nation from enslavement by the Egyptian empire. Paradoxically, Egypt was the country of her birth.

Yahweh hears the cry of Hagar and her son and appears to Hagar. Yahweh saves both the child and Hagar herself, freeing her from her slavery in Israel and blessing her with the promise of numerous descendants.

This epiphany of God is the only one in the Bible that happens to a woman. It is interesting to reflect on this point, because it reveals some important factors:

• God is in solidarity with the poor and oppressed.
• God is in solidarity with the poor of other peoples, of despised races and ethnic minorities.
• God is in solidarity with women.

Why do biblical commentators studying the biblical epiphanies omit the one to Hagar? Is it perhaps because they cannot understand how God would permit himself to be seen and experienced by an oppressed person, by a woman? Or perhaps they cannot accept that the true God is manifested even to those outside the "chosen people"?

Let this reading of the story of Hagar from the perspective of the poor and oppressed of the Third World be a challenge to the traditional interpretations in our churches and seminaries.

Magnificat
Luke 1:46–55

Tell out, my soul, the greatness of the Lord,
rejoice, rejoice, my spirit, in God my saviour;
so tenderly has he looked upon his servant,
   humble as she is.
For, from this day forth,
all generations will count me blessed.
  O God,
   look upon the downtrodden of Asia,
   especially the women,
   who are exploited, raped, and sacrificed
   every day to heartless idols,
   we pray.
Response: God of compassion, God of freedom, hear our prayer.

So wonderfully has he dealt with me,
   the Lord, the Mighty One.
   His name is Holy.
   Do great things for the people, especially the women,
   of Africa, in their search for authentic identity,
   in responding to your call, hallowing your name,
   we pray.
Response: God of compassion, God of freedom, hear our prayer.

His mercy is sure from generation to generation
   toward those who fear him;
the deeds his own right arm has done
   disclose his might:
the arrogant of heart and mind he has put to rout.
   Have mercy on the people, especially the women,
   of North America, the discouraged, the deprived,
   the little ones who take up the struggle
   against the demonic powers of violence, untruth, and greed,
   we pray.
Response: God of compassion, God of freedom, hear our prayer.

He has brought down monarchs from their thrones,
>   but the humble have been lifted high.
>   Lift up the lowly among the people of Central America,
>   especially the women,
>   that they may rise in strength and hope,
>   in their struggle for justice and freedom,
>   we pray.

Response: God of compassion, God of freedom, hear our prayer.

The hungry he has satisfied with good things,
>   the rich sent empty away.
>   Feed the people of Europe,
>   especially the women,
>   who hunger not for material wealth
>   but for the vital nourishment of their being,
>   we pray.

Response: God of compassion, God of freedom, hear our prayer.

He has ranged himself at the side of Israel his servant;
>   firm in his promise to our forefathers.
>   In your mercy may you be a true Helper,
>   a Deliverer and Liberator to the people of Latin America,
>   and especially to the women,
>   who are crushed by manifold oppression,
>   we pray.

Response: God of compassion, God of freedom, hear our prayer.

He has not forgotten to show mercy to Abraham
>   and his children's children, forever.

Let Us Pray

Mother/Father God,

We come to you with adoration, praising you because you are God our Creator, God our Sustainer, God our Liberator.

You have created us black, brown, yellow, white, and red; male and female. We praise you because, in the midst of oppression, trials, tribulations, pain, and injustice—caused by sinful human beings—you reign as our Sustainer.

As in the resurrection of Jesus Christ, you have shown us that suffering is not the end but that you are the supreme and final Liberator, who will free us from all that shackles and pains. You struggle with us so that our struggle is your struggle and your struggle is ours.

And now as we move into the work of the day to better understand our hour of history, we solicit your presence through your Holy Spirit.

Give us love where there is hate,
Strength where there is weakness,
Tolerance where there is impatience,
Openness where there is inflexibility,
Hope where there is discouragement.

This is our prayer. Amen.

PART V

FINAL STATEMENT

14

The Irruption of the Third World: Challenge to Theology

*Final Statement of the
Fifth EATWOT Conference,
New Delhi, August 17–29, 1981*

INTRODUCTION

(1) The fifth conference of the Ecumenical Association of Third World Theologians met in New Delhi, from August 17 to 29, 1981. The participants, fifty in all, came from twenty-seven different countries representing Africa, Asia, Latin America, the Caribbean, and minority groups in the U.S.A. They included observers from Europe and the U.S.A. We thank God for bringing us together within a common concern for the oppressed and suffering peoples of our continents. We are grateful for the experiences we have shared and the tasks to which we have been challenged.

(2) EATWOT was formed in Dar es Salaam, Tanzania, in August 1976, to foster the growth of theologies relevant to the lives, religions, and cultures of our people and to their struggles for full humanity.

(3) In Dar es Salaam we examined the political, social, economic, cultural, racial, and religious contexts of the Third World. We took note of the challenge they pose to Christian theology and to Christian witness to the gospel of Jesus Christ. We proposed new approaches and tasks to the theologians of the Third World. We also made an appeal to the churches for a self-evaluation before God in the face of global oppression.

(4) The conference in Accra, Ghana (December 1977), Wennappuwa, Sri Lanka (January 1979), and São Paulo, Brazil (February 1980), continued this work with special reference to the context of each of the three continents.

(5) It was after five years of theological research and reflection that we met

191

in New Delhi to evaluate our work, to put our insights and resources together, and to seek new direction for the future.

(6) India was an appropriate venue for this conference. The second most populous country in the world with 680 million people, it has played a leading role among Third World countries in their struggle for independence and autonomy. The enormous richness of its traditional cultures, the variety of its ancient religions, its industrial and technological development, and the wide contrast between its rich and its poor, make India a typical representative of Third World realities, challenges, and hopes.

(7) Our point of reference was always the Dar Es Salaam Conference of 1976, where EATWOT was formed and its program formulated. The unanimous decision of the group was to reaffirm the basic thrust of the Dar es Salaam and the subsequent conferences. This time in Delhi we deepened our Christian fellowship and discovered new common traits in our theologies, but we also saw that in language and approach these theologies had considerable differences. We came to realize that it was premature to talk of a synthesis of the past five years, or to describe Third World theology as one.

(8) The present document is a working instrument for further study and reflection—a document of transition from the first five-year period to the new program of another period of five years. From the many theological issues discussed, a few have been selected for inclusion here because of their importance for theology in the Third World. These issues, to be further refined and deepened, will be the core of our work for the next five years.

CHALLENGE OF REALITY TO THEOLOGY

(9) The analysis of the situation of the Third World countries presented in reports from the various regions and continents disclosed a general agreement that poverty and oppression are the most glaring characteristics of the Third World: massive poverty surrounding small islands of affluence and an oppressed majority vis-à-vis a powerful elite.

(10) Massive poverty grows and spreads like a mortal plague over the Third World where the majority of humankind lives. But this poverty is not an innocent social fact. It is the result of structures of exploitation and domination. Much of it stems from centuries of colonial rule and is reinforced by the present international economic system.

(11) Third World peoples are dominated by local elites in such a way that the masses are subjected to a double oppression: at the national as well as the international level. Local elites, in conjunction with international capitalist forces, determine patterns of development for the people, sacrificing the common good in favor of exhorbitant profits for the few.

(12) The underdevelopment of the Third World is the result of a process of international exploitation and accumulation by the rich countries. The rich world imposes an ordering of international relationships that throws the Third World into extreme misery that worsens every day. What makes this

situation more difficult is that technology, an essential element for our development, is controlled by the rich nations, deepening our dependence.

(13) This situation has brought about not only untold suffering and constriction of every aspect of the people's life—economic, political, cultural, racial, religious, and spiritual—but also untimely death to children, men, and women by the millions. Poverty dehumanizes not only the countless poor, but also the rich in that they benefit from the suffering of countless others and grow insensitive to the claims of life.

(14) Although material deprivation and economic exploitation are blatant and shocking realities of the Third World, other types of poverty and oppression are interwoven and interrelated with them. Classist oppression is compounded by discrimination based on race, color, sex, and caste.

(15) Caste is a mighty, divisive, and oppressive institution in India, deeply entrenched in the very flesh of the people and infecting all the limbs and movements of the nation. As a stratification of society in a hierarchical pattern of relationships, the caste system has its peculiar features, but it also has elements common with racist and classist structures elsewhere. Used for long as a tool and technique of "divide and conquer," caste still acts as the main obstacle to the unity and organization of all the exploited for an effective struggle against oppression in India.

(16) Racism is an evil still present in many societies in the world, expressing itself in various forms of dehumanization and segregation. Racist attitudes and policies have condemned the colonized and subdued populations to a subhuman condition. In South Africa especially, the ideology of apartheid ensures that at all levels whites dominate. Furthermore, the usurpation of the lands of the black peoples by the whites has placed them in a frightening state of dependency.

(17) Women everywhere and at all levels suffer immensely from male-dominated patterns of culture and social organization. Although women have contributed to the development of Third World countries, they have been accorded minority or inferior status. Women's oppression has been made more evident by their general absence in decision-making positions even on issues that radically affect them. This is true not only in society at large but in the churches as well. All religions without exception are guilty of discriminating against women.

(18) With the coming of capitalism and modernization in our Third World societies, there is additional evidence of women's inferior status: inequality in job opportunities and remuneration. Society on the whole has not recognized the economic value of women's full-time employment in rearing children and maintaining households. In Asia in more recent times, with the mushrooming of international tourism and free trade zones, Asian women have been forced to become part of the cheap labor market with inhuman and dangerous working conditions making them vulnerable to sexual exploitation that eventually leads to prostitution. In the case of migrant laborers to the Middle East, women are subject to abusive treatment especially in their

role of housemaids. Worse, there is hardly any provision for the legal defenses of their human rights.

(19) Poverty was not a univocal term at the conference. Although the majority stressed material poverty, others, particularly the Central Africans, emphasized anthropological or cultural poverty. For them this means the general impoverishment of their people. Colonialism brought about a loss of their identity and a diminishment of their creativity. It indiscriminately disrupted their communal tribal life and organization and destroyed their indigenous values, religious beliefs, and traditional culture. This result of the ravages of colonialism is now maintained by economic and cultural neocolonialism.

(20) Western domination has also harmed native cultures and religions. Changes in the mode of production have affected and often damaged the patterns of social and religious values that have shaped our communities for centuries. This has had serious consequences on the Indian and black populations of Latin America, the tribal societies in Africa, the millions of adherents of other world religions in Asia, and marginalized groups everywhere. Missionary enterprises and traditional theology, by imposing Western values, have also contributed, sometimes unwittingly, to the cultural impoverishment of the Third World.

(21) U.S. minorities find themselves in a difficult position as "internal colonies." They are discriminated against by the dominant Anglo-Saxon political and cultural system and at the same time identified with the First World by their Third World brothers and sisters. The Caribbean is the center of a new offensive of American cultural and economic imperialism.

(22) The rich countries are not without their serious problems. The process of accumulation of wealth and power in the hands of a few transnational corporations and rich nations is leading to a new crisis at the very center of capitalism. Recession, inflation, and large-scale unemployment are signs of this crisis. This crucial situation forces the capitalist countries to defend their economies in ways injurious to the Third World.

(23) Moreover, there is also a crisis of culture in the capitalist countries. There is a curtailment of quality of life and human relationships. This shows itself in youth unrest, exaggerated individualism, alcoholism, drug addiction, violence, loneliness, increasing suicide rate, wasteful lifestyles, and the like. The wasteful lifestyle of the affluent in the capitalist countries is leading to an escalating despoliation of nature and depletion of natural resources, dangerously threatening the future of nature and human life itself.

(24) In view of this gloomy picture of the capitalist world, socialism seems to offer the only viable alternative. However, socialist countries in both the Second World and the Third World have their own problems to solve. From the Dar es Salaam Conference to today, we have experienced a growing concern about the way socialism is being implemented. Struggle for civil and political rights, demands for greater participation, unemployment, internal power struggles, conflicts among socialist nations themselves, dependence on

capitalist economy, and remnants of feudal-capitalist mentalities and institutions are some of the issues present-day socialist countries have to face.

(25) Our present reality is more threatening due to the immediate danger of nuclear annihilation that faces all of humanity today. Humankind is faced as never before with the alternative of survival or annihilation. The arms race and nuclear buildup are not isolated phenomena. They are organic consequences of the new crisis of the global capitalist system. Structurally, capitalism needs arms production and warfare. But even though the initiative for the arms race comes from the West, it has forced socialist countries such as the U.S.S.R. into an arms buildup just as ruinous. This competition has become a threat and a burden to all countries of the world. We believe that to survive, the only wise course for Third World nations is to stay out of this ruinous race; to resolve their own problems peacefully, without being trapped by industrialists who promote wars; and to help create an international movement against war, arms buildup, and nuclear threat.

IRRUPTION OF THE THIRD WORLD

(26) Over against this dramatic picture of poverty, oppression, and the threat of total destruction a new consciousness has arisen among the downtrodden. This growing consciousness of the tragic reality of the Third World has caused an irruption of exploited classes, marginalized cultures, and humiliated races. They are bursting from the underside of history into the world long dominated by the West. It is an irruption expressed in revolutionary struggles, political uprisings, and liberation movements. It is an irruption of religious and ethnic groups looking for affirmation of their authentic identity, of women demanding recognition and equality, of youth protesting dominant systems and values. It is an irruption of all those who struggle for full humanity and for their rightful place in history.

(27) Inasmuch as the vast majority of the Third World people are those of other faiths, the irruption of the Third World is an irruption of a world that is not Christian. It is bursting into history with a voice of its own, demanding justice and equality, reaffirming its age-old religions and cultures, and challenging the West-oriented and narrowly Christian understanding of the world and of history. No social revolution in the Third World can be effective or lasting unless it takes into account and incorporates the religious experience of the people. This dawned upon our conference with a tremendous impact.

(28) The struggles of the oppressed for liberation throughout history have not been accidental or isolated events; they are part of a dialectical process. They are a reaction to overwhelming oppression, and, as a consequence, they elicit the violent counterreaction of oppressors. Threatened by the rising tide of the Third World, the powerful centers of capitalism, together with their local allies in our countries, have used every means to squelch all efforts toward liberation; they have stepped up repression and redoubled their ca-

pacity to destroy and to kill. Human and social rights have been suppressed. Summary imprisonment, torture, disappearances, and outright murder have become commonplace in many of our countries. Millions of our people have been displaced, expelled, or forced into refugee camps, uprooting them from home and families. In many countries of the Third World, military and dictatorial regimes, under the ideology of the national security state, have been set up to counteract the irruption of the masses. Police and paramilitary groups act with impunity against their own people, strengthened by the latest technology and systems of amassing information and the most modern instruments of torture and repression. To aggravate matters for Christians, there has been an upsurge of reactionary forces within Christianity in opposition to liberation struggles of all forms, reinforcing the repressive stance and policies of their governments.

(29) Our analysis of the world situation and especially of the Third World looks grim and discouraging. But as believers in the person, message, and power of the risen Christ, we see at the same time signs of life and hope amidst the darkness and injustice. We see hope in the rise of popular movements and the growth of basic Christian communities in Latin America, the anticolonial struggles and the revival of traditional religions and cultures in Asia and Africa. We see some hope in the pressure for a New International Economic Order and the demand for an effective North-South dialogue. We see as promising some of the socialist experiments in the Third World and the movement toward people's democracies with a strong anti-imperialist thrust.

The struggle against racism and sexist domination has become reinforced. Marginalized cultures and religions are asserting their will to autonomy and freedom. Communities of Christians and of those of other faiths, by their commitment to the poor and oppressed, are proving that religion is not the opium of the people. Bonds are deepening between the oppressed of the Third World and the exploited minorities of the rich countries. We are encouraged by developments in the First World, such as the feminist movement, the search for alternate lifestyles, the ecological defense of nature, antiwar and antinuclear organizations, and the networks of solidarity with Third World causes.

(30) Lastly, we are strengthened by the reaffirmation of our commitment to the gospel of life, love, and justice. We believe that life can be more authentically human and in keeping with biblical revelation through a more egalitarian and communitarian reorganization of our societies. We believe that the fundamental intuitions of pristine socialism are closer to the gospel teaching than are the tenets of capitalism. Yet we are critical of the weaknesses of the present and past attempts to implement socialism, though appreciative of their accomplishments. Socialism has to face these weaknesses; they need to be seriously analyzed and evaluated, and, where possible, challenged by prophetic witness to the gospel values.

(31) We reject the capitalism that has been responsible for most of the evils of our societies both from within and without. The challenge to the Third

World countries is to work out viable forms of socialism that would bring about economic development, as well as respect their religions, cultures, and human freedom. We commit ourselves to this search with hope and determination and in collaboration with all peoples struggling for the same ideal.

INADEQUACIES OF TRADITIONAL THEOLOGY

(32) After the study of our reality and its challenges, we looked at the response of the church and theology. We saw that the official mainstream theology of the Christian churches continues to be Western, with little relevance to our Third World situation. Though this traditional theology has provided an impetus for personal spirituality and for tremendous missionary expansion, it has been incapable of responding to the social problems of the First World and to the challenges of the Third World. For the Third World, this theology has been alienated and alienating. It has not provided the motivation for opposing the evils of racism, sexism, capitalism, colonialism, and neocolonialism. It has failed to understand our religions, indigenous cultures, and traditions, and to relate to them in a respectful way.

(33) The tools and categories of traditional theology are inadequate for doing theology in context. They are still too wedded to Western culture and the capitalist system. Traditional theology has not involved itself in the real drama of a people's life, or spoken in the religious and cultural idioms and expressions of the masses in a meaningful way. It has remained highly academic, speculative, and individualistic, without regard for the societal and structural aspects of sin.

(34) The Bible itself has not always been used to convey the liberating message of Jesus. Often it has been used to legitimize Christian participation in oppression, and to benefit the dominant group, class, and sex.

(35) Theology has often been unable to dialogue with other world religions in such a manner as to be enriched by the centuries of wisdom and profound faith experiences of their followers. It has generally failed to recognize worldviews that do not correspond to that of the West.

(36) To make theology relevant to the lives of our people, new approaches and perspectives are necessary. In recent years there have been attempts in the Third World to evolve a theology based on biblical reflection on struggles for liberation. There are also efforts toward the inculturation of theology from the anthropologico-cultural perspective.

(37) In the past five years we have noted some changes in theological approach in the First World. For the first time, some European theologians are talking about *European* theology, as distinguished from the old concept of universal theology. Some theologians in the U.S.A. are reviewing their theology and accepting the challenge posed by Latin American liberation theology. They are responding to the exigencies of their own situation as the center of the capitalist world and at the same time the home of many oppressed minorities. Churches and assemblies in both the First and Third

Worlds have begun to undertake the task of revamping their theology to make it more relevant to the times and to their constituencies.

ELEMENTS OF AN EMERGING METHODOLOGY

(38) We have realized the inadequacies of traditional theology, and in the last five years we have made some efforts to develop some general criteria that will make our theology more relevant. In our conference, we both reiterated and reformulated some of the elements of an emerging methodology.

(39) Action in service of the people is necessary for genuine theological reflection, but equally necessary is silent contemplation. To be committed to the people's struggle for social justice and to contemplate God within this involvement—both form the essential matrix of theology. Without this prayerful contemplation, God's face is only partially seen and God's word only partially heard within our participation in God's liberating and fulfilling action in history.

(40) The poor and oppressed are emerging from their culture of silence to speak their word in the world that has long tried to deny their existence. They have the elementary right to think. To reflect on their own lives and their own faith in God, the Liberator, is part of that right to think and exist. In this context, to do theology is no academic exercise. Many groups of grassroots Christians are engaging in this kind of reflection from their own liberating praxis—at times together with persons of other faiths and persuasions.

(41) The faith-based life interpretations of the masses, expressed in their cultural idioms, liturgies, workshops, storytelling, drama, songs, and poems, constitute genuine theology. In its formal sense, as an art and a science, theology is a discipline that requires technical or academic competence—but both forms of theology are relevant only if they stem from involvement and a liberated consciousness.

(42) The Bible is an integral basis of our faith reflections. There have been attempts to reread the Scriptures from the underside of history. Some critics consider this method of interpreting the Bible too subjective. With the help of the biblical scholars at the conference, we examined the broad principles of hermeneutics. Among other things, we were reminded that a religious text is based on an event, the praxis of a specific group—for example, the exodus. The text, however, does not exhaust the meaning of an event. Every reading is done from the perspective or mind-set of the reader. Even the technical scholar reads out of a particular perspective. The exodus itself, as the foundational event of the life of Israel was read differently at different stages in the history of the Jewish people, in the Old and New Testaments. So a reading today will be conditioned by our historical experience. And even our present reading will not exhaust the total meaning of this event.

(43) Social analysis is an indispensable mediation and basic equipment for a liberating theology. It indicates the way in which the values of the kingdom of love, justice, and truth are being realized or denied in diverse situations.

Without an adequate understanding of our societies, theologians cannot interpret the will of God for our societies and our times.

(44) We are convinced that a relevant theology for the Third World should include both the cultural and socio-economic aspects of the people's lives. In most theological efforts today, stress is on one to the near exclusion of the other. Most of the Latin Americans realize that their liberation theology has failed to include the cultural dimension of their people and the aspirations of marginalized groups of their continent. Some Africans, on the other hand, in stressing anthropology, traditional cultures, and religions, tend to give little consideration to the contemporary economic and political plight of their peoples. At the EATWOT Conference in 1979, it was strongly emphasized that Asian theology must focus both on Asia's poverty and Asia's religiousness. Clearly a synthesis of the religio-cultural and socio-economic elements remains a necessary task of Third World theology in the future.

THEOLOGY FROM THE OPPRESSED

(45) The starting point for Third World theologies is the struggle of the poor and the oppressed against all forms of injustice and domination. The committed involvement of Christians in this struggle provides a new *locus* for theological reflection. Their participation is faith in action and the manifestation of Christian commitment, which constitute the first act of theology (see the Dar es Salaam Statement).

(46) The struggle for a just world and full humanity is a participation in God's creative plan. God the Creator, Father/Mother of humanity, entrusted the earth to the whole human race to be developed as a means of life and fulfillment for all (Gen. 1:28–31). It is also a participation in Jesus' mission to bring to humankind life in abundance (John 10:10). It is one of the highest expressions of Christian love inspired by faith, leading even unto death for the sake of the other (John 15:12–13). It is a new dimension of a long tradition of love and service to one's neighbor that has deep biblical roots (Lev. 19:9–18; 1 John 3:11). Effective love and work toward a world of justice for our neighbor is more acceptable to God than are holocausts and burnt offerings (Hos. 6:6; Jer. 6:20; Mark 12:33).

(47) Poverty as experienced by the majority of God's children is a degradation of the divine image on earth and a diminution of human dignity and personhood. It is a social sin, to be attacked and eradicated. The exigencies of the gospel of love and sharing can best be experienced and articulated by those who are in need, by those who suffer, by those who are abused. It is the wounded who know the pain of wounds. The oppressed are those who best understand and are receptive to the promises of the kingdom (Matt. 5:3–11; Luke 10:21). The oppressor is insensitive to the demands of justice and love.

(48) Poverty and oppression are universal phenomena in the Third World. The groanings, yearnings, and cries for liberation of the masses reach out to heaven, and, as in the days of Moses, God continues to be Yahweh the Liber-

ator, who sees the affliction of the people and comes to deliver them (Exod. 3:7-9). In the struggle against oppression, God is revealed to be the saving God who acts in history. The experience of the Third World as a source of theology must be taken seriously.

(49) Women are especially discriminated against in the Third World. Theology both in the First World and Third World has for too long been a male, white theology, and should be liberated from these constraints. The sexist interpretation of Scripture to legitimize the subordination and oppression of women must be recognized as sinful and seriously falsifying the biblical revelation that God created the human being according to the divine image: Male and female God created them (Gen. 1:27). Theology and the church should be sincere in expressing this act of divine creation, and not merely making more room for women in ecclesiastical disciplines and institutions that continue to be patriarchal at heart. The common human experience of women in their liberational struggle constitutes a true source of theology. Christians must seriously consider the grave injustice toward womankind in their action and include women's perspectives in their theological reflection. Otherwise there can be no truly relevant theology, no genuine social transformation, no holistic human liberation.

(50) Racism is another form of oppression for millions of men and women all over the world. It is especially felt in South Africa where, to many blacks, Christianity is the religion of the oppressor, which has long supported the prevailing ideology of apartheid. When black peoples struggle to regain their humanity both by their fight against the socio-political structures of apartheid and by their challenge to the distorted image of Christ, God is involved in that struggle, and theology cannot ignore this dimension of God's presence. God works justice for all who are oppressed (Ps. 103:6).

(51) God has condemned oppression and has rejected every form of injustice. God assumes the suffering of the weak and powerless in Jesus Christ (Isa. 53:4-6). The oppressed are the presence of the crucified God. But the crucifixion is not the culmination of Jesus' life or of our faith. He was raised from the dead and, once and for all, he pronounced victory over the forces of darkness and death. In the struggle of the weak and powerless for light and life, the resurrection of Jesus becomes a historical experience and the resurrection of the downtrodden begins.

(52) This is the liberative praxis of the oppressed of the Third World. The faith reflection on this experience is authentic theology, and theology born of praxis is theopraxis. In the Third World, the poor and oppressed themselves are beginning to articulate their own reflections in both verbal and nonverbal forms. Though unsystematic and nonprofessional, this theopraxis—this faith-based interpretation of the struggle and religious experience of the poor by the poor—is a rich source of theological formulations in the Third World. Inasmuch as the poor are truly irrupting, then the God-image and expression of the poor must equally irrupt as the most meaningful image and expression of God in today's world.

CULTURE AND THE THEOLOGY OF RELIGIONS

(53) Culture is the foundation of the creativity and way of life of a people. It is the basis and bond of their collective identity. It expresses their world-view, their conception of the meaning of human existence and destiny, and their idea of God. It includes the historical manifestations of the people's creativity, such as their language, arts, social organization, philosophy, religion, and theology itself. Thus religion is culturally conditioned.

(54) Though in Latin America and the Philippines most of the population is Christian, in the rest of Asia and in Africa, which constitute three-fourths of the population of the Third World, the vast majority belong to other faiths. If this majority are irrupting into the Christian world, then Third World theology, to be truly meaningful and liberational, must speak to and through this world that is not Christian. Otherwise theology becomes an esoteric luxury of the Christian minority. Third World Christians are under the obligation to be alert to the claims of the oppressed of other faiths and to grasp the implications of their demands for the liberation of humankind, as well as for a more profound understanding of God and of history.

(55) The religions of the Third World peoples have shaped their life and thought for centuries. And these religions have been misrepresented and marginated by colonialism, the missionary enterprise, and traditional theology. History shows that the world religions have generally contributed to the alienation of the masses. But at different moments of history, they have also proven to be powerful motivational forces in popular struggles for independence and self-determination. Religion thus plays an ambiguous role in the lives of the people. Its potential for revolutionary change has been tapped by some, but it has been utilized by others to legitimate injustice and the status quo. The task lies before us to identify the liberating aspects of religions and cultures on the one hand, and their alienating, domesticating features on the other. It is a regrettable fact that in Asia, the birthplace of all world religions including Christianity, no serious, critical study of the Asian religio-cultural complex has yet been done.

(56) It is well known that liberation *(mukti)* has been a perennial quest of the world religions. Although the emphasis has been on internal and spiritual liberation, their search also includes dimensions with social relevance: the stress on freedom from greed as well as from overattachment to material or mental possessions and to one's private self. Voluntary poverty, so central to Asian religious ideals, and the simplicity of lifestyle it implies, are powerful antidotes to capitalist consumerism and to the worship of mammon.

(57) Christian theology must be open to learn from other religions. In the Third World, theology must develop in deep communion with the religions and cultures of the people. Unfortunately, the Christian evangelization of our part of the world was brought about by an aggressive Western culture that lessened our own appreciation of our indigenous cultures. For Christian

life and theology to become relevant for us in the Third World, the gospel of
Jesus should be able to meet our peoples in and through our cultures. To
make this possible, the core of the gospel must be disengaged from its Western, elitist wrappings and re-expressed in the cultural idiom of the poor and
oppressed of our continents. This work has already been initiated in Africa
and Asia.

(58) In our attempt to disengage our theology from its Western, dominant
moorings and to relate it to the other religions, we should learn from the
inadequacies of some attempts in Asia in the past.

"Fulfillment theology" (Christ is the fulfillment of all religions) was elaborated in the 1930s under Indian initiative to counteract the long-standing
"civilization theology" of the Western missionaries and colonizers, which
taught a Christ who was against all but the one true religion. Fulfillment
theology did not take into account the pervading poverty of Asia and failed to
recognize the Christ-of-the-poor, although it acknowledged the Christ-of-
the-religions.

The ashramic movement of the 1960s was a reaction to the development
theology of the West. Both recognized the poverty of Asia. Development
theology saw the cause as lack of economic growth; the ashramic movement
discerned the enemy as greed. The movement was unable, however, to move
from the micro-ethical level to the macro-structural, because it failed to see
the structural greed of systems and institutions. Lacking the full perspective,
members of the ashramic movement remained in passive solidarity with
Asia's poor and oppressed without actually participating in their struggle.

The most recent attempts to emphasize "inculturation" in opposition to
Latin American "liberation theology," gaining popularity in Asia, again
have their shortcomings. The church and theology must indeed be inculturated, but the advocates of inculturation fail to see the class culture they have
identified with. Culture and religion are not monolithic in Asia or anywhere
else. There are many cultures within one religion, and many religions within
one culture. Likewise there are different class positions in one religion.

(59) Adherents of other religions and beliefs also reveal some aspects of the
will and message of God for our times. As we Christians recognized God's
action in the events of Jewish history, so we must learn to discern God's
presence among the oppressed of other faiths as they struggle for full humanity in the Third World today. Their sacred scriptures and traditions are also a
source of revelation for us. This consideration of divine revelation enables us
to see that the concept of the "people of God" should be widened to include
not only believers of other faiths but the whole of humanity—all of whom the
God of the Bible wishes to bring to life and self-understanding.

(60) We favor ongoing dialogue between Christians and the members of
other religions. But this dialogue cannot remain only on an intellectual level
about God, salvation, human fulfillment, or other such concepts. Beyond
dialogue, there must be collaborative action for the integral liberation of the
oppressed, not only action to change unjust and oppressive social structures

but also attempts to regain our lost identity and life-giving values. Our common praxis with the people of other faiths is a valid source of theology in the Third World.

THE GOD OF LIFE AND THE KINGDOM

(61) Poverty and oppression in the Third World are not just a situation of deprivation; they bring unjust and untimely death to millions of women, men, and children through hunger, disease, and repression. But death in the Third World is not only physical. Countless persons are degraded and have suffered the loss of their identity, dignity, and personhood. Not only individual persons are killed, but also entire cultures and religious traditions have been annihilated by colonialism and by more modern forms of repression. The poor and the oppressed are struggling not only for a better economic standard but for freedom and dignity, for life and full humanity. They risk their life for the sake of life, and undergo death to undo the powers of death.

(62) We find in the Third World a dialectical tension between life and death, manifested in different ways. In Asia, despite the tendency to reconcile and harmonize opposites, this tension between strong affirmation of life and emphatic renunciation of life continues. In the African worldview, the cosmos is seen as a permanent struggle between life and death. In Latin America, physical death of the victims of repression has become a source of life for the Christian community. This dialectical relationship challenges us to deepen the meaning of our faith in the God of life. Third World theology is thus led to a constitutive dimension of our biblical faith: through Jesus' death, God overcame death (2 Tim. 1:10). God has overcome death in all its forms and shapes. This is the source of our hope that life-giving forces will finally triumph. To believe in this God of life is to believe in love, justice, peace, truth, and human fulfillment. It is to denounce the causes of the dehumanization of our people and to fight against the systems that shorten and extinguish the lives of so many.

(63) To proclaim a God who does not see the plight of the poor and does not act in their favor is to preach a God of death, a dead God. When the forces of death are free to kill, God's reality is not recognized. When life is ignored or cruelly crushed, false Gods are set up. This is idolatry (Exod. 20:2–6). In the Third World, the opposite of faith is not atheism but idolatry.

(64) We cannot separate God from the kingdom of God. Jesus did not bear witness to himself but to the reality of God and the kingdom. The kingdom of God is the kingdom of life. In inaugurating the kingdom, Jesus performed signs of life: healing the sick, feeding the hungry, restoring the outcast, and setting the downtrodden free (Luke 7:22). He came to give life—in abundance (John 10:10).

(65) The kingdom of life is revealed above all in the resurrection of Jesus. The resurrection means that new life and new humanity is taking shape right within the struggle of the victims of injustice, even in their death. This is the

historical realization of the paschal mystery in the Third World (Rom. 6:5-11; 1 Pet. 1:3).

(66) To be a follower of Jesus is to witness to his life, death, and resurrection. Discipleship calls for participation in the struggle of the oppressed for the transformation of social structures and the renewal of cultures. At the same time it demands a conversion of ourselves and of our distorted relationships. This is what it means to love one's neighbor; this is what it means to be a Christian in the Third World today (1 John 3:18).

(67) A renewal of theology should bring about not only new articulations but a new spirituality deriving from the positive inspirations of our cultures and of our struggles. Different regions have different emphasis in the expression of their spirituality. Two examples: the report from Central America states that many Christians in that area are reliving the exodus, the covenant, and the paschal mystery, and discovering the saving God in that experience. The report from India makes an effort to link Christian spirituality with the different ways of experiencing the divine in the Indian traditions: the cosmic, the gnostic, and the totalizing. The report stresses the need to recapture the very Indian and positive dimension of all three and hold them in living unity, liberated from every kind of alienation and misuse.

(68) At the daily worship during the conference, the continental groups showed a variety of ways to express their search for God and their own spirituality. The worship service prepared by the women reflected the women's perspective in Christian prayer and in rereading the Bible. A few at the conference questioned the reinterpretation of the biblical message in nonsexist terms, but in the end it was generally acknowledged that this was an integral part of the women's attempt to express their reflections and spirituality arising from their specific struggle.

(69) The values of the kingdom and new ways of spirituality are being lived and experienced in small Christian communities. Though more widely known in Latin America, these communities are a sign of renewal and hope in many Third World countries. Christians get together to pray, study the Bible, share their pain and joy, celebrate the Eucharist, and strengthen their commitment to the people (Acts 2:42, 46, 47). In a growing number of these communities a new form of ecumenism based on common praxis and a new synthesis of faith and political action are developing.

(70) When Christians in the Third World actively engage in changing structures and the mind-sets behind them, they face opposition and sometimes persecution. In many countries, the commitment of Christians is felt as a threat by economic and military powers, who have made them a special target of their repressive activities, inaugurating a new era of persecution and martyrdom (Luke 21:12; John 15:20). As in the early centuries, Christians are accused of being subverters of their societies and made to pay with their lives for the crime of supporting the people's struggles. They are rejected and ostracized by some in their own worship communities for siding with the masses (Luke 21:16-17).

(71) The era of persecution is becoming a new era of the Spirit in the Chris-

tian communities of the Third World. The words of Jesus about losing one's life, taking up the cross, and following his path have become a dramatic reality in many countries (Matt. 10:38–39). But suffering and death do not have the final say (John 3:14,16). We thank God that in our time many Christians have joined the oppressed in their struggle for justice (Matt. 5:10–11). We humbly ask of God the grace to follow the path traced by the blood of our martyrs.

CONCLUSION AND ORIENTATIONS

(72) The irruption of the poor and oppressed does not automatically lead to the victory of justice. Besides direct acts of violence against them, divisions among the oppressed are manipulated to pit them against one another. As Third World Christians and theologians, we wish to stand with our people in resisting the forces that try to divide, to weaken, and to destroy them. We want to place our energies and theological resources at their service for the greater realization of justice and freedom in our world. This is to participate actively in the liberating mission of Jesus (Luke 4:18–19).

(73) After our days of work, prayer, and fellowship, we decided to recommit ourselves as an association to continue our work toward a more relevant theology for the Third World for a period of another five years. Among our program goals for this next five-year period, we see as priorities:

   a. evolving a process of doing theology in and from the situation of struggle in our lands and helping to orient Christian and ministerial formation in this direction;

   b. developing a synthesis between the two major trends in Third World theologies: the socio-economic and the religio-cultural, both of which are essential for integral liberation;

   c. supporting women's struggle for equality in and through theology.

   We agreed on three concrete ways of implementing our goals:

   a. working commissions on the continental level;

   b. international dialogues with special groups;

   c. an intercontinental conference and assembly at the end of the next five-year period.

(74) Our tasks, general and specific, include:

   a. preparing a dialogue with First World theologians on how the struggles of the oppressed lead to a better understanding of God in different contexts;

   b. forming continental working groups on cultures and religions and their relationship to integral liberation, and on church history from the perspective of the oppressed;

   c. organizing a theological conference on women to further their liberation efforts in the churches and in society;

   d. initiating a program of interchange among Third World theologians through longer transcontinental visits, the translation of their works, and the publication of bibliographies;

   e. denouncing antijustice evangelistic efforts that unfortunately divide

Christians and prevent the development of a more relevant theology for our times;

f. communicating demands of justice by the oppressed to the churches at the centers of power;

g. cooperating with international agencies promoting the values of justice, freedom, equality, and peace, human and social rights, the rehabilitation of refugees, and the preservation of nature.

(75) Coming to the end of our document, we wish to express our gratitude to God for the guidance and insights we have received. We also thank all those in New Delhi and elsewhere who have made our coming together possible. We want to share this document with our brothers and sisters who quest for a meaningful Christianity in our world and a full human life for all. May the God of Life, the source of our strength and our hope, be with us in our quest.

PART VI

EVALUATION AND INTERPRETATION

15

Reflections from an Asian Perspective

J.C. Duraisingh and K.C. Abraham

In Asia we are increasingly aware of our theological task as primarily articulating the liberative potentialities of the gospel in a context that is being
shaped by persons and cultures of other faiths and ideologies. Our commitment is to the liberation of persons and societies.

In the past decades we have made some attempt in the area of indigenization, taking seriously the philosophical and existential questions of the situation. We recognize this as still valid and necessary, but we are aware that the
new situation emerging in our countries as a result of the irruption of the poor
and oppressed has raised a new set of questions and challenges. Theologies
responding to this new situation have to make a preferential option for the
poor. For many of us this is a new and exciting task—a task that involves a
definite breakaway from the style and method of theologizing in the past.

Although we are clear as to what we want to reject, we are not quite certain
about the future. We are also bewildered by the complexity of our situation,
which in a way is intensified by the impact of resurgent forms of religions and
ideologies. It is, therefore, with a sense of the demand of the context, a not
too clear sense of direction and a desire to learn from a group of theologians
who have made the option for the poor, that we ourselves participated in the
1981 EATWOT Conference. Our participation was rewarding and stimulating. It brought us in contact with theologians from three continents, the
Caribbean, and the U.S.A. who are struggling with questions of contextual
theology. It has raised new questions and challenges for our own task. The
reflections that are given below are personal, although we hope they may
represent the concerns of many fellow theologians in Asia.

THE THIRD WORLD REALITY

The factors that unite Third World countries in their struggle for justice
were clearly brought to our attention in the conference. The colonial past and

the continuing exploitation by neocolonial forces generate identical problems of economic domination in the international context. We all seem to be caught up in the power game of superpowers and, much against our will, we are divided among ourselves. This makes it impossible for us to tap the inherent potentialities of our unity.

The poverty of the masses in all these countries is appalling. There is the dominance of elites, a minority over the masses, which perpetuates the misery of poverty, unequal distribution, and plummeting unemployment. What is also significant about these situations is the awakening of the masses to their rights and a new determination to fight the forces of economic domination and social oppression. In this sense the irruption of the poor and the oppressed is the most significant development in the Third World. The struggle against various forms of death is going on in these countries. We affirm these common characteristics in any analysis of Third World reality.

One cannot, however, ignore the specificity of each continent. Latin American countries are economically exploited by capitalist forces. The dehumanizing process that sets in as a result of it can be analyzed and combatted against on the basis of an ideology that "makes sense" about economic developments in the modern world. Many Asian countries, although the economic factor has assumed a certain preponderance in their recent histories, have to contend with oppressive and dehumanizing forces of age-old traditions and religions in their fight for a just order. As the Asian document has clearly stated, our problem is the problem of poverty *and* religion.

It was also a discovery for at least some of the Asian participants that there was a wide difference in the climate and ethos within which the theologians of Latin America and Asia were theologizing. The so-called Christian context in the former may make it easier for theologians to interpret biblical symbols and language. Most of the Asian countries, as we know, are non-Christian and the majority religion in each country determines its common culture, language, and symbols. This also raises in a unique way for those of us from Asia the question of our identity. We are involved in the liberative praxis along with fellow Asians who use symbols and idioms drawn from traditions other than Christian to articulate their concerns. In the Delhi conference this was not a major concern for many. In an Asian agenda of theological reflection this should be seriously considered.

Ambiguities and uncertainties about the nature of the political order one strives for in one's own context were paralleled in the discussions at the conference. Among the participants there were many who were very sure of their ideology and therefore sure of the response they should make. But there were others still struggling to find an adequate framework that took into account all the dominant elements of their situation. There were committed socialists, and others who were disillusioned by the socialist system. There were revolutionaries talking the language of politics; there were others searching for forms of radical spirituality for their struggles. In short, the conference was a forum that used different idioms and languages, and therefore at times the dialogue tended to be frustrating.

Even though no notable progress in the ongoing task of theological reflection in the Third World was made by the Delhi conference, it has raised many important questions for us. In this short reflection we will attempt to mention some of them and indicate their relevance to our task in Asia.

THE NEED FOR AN ADEQUATE FRAMEWORK
OF INTERPRETATION

It is agreed that conditions of poverty are the effect of unjust structures and a false system of economy. To make us aware of these structures of domination and to provide a perspective for action, we need ideologies based on an analysis of social and economic forces of a given context as they interpenetrate with global realities. Marxism has played a specific role in providing an understanding of the economic forces at work and their impact on history. The growth of capitalism and the continuing misery it causes, even to the extent of taking the entire world to the brink of total destruction, are sharply brought to light by Marxist analysis.

All the participants seemed to have agreed about the continuing relevance of Marxist analysis, but there was the feeling that it was not comprehensive enough to respond to certain issues that were specific to some situations. We share this doubt about the adequacy of Marxian ideology for interpreting the cultural and religious realities of Asia. For example, even responsible Marxist thinkers in India will agree that caste structure and its manifestations in the power politics in India cannot be understood solely in terms of the classic Marxist theory of class conflict. It should be modified in the light of Indian experience.

This and other similar concerns have prompted a group of Christian activists in India, who have taken Marxian insights for their interpretation of Indian reality and for their action, to say that there is need for a "critical understanding of Marxism in the Indian context" and for evolving "a relevant revolutionary ideology for India."[1] Again, Aloysius Pieris of Sri Lanka has repeatedly drawn our attention to the occidental character of Marxism and its incapacity to come to terms with the religious reality of Asia. He affirms that "a liberation theopraxis in Asia which uses only the Marxist tools of *social* analysis will remain un-Asian and ineffective until it integrates the psychological tools of *introspection* which our sages have discovered."[2]

It should also be pointed out that many of the participants at the Delhi conference expressed their uneasiness about the socialist system that is at work in the so-called socialist countries. All will agree that these countries too are a party to the present arms race and contribute their share to the resultant crisis. We too are committed to the socialist society, but we find it difficult to identify with every manifestation of it. The problem is more acutely felt in Asia, which has become the scene of continuing exploitation by all the superpowers and the *locus* of their competitive display of military strength creating new tensions.

The final statement of the Delhi meeting reflects this dilemma. It has to be faced in concrete situations. Certainly in many countries in Asia a critical look at Marxian ideology and the search for a more adequate framework will open up a fruitful dialogue between all who are committed to the liberation of the oppressed.

SPECIFICALLY ASIAN QUESTIONS

In sharp contrast to its earlier gatherings, the EATWOT meeting in Delhi endeavored to respond to the religious question. We recognize this as a new beginning for EATWOT's theological task. The Final Statement has given a pointed expression to this:

> To be committed to the people's struggle for social justice and to con-
> template God within this involvement—both form the essential matrix
> of theology. Without this prayerful contemplation, God's face is only
> partially seen and God's word only partially heard within our participa-
> tion in God's liberating and fulfilling action in history.[3]

The positive attitude toward other faiths and a newer appreciation of the humanizing elements within them are significant for the theological task in Asia. When the hitherto submerged masses in Asia are awakened to the task of nation-building, there comes a new resurgence of their religious and cultural heritage. Values enshrined in old religions and traditions are sub-jected to critical scrutiny. Some are rejected, some are reinterpreted, and others are reaffirmed with renewed vigor. Not only the protest movements of the past, but also a contemporary social protest by the untouchables in the form of mass conversions to Buddhism and Islam clearly show the re-ligious matrix of liberation experience in India. We need to enter into this process and discover the liberative potentialities of religious experience in Asia.

However, we also affirm the ambiguous nature of our religious and cultural heritage, as the Delhi conference has correctly observed. We in Asia are prone to the danger of romanticizing the ancient religions and accepting them uncritically.

For example, India is a land of great religions. Its seers and saints have made important contributions to heightened human self-awareness and awareness of the world. But this land has also seen the worst of these reli-gions. They have been used for exploiting the masses and for protecting the vested interests of the high and mighty. For example, contemplation and silence have been used to suppress the masses. The masses were made to accept passively their suffering, resorting to other-worldly flights from real-ity.

We need to probe further into the essential character of Asian spirituality. Here it is difficult to enter into a detailed inquiry, but we want to mention a few aspects of Asian spirituality that pose a challenge to Christian theol-ogy.

Transcendence

The Asian religious heritage teaches us that until we are enabled to recognize the inseparability of our concrete action of liberation and the ultimate ground of it—God—there can be no authentic *mukti*, liberation. Although the conference rightly occupied us with urgent issues calling for immediate action, very little time was spent together in prayer and faithful celebration of God, the ultimate source of our liberation. The little we did—notably, the Indian Mass—powerfully highlighted the relevance of this conscious reminder to ourselves that our praxis is rooted in the just and liberating God. This dimension of ultimate reality—transcendence—is necessary for any process of authentic humanization.

M. M. Thomas in his analysis of modern ideologies has helped us to see how "self-sufficient secularism," which "rejects the dimension of transcendence for human existence, became closed and dehumanizing."[4] He calls for a spirituality that is open to the dimension of the "beyond" and at the same time takes us to the liberation struggles in history.

Within such a spirituality the search for personal meaning can find expression in its relatedness to the process of total liberation. The gospel of Jesus Christ is inclusive, not exclusive, in its taking up of the questions of bondage, sin, and death as they are experienced in the personal as well as the social realities of our lives.

Suffering

The heart of Asian spirituality is to be found in its response to human pain and suffering. The genius of Buddha, for example, was that he provided a new perspective on the creative meaning of suffering. Great saints and gurus were one with the people in their pain. Theirs is not the spirituality of manipulative power and strength, although there is much of it in Asian tradition, just as it is present in every other religious tradition. But they insisted on the value of sacrifice and the strength of love and truth.

Powerlessness

Asian spirituality challenges us to take a new look at our concept of power. Asian mythologies are full of stories that show how the ruthless power of despotic rulers is thwarted by the patient suffering and tears of ordinary men and women. This is the *kenosis* principle (Phil. 2) of God's solidarity with humankind found in Christian tradition. Christ, who was all-powerful and all-privileged, was willing to empty himself. God's powerlessness can be transformed into powerfulness by love. Life gains its fulness in giving, not in having. Hope is experienced in the midst of suffering. This very Asian and at the same time Christian idea of power and fulness of life should provide a new direction to our theology.

Recently C. S. Song of Taiwan has given expression to this concern in his theological interpretation of a Chinese folk tale called "The Faithful Lady Meng." He ends his reflections with these poignant words:

> Our political theology is located in the spaces created by the spiritual power of Asian people in suffering. And our power ethic is the ethic that believes in the Ultimate victory of God who lives with people and gives them the power of truth, love and justice. If this is God's politics, it should be ours also.[5]

Wholeness

Asian spirituality confronts us with a vision of the whole of human nature that takes seriously our relationship with our fellow humans and with the cosmos. To be preoccupied in our theology with the dimension of history in isolation from the cosmos is inadequate. The vision of Christ, the Lord of the cosmos, who initiates a process of transformation that moves toward cosmic release, stands at the very center of our Christian affirmation.

In Asia and elsewhere the plane of human history and the plane of nature can never be set in opposition. It is in the search for the liberation of all aspects of human life, culture, and natural environment that we can truly affirm that salvation is the wholeness of all God's creation.

The suffering and hope of Asia's teeming multitudes cannot but be the central focus of our theological reflection. Our commitment is not primarily to programs of liberation but to human beings. We also recognize that the church in Asia is part of the total movement of Asian peoples for liberation. This concern is forcefully articulated by Korean Christians in their *minjung* theology.[6]

A NEW DIRECTION

We consider it significant that the Delhi conference raised hermeneutics as one of its primary concerns. We affirm that our theological enterprise consists in discovering and articulating the liberating presence of God in the history that peoples are forging through their struggle against oppression of every kind. The question is, how to do this?

Theology in Popular Idiom

Theology need not be rational discourse on philosophical questions about humankind and God. In fact we are increasingly convinced that settling questions of logic and truth that have no direct relevance to human liberation need not be our concern.

The faith articulation of a people involved in the struggle for freedom can perhaps be best expressed in story, song, symbols, and drama. Theology in the liberating idiom of the people can equip the people for the struggle, can arm it with vision, discernment, motivation, hope, and courage.

Theology in a Real-Life Context

However, theology is more than storytelling and description of events. Stories and facts must be interpreted in the light of text and tradition, and in interaction with concrete situations and new contexts. The question is how to interpret the biblical materials in terms of a dominant concern for the contemporary situation—namely, the removal of present oppressive structures. Biblical symbols, stories, and narratives are peculiarly relevant to such a task, for they emerged out of a people's struggle in a concrete situation. They describe the agonies and joys of a real people; their questions and answers. Today this "people character" of the Bible is made obscure by professionals. There should be a process by which the Bible could be reappropriated by a people, to be used by it for the articulation of its faith.

In this we are encouraged by the testimonies of some of the Latin American delegates to the conference who are involved with ordinary persons in interpreting the Bible and tradition in the context of their struggle. We are challenged that in many of our Asian countries we have yet to discover this people-character of the Bible. It is disheartening to observe that we do not yet have in India, for example, commentaries on the Bible that arise out of the context of a people's struggle.

It should be mentioned that in this interpretative process we are not alone. We are aware of the various attempts in our histories to interpret our religious and secular memories, myths, and symbols from the standpoint of social and liberating praxis. EATWOT has not done all it could to explore and make known such hermeneutical experiments in Third World religious and social histories.

We feel that Asian theologians have a special responsibility to search for paradigms, folktales, and symbols in other faiths and traditions, to bring out their liberative potentialities.

A prerequisite for the above is, we feel, a correct perspective on religion. The task of developing a liberative idea of religion in conversation with adherents of other faiths is incumbent on Asian theologians. We have not paid sufficient attention to this.

THE ROLE OF EATWOT

Our final comments are on the structure and the continued usefulness of EATWOT.

We are convinced that the movement character of EATWOT should be maintained in order that it may continue to play a creative role. Preoccupation with organizational and constitutional matters can be self-defeating.

What we need is a flexible structure that is ready to seek and initiate new ways of theologizing.

It is important for EATWOT to maintain the distinct identity of each constituent body within its fellowship. To strive toward a monolithic structure and to endeavor to speak with one voice to the world may not fully express, and even smother, the dynamism of the inner dialogue of fellowship. A forum such as EATWOT should facilitate participant groups to bring to the fore their specific concerns to bear on the overall task of liberation. Such an enterprise will necessarily be marked by tension and at times the process of collective thinking will be slow. But creative contributions can come only by a free encounter between partners who respect each other and are willing to learn from each another. The decision to promote regional fellowship and study commissions will go a long way in meeting this need.

We are impressed by the fact that many of the creative contributions in theology are by persons who are involved at grassroots levels in pastoral ministry and concrete struggles of liberation in different parts of the Third World. This leads us to affirm that genuine theology is born out of a people's struggle for liberation and therefore no Third World theologian can remain in isolation from the people. EATWOT is a fellowship of committed theologians, not an academic professional society.

This perspective has serious implications for theological education—its method, curricula, and pattern of teaching, especially for Asian churches. Our hope is that other conferences like the Delhi meeting will provide enough impetus to face them and to respond to them in a creative way.

It is essential to maintain the ecumenical character of EATWOT. The recommendation of the Delhi conference to initiate a dialogue with First World theologians who are concerned about liberation is a step in the right direction to help the association to widen its horizon of experience. We want to suggest that such dialogue should also be started with people of other faiths and ideologies who are actively participating in concrete struggles for liberation. A genuinely people-oriented theology can evolve only when Christian theologians enter into active communion with concerned and committed persons with other faiths and ideologies.

NOTES

1. "Political Process and Action Groups in India—A Statement of Consultation" (New Delhi: Forum for Christian Concern for Peoples' Struggles, July 6–10, 1981), p. 9.

2. Aloysius Pieris, "Towards an Asian Theology of Liberation: Some Religio-Cultural Guidelines," in Virginia Fabella, ed., *Asia's Struggle for Full Humanity* (Maryknoll, N.Y.: Orbis, 1980), p. 88.

3. No. 39.

4. M. M. Thomas, *Salvation and Humanization* (Madras: CLS, 1971), p. 43.

5. C. S. Song, *The Tears of Lady Meng* (Maryknoll, N.Y.: Orbis, 1982), pp. 65–66.

6. For a detailed discussion, see Kim Yong Bock, ed., *Minjung Theology* (Singapore: Christian Conference of Asia, 1981; rev. ed.: Maryknoll, N.Y.: Orbis, forthcoming).

16

Third World Theology—
What Theology? What Third World?:
Evaluation by an African Delegate

Engelbert Mveng

From an African delegate's viewpoint, the New Delhi Conference was a new beginning, on two levels in particular. First, it enabled EATWOT to dispel all the misunderstandings that had plagued it since its foundation. Secondly, it laid the groundwork for a truly joint enterprise in the area of Third World theology—an enterprise that will both transcend and respect the peculiar differences of each continent. (This is the only legitimate meaning of "contextualization.") One may say, then, that New Delhi gave birth to great hopes—meaning, not hopes for us, the "marginalized by definition," but hopes for the worldwide church, as it turns toward the Third World today with mixed sentiments of uneasiness and hope.

First, New Delhi enabled us to dispel misunderstandings—historical misunderstandings. EATWOT is in its origin neither Latin American nor Asian. It is of African inspiration. It was an African project. It was born in Louvain, of confrontation and dialogue among young African theologians (its inspirers) in company with their Belgian, Latin American, and Asian colleagues. We are grateful to Father Bimwenyi Kweshi for having dispelled all misunderstanding on this point.

Many another misunderstanding lurked within the first. For a number of ill-informed elements of the world press, EATWOT is simply an institutionalization of the Latin American theology of liberation. Here, then, was another point on which we had to be very clear. Long before our association came into being, various currents of liberation theology existed—in Latin America, in the United States, in Africa (especially in South Africa), and in Asia. These currents, very different from one another in their context, their methodology, and their analyses, did not depend on, did not flow from, the Latin American current.

An organized group of Third World theologians can legitimately constitute no more than a locus of discussion and dialogue, based on their sometimes analogous, sometimes convergent—but always different—experiences.
It cannot constitute a "school," and least of all a school of theology, where
some are masters and the others, the herd, are students or disciples.

During the first five years of its existence, the association lent a ray of
verisimilitude to these misunderstandings by the manner in which it conducted itself. We had provisional statutes, but they were hardly ever applied.
We had an intercontinental Advisory Committee, but only two or three of its
members were active, and they often acted without the knowledge of the
(Asian) president, and almost always in the absence of the African member,
who was never invited to its meetings. On the eve of the New Delhi conference, no directorial report had been forthcoming in five years. And,
strangely, although the program of this general assembly made provision for
the presentation of a theological report by all the other continents, Africa was
excluded. Our delegation was invited in the capacity of auditors.

Evidently, Africa is not taken seriously. Even in the Third World itself, in
an association of theologians, Africa remains the everlastingly marginalized
—not to say forgotten!—continent.

This oblivion concealed still further misunderstandings and ambiguities.
We hear much about the "Third World." But whose definition of the "Third
World" are you going to use? One had the impression—and heaven grant
that it be only an impression—that, behind this concept of a "Third World,"
new struggles for hegemony lurked. Who is going to assume leadership in the
Third World?

For some, there seemed already to be an answer to this question as far as
theology was concerned. Who has the right to speak in the Third World?
Why are there so many absent, so many forgotten? Is it too early to invite the
Australian aborigines? The blacks of Brazil, and the native Latin Americans—all the descendants of the Incas, the Aztecs, and all those basic Christian communities that dot the rainforests, the mountain ranges, and the
pampas—where are *their* representatives? What about *their* way of encountering Christ or turning from him, of *their* way of building, and living,
church, of being the people of God—who will tell us of all this if they are
absent? How shall we fashion a theology of the Third World without them?
What kind of "Third World theology" would we have if it were a theology
they would not recognize?

And here is where the basic ambiguity of the theology of liberation comes
to light. Liberation is the liberation of all these absent ones, all these persons
who have no right to speak. We have a problem here. The problem is not the
liberation, the deliverance, that constitutes the very essence of revelation, the
freedom that Christ has won for all human beings at the cost of his passion,
death, and resurrection. The problem is to know what that liberation of his
means concretely for each and every human being, in his or her actual situation today.

"Liberation" is a confusing notion for many. Why? Because the poor, the oppressed, the marginalized, have no right to speak out and tell us what liberation means for them. There are as many "liberations" as there are concrete situations of oppression, domination, and contempt. Let us never forget that the rejection of the gospel law of love of one's brothers and sisters has become institutionalized. The situation of the black minorities of the United States and the Caribbean, the situation of the blacks of South Africa (indeed of all Africa), the situation of the exploited masses of Latin America and Asia—all this constitutes the state of sin that obtains throughout "civilization" today. All these victims have a thousand reasons for solidarity. Indeed this is one of the basic premises of the Ecumenical Association of Third World Theologians.

Not everyone, unfortunately, has the right to speak. Hence those who do speak may not be allowed to simplify things to the point of universalizing their particular cases, and to present themselves as type, model, and only true instance of the matter at issue, as if they were capable of recapitulating in their own particularity the limitless diversity of all world situations.

Hence the rise of the specter of intellectual, cultural, sociological, economic, and religious imperialism, which manufactures its models and imposes them on the world. This is what I referred to above: the temptation to hegemony. This temptation secretes the myth of the "civilizing" (or "liberating") peoples. It deprives the poor, the oppressed, the marginalized, of their one chance for salvation: to liberate themselves. Thus new types of paternalism are born, and one of them is the attempt an intercontinental association might make to take a continental association under its tutelage. Our Ecumenical Association of African Theologians, for its part, refuses to be taken under another association's tutelage.

Then let that other association cease forthwith to pretend to speak in our name, to represent us, to take up collections for us, as if we had no existence of our own. Those who wish to take Africa seriously will dialogue with Africa, and not with intermediaries—especially unauthorized intermediaries.

This temptation to hegemony, in its own turn, entails still other types of misunderstandings and ambiguities. For example, a vocabulary—a discourse—is now formed that seeks to impose itself upon the Third World. Methodologies and systems of analysis are proclaimed that are said to be "universal." Appeal is made to the humane sciences, to structuralism, and to the new exegesis, in order to "teach" us, everlasting school children that we are. All these things are fine, of course—for *their* schools. The only problem with them is they contribute nothing to the solution of *our* problems. We have not gone that far. That is, we have gone much farther than that.

Here, then, we Africans are existentially and tragically alone. No one can do our encounter with Christ for us. Nor can anyone else take responsibility for what we do, because we believe we must.

The debate at New Delhi was an ebullient one, from every standpoint. And yet, all passions were surmounted and transcended, and we entered into a dialogue.

The first hurdle to be cleared was the temptation to spin around in circles in our evaluation of our various situations, by practically repeating what had already been said in Dar es Salaam, Accra, Wennappuwa, and São Paulo. To be sure, far from having improved over the last ten years, the world has only seen its chains of oppression grow heavier still. But the basic problem resides in the transition from analysis to praxis. Are we simply to describe and criticize the situation in the world and the church, or are we to change it? And if we are to change it, how, and by what means?

Let us face the facts: on the level of transition to praxis, reflection often lacks a certain maturity. We thank our colleagues for sharing with us, over the years, their Marxist analysis, their socialist projections for the society of the future, and their contextual reading of the Bible. But we are not satisfied. First of all, the basic problem remains the foundations of Western anthropology, which would impose themselves upon the world. The concept of the human being that the West seeks to export to us is based on domination, power, death struggle, and so on—the triumph of death over life. There has never been a way to avoid an impasse. It is not easy to see how all this can be reconciled with the gospel.

We hear of the church of the poor, and we are directed to the Beatitudes. But poverty is defined first of all in function of one's conception of the human being—and here we are back with anthropology again. Of course there is capital, of course there is the class struggle, of course there is the exploitation of human being by human being. And so of course there is a theology of violence, just as there is a theology of the rationality of the state. But for us Africans, the world's institutionalized poverty has other roots as well, and it is perhaps these other roots that are more serious, more important, and more relevant to the present moment: slavery, colonialism, neocolonialism, racism, apartheid, and the universal derision that has always accompanied the "civilized" world's discourse upon and encounter with Africa—and still accompanies it today.

Strange, is it not, that in the immense literature that we have on the poor today, Africa is always looked down upon and derided? There is a type of poverty that I call, "anthropological poverty." It consists in despoiling human beings not only of what they have, but of everything that constitutes their being and essence—their identity, history, ethnic roots, language, culture, faith, creativity, dignity, pride, ambitions, right to speak . . . we could go on indefinitely.

There is a more serious form of impoverishment. It weighs not only upon Africa, but upon a very great proportion of humanity. This is the impoverishment that, when confronted with the gospel, is seen to be its negation pure and simple. It ought to constitute a serious subject for the reflection of theologians, because "anthropological impoverishment" can take on "theological" forms as well: it drains, voids, persons of everything that can enable them to recognize Christ as a person. Others have spoken of pseudoevangelization. There is no need to repeat here what they have said.

The final misunderstanding, or ambiguity, to which we shall here address ourselves is that of "inculturation." It is in this area, doubtless, that the theological debates have been the most ample, the most elaborate and complete. To be sure, we are astounded to discover this immense continent of Asia—and especially India, this sacred land, this cradle of religions, where thinkers, saints, and mystics are more numerous than anywhere else on the face of the earth. We have discovered the material misery of the Indians, too. Even in its most brutal forms, this misery, blending with such great mysticism and holiness, has the aspect of the holy, the sacred.

But what strikes us most of all is the extent to which Christianity in India has preserved its foreign complexion. Amid the splendor of all this ancient Indian architecture, our churches are ugly—"exotic" in the original sense of the word. We assisted at the Sunday Eucharist in the cathedral. The Mass was in English. The community appeared to be altogether Westernized. But we also had the unique opportunity of participating in a Eucharist celebrated in Indian style by Father Rayan, an Indian Jesuit. There was Indian music and Indian singing. We were all seated on plaited mats around the gifts of the Lord's supper. A sea of candles burned in their sunburst, with Indian incense, the infinite grace of Indian women dancing around the altar, and readings from the sacred texts of the holy sages of eternal India. It was like the beauty of another world. But it all revealed to us a new face of the church, the people of God, and brought us so close, so present, to all the Christians of India—of whom a dozen at most participated in the ceremony.

This celebration—purely "experimental," as we say in official parlance—took place in a humble little meeting room, almost in secret. And we were assured that the Christian masses of India had practically nothing like it anywhere else. Indigenization? Inculturation? Where were they? When shall we move from analysis to praxis? When shall we *really* inculturate and indigenize?

The New Delhi debates enabled us to recognize one another in the truth. It was too rich an experience for us to be able to set forth all its lessons here. The EATWOT theologians dispersed, rejuvenated and confirmed, with a vast program before it—whose most exciting point will be the January 1983 encounter of Third World theologians with their counterparts from the West. Turn the page. A new dialogue is about to begin.

—Translated by Robert R. Barr

17

Reflections from a
Latin American Perspective:
Finding Our Way to Talk about God

Gustavo Gutiérrez

In the years between the EATWOT conferences in Dar es Salaam (1976) and New Delhi (1981) something unusual occurred in the churches of the Third World. Christians who had shouldered ecclesial responsibility and the task of theologizing in those countries, and among the black and Hispanic minorities in the United States, began to get together to share their diverse reflections on their common faith in the God of Jesus Christ. In the past they had customarily met as students in the major theology departments of Europe and North America, or had occasionally been invited to meet in those surroundings. Now they were meeting on their own initiative in the setting of poor countries. This many-faceted initiative was carried through time and again by Sergio Torres, who has displayed much perseverance and creativity in the process.

The first country to host these meetings was Tanzania, a small country inhabited by a poor, very poor, population. Its people bears the marks of a harsh past involving colonial rule and racial contempt. But Tanzanians have also shown much courage and creativity in undertaking a thoroughgoing process of liberation. Exploring their roots in their native African tradition, they have set out on their own to construct a just and humane order. This accounts for the disproportionate moral authority exercised by that small nation and its president, Julius Nyerere, in the concert of nations. The achievements of the Tanzanian people enable us to perceive and concretely experience the significance of the poor in history.

After continental meetings in Africa, Latin America, and Asia, a tricontinental meeting was held in New Delhi. There in India we encountered a country whose vastness is both geographical and historical in nature. We were deeply impressed by the poverty of its people, and the thin bodies of New Delhi are still before our eyes. But we were also deeply impressed by its rich cultural and religious heritage. Held in the midst of a small minority of native Christians, our meeting of theologians became aware of its own insignificance. The people of India, poor and profoundly religious, brought us back forcefully to the center of our faith: the mystery of God.

Thus Tanzania and India were not just different geographical locales and different cultural landscapes. They were real theological lessons. The peoples of those countries were living witnesses of God and the poor. For us those experiences represent the starting point for a theology that seeks to combine diverse efforts into a process of reflection carried out from the underside of history. As was the case in the Bible, God and the poor are its great themes.

Some may well see all this as an obsession, feeling that it is time to move on to new questions. But the fact is that poverty, the result of unjust national and international structures, is our historical territory. It is there that our peoples affirm their faith and hope in God. If our theology is not framed in the context of the salvific dialogue between God and the poor, then it ceases to be the word of God in history about the gift of faith.

It is within that context, therefore, that I shall offer a few disparate observations here. I make no claim to offer a full account or reckoning. Although the following observations may delve into any evaluation necessary, the process of evaluation itself must be the joint effort of many.

THEOLOGIANS OR THEOLOGIES?

When we began in Dar es Salaam, we said in the Final Statement, "We are prepared for a radical break in epistemology which makes commitment the first act of theology and engages in critical reflection on the praxis of the reality of the Third World."[1] The point was spelled out a bit further on in the same statement: "Our conviction is that the theologian should have a fuller understanding of living in the Holy Spirit, for this also means being committed to a lifestyle of solidarity with the poor and the oppressed and involvement in action with them."[2] The New Delhi document picks up the same perspective:

The starting point for Third World theologies is the struggle of the poor and the oppressed against all forms of injustice and domination. The committed involvement of Christians in this struggle provides a new *locus* for theological reflection. Their participation is faith in action and the manifestation of Christian commitment, which constitute the first act of theology.[3]

Clearly then, this view of the theological task is of the utmost importance in all those theologies that seek to combine reflection with solidarity in the various struggles for liberation. Here I should like to point out some of the consequences of such an approach, consequences that have cast a shadow over our work, created difficulties, and posed problems as yet unsolved.

Academic Theology and Christian Grassroots

To say that commitment is the first act of Christian living is to say that the reflection of faith on it must be deeply rooted in the Christian community. It is the assembly of the Lord's disciples as such that is responsible for the proclamation of the gospel message in words and deeds. One is a theologian insofar as one is linked to the life and commitments of a Christian community. Only within such a community does one have a theological function to carry out; that function is an ecclesial task.

This view necessarily makes for a more fluid boundary between those we usually call theologians and those we regard as committed Christians with some sort of ecclesian responsibility. In the broadest and most basic sense, every Christian is a theologian. The first and primary initiator of discourse on the faith is the Christian community located within nations and peoples who are struggling to assert their dignity as human beings and children of God, and to build a just society. And that is our situation, of course.

It is here that we are confronted with various questions, if our theological reflections are supposed to be based on the concretely experienced life of the poor in our world. Can we convene only those who are professionals in the theological world: professors, authors, and so forth? Or should we also invite other Christians involved with other functions within the Christian community? And there is another uncomfortable question raised by the Dar es Salaam statement about a "radical break." If we take that seriously, must we not restrict the kind of theologian we invite to these meetings? And if we do, what effect will that have on strictly theological work?

I do not think we have fully faced up to those questions or answered them yet, which is not surprising. But there the questions stand in any case, forcing us out of our old certainties and opening up new pathways that we must travel one step at a time.

Let me give one example. Our new way of conceiving the work of theologizing has prompted us to hold joint meetings between those whose focus and specialty is theology and those whose work is basically on the grassroots level. Continental meetings, in particular, have tended to be joint meetings of that sort. All of us have gained a wider, overall vision and found our reflection enriched by such joint meetings. But it cannot be denied that they have also given rise to certain tensions.

It is our deep and irreversible conviction that we must avoid an academic theology dissociated from grassroots work, where the "first act" of theology is taken. The point is important and bears stressing. Such a dissociation is ruled out, not just because we want to elaborate a committed theology, but even more importantly because we want to develop a discourse on faith that will respond to the real questions raised by the contemporary world and the

Christian community living in it. In short, we rule out such a dissociation because we want a truly serious and scientific theology. By the same token, however, we must acknowledge that the work of theologizing, if it is to be rigorous in its elaboration and universal in scope, calls for a painstaking knowledge of Scripture and careful correlation with both the Christian tradition and contemporary theology. But proper handling of those theological fonts and all the requirements entailed in the process are not always fully appreciated from the standpoint of grassroots urgencies.

These differences in emphasis have sometimes led to sharp debates at our meetings, and the resulting tensions have not been completely resolved. The point I want to stress here, however, is that such confrontations are basically sound and healthy. They are to be found not only in and between groups but also inside every Christian individual who wants to be committed and at the same time wants to reflect on the faith. In short, this tension is to be found in all those persons we call theologians. In the last analysis it is a very beneficial and enriching thing, stemming from our new way of viewing theology rather than from minor or transient issues. In our conception there is really no place for the old circle of theologians as a separate, clearly defined and delimited group within the Christian community.

We may have come up with facile formulas, but they will not get us very far. For example, what exactly does it mean and imply to say that the poor as such are the producers of their own reflection on the faith? Real articulation and correlation of the various levels and agents involved in elaborating theology is a task that still lies ahead of us. We are still in the process of perceiving all the implications of our epistemological break. In our meetings we have met with successes and come up with tensions and impasses. Most of all, though, we have seen the outlines of the road ahead taking shape.

Our Method Is Our Spirituality

When we say that commitment to the struggles of the poor for decent and just living conditions is an indispensable precondition for a sound, intelligent understanding of the faith, we are not simply raising a question of theological methodology. We are talking about a specific way of understanding what it means to be a Christian. We are framing method (Greek *hodos*, "way" or "path") within the broader context of the Christian life. And in the Acts of the Apostles we find that the Christian life is actually described as "the way" initiated by Jesus (Acts 9:2, 18:25, 19:9). The Christian way is prior to the theological way.

The first and most basic thing in this process is charity or love, the only thing that will perdure (1 Cor. 13). The discourse of theology, which in the last analysis is always reflection on God, comes from and moves toward the love of God. That love implies contemplation and practice: we worship God and we put his will into practice by accepting the gift of his kingdom. Only then is it time to bring up discourse about God. To put it in our by now familiar terms: contemplation and practice together constitute the *first act*; theologizing is the *second act*. First comes the mystical life and practice; only then can we have any authentic, respectful reflection about God. The mystery of God comes to live in contemplation and in practice (i.e., in solidarity with the poor). Only then, in the second stage, can that way of life give rise to a reasoning process, a discourse.

Contemplation and practice make up the moment of *silence* before God. Theology (Greek *logos*, "reason," "word") is a reasoned *talking* about God. We personally experienced the importance of silence and its contemplative dimension in India. There we saw the attitude of its poor but dignified people toward life and its deeper meaning. There we learned the stance of its theologians, who are so deeply marked by the grandeur of God. But to this contemplative aspect of silence we must add the dimension of committed solidarity with the poor and their efforts to end centuries of oppression. We know that from the witness of the poor in our nations, of which Tanzania and its people are one example. Both dimensions of the "first act" are to be found in the concrete experience of the poor, and they are mutually related.

Silence, then, is one of the preconditions for any talk about God. And distinguishing between these two moments is not simply a question of methodology, as I noted above; it involves a particular style of life. It is a particular way of living our faith in the Lord, of living according to the Spirit. It is a question of spirituality in the strict sense of the word. Our epistemological break in the work of theologizing, as proclaimed in Dar es Salaam, also entails a break in the way we live as Christians and theologians. We must not forget that exigency if we wish to be faithful to the Lord and our peoples.

This way of viewing our theological approach only serves to emphasize the point I made earlier: the close tie between the process of discoursing on the faith on the one hand, and the life of the churches on the other. It becomes clear that our experiences over the past five years entailed more than meetings between theologians, they were confrontations between theologies. They were efforts to link the life and death, the hopes and struggles, of this world's poor to salvation in Jesus Christ. And the primary agents of such efforts are the poor themselves and the communities in which they share their faith in a liberating God. Such a theology imposes an obligation on those Christians who engage in the specific field of theology. It demands that theologians have deep, ongoing involvement in the evangelizing work of their churches and in the struggles of their peoples. Only then can they be both bearers and articulators of the faith-understanding arising from the underside of history.

THE COMPLEX ROAD OF DIALOGUE

An encounter between theologies, and between the churches and peoples behind them, is a step forward on the road of dialogue and mutual enrichment. And another factor in this dialogue is the way we picture the relationship between these theologies and the discourses about the faith that have prevailed in the churches up to the present.

Two Perspectives

In the Final Document of the Dar es Salaam Conference we said:

The theologies from Europe and North America are dominant today in our churches and represent one form of cultural domination. They must be understood to have arisen out of situations related to those countries, and therefore must not be uncritically adopted without our raising the question of their relevance in the context of our countries.[4]

Despite all that has been written about this matter in recent years, the phenomenon is still new. For the first time in centuries a new type of theological reflection is arising outside the major European centers of theological work and their North American extensions. The fact still evokes surprise, if not skepticism, hostility, or paternalistic condescension. These varied reactions are not confined to theological circles in Europe or North America. They can also be found in churches of the Third World and churches ministering to minorities in the United States. In all of them some segments still follow and respond to the dominant theologies, for a variety of reasons.

Given that situation, we can readily understand why our advocacy of a new approach to theological reflection might spark controversy. Such controversy is inevitable and necessary in certain circumstances; but it is not the fundamental thing, and it is not without its own ambiguities. The really crucial thing is to realize and appreciate the fact that there are different perspectives associated with different historical situations and different interlocutors.

I have offered my own characterization of the difference in approach between our theology and that of the affluent countries. In the churches living in affluent countries, theology more attentive to contemporary problems tends to regard the *modern mind* and spirit as its chief interlocutor. It addresses itself to the modern person, who is an unbeliever in many instances, and to the liberal ideology espoused historically by the middle class. By contrast, theology deriving from the poor majorities of the human race seeks to answer the questions raised by those "without history," by the *"nonpersons"* who are oppressed and marginalized specifically by the interlocutor of the dominant theologies. So the issue is not simply one of theological niceties. We are talking about two theological perspectives that respond to different needs and questioners.

When theologies take shape as reflection on the faith insofar as it is lived out in solidarity with the lives and struggles of the poor, they are not being driven by any terrible itch for originality in their field. They are simply trying to be loyal to the Lord of history, to lend their support to the proclamation of the gospel and the liberation efforts of their peoples.

Theologizing is both a right and a duty for any people that is both poor and Christian. To evade that task is to create a vacuum that will quickly be filled by reflections centered around other categories, interests, and goals. Such was the case in the past, and it remains the case today. To evade the task would be to betray the experiences and aspirations of the poor and oppressed. Thus the aim of our new reflections is not to challenge some other discourse on the faith out of a frivolous desire to indulge in self-assertiveness. The whole thrust of our effort is a direct result of the starting point we have chosen—that is, the faith as it is lived by the poor who are fighting for their liberation and their dignity as human beings.

It must be clearly perceived that we are dealing with two distinct theological perspectives rooted in two very different historical blocs rather than in merely academic discrepancies. Only that realization will permit healthy dialogue between the two viewpoints, and that sort of dialogue is in fact in progress. As the New Delhi Final Statement points out:

> In the past five years we have noted some changes in theological approach in the First World. For the first time, some European theologians are talking about *European* theology, as distinguished from the old concept of universal theology. Some theologians in the U.S.A. are reviewing their theology and accepting the challenge posed by Latin American liberation theology. They are responding to the exigencies of their own situation as the center of the capitalist world and at the same time the home of many oppressed minorities.[5]

Much more needs to be done, but this is an important beginning.

Pointing up this difference in theological perspectives makes matters clearer. It also allows for a dialogue that will be truly advantageous, not for theologians of the First and Third Worlds, but for their respective peoples and churches. This is not only the context but the very point and meaning of dialogue between theologies.

Being Listened to or Listening?

The poor have a basic right and claim that the powerful tend to disregard—namely, recognition of their very existence. A famous text published a few years ago in the United States began by saying that blacks affirmed the fact of their own existence. The text came from officials in black churches, churches of a people that has had the sad distinction of not being recognized as truly human for centuries by the dominant sectors of humanity. Much the same self-affirmation could be made by many other peoples and ethnic groups—and by their women in particular, who are doubly marginalized and oppressed.

Reflection on faith in God that arises out of these real-life situations must mirror them. And it must do more than that. Theology of this type is an expression, however modest, of a people's right to exist. Their will to exist finds expression in and through their claim to the right to think their own thoughts, to ponder in their own terms the reality of their faith in a liberating God. We cannot underestimate the immense burden of suffering involved, nor can we minimize the ebullient hopes of the poor.

Given this situation, we can understand the reaction of these peoples and the theologies embodying some portion of their experiences. They are demanding to be heard by a world that has been deaf to their voice and blind to their existence. This is an added reason for the atmosphere of controversy surrounding the confrontation between the two different theological perspectives under consideration.

As we all know, however, the accent is not on dialogue with the First World in our ecumenical meetings. It is on dialogue between theologians (or theologies!) coming from the poor sectors of the human race. And although they share much in common, there is no dearth of real differences between them. This point was made tactfully and accurately at our Dar es Salaam meeting:

> There was a considerable measure of agreement in the area of the need to do theology in context as described above; furthermore, we recognize that our countries have common problems. The analysis of the social, economic, political, cultural, racial, and psychological situations showed clearly that the countries of the Third World have had similar experiences of which account should be taken in the task of theologizing. Nevertheless, obvious differences in situations and consequent variations in theology were also noted. Thus, while the need for economic and political liberation was felt to offer a vital basis for theologizing in some areas of the Third World, theologians from other areas tended to think that the presence of other religions and cultures, racial discrimination and domination, and related situations such as the presence of Christian minorities in predominantly non-Christian societies, reveal other equally challenging dimensions of the theological task. We are enriched by our common sharing and hopefully look forward to the deepening of our commitment as Third World theologians.[6]

There are indeed different approaches and focal points, and we would all agree that they are enriching, as the above text indicates. They are another expression of the will to be and the demand for recognition that I mentioned earlier. Such realities as culture, race, sex, and class are important; and the fact is that exclusive concentration on one of them tends to cause us to overlook the others. This is another reason for lively reactions to a given viewpoint in our meetings, which must be viewed as a healthy and constructive thing.

But the existence of different approaches and viewpoints does raise another question: What criterion tells us that we are making progress in dialogue? We might be inclined to say that there is progress to the extent that our *own* viewpoint is heard and that we make every effort to make it heard even more convincingly. We feel that something is really being accomplished when the validity of our *own* emphases is recognized by some other theological standpoint. This, then, is the temptation that faces us. We are tempted to measure progress in dialogue over the past few years in terms of our own ability to get a hearing for our own viewpoint, in terms of the relative openness or resistance of our interlocutors to our point of view.

The temptation is understandable enough, but we might well ask ourselves to what extent this attitude is influenced by our long and continuing confrontation with the dominant theologies. In that confrontation we have felt that it is of primary importance to vindicate our own right to existence. Such a standpoint remains proper and obligatory in dialogue with various theologies elaborated in terms of the poor and their struggles for liberation, to be sure. We are well aware that such theologies still harbor First World categories and perspectives that must be rejected. However, there must be a change in the style of our dialogue if we want to keep moving forward, and I think we have perceived some hint of that fact in the years between Dar es Salaam and New Delhi.

My impression is that *listening* to what sister theologies have to tell us is increasingly becoming the prime criterion of progress in our dialogue. Acceptance of, and listening to, the other party is beginning to replace self-affirmation and an imperious (though legitimate) need to communicate our own experiences. This ground has scarcely been broken, much less tilled, in the last five years. It will bear fruit in our meetings only insofar as we lend an ear, not only to the reflections of theologians, but also to the theologically articulated faith-experiences of the oppressed. Faced with the sufferings and hopes of the poor, whatever their race, sex, or culture may be, theologians can only listen respectfully. To do that is to pay attention to what God is trying to say to us, and that is the starting point of all theology. I do not mean to imply that our own experience and that of the people we somehow represent should be minimized. My point is that when our experiences are compared and contrasted with those of others, we can situate them more realistically on the map of humanity's sufferings and struggles for liberation. In that way we gain a better understanding of our own personal experiences and those of our people.

As a Latin American, I myself have been goaded by the life and death of my people. I have been awestruck by the rich welter of Christian communities that have arisen to bear witness to the Lord in Latin America, even to the point of martyrdom. I must confess that I had a tendency to shut myself up in those realities. But at these meetings I have come into contact with the forms of oppression experienced by other peoples, and with their approaches to liberation and reflection on the faith. I have gained enormously from that contact, not only in hope but also in sadness—strange as it may seem to talk about gain in terms of sadness.

When we began to talk explicitly about liberation theology in Latin American (in 1968), we used three terms to talk about the poor and oppressed on our continent: class, race, and culture. This initial perception has acquired fresh urgency and content from our direct contact with other theologies and realities—that is, those of Africa, Asia, and the black and Hispanic minorities in the United States. Moreover, this contact has enabled us to better understand and appreciate certain features of our own people, which might otherwise have remained in the chiaroscuro of a theory with little or no relationship to practice. Something similar has happend with that specific form of oppression and marginalization embodied in the present condition of women, particularly those women from social strata that are exploited and degraded.

When we listen to those who speak from the reality of other poor peoples, we gain a keener and more in-depth insight into the people to whom we ourselves belong and whose life of faith we are seeking to express. To listen to other realities is to let our own reality speak. That is what we are now beginning to understand clearly and convincingly, even at the price of self-renunciation and occasional lapses.

To sum up once again, these dialogue possibilities presuppose a shift in our approach to theologizing. It must increasingly be linked up with the human and Christian experiences of our people, which in turn must be measured against the Bible, church tradition, and contemporary theological awareness. It is a complicated theological task in which personal effort is submerged in a collective adventure. In the last analysis, then, progress in our theological dialogue must be measured in terms of the following question: Has there been real gain in the liberation of our peoples, or in the faith in the Lord witnessed to by our churches?

A PASCHAL THEOLOGY

This theology stemming from the poor and their breakthrough into church life and world history is necessarily framed in terms of the dialectic between life and death. It is from there that it seeks to talk about God, the ultimate ground of the meaning that the poor have for any and every Christian.

Death versus Life

Solidarity with the human struggle against poverty and for a more just and humane social order presupposes an option for life. One thing, at least, is becoming increasingly clear to our peoples: poverty means death. We see the untimely and unjust death of the vast majority of humanity produced by a socio-economic system that is international in scope. That majority is made up of the poor people in Third World countries and the oppressed minorities in affluent nations. We see death occasioned by starvation, illness, and the repressive measures of those who find their privileged position threatened by every effort at liberation on the part of the oppressed. To physical death is added cultural death. The ruling sectors seek to destroy everything that will give unity and strength to the deprived sectors, so that the latter may more readily fall prey to the machinery of oppression.

All this is implied in our talk about poverty and the destruction of persons, nations, cultures, and traditions. When the poor seek to liberate themselves from those death-dealing conditions, which some are euphemistically calling "living conditions," they are expressing their will to live. Contrary to what is sometimes thought, the challenge facing us is not simply that of a "social situation." It is not something wholly extraneous to the basic demands of the gospel message. Instead we face a situation that runs directly contrary to the kingdom of life proclaimed by our Lord.

In the mystery of Jesus there is revealed to us a dialectic between death and life. That same dialectic pervades our historical situation, surprising us by its current relevance and its demands. Our discourse of faith arises out of our involvement with the reality of the poor—their premature death and their struggles for liberation. Such a discourse, such a theology, cannot help but be an affirmation of life. To be more specific, it cannot help but be a paschal theology dealing with the passage from death to life.

The conditions surrounding the life and death of the poor bring us back to the essence of the biblical message: paschal faith in the life-giving victory of the risen one over death. In a real sense we cannot depart from that central theme if we want to forge what our Asian brothers and sisters call a relevant theology. Because of our focus on this essential message of the gospel, our theology may be very unsophisticated and indeed elementary. This only makes for closer ties between theologians and nontheologians in the Christian community.

A Way to Talk about God

Proclamation of Christ's resurrection is the heart of the gospel message because it fully and forcefully reveals the kingdom to be a kingdom of life. That message calls us together as church, as a community of witnesses to the fact that death is not history's last word. As the perplexed disciples stood before the empty tomb, they were asked: "Why search among the dead for one who lives?" (Luke 24:5). To be witnesses to the resurrection means to give life, and bearing witness to life takes on special importance from the standpoint of Third World poverty.

Such witness compels us to find a way to talk about God. We need a language rooted in the unjust poverty that surrounds that vast majorities, but also nurtured by the faith and hope of a people struggling for its liberation. We need a language that is both contemplative and prophetic: contemplative because it ponders a God who is love; prophetic because it talks about a liberator God who rejects the situation of injustice in which the poor live, and also the structural causes of that situation. As was the case in the book of Job, both idioms arise in Third World countries out of the suffering and hope of innocent victims.

How are we to talk about God in terms of such a state of affairs? Here we come to what may well impress and exasperate the ruling classes most. It is the fact that the poor see their struggle for liberation as a way of "holding fast to God," to echo a phrase from Deuteronomy in which the fundamental dilemma of a believing life is brought vividly before us:

Today I offer you the choice of life and good, or death and evil. . . . I summon heaven and earth to witness against you this day. I offer you the choice of life or death, blessing or curse. Choose life and then you and your descendants will live; love the Lord your God, obey him and hold fast to him. That is life for you and length of day in the land which the Lord swore to give to your forefathers, Abraham, Isaac, and Jacob [Deut. 30:15, 19–20].

The fight for liberation is an option for life and a rejection of untimely and unjust death. What is more, the poor and exploited see this fight as an exigency of their faith in God the liberator. As the New Delhi Final Statement puts it:

We find in the Third World a dialectical tension between life and death, manifested in different ways. . . . This dialectical relationship challenges us to deepen the meaning of our faith in the God of life. Third World theology is thus led to a constitutive dimension of our biblical faith: through Jesus' death, God overcomes death (2 Tim. 1:10). . . . To believe in this God of life is to believe in love, justice, peace, truth, and human fulfillment. It is to denounce the causes of the dehumanization of our people and to fight against the systems that shorten and extinguish the lives of so many.[7]

A new prophetic and mystical language about God is arising in these lands filled with exploitation and hope. We are learning anew how to say "God." We are seeing the first stages of a process of reflection that seeks to give expression to the life of faith and hope being lived by the oppressed everywhere. It is the language of those in whose faces, noted the Puebla Conference, "we ought to recognize the suffering features of Christ the Lord, who questions and challenges us."[8]

This new language reminds us that the ultimate reason behind our option for the poor and our solidarity with their struggles is the God in whom we believe. There may well be other reasons for this privileged commitment. For the follower of Christ, however, this solidarity is ultimately rooted in our faith in the God of life. Above and beyond all the efforts, limitations, and achievements of our theologizing from the standpoint of the poor, we find that something fundamental is at stake: our very faith in God.

Ours is an effort to speak from the standpoint of the poor and their silence. If those who have the role of theological articulation mean to do that, then they must share in that silence of contemplation and practice; they must participate in the sufferings of the innocent poor. Otherwise our theology will merit the same reproach that Job hurled at his pompous friends:

I have heard such things often before, you who make trouble, all of you, with every breath, saying, "Will this windbag never have done? What makes him so stubborn in argument?" If you and I were to change places, I could talk like you; how I could harangue you and wag my head at you! But no, I would speak words of encouragement, and then my condolences would flow in streams [Job 16:2–5].

—Translated by John Drury

NOTES

1. Sergio Torres and Virginia Fabella, eds., *The Emergent Gospel* (Maryknoll, N.Y.: Orbis, 1978), p. 269.

2. Ibid., p. 270.

3. Final Statement no. 45.

4. Torres and Fabella, eds., *Emergent Gospel*, p. 269.

5. Final Statement no. 37.

6. Torres and Fabella, eds., *Emergent Gospel*, pp. 270–71.

7. Final Statement no. 62.

8. John Eagleson and Philip Scharper, eds., *Puebla and Beyond* (Maryknoll, N.Y.: Orbis Books, 1979), Final Document, no. 31, p. 128.

18

Reflections from the Perspective of U.S. Blacks: Black Theology and Third World Theology

James H. Cone

BEGINNINGS OF BLACK AND THIRD WORLD THEOLOGY

All Third World theologies began as a reaction to the dominant theologies of Europe and North America.[1] Whether one speaks of Latin American, African, Asian, or Caribbean theologies—all of these recent theological developments in the churches and seminaries of Third World nations signal the rejection of the missionary theologies of their former colonizers.

Instead of accepting the prefabricated theologies of Europe and North America, Third World peoples are developing their own theologies. Most of them show a special interest in liberation, understood as the attempt of a poor people to gain its freedom. The focus on liberation is partly a reaction to the missionary emphasis on spiritual salvation, as if the gospel of Jesus had no interest in the material conditions of life. Almost universally, awakened Third World peoples began to realize that the Bible is concerned about the salvation of the whole person, including his or her physical well-being. The neglect of the political and economic aspects of the gospel by European and North American missionaries came to be understood as a deliberate cover-up by oppressors so that Third World victims would not challenge the unjust international economic order.

As long as Third World peoples believed that the meaning of the gospel is defined by Europe and North America, they could not develop theological perspectives that would challenge their domination by the First World.

The rise of Third World theologies, with their almost universal interest in

235

liberation, is directly related to the emergence of national, political movements of liberation in the countries of their origin. When grassroots peoples
of the Third World began to rebel against colonial rule by insisting, sometimes through armed revolution, upon self-rule, theological perspectives also
began to develop with a similar focus.

It was no accident that Third World theologies of liberation began in the
context of struggles for political liberation. The precise character of the liberation sought depended upon the political needs of the country as defined by a
people struggling to liberate itself from foreign domination. Africans began
to speak of a distinct African theology with a special interest in the africanization or indigenization of the gospel so that they would not have to become
European in order to be Christian.[2] Latin Americans spoke of theology with
an emphasis on liberation as defined by Marxist class analysis.[3] Asians also
used the term "liberation" in defining Asian theology, but they included in
its meaning a special focus on their culture as defined by their great religions.
They spoke about contextualization instead of indigenization, and began to
relate it to an Asian Principle.[4] Although Caribbean peoples have not developed a distinct theological perspective comparable to Asian, Latin, and African theologies, there are several indications that they also share many of the
concerns for liberation as found among other Third World peoples. Perhaps
Caribbean theology will be a theology of liberation that will address itself to
the issues of imperialism, classism, and racism.[5]

It is clear that all Third World theologies began as a direct reaction to the
theologies of the First World. A similar point can be made regarding theologies of liberation among the oppressed in North America. Black, Asian, Hispanic, and native North American minorities have begun to develop distinct
theologies of liberation as defined against oppressive white North American
theologies.[6] Like Third World peoples in Asia, Africa, Latin America, and
the Caribbean, the oppressed peoples of North America do not believe that
white oppressors can define for them what the gospel of Jesus is.

Included among our liberation theologies of North America is also a distinct feminist theology that seeks to address the evils of sexism.[7] Although
feminist theology began among white North American women, some of the
aspects of this theology have been adopted by minority women as well.[8] Although minority women have not, for the most part, adopted the extreme
radical rhetoric of some white women, minority women do realize that their
men are not exempted from sexism. Furthermore, minority men have internalized many of the sexist values of the white male culture that defines the
woman's place as the home, thereby limiting her contribution in the liberation struggle.

Although the theologies of liberation have been in dialogue with the dominant theologies of North America and Europe, they have not been, until
recently, in dialogue with each other. They have been so preoccupied with
correcting and uncovering the hypocrisy of Euro-American theologies that
they have tended to ignore their relationship to each other. Like their coloni-

zers and oppressors, unfortunately, many Third World persons do not believe that they have anything intellectual to learn from another oppressed people. Although some Third World peoples may turn against their white colonizers and oppressors, as is true also of liberation theologians, they are not likely to turn to their Third World brothers and sisters on other continents for intellectual resources of liberation. What they know about each other is often determined by white missionaries and other European mediators. This is tragic because missionaries are just as prejudiced against one Third World people as they are against another. The information supplied by white missionaries becomes suspect, because they do not intend for Third World peoples to build a coalition among themselves.

If Third World people were to build a coalition among themselves in their common struggle, it would be more difficult for Europeans and North Americans to control the Third World. When Third World persons become Christians, they must be persuaded that Europeans and North American whites are the only ones who know what Christianity means. Whatever the oppressed attempt to do, their oppressor must convince them that they need their help. The control of a people's thinking is an essential element in socio-political oppression.

When I first began to write black theology, in 1968, the first thing white theologians and ecclesiastics told black and other Third World persons was that there is no such thing as black theology, because theology does not come in colors. What was so amazing is that many blacks rejected black theology, because white theologians, missionaries, and preachers said black theology was not "real" theology. It is unfortunate that many Third World persons even today ignore each other because they do not think that they could have anything of theological value to say. Even today there are still some Third World and North American black seminaries that offer courses in systematic theology but do not include their own theology or that of other oppressed peoples alongside North Atlantic theologies. Some North American black theologians are black in color only, not in their thinking, because they still contend that only Europeans and others who think as do they are "real" theologians.

It is very difficult for Third World persons to liberate themselves from a dependence on European thought, because we were trained by them and thus have a certain—inordinate—admiration of their thought processes. Even when we rebel against Europeans or North American whites, our rebellion is often limited to negative reactions.

My interpretation of black theology during the late 1960s and early 1970s is an example of this weakness. When one reads *Black Theology and Black Power* (1969) and *A Black Theology of Liberation* (1970), my dependence on white theological concepts is obvious. And my black colleagues were quick to point out this contradiction in my perspective. Since the publication of *The Spirituals and the Blues* (1972) and *God of the Oppressed* (1975), I have been struggling to incorporate the experience and culture of the oppressed into the conceptual raw material for articulating black theology. For I contend that our rebellion against a European mentality should lead to a second step— namely, to an affirmation of our own cultural resources as well as those found among other oppressed peoples who have had similar experiences of oppression.

As a North American black theologian, I have emphasized the need for oppressed Christians of the world to begin to develop structures of coalition among themselves so that we can pursue a common struggle for freedom. In an organization called Theology in the Americas, oppressed black, native American, Hispanic, and Asian Christians have begun to dialogue on their common plight of oppression.[9] In the Ecumenical Association of Third World Theologians, Asians, Africans, Latin Americans, and oppressed minorities of North America have begun to dialogue with each other. It has been within the EATWOT context that black theology has developed a dialogue with other Third World theologies. Other settings for dialogue include the World Council of Churches and the individual efforts of black and Third World theologians to be in conversation with each other.

In the next two sections of this paper, I want to focus my attention on the similarities and differences of black theology when compared with some literary expressions of Third World theologies in Asia, Africa, and Latin America. (I have not included Caribbean theology, because its distinctive features are still at an early stage of development.)

BLACK AND THIRD WORLD THEOLOGIES: SOME SIMILARITIES

Black and Third World theologies are in agreement that the dominant theologies of Europe and North America must be rejected. In their rejection of the white theologies of North America and Europe, black and Third World theologians used the term "liberation" as a focus of their theological concern.

The earliest references to liberation, as the heart of the gospel and as a definition of Christian theology, were made by black and Latin American theologians and church persons. It is important to note that black and Latin theologians began to use the term "liberation" almost simultaneously but independently of each other. Liberation became the dominant emphasis of black theology from its beginning with the publication of my *Black Theology and Black Power* (1969) and *A Black Theology of Liberation* (1970). One year after the publication of the second book, the Spanish edition of Gustavo Gutiérrez's book, *A Theology of Liberation* (1971), was published. Other black and Latin theologians followed with an emphasis on the same theme.

The theme of liberation is not limited to Latin and black theologies. A similar concern is found among Asian and African theologies as well. The common concern of rejecting the dominant theologies of Europe and North America and the emphasis on liberation led Third World theologians to organize EATWOT. In the New Delhi meeting, efforts were begun for the development of a Third World theology within the context of the non-Christian world. When one analyzes the Final Statements of the five EATWOT conferences to date, the rejection of European theology and an affirmation of liberation are common characteristics.

In addition to the rejection of European theology and the affirmation of liberation, black and Third World theologies also stress the need to reread the Bible in the light of the struggles of the poor for freedom. They have begun to speak of the "hermeneutical privilege" of the poor, and of God's option for the poor—that is, God's decision to reveal himself to all humankind preferably in and through the poor. Rereading of the Bible in the light of God's option for the poor has led to an emphasis on the exodus, the prophets, and Jesus Christ as the liberator of the poor and the downtrodden.

It has been within the context of our attempt to reread the Bible in the light of the struggles of the oppressed that the theme of the "suffering God" has become important in our theological reflections. Jürgen Moltmann's writings on the "crucified God" have stimulated our theological imagination, as has also Luther's distinction between the "theology of glory" and the "theology of the cross." But it has been the actual suffering of the oppressed in Africa, Asia, Latin and North America that has been the most decisive influence in our reflections on the cross of Jesus Christ. As Gustavo Gutiérrez has said: "We cannot speak of the death of Jesus until we speak of the real death of the people." It is in the deaths of the poor of the world that is found the suffering and even death of God.

The political implications of Luther's insight on this point seems to have been completely distorted with his unfortunate emphasis on the two kingdoms. Contemporary Lutheran scholars are even worse, because they appear to turn the cross of Jesus into a theological idea, completely unrelated to the concrete historical struggles of the oppressed for freedom. For most Lutheran scholars, the theology of the cross is a theological concept to be contrasted with philosophical and metaphysical speculations. It is a way of making a distinction between faith and reason, justification by faith through grace and justification through the works of reason.

But when the poor of the Third World and of North America read the passion story, they do not view it as a theological idea but as God's anguished solidarity with the victimized of the world. Jesus' cross is God's election of the poor, taking their pain and suffering upon himself. This is what Third World theologians mean when they say that "God is black," "God is red," "God is rice," and other strange ways of speaking when compared with the metaphysical reflections of Europeans. This apparently crude anthropomorphic way of speaking of God is the Third World theologian's way of concretizing Paul's dictum: "To shame the wise, God has chosen what the world counts folly, and to shame what is strong, God has chosen what the world counts weakness. He has chosen things low and contemptible, mere nothings, to overthrow the existing order" (1 Cor. 1:27-28).

Another common emphasis among black and Third World theologians is their de-emphasis, though not complete rejection, of the Western theological tradition and an affirmation of their own cultural traditions. If the sufferings of God are revealed in the sufferings of the oppressed, then it follows that theology cannot achieve its Christian identity apart from a systematic and critical reflection upon the history and culture of the victims of oppression.

When this theological insight impressed itself upon our consciousness, we Third World theologians began to realize that we had been miseducated. In fact, European and North American theologians and missionaries stifled the indigenous development of theological perspectives of Third World peoples by teaching them that their own cultural traditions were not an appropriate source for an interpretation of the Christian gospel. Europeans and white North Americans taught us that the Western theological tradition, as defined by Augustine, Aquinas, Luther, Calvin, and Wesley, is the essential source for a knowledge of the Christian past. When black and Third World theologians began to concentrate on distinct black, African, Asian, and Latin theologies, they also realized that their own historical and cultural traditions are far more important for an analysis of the gospel for their struggle of freedom than are the Western traditions that participated in their enslavement.

African traditional religions and the African independent churches have played a vital role in the development of African theology. Black spirituals, blues, and folklore as well as radical nineteenth-century black freedom fighters played a special role in the rise of North American black theology. The major religions of Asia, including Hinduism and Buddhism, are being integrated into the current shape of Asian theology. In Latin America, the most Western of all liberation theologies, theologians have also turned to their own cultural history for guidance and inspiration.

All Third World theologians began to realize that those responsible for our enslavement are not likely to provide the resources for our liberation. If oppressed peoples are to be liberated, they must themselves create the means to make it happen.

The focus on our culture in the light of our liberation struggle has led to an emphasis on praxis as the context out of which Christian theology develops. To know the truth is to do the truth—that is, to make happen in history what is professed in church. All proponents of liberation theology contend that the masses are not poor by accident. They are *made* and *kept* poor by the rich and powerful few. This means that to do liberation theology, one must make a commitment, an option for the poor and against those who are responsible for their poverty.

Because liberation theology is not simply something to be learned and taught in colleges and seminaries but something to be created in the struggles of the poor, social analysis becomes a critical component of all forms of liberation theology. How can we participate in the liberation of the poor from oppression if we do not know who the poor are or why they live in poverty? Social analysis is a tool that helps us to know why the social, economic, and political orders are composed as they are. It enables us to know who benefits from the present status quo. Unlike European and North American theology, whose interlocutor is philosophy, liberation theologians dialogue with sociology. Agreeing with Karl Marx's eleventh thesis on Feuerbach, they say: "The philosophers have only interpreted the world in various ways; the point, however, is to change it." Black and other Third World theologians have been searching for ways in which they can change the world together.

In our use of the tools of the social sciences for an analysis of the social, political, and economic structures that dehumanize the poor, Third World theologians almost universally endorse democratic socialism and condemn monopolistic capitalism. When we speak of democratic socialism, we do not have in mind Soviet Russia, Eastern Europe, or any other so-called socialist country under the influence of the Soviet Union. Socialism by definition means democracy, and the U.S.S.R. is not a political democracy. Many Third World thinkers refer to Russia as an example of state capitalism.

Although there are no perfect exemplifications of our socialist vision, its authentification is based upon the struggles of the poor in the Third World who believe that there is no invincible reason why the present unjust order must continue. And the struggles of the peoples of Tanzania, Zimbabwe, Nicaragua, and other Third World countries symbolize the partial realization of our socialist vision.

For what we do know is that monopolistic capitalism is evil and must be opposed. Latin American liberation theologians have taken the lead in condemning and exposing the international capitalism of the U.S.A. and Europe, and their voices have been joined by Asians, Africans, Caribbeans, and Third World theologians in the U.S.A. Our discussions together have widened our vision and enabled us to analyze more clearly the complexity of the international machinations of monopolistic capitalism.

Although Africans, Asians, and black North Americans have emphasized the role of culture in the bestowal of identity in the struggle for freedom, we also see more clearly now the importance of Marxism and the role of class analysis in the doing of theology. Both race and class analyses are important, and their importance is reflected in our support of each other.

BLACK AND THIRD WORLD THEOLOGIES: SOME DIFFERENCES

Although black and Third World theologies share many common concerns, they are not identical. The differences between black theology and Third World theologies in Asia, Africa, and Latin America can be classified in two general areas. There are differences that alienate us, and there are others that complement and enlarge our liberation perspectives. Both kinds of differences are present in the relationship of black theology with African, Latin American, and Asian theologies.

The two main focuses around which our differences have shown up are socio-political liberation, on the one hand, and cultural liberation, on the other. In our dialogue with African theologians, North American black theologians have placed more emphasis on socio-political liberation, and Africans have stressed cultural liberation. Our dialogue began in 1971 and has continued to the present. In each of our meetings, Africans have shied away from the term "liberation," because they say that the gospel is not political. It is not an ideology of the oppressed. Some have even said that the gospel is concerned about all—the rich and the poor alike.

In lieu of liberation, Africans often prefer the terms "africanization" and "indigenization," because they locate the problem at the point of culture, not politics. But black theologians have been adamant in their insistence that the God of the Bible is a political God who has identified divine righteousness with the bodily liberation of the poor. The differences between African and black theologians on this point have led some African theologians, such as John Mbiti, to say that African and black theologies have nothing in common. But the presence of black theology in southern Africa has cast a shadow over Mbiti's statement. Desmund Tutu, the present director of the South African Council of Churches, says that black and African theologies are soulmates and not antagonists. A similar point has been made by black Lutheran Bishop Manas Buthelezi.[10]

The concern of North American black theologians has not been to reduce theology and the gospel to blackness or political liberation. Like our African brothers and sisters, we believe that there is a spiritual ingredient in the gospel that transcends the material conditions of human life. What we reject is the tendency, among some African theologians, to reduce the gospel and theology to a spirituality that has not been carved out of the real-life sufferings of the poor who are engaged in political liberation. When the sufferings of the poor are individualized, privatized, it becomes possible to identify their sufferings with God without challenging the existing socio-political structures responsible for their suffering. A suffering God and Jesus' cross become mere intellectual, theological concepts totally unrelated to the daily life of the poor. This is precisely José Míguez Bonino's and other Latin theologians' critique of Jürgen Moltmann's writings on the "crucified God."[11] A much more severe critique can be made of contemporary Lutheran reflections on Martin Luther's theology of the cross. Some liberation theologians would even make the same critique of Martin Luther because of his failure to extend his theological analysis of the cross to society.

Whether it is Moltmann's crucified God, Luther's theology of the cross, or African theology's theme of indigenization, the question of the socio-political ingredient of the gospel must be faced head-on. This has been and still is black theologians' chief concern in our dialogue with African theologians.

In the dialogue between black theology and Latin American liberation theology the opposite pole has been stressed. The main question has been: What is the relationship between race and class oppression? Because the Latin Americans are Marxists, they emphasize class oppression, almost to the exclusion of race oppression. Inasmuch as black theologians live in the white racist society of North America, with a heritage of two hundred fifty years of slavery and over a hundred years of white capitalist oppression, it is not likely that they will ignore cultural oppression as imposed by white racism.

Unfortunately black theologians have not always been sensitive to class oppression or to the role of U.S. imperialism in the Third World. Sometimes we have given the impression that all we want is an equal piece of the North American capitalist pie. Therefore Latin Americans have rightly asked for a social analysis in our theology that criticizes capitalism. In this dialogue with Latin theologians, we have come to realize the importance of Marxism as a tool for social analysis.

As Latin Americans have pressured us on the issue of class analysis, we have pressured them on the importance of race analysis. Similar to black theologians in their approach to Marxism, Latin theologians have not taken up race analysis enthusiastically. Our dialogue began in 1973, and we have struggled with the issue of race versus class since that time. Although the tensions between us have been high, we have learned a lot from each other and intend to carry on the dialogue.

It is revealing to note the changing dynamics and emphases in black theology and its dialogues with African and Latin American theologies. With Africans, we black theologians often appear very "political" in our view of theology, and the Africans seem more "cultural" and "spiritual." In our conversations with the Latins, black theologians seem very "cultural" and "spiritual," and the Latins appear to reduce theology to politics. The reason for these differences in dynamics and emphasis is partly due to the way we read the Bible and analyze the gospel with our respective situations in view. Another reason is our limited knowledge of each others' situation and the role of our theologies in our liberation struggles. Sometimes we try to impose our particular theology upon another situation.

The crucial issue is whether our theological perspectives have achieved and still retain their identity out of the struggles of the poor. For I contend that any theological perspective that does not remain committed to the liberation of the oppressed cannot be Christian. It does not matter on what continent a theology may be found. What is crucial is *whom* it represents: the poor or the rich, the black or the white, the First or Third World?

There has been less dialogue, and almost no conflicts, between black and Asian theologians. Asians do not know much about North American blacks, and we do not know much about Asians. The differences in culture and geographical distance are so great that we seldom have much to say to each other. This situation began to change when I was invited in 1975 by the Korean Christian Church in Japan to lead a three-week workshop on the theme "The Church Struggling for the Liberation of the People." Since 1975 I have returned to Japan and South Korea several times. Black theologians have met with Asian theologians in the Ecumenical Association of Third World Theologians. We found that we have many differences and similarities that complement each other.

Important for my perspective on Asia have been my colleagues Kosuke Koyama and Preman Niles of the Christian Conference of Asia, both of whom have done much to teach me about Asian theology. In addition to Koyama and Niles, I must also mention Asian students who have been in my classes at Union Seminary. Their presentation of the Asian reality and their commitment to participate in the struggle to liberate the oppressed on that continent have done much to illuminate my perspective on Asian theology. Like black theology, Asian theology seeks to bring together in dialectical tension the commitment to cultural identity and socio-political liberation. As I have suggested in my discussion of African and Latin theologies, they seem to be in danger of minimizing one side: the Africans socio-political liberation and the Latins cultural liberation. In Asian theology, there is a recognition of the importance of both these elements. My perspective on black theology has endeavored to recognize both elements as well.

Because our differences and similarities seem to complement each other's perspective, black and Asian theologians have begun to discuss the possibility of a dialogue with each other outside the Ecumenical Association of Third World Theologians. Preman Niles has explored this possibility among Asian Christians, and I have done a similar exploration within the context of the Black Theology Project of the Theology in the Americas. No dates or agenda for a dialogue have been decided, but we are both anxious to initiate it, because we believe that we will have much to learn from each other.

Because black and Asian theologians have had few conflicts in our dialogue, we have been able to transport this experience of mutual support to our respective dialogues with Africans and Latin Americans. Why should we fight each other when we have so much to lose in division and so much to gain in unity? Asians and blacks seem to recognize that point in our theological conversations, and this recognition has enabled us to move to a deeper understanding of each others' struggles.

On the basis of Third World theologians' dialogues together, it is clear to us all that the future of each of our theologies is found in our struggles together. I am firmly convinced that black theology must not limit itself to the race struggle in the United States but must find ways to join in solidarity with the struggles of the poor in the Third World. The universal dimensions of the gospel message require that we struggle not only for ourselves but for all. For there can be no freedom for any one of us until all of us are free. Any theology that falls short of this universal vision is not Christian and thus cannot be identified with the Jesus who died on the cross and was resurrected so that everyone might be liberated in God's emergent kingdom.

NOTES

1. The term "Third World" is the object of much discussion. When I use the term in this essay, I am referring primarily to Asia, Africa, and Latin America. For a discussion of this term in a theological context, see Sergio Torres and Virginia Fabella, eds., *The Emergent Gospel: Theology from the Underside of History* (Maryknoll, N.Y.: Orbis, 1978), pp. vii–xxii.

2. For one of the earliest texts on African theology, see Kwesi Dickson and Paul El-lingsworth, eds., *Biblical Revelation and African Beliefs* (London: Lutterworth, 1969); see also Henry Muzorewa, *African Theology: Its Origin and Development* (Orbis Books, forthcoming).

3. One of the best introductions to Latin American liberation theology is that of José Míguez Bonino, *Doing Theology in a Revolutionary Situation* (Philadelphia: Fortress, 1975).

4. A good introduction to Asian theology is that of Douglas J. Elwood, ed., *Asian Christian Theology: Emerging Themes* (Philadelphia: Westminster, 1980).

5. For the emerging themes in Caribbean theology, see Idris Hamid, ed., *Troubling of the Waters* (Trinidad: Ruhaman Printing, 1973).

6. For an introduction, see Gerald H. Anderson and Thomas F. Stranksy, eds., *Mission Trend No. 4: Liberation Theologies in North America and Europe* (New York: Paulist, 1979).

7. Writings on feminist theology among whites are well known. For a good introduction, see Carol P. Christ and Judith Plaskow, eds., *Womanspirit Rising* (San Francisco: Harper & Row, 1979).

8. For an emerging black feminist theology, see "Black Theology and Black Women," in G. S. Wilmore and J. H. Cone, eds., *Black Theology: A Documentary History, 1966–1979* (Maryknoll, N.Y.: Orbis, 1979).

9. See Sergio Torres and John Eagleson, eds., *Theology in the Americas* (Maryknoll, N.Y.: Orbis, 1976), for information on the origin of this organization. For information on Detroit II and the Inter-Ethnic/Indigenous Theologies' Dialogue, see "Message from the Haudenosaunee Dialogue/Retreat" (New York: Native Self-Sufficiency Center); see also Gregory Baum, "Theology in the Americas: Detroit II," *The Ecumenist,* Sept.–Oct. 1980; C. West, C. Guidote, M. Coakley, eds., *Theology in the Americas: Detroit II* (Maryknoll, N.Y.: Orbis, Probe Series, 1982).

10. See John Mbiti, "An African Views American Black Theology" in Wilmore and Cone, *Black Theology: A Documentary History,* pp. 477 ff.; Desmond Tutu, "Black Theology/ African Theology," ibid., pp. 483ff.; Manas Buthelezi, "An African Theology or a Black Theology?" in *Black Theology: The South African Voice,* Basil Moore, ed. (Atlanta: John Knox, 1973), pp. 29ff.

11. See especially Míguez Bonino's *Doing Theology in a Revolutionary Situation.*

19

Reflections from a Third World Woman's Perspective: Women's Experience and Liberation Theologies

Amba Oduyoye

A TALE OF TWO HALVES

Once there lived on earth Half and Half, each of them only half a human being. They spent all their time quarreling and fighting, disturbing the rest of the village and trampling upon the crops. Every time a fight began cries went up to Ananse Kokroko: *Fa ne Fa reko o!*¹ "They are at it again, Half and Half are fighting." So one day God came down, brought Half and Half together, and a whole human being appeared.

This fable, rich with the imagery of the desirability of unity and peace, is my image of what is happening to male/female relationships in our world. The question is, What kind of unity and peace, and at what expense? Today we begin to be aware of concepts such as unity in diversity, difference in sameness and sameness in difference, unity within difference, and more will come, as we search for language with which to express this experience.

But not all are prepared to see difference within unity. I was talking with a German woman recently on the use of the term "Third World," which she does not like and which some Third World persons too have declared anathema. She told me about a poster used by Bread for the World; it states that we have only "one world." We do have one *earth*, granted, but it is also true to say that we live in *different* worlds. The world of the rural woman in Ghana has little in common with that of the rural woman in Germany, nor does the world of the white woman in South Africa bear comparison with that of her black compatriot.

In our desperate attempts at "being one" and being "at peace," we forget how God put an end to the ideology of the Tower of Babel, replacing it later with the more meaningful and community-building diversity of pentecost—life in the Spirit of God as opposed to the mentality of "let us . . . make a name for ourselves" (Gen. 11:3–4) and build structures that will never be changed. To strive for unity in diversity is a task we cannot evade—and there are no shortcuts.

In EATWOT our recognition of this fact prevents us from embarking on the construction of a single Third World theology. In spite of our common experience of exploitation and oppression, we have recognized that sources and manifestations vary, and so does experience. Yet we are united in our reading of biblical motifs and imagery—the exodus, the Magnificat, the proclamation from Isaiah that Jesus read at Nazareth. Women too have been reading the Bible and cannot come to these experiences except through their own experience. Hence the "irruption" at New Delhi, on which I have been asked to reflect.

THE IRRUPTION WITHIN THE IRRUPTION

The person who sleeps by the fire knows best how intensely it burns; so runs an Asante proverb. The irruption of women in church and society is an integral part of the voice of the earth's voiceless majority that is beginning to penetrate the atmosphere and disturb the peace of the principalities and powers that hold the structures of our so-called one world in their hands.

It sounded like a joke to some when Marianne Katoppo of Indonesia, author of *Compassionate and Free,*[2] called the attention of the session to the necessity to watch our language about God and before God. It was not intended as comic relief; it was the irruption within the irruption, trumpeting the existence of some other hurts, spotlighting women's marginalization from the theological enterprise and indeed from decision-making in the churches.

EATWOT had come face to face with the fact that the community of women and men, even in the church and among "liberation theologians," is not as liberating as it could be. That "irruption" could only have come from a woman. But why at New Delhi and not before? The answer is simple; the process of involving women in meaningful roles in EATWOT did not begin at the initial stages. So until Virginia Fabella undertook the assignment of program co-ordinator EATWOT was virtually a male enterprise.

It was Virginia Fabella in her role as co-ordinator who explained EATWOT to me and urged me to get involved in the enterprise. Talking to me of the concerns of the association she repeated several times "it is our responsibility to get more women involved." Whether or not this was part of her official mandate as coordinator, she did get more women and encouraged their contribution with "don't disappoint the women." My experience is that it has always taken women to ensure the representation and voice of women, at least in the church and other related bodies. Of course not every woman in EATWOT was called in by a woman.

The theory of our unity and equality in Christ often pales in the structures we create, thus the necessity for more visibility demanded by and for women. It is also a fact that even when "a place" has been found for the contribution of a woman, it is often on women, or so-called women's issues: home and family, children and education. The concerns and experience of women as women are yet another *locus* for liberation theology. The presence and contribution of women as women have not been fully appreciated or respected. This was the problem in Delhi. The outburst came not because women were being treated as mere spectators at the meeting, but because the language of the meeting ignored our presence and therefore alienated some of the women present. But language was not the only issue; it was an index of other deep-seated criteria for assigning roles. Even the periods of relaxation were painful at least to me, as I listened to African misogynist fables being enjoyed by all and sundry.

To some the "outburst" was uncalled for. After all from Dar es Salaam to Delhi women have not been absent from EATWOT meetings, and never have they been prevented from contributing. Conceived at Louvain, it seems to have had an all-male genesis and could have become an all-male enterprise but for the presence of Sister Virginia Fabella, who coordinated the study process through the journey from Dar es Salaam to Delhi.

The general pattern, however, has given the impression that women do not form a legitimate part of the human community but are beings who are to be benevolently listened to and then passed over. Occasionally a woman will beat men at their own games and have to be admitted to contribute to central issues. It happens in politics and theology. Women are supposed to feel flattered when it is said of them "she is as good as a man," "she can hold her own against any man." These are simply indications of the male-oriented nature of our common consciousness.

It was such language that sparked off the feminism discussion at Delhi. Yet more glaring perhaps was the fact that none of the formal papers was assigned to a woman. Presumably we were dealing with more "central issues," which, until Delhi, did not specifically include sexism and therefore no "competent" woman could be discovered.

That session became for me one more example of the manifestation of the entrenched mind-set of Christians, both women and men, which hinders listening to a rereading of the Bible especially by a woman. Just point out that in none of the gospel narratives was "the woman who was a sinner" identified as a prostitute, or as Mary of Magdala, and you might have a minirevolt on your hands. Women's sinfulness has to do with their sexuality. Thus gender has become one of the challenges to our attempts at building a community in which a person can function as a human being, helped rather than hampered by his or her sex.

Among theologians working for the liberation of theology so that it may serve God's liberating work among "the poor of the land," I was shocked to discover that some saw the "irruption" of women upon the Christian theological scene and their call for a clean-up of the language of theology and its effects on church practices, especially in liturgy, as one big joke. Part of the agenda of New Delhi was to assess EATWOT's contribution to the renewal of theology in the Third World and to plan for the future. Will sexism-in-community become an issue for Third World theology?

There have been several international meetings at which Third World representatives have said that antisexism is not their priority. At times they have even said it is not an issue in their world, where men and women *know their place* and *play their role* ungrudgingly and no one feels suffocated by society's definition of feminity and masculinity. Issues of sexism are supposed to belong to a minority of disgruntled, leisure-saturated, middle-class women of the capitalist West. The few Third World women who speak that language are just allowing themselves to be co-opted. The fact is that sexism is part of the intricate web of oppression in which most of us live, and that having attuned ourselves to it does not make it any less a factor of oppression. Most Third World women, being literally close to the earth and to the maintenance of their race against classist and racist aggression, have opted to find complete fulfillment in this sacred duty and why not? But that does not mean an approval of sexism. Brigalia Bam puts the choice this way:

> To understand that while you are preoccupied with, say, equality or abortion rights, your sister is anxiously awaiting her husband's release from South African police detention is consciously to accept responsibility for *her* freedom in her terms. What is important for you may be merely incidental for her by comparison with the suffering she experiences because of the color of her skin. . . . I am not saying that the issues which affect us as middle-class women are unimportant, but I am saying that, if we have platforms, we must also speak on behalf of others who have no platform. . . . *We simply have no place for our freedom if there are still black women working like slaves under the impossible conditions of racial injustices.*[3]

Third World theologians, women and men, occupied with the study and exposure of sexism as a factor of oppression, and those attempting to discover community-building concepts from Christianity and other religions, should take their full place in EATWOT. The struggle for a wholesome and life-expanding community of women and men in church and society is bound to be enhanced by viewing feminism in theology as a theology of relationships, and a Third World perspective on it will be a contribution to the global effort. Feminism is anything but the imperialist ploy some would like us to take it for. There may be a lot of red herrings to come, but feminism is certainly not one of them. It is a fact of experience, not a thesis.

THE ASPIRATIONS OF DELHI

The experiences that have informed the doing of theology in the context of EATWOT have been mainly socio-economic and political and have led largely to the analysis of the roots of classism and racism. The religio-cultural concerns of Africa and Asia and of the indigenous peoples of the Americas have been marginal. This I believe has been one of the reasons why sexism, often anchored on religio-cultural perceptions, had not surfaced before. It will be interesting to see how the recognition of "anthropological poverty" as a negative factor in the struggle for full humanity will deal with the sexist elements in African culture. The same applies to our commitment to seriously study the role of other religions in this quest, bearing in mind that the same religion can be used to alienate as well as to liberate. What has religion done with the full humanity of women?

EATWOT has a structure and an atmosphere suited to liberation discussions, for within the membership and among the participants at its conferences are women and men who have personal experiences of various types of oppression and who are therefore equipped to see the interrelatedness of the struggle for liberation. To deal with "women's issues" in isolation and, even worse, to assign only women to do that job will be unrealistic. Overcoming sexism in theory and practice will demand the joint search of women and men, not only in a conference taking up that challenge but wherever sexism appears in other areas of emphasis. It is not necessary that we should all speak with one voice on the preoccupations of feminist theologians or any other concerns, but as seekers after the truth we are in duty bound to examine them. Conflicting perceptions will be the seeds out of which a clear vision of the new humanity will emerge.

EATWOT claims to work in the context of the challenges of reality to theology. As such, the feminist claim that "the male-dominated patterns of culture and social organization" oppress women in society and manifest themselves in the life and theology of the church has to be examined. This is not simply a challenge to the dominant theology of the capitalist West. It is a challenge to the maleness of Christian theology worldwide, together with the patriarchal presuppositions that govern all our relationships, as well as the traditional situation in which men (male human beings) reflected upon the whole of life on behalf of the whole community of women and men, young and old.

Because EATWOT has recognized that it is premature to consider the emergence of a synthesis called Third World theology, in spite of the various common oppressions and convergences of understanding, there is still room for further, in-depth probes to be undertaken. The events and deliberations of Delhi confirm this conclusion, for there it became clear that we cannot assume that African men and African women will say the same things about African reality. But also just as African men do not speak with one voice on

Africa, so African women should not be expected to speak with one voice. The diversity we are dealing with ought to be fully recognized and as many experiences as possible incorporated into EATWOT, provided they are anti-domination and foster full participation and mutual critical relationships and cooperation—the things that unite us in EATWOT. In this way the experience of "women and other outsiders to traditional theological discussions may become occasions for discovering new dimensions of unity."[4] EATWOT is clearly a newcomer as far as sexism is concerned.

THE STORY OF A DESK

One of the several roads along which the concern for unity of the church has led the World Council of Churches (WCC) is the establishment of "a desk" called the "Cooperation of Men and Women in Church and Society." To trace this journey is to understand better the struggles of the WCC to take women seriously in its structures and in those of the member churches. It is also to get a valuable insight into how crucial the factor of sexism is in our search for the unity and renewal of church and the human community at large.

The factor of sexism appears right from the beginning and is a study of how women have always had to announce themselves before men would recognize their presence. It was the efforts of women that led to the French Reformed Church's asking that the subject of women in the church be put on the agenda for the WCC Amsterdam assembly.[5] Here also began the strategy of women's preassembly consultations, for it became clear that women needed them in order to contribute effectively to the concerns of the whole council.

The founding assembly of the WCC at Amsterdam in 1948 had this to say: "The church as the Body of Christ consists of men and women created as responsible persons to glorify God and do his will." But the same assembly recognized that "this truth, accepted in theory, is too often ignored in practice." It appears that once more it would have been ignored by the founding fathers of the WCC if church women and the YWCA had not organized to ensure that the role of women in the church be explicitly taken up by the nascent council. It was both realistic and prophetic that the concerned women of the time saw the issue as that of "women in relationship with men" and placed it squarely on the table of the WCC rather than on that of the YWCA. It is a community issue.

This was also highlighted by the late D.T. Niles, a well-known figure in the ecumenical movement, who by comparing men/women relationships in Sri Lanka and northern India at a meeting in 1953 led the participants to the realization that in studying the contribution of women one is simply aiming at redressing a balance. Nor was it to "suggest the promotion of noncommunicating parallel groups acting autonomously within the larger church."[6] The result was that when eventually "a desk" was created it was to deal with "the cooperation of men and women in church and society." It was through the efforts of this "desk" that the WCC is now studying "The Community of Women and Men in the Church," which had its origin in the Berlin 1974 consultation on "Sexism in Church and Society"—organized by the "desk." The findings of this study will be another source for further research and even more important for strategies for implementation of our longing for community.

The World YWCA and the World Student Christian Federation have had to face the theory and practice of how the common humanity of women and men should govern our interaction in human community. Issues that have surfaced through the efforts of these ecumenical bodies have been political, economic, socio-political, and legislative, as well as psychological, cultural, and theological. Space limitations prevent the giving of samples from all fields, but, inasmuch as EATWOT has listed as one of its program goals to support women's quest for equality "in and through theology," here are a few theological issues chosen at random from various stages of the search:

(1) Examination of the language, imagery, and symbols of Scripture, worship and theology in reference to God.

(2) The representation of Christ in the ordained ministry in relation to the ordination of women.

(3) Christian *diaconia* and ordination to sacramental ministry.

(4) Evidence in Scripture and tradition with regard to the participation of women and men in the church.

(5) The importance of cultural traditions in the shaping of community in the church. Mariology and the Magnificat.

(6) The authority of Scripture.

(7) Theological anthropology: toward a theology of human wholeness.

The global perspectives of these issues should not hide the concerns of specific situations, which one finds in the documents available in the WCC, especially as illustrated by the statement from Third World participants at Sheffield, which provoked a very intense dialogue within that consultation.[7]

UNPICKING THE WEB OF OPPRESSION

Does the feminist movement have any meaning in Africa? The accepted position is that it does not. This was the general tone of the religious studies conference that took place at the University of Ibadan in 1974. The theme was "Women from the Perspective of Religion." A paper, "Continuity and Change in the Status of Women," given by Folanke Solanke, a Nigerian legal luminary, ended with: "Ladies and gentlemen, there is no need for confrontation." There was loud and sustained applause. She had hit at the reason for wanting to isolate Africa from the sexism debate, and the opinion columns of Nigerian dailies in the International Women's Year confirm this.[8]

From April 26 to 30, 1976, at the Conference Centre of the University of Ibadan, a national conference was held. The theme was "Nigerian Women and Development in Relation to Changing Family Structure." Prof. Ogunseye, in her keynote address, expressed the same sentiment: "I hope the popular belief that there is a conflict between the sexes will not be allowed to surface and mar the discussions." But should we not rather bring popular belief to the surface in order that we may examine it critically?

There is yet another way of avoiding this so-called conflict. B. Onimode, an economist, in his paper "Capitalist Exploitation, Women and National Development," quotes Samora Machel as pointing out that "the antagonistic contradiction is not between women and men, but between women and the social order." Therefore, Onimode continues, "men and women should unite to fight the exploitative society they have together created." This would be my own focus, except that it leaves the women who believe that "the hand that rocks the cradle rules the world" to rest content, for if this saying holds good, then women have exactly the world they want. Here I part company with some of my sisters. I did a study of Akan proverbs in which I attempted to demonstrate that women fall victim to linguistic imagery that socializes them to accept *their place* in society and to view with caution any call for more space.

In the process of the noble and I believe necessary battle to maintain the institution of the family, women's personal development is curbed because "their domestic labors are *required* by the male folk to make their own participation and progress in the modern labor force possible and comparatively easy." Dr. Aboyade, from whose contribution to the conference I have just quoted, also points out that an unmarried woman is considered a social failure. Should we not reexamine our assumptions about marriage and family life?

There are therefore voices from Africa that would suggest that we too have a problem, and not one that was created only by the arrival of Islam and Christianity, but is an integral part of our African worldviews. F. Solanke, quoted above, was present at the conference and in her paper "Legal Rights of Nigerian Women in Decision-Making" made the following recommendation: "We should call for more research . . . and encourage the Obas [kings] and the aged men and women to speak candidly on these matters in order to have a clearer picture of the traditional role of Nigerian women."[9]

A similar situation exists in Asia, as was stated in a press release issued by a consultation held in Bangalore in August 1978: that "cultural and traditional structures along with misinterpretation of Scripture have kept women in subordinate roles both in the church and in society was the consensus opinion expressed by all papers that were read."

By now it ought to be quite clear that I welcome "the irruption" and the move of EATWOT to be involved in these struggles. Those who will examine our language, proverbs, myths, and fables cannot exalt our African culture into one that backs up the woman who seeks a fuller participation in her community, or for that matter the man who finds so-called feminine roles fulfilling. But this may be discovered to apply in various degrees to the cultures represented in the Third World. The Chinese ideograms translated below illustrates the power of language and symbolism over our lives:

(1) Three women together means noisiness, badness.

(2) Woman under a roof means peace.

(3) Woman combined with littleness means exquisite, whereas a young woman and a man means wickedness because *she* seduces the man.[10]

The word "feminism," which jars on the ears of so many, and the expression "feminist theology," which sounds like some kind of heresy, have been occasioned by women's experience of how Christian anthropology and upbringing have required them to be content with being subsumed. Those who speak out, do so from a Jeremian cloud, which threatens to consume them. It becomes for them the sin of omission. No, persons labeled feminists, rather than being shunned or feared, are to be welcomed as persons who seek to define more realistically what it means to be human. This has to be a common search, of women and men, of the northern and southern hemispheres; all have to bear their part of this responsibility.

The way forward is a "new community of men and women," not reversal; participation, not takeover or handover. Feminism in theology springs from a conviction that a theology of relationships might contribute to bring us closer to human life as God desires it. In the same way as most accepted traditional Western theological categories went without question until they were examined in the light of the peculiar contexts of the Third World, so Christian women have begun to see that from their experience they cannot confess the same sins or affirm the same reading of the Christian faith. Is this not what a liberating theology is about, a hermeneutic that enables us to get the most out of the confrontation of texts and contexts as well as their interaction?

To benefit fully from this hermeneutical figure of eight requires that women's experience, hitherto marginalized, should become a part of the "community of interpretation,"[11] not only of Scripture but of the whole Christian tradition. We pray fervently for the Holy Spirit to lead us to the truth and we thank God for each step taken toward God's will for our human community.

NOTES

1. In Asante fables, Anase (the Spider) is the chief "human" character, whereas Ananse Kokroko (the Great Spider) is the name of God. It serves the same purpose as Adonai in biblical narrative.

2. Maryknoll, N.Y.: Orbis Books, 1980.

3. Susannah Herzel, *A Voice for Women* (Geneva: WCC, 1981), p. 64. Brigalia Bam, a South African woman, directed the WCC subunit on "Cooperation of Men and Women in Church and Society" from 1967 and is now on the staff of the World YWCA.

4. See Lettie Russel, "Women and Unity: Problem or Possibility," in *The Unity of the Church and the Renewal of Human Community* (Geneva: WCC, Faith and Order study document no. 81, 1981).

5. See Herzel, *A Voice,* p. 9. For this and other historical references I have depended on this work, which is less than 200 pages. It provides a chronological account of the subunit ("the desk" of this paper) as well as interviews with the women involved and a valuable bibliography.

6. Ibid., pp. 6–13, 23–24.

7. A number of these concerns are gathered in the recommendations of the Sheffield Consultation held in Aug. 1981. See Doc. CWMC 03/1 (WCC/FAO) and *Ecumenical Review* (Geneva: WCC), Oct. 1981.

8. *Orita-Ibadan Journal of Religious Studies,* 10/2 (Dec. 1976), carries the papers given at this conference.

9. Papers from this conference are yet to be published but are available at the University of Ibadan Conference Centre.

10. Herzel, *A Voice,* p. 78.

11. Mary Tanner, "The Issue of Scripture in the Community Study" (FOCL [WCC], 82/2/12, unpublished paper). For hermeneutical principles that demand our taking up the subject of this paper in EATWOT, see J. Severino Croatto, *Exodus: A Hermeneutics of Freedom* (Maryknoll, N.Y.: Orbis, 1981), pp. 1–11.

20

EATWOT and Its Significance: A European Perspective

Dirk Döring and Erhard Kamphausen

A new ghost is stalking Western society and perplexing its theologians. It has been haunting European theologians ever since Christians of the Third World, who have been on the underside of history up to now, have suddenly started to speak up about their own theological concepts, even claiming to have a right to criticize traditional Western theology from their own point of view. This specter is called "Third World theology."[1] The necessity of and justification for a Third World exodus from Western domination in the sphere of theology was emphatically endorsed by the fifth EATWOT conference, held in New Delhi in August 1981.

This same conference stressed and strengthened objections to and criticism of Western theology—essentially, European theology—objections already expressed from time to time in a variety of other connections.

And so European theologians find themselves confronted with a challenge: critically reflect on your tradition in the mirror of the Third World! Especially, answer for the historical effects your theological statements have had, in all areas of society!

This very challenge shows the significance of the advent of Third World theology. Here is a chance to be done with European-centered "solipsism" in our theology. Here is a chance to bring new perspectives, oriented to the global situation, into the well-worn systems of European theologians.

The first reaction here was one of surprise. This was a new state of affairs indeed. By and by, small circles of theologians began to take up the Third World challenge and to react to it. A new process of learning and awareness was underway, a process whose relevance for the construction of a consciously and genuinely ecumenical European theology is not yet altogether clear.

We have been asked to write a reflection on the EATWOT conference from

256

a "European perspective." To us, this means an investigation of the meaning that these waxing, ripening challenges from Third World theology (we think of it as a "theology of the poor") have for our theological self-understanding. Serious reflection is doubly important because we are convinced that neither benevolent applause of unconventionality and daring, nor narrow-minded parochial criticism could do justice to the peoples of the Third World in their struggle for new forms of active faith and theology.

We set out, then, with the intention of either accepting or showing ourselves exempt from the demands raised by the "irruption" of the Third World into the world of our theology. We shall consider how this challenge to dominant Christianity and its theological bulwark is received in Europe. In this way we hope to get an idea of the relevance of the "theology of the poor" for the critical remodeling and reconstruction of theological traditions in Europe. Our interest, then, is in a dialogue with the EATWOT theologians, and not in an apologia for Third World theology in reference to our own theological environment.

FAREWELL TO A THEOLOGY OF DOMINATION

European theologians have been known to describe the questions and theological controversies abroad in the ecumenical world as "European theology talking to itself, with audience participation,"[2] or as the "reimportation" of earlier European thinking.[3] But one wonders whether this approach does not miss the reality of Third World theology.

If the common feature in Third World theology is adequately characterized as a "theology of the poor," then the striking solidarity and accord evident at the New Delhi conference—in spite of all the differences—signals the dawn of something basically new under the sun. For the first time in the history of Christianity, the poor two-thirds of the world have set about the business of proclaiming the liberating force of the gospel in the strenuous battle to alter its lethal predicament. The "wretched of the earth" (Frantz Fanon) are proclaiming the gospel's rightful place on their side of the chasm that divides the haves from the have-nots in the global class struggle. The gospel of Christ Jesus, who devoted himself to the poor and those stripped of their rights, is now removed from its position of neutrality vis-à-vis the two-thirds of humanity suffering under dependency and oppression, and put into its authentic context of oppression/liberation.

As European theologians we must be altogether clear on the urgency of the questions concerning our theological traditions:

The challenge is, will the Church identify with this community of the poor in their struggle for liberation or will it choose the option of being neutral towards the problems of the poor? . . . "Is Jesus still in the church?" Some have suggested that it is the church that is dead, not God or Jesus Christ. God in Jesus Christ is alive and actively involved in human history, reconciling the world unto himself; but his presence is no longer clearly manifested in ecclesiastical institutions.[4]

These are basic questions put to our theology—that is, a theology in "bourgeois imprisonment." In view of the growing misery in the Third World, some claim that European theology itself has become a bolstering and legitimating "theological ideology" for the prevailing mechanisms of exploitation and repression. This ideology prevails because it is a theology of domination—a theology molded by religious power relationships to serve the dominant classes of developed societies and totally orientated to the enhancement of their might and power. It serves as a means of economic exploitation and ideological indoctrination of the oppressed masses, in rich countries as well as in Third World countries.[5]

Thus the indictment of Western theology by non-Western theology is only one particular instance of what Catholic missiologist Ludwig Rütti describes as a common Western identity crisis:

Western identity in modern times, both as actuality and as self-understanding, bore (and bears) the stamp of a relationship essentially of conquest and domination, in manifold forms, direct and indirect, overt and covert. That is why the indictment of Western dominance does not just have to do with a particular, perhaps only secondary, facet of the West, but with the very core of Western identity.[6]

As for the indictment that "Western theology is talking to itself, with audience participation," or, indeed, "pursuit of mission by other means,"[7] we can only cite James Cone:

You are not in a position to understand our situation. Only those who know and share the need, humiliation, and repression of their people can practice theology today. Your theologies and churches are bankrupt and bourgeois. You have had your chance, and you missed it. Your time is up.[8]

Heading for a New Reformation

The theology of the poor is calling Western theology into question—very severely. These sharp confrontations, with their massive challenges, bid fair to lead to a "second Reformation" in the history of Christianity, whose importance and influence will surpass that of any messianically inspired liberation movement ever known.

Like the theology of the Reformation, the theology of the poor rests upon basic theological propositions that become a canon within a canon, propositions that became the key to all theology. Again and again it emphasizes the primacy of practical commitment over critical reflections, and insists that purely academic theology, divorced from action, is irrelevant—especially when it seeks to shirk responsibility for the de facto effects of its statements in the past. New Delhi reasserted the conviction that the uncritical adoption of European and North American theologies in the Third World is not acceptable:

> The tools and categories of traditional theology are inadequate for doing theology in context. They are still too wedded to Western culture and the capitalist system. Traditional theology has not involved itself in the real drama of a people's life, or spoken in the religious and cultural idioms and expressions of the masses in a meaningful way. It has remained highly academic, speculative, and individualistic, without regard for the societal and structural aspects of sin.
>
> This traditional theology . . . has been incapable of responding to the social problems of the First World and to the challenges of the Third World. . . . It has not provided the motivation for opposing the evils of racism, sexism, capitalism, colonialism, and neocolonialism.[9]

Hence theologians of the Third World are ready to effect a break with First World theology, "a radical break in epistemology which makes commitment the first act of theology and engages in critical reflection on the praxis of the reality of the Third World."[10]

Hence the impossibility of a "neutral" theology, New Delhi maintains. Theology originates in dependency on the socio-cultural context in which it has developed and by which it is molded. Thus an interdisciplinary analysis of the prevailing context belongs to theology, for it permits the theologian to recognize the mechanisms of domination, repression, and exploitation that lead to human enslavement and depersonalization:

> Theology working for the liberation of the poor must approach its task with the tools of social analysis of the realities of Asia. How can it participate in the liberation of the poor if it does not understand the socio-political, economic, and cultural structures that enslave the poor?[11]

At the same time this analysis demands from theologians a critical self-analysis of their own position in a social class, and their standpoint vis-à-vis theology's privileged objects: human beings and the tragedy of human life.

Here is where Christian mission comes face to face with its very essence. The task is to liberate the victims of the sinful structures of oppression and to reestablish them uninjured, whole, and in the image of God. The curtain has fallen on "spectator theology." The main goal, the utopia, of a liberating theology consists in the creation of a new human being. Frantz Fanon has summed up that goal in the context of the emancipation process in Africa: "For Europe, for ourselves and for humanity, comrades, we must turn over a new leaf, we must work out new concepts, and try to set afoot a new man."[12]

The critical potential latent in these "basic propositions of the theology of the poor" has as yet won but little notice in European academic theology. Instead, the attempt has been to integrate the *novum* of Third World theology into the European theological model itself, in order to perfect the set of traditions transmitted by Christianity.[13] Now the order of the day is openness to dialogue and the new catchwords are "context" and "situation." How can anyone accuse us of aiding and abetting the oppressors of the Third World now? Now the 2,000-year-old organic process of Christian tradition in the North, with its European stamp, presents an isolated, self-contained set of traditions, separate from the Christian theologies of other parts of the world.

As an example of this outlook we can cite the Austrian systematic theologian Wilhelm Dantine who, facing the challenge of black theology, maintains:

> Christian doctrine could develop only by putting to use the thought and language models common and possible at that time. One might say it had to become incarnate in the flesh of the Christianity of that time. . . . The historical character of the revelation in Christ corresponds to the historical character of its conceptual understanding within the development of the church.[14]

Dantine then pleads for still more independent theologies, alleging their necessity for "a meaningful development of the Christian faith as we move forward into the future."[15] Completely oblivious of the dependence of Third World theological development on European missionary and colonial history, and of the consequent justification of a critique of Western theology by the theology of the poor, on the grounds merely of this history of injustice, Dantine sees adequate basis for future "regional" and "continental" theologies in "Christianity's historicity and claim to universality."[16] If the new "regional" and "continental" theologies also fulfill Dantine's criteria for an "actually independent" theology,[17] there results a theology that "claims to accept the different points of departure of non-Western theologies."[18]

The first result of such a procedure, as proposed by Dantine, is to render European theology, of the language and method as well as its theological contents and dogmatic and moral norms, immune to criticism. "Context" for Dantine means merely a particular cultural or religious tradition. All one needs to do, then, is to develop an independent theology for every "context." Now Western theology can, and must, be understood as one such culturally determined theology among many.

However, such a view of the problem—as the criticism based on the situation of dependency demonstrates—is too abstract to mean anything in a *global* context.

Therefore, Ludwig Rütti is right when he points out that

> The structure of dependency proceeding from and founded by the West never spared any "isolated context," at any time in the history of Western expansion. Western theology and the Western church cannot get themselves off the hook now merely by appealing to their "specific cultural context."[19]

And he adds:

> Even talking about "contextualization" can function as a defense mechanism, if it distracts attention from the global structures of dependency that ultimately determine even religious and cultural relationships to the non-Western world. A real and effective contextualization, self-reliance, and self-discovery cannot be created by the simple proclamation of the "particularity" of Western theology, when this same theology provided and (although denying it) still provides a foundation for the expansionist, universalistic, and paternalistic character of the West.[20]

And so Rütti calls for an overcoming of "third-worldism":

> The conceptualization that particularizes and regionalizes the problems of the non-Western world, particularly the Third World, characterizing them as someone else's problems, is to be overcome. It may sound paradoxical, but the West must begin with the West, and discover the presence of the "others" right there.[21]

Hence if we hear of the "perfectibility" of Christianity, or of theology, in this connection, it can now mean only testing the articulation of one's understanding of faith in the concrete historical situation, paying attention to that articulation's possible or actual political or ideological function. Looking at the historical patrimony of Western theology, the question forces itself upon us: In what can the renowned progress of theological knowledge have consisted, when repression, exploitation, and humiliation to the point of dehumanization, rampant through centuries of European world domination, is tirelessly and relentlessly justified by that theology down to our very day? What progress have the everlasting battles of the theologians, or what profit has what Tillich called "the Age of Protestantism," ever brought toward the attainment of the humblest claims of a right to life or survival?

The Reformation did not change the fate that Europeans prepared for the world. German systematic theologian Helmut Gollwitzer writes:

The Reformation did not change a thing in the fate white people prepared for the colored peoples of the world. Whether Rome, Witten-
berg, or Geneva prevailed, whether justification before God occurred
through works or through faith, whether *est* or *significat* was correct,
whether the Canons of Dort or the declarations of the Remonstrants
became accepted church doctrine, whether Cromwell or Charles I
won—for the red, the yellow, and the black all this was irrelevant. It did
not change their condition. For the white confessors of the faith, regardless of their particular Christian hue, the people of color were all
destined for bondage; "oneness in Christ" might pertain to heaven, but
certainly not to this earth.[22]

European theology will not be able to squirm out of a critical confrontation with this heritage, which has always seemed to lead it to a pass in which
Christ—the one who came into the world to seek his own, and turned especially toward the outcasts of society—is more and more estranged from that
world, to the point where he can even be invoked to justify the subjugation
and economic exploitation of a foreign people, to justify slavery, mass murder, and all the rest.

Third World theologians put it this way:

In the early phases of western expansion the churches were allies in the
colonization process. They spread under the aegis of colonial powers;
they benefited from the expansion of empire. In return they rendered a
special service to western imperialism by legitimizing it and accustom-
ing their new adherents to accept compensatory expectations of an
eternal reward for terrestrial misfortunes, including colonial exploitation. . . . The gospel was thus used as an agency for a softening of
national resistance to the plunder by the foreigners and a domestication
of the minds and cultures of the dominated converts.[23]

The Western Church and Secularization

The conditions necessary for the development of a theology so open to
manipulation have been present in ecclesiastical tradition since the Enlightenment, when religion and the church lost their leading role in public life, especially in politics. The appearance of a new secular society, seeking to divorce
itself entirely from the tutelage of the church, brought theology and the
church face to face with the task of preserving the church's social influence
within the new leading social class, the educated bourgeoisie.

But a religious worldview proved to be especially awkward for the up-and-
coming bourgeoisie in that it hindered the continued development of productive capabilities within the new capitalist production system. As Marburg
sociologist Richard Sorg puts it, the new middle class had two battles on its
hands at the same time:

One against theology's control of natural science, the other directly against religion and the church as the primary agents underpinning feudal supremacy. To the extent to which the bourgeoisie gradually gained control over the forces of nature . . . and in its struggle against feudalism, it recognized the obstacles to progress thrown in its path by religion. Therefore, the authority of religion in this class began to dwindle away.[24]

The church sought to come to grips with its loss of influence by adapting to the times. It bade farewell to state and society, leaving them to their progressive secularization (to their "coming of age," as Bonhoeffer put it). Henceforward they were abandoned to their destinies and to the constraint of circumstances. Of course, the church thereby forfeited the privilege of passing theological judgments on social processes.

At the same time theology and the church made themselves serviceable for the goals of the new middle class:

[This class] having become the ruling class of society, used religion as the ideological underpinning of its supremacy over the newly vociferous proletariat. Both the active role of the proletariat in the production processes of bourgeois society, as well as its experience during its struggle with the bourgeois class, which used religion and the church once again to support its own claims of domination, led the working class to turn away from the church in ever increasing numbers. Religion lost more and more ground.[25]

The price the church had to pay for the privilege of dividing the world in two—a secular world left to its own ideological self-interpretation and a sacred world characterized by individualized churchly piety—was a high one indeed: The church became irrelevant.

The "Theology of Difference" and its Consequences

The theological foundation and interpretation of the dichotomy between church and society derives from a tradition that, according to social ethicist Wolf-Dieter Marsch, can be traced back to the nineteenth century.[26] This tradition is known as the "theology of difference" (*Differenztheologie*) inasmuch as it considers the determination of "differential phenomena" as the starting point of theological reflection.

The most significant and consequential model of the theology of difference in recent theological reflection is doubtless that of "dialectical theology." Here, opposing positions are raised to the level of basic antitheses that ultimately determine the structure of all thought, language, and behavior. As a result, thinking cast in antithetical structures was for decades the only "legitimate" form of theological thought structure. Still today theologians follow this thought structure to deduce church praxis exclusively, via dogmatic theology, from an order flowing somewhere in the realm of the "transcendent." Others, more concerned with a "synthesis of difference," stress the priority of exploring the church's actual function in society, and of regulating conduct.

The dialectical tension between empirical experience and the transcendental nature of the church as a basic ecclesiological problem is generally accepted on the theoretical level. In practice, however, a normative dogmatics or exegesis is given priority over concrete experience determined by the methods of the social sciences. Thus, for example, the Bonn New Testament scholar Erich Graesser sees in such theological systems a "barbaric misunderstanding of New Testament eschatology." They emphasize the social relevance of theology and its practice. He suspects in them a one-sided, Marxist-inspired obsession with the "ideology of structure."[27] Empirical and historical theological positions are thus disqualified as "pseudotheology," which "can only be unmasked through theology."[28] The only theology Graesser recognizes is the "theology of the word of God."[29] This is the only norm for the evaluation of concrete experience, and it is only within these confines that empirical reality is accepted as being relevant either for theory or for praxis.

Wolfhart Pannenberg warns against misusing Christian theology by accepting a principally Marxist-oriented social analysis, which calls for revolutionary change in the social system.[30] Pannenberg questions the very existence of any economic "neocolonialism" and doubts that an increase in the economic power of individuals or societies causes or reinforces the poverty of others. Further, Pannenberg rejects, as an outmoded rhetoric of Marxist authors, the theory of dependency of Latin American theologians, according to which capitalist countries cause the underdevelopment of the poor nations of the southern hemisphere. He states that it is incorrect to assign a negative value to any and all dependency.[31] In order to reach a balanced judgment on "questions of the order of social relationships of this world," as well as to avoid a situation in which "theology and the church unwillingly serve ideologies whose goals are altogether different from those that serve the kingdom of God proclaimed by Jesus Christ," Pannenberg recommends that a "corrective for the one-sided Marxist-oriented presentation of the state of economic and economico-political affairs" should be developed by non-Marxist economists.[32]

Other theologians consider it unacceptable to combine "Christian faith and ecclesial proclamation with political analyses and programs of action," even when these programs are based on a sound analysis of the facts, as in the case of the WCC Program to Combat Racism. For Erwin Wilkens, former vice-president of the chancery of the Evangelical Church in Germany, this is "a way of retheologizing secularized doctrines of salvation," which must be rejected.[33] Empirical reality is thus automatically and categorically disqualified as a starting point for theology.

Inasmuch as the premises of dogmatic discourse are irrefutable by definition, the question of whether these premises are legitimate is answered in advance, in the affirmative. Bonn theologian Hans-Dieter Bastian has applied this principle to "practical theology" in this way:

> Either . . . practical theology follows the doctrine of the word, and gains certitude (dogma) but loses reality (praxis), or it turns from the axiomatic word to human words, takes responsibility for their power or lack of it, and radically subjects church conduct to empirical analysis.[34]

It seems to us that European theology's approach to reality largely on transcendental and universal terms constitutes a decisive weakness in our tradition and causes us to cut off from our field of vision whole areas of theological challenge. This does not mean, however, that European churches are not concerned with societal realities. Their interest is not to change these realities by relating them to new theological challenges but rather to save the continuity of their institutional structures within the given status quo. Therefore, renewal is desirable only if it is in harmony with institutional stability, as the study of the Evangelical Church of Germany, "How Stable is the Church?," clearly demonstrates.[35]

Theology and Capitalism

Actually, as an encounter with Third World theology opens our eyes to the matter of situation and context, our own European circumstances show us how situational and contextual theology is right here. Of course, our theology is not tied to a situation of struggle for liberation, as Third World theology is. Ours is locked up in a society that not only brought forth oppression and violence in the past, but, under the increasing pressure operative in the system at present, seeks more and more to further its own interests and to perpetuate unjust conditions bound up with those interests.

The church in Germany was, and still is, bound into this system. We Christians and theologians, then, also participate in the tensions, internal contradictions, and dependencies of modern capitalism. Our understanding of the gospel of Jesus Christ as the proclamation of the coming kingdom of God is obviously corrupted by our involvement in this system.

Our theological existence is defined and legitimated by the fact that the official German church sees itself as a *Volkskirche*, a kind of national church, which directs its message and ministry, generally and across the board, toward society as a whole. This claim to be a universal mediator of meaning in society has had two important consequences for the church, ever since the social question was raised in Germany, and has these consequences still.

First, the church has carried on its dialogue with socialism essentially as a "reaction of church representatives to the diminishing influence of the Christian religion on the masses in the wake of industrialization.''[36] Where, however, a socialist movement made itself manifest—as with the religious socialists—this breakthrough either failed to have a practical impact on society, or met its provisional end at the hands of fascism.[37] The Protestant contribution to the discussion with Marxism after World War II repeated the old historical confrontation. Thus the opportunity of the second great crisis of the capitalist system, whereby a new socialist order might have been established in Germany, was allowed to slip away, while forces working for the restoration of the old order carried the day.[38] It was precisely in ecclesiastical and theological circles in Germany that the real enemy of a new social order managed to escape attention. The true social alternatives were put in a false light by the claim that there was an imminent and inescapable choice to be made between the Christian and the Marxist worldviews.[39]

The second consequence of the claim of the German church to be a *Volkskirche* causes what is known as the ''bourgeois imprisonment of theology.'' The institutionalization, bureaucratization, and public support through taxation, all necessary to the maintenance of such a church, led to a dependency on secular power politics and financial strategy.

And here is precisely where the double moral standard of church decisions stands out like a sore thumb. The church, for instance, refuses to take an unambiguous position on economic sanctions against the apartheid regime in South Africa, arguing that the result would be the mass exodus of members and tax payers. Church leaders and theologians seem to prefer to secure the benefits deriving from our society's wealth and from the often inhumane and life-destroying conditions that this society produces at home and abroad.

It is an idle question whether the church has any business involving itself in economic affairs. A church that disposes of a budget of over four billion marks a year, as the member churches of the Evangelical Church in Germany do, exercises enormous economic power.

More important is the discussion on the church's ethical position on economics in an industrial nation whose well-being depends to a decisive extent on its international economic relations. Can the church be indifferent to the moral premises and judgments of economic processes when the wealth of the people whose church this *Volkskirche* seeks to be rests to a decisive extent on these same economic processes, and when countless members of this church participate in the management of this wealth?[40]

Against this background, it is most embarrassing when ''neutral'' and ''objective'' European theologians confronted with the theology of the poor think they have a duty to persuade their constituency that the gospel is, after all, for the rich, too.

Thus it comes about that the irruption of the poor into our church and society brings with it the challenge to take an honest look at our corrupt situation. This situation makes it very difficult, practically as well as theoretically, to take sides with the poor at home as well as in the Third World.

Theology in Germany today has to work from a starting point that in itself paralyzes our theological perception and judgment in certain areas. The general, oft-remarked, societal function into which the church has allowed itself to be maneuvered as a member of the "church-state cartel" is pernicious. Richard Sorg analyzes the church's dilemma:

The church's still strong and privileged position in society is less and less a matter of religion of the masses. The church has and holds its social position because (and as long as) it demonstrates its utility to the dominant classes, especially by securing the ideological basis of their dominance. But if the church does this too openly, it loses still more influence with the masses. If it loses influence with the masses, it is less and less able to carry out its assigned function, and thus its importance for the dominant classes declines.

The church's concern for its survival in this dilemma forces it to accommodate itself in various ways. One such measure is the attempt of the church to present itself as an institution independent of parties and classes—as a third possibility. Neutrality, however, in a world divided into classes is impossible.[41]

Wolfgang Huber's observation is applicable with regards to the public functions of the church:

In retrospect, one cannot help but decide that the "claim of universality" of the church, whereby it came to use its status as a social superorganization to further its own particular interests, has damaged the "claim of universality" inherent in the gospel.[42]

Challenges to European Theology

The demand of Third World theologians that theological reflection start out from concrete situations of life is winning a place in our consciousness only very gradually.

The social, political, and cultural shifts taking place before our eyes still hardly make their way into our reflection. A pseudo Third World interest often covers up the situation of our "guest workers" in their deplorable living and working conditions, the tightening up of the regulations under which their families can join them in Germany, and the dismantling of the right of asylum. Our capitalist system is not only losing strength, it is entering a state of structural crisis. We are beginning to realize that "European capitalism in its crisis [offers] the peoples of Europe and the world only blind alleys" and that the only real hope depends "on a break with a system whose further development, bolstered by more and more violence, would mean fatal steps in the direction of even more injustice."[43] For the moment, politicians and bureaucrats are still handling the situation with "crisis management." Protesting groups can still be held in check by allusions to the miserable situations in other countries, or with the "vital national interests" argument. The exploitive international division of labor is still working to the profit of capitalists. The arms race can still be legitimated by the threat of world communism. We can still justify limited, regional "conflicts" (costing thousands of lives), and welcome them as an occasion for multiplying profits and influence.

Deaths that have become commonplace, the disappearance, destruction, and plundering of millions of human beings—whole cultures and societies—still fail to impress most European theologians and Christians. Clearly, science and professionalism, left to themselves, are too smug, too insensitive, too easily taken up with their own routine, and too unconcerned with the plight of our world. But we shall not get away with it. Despite all the efforts of European theology to build its own closed world, there are chinks appearing in the fortress walls, and the battering-ram strikes daily.

One of the best things about the uneasiness we feel today as Western theologians under indictment is that it seems to bring us a giant step closer to a response to the challenge made by injured lives. The critical questioning to which we have been subjected has led us to the discovery of the Third World right here on our own shores. It has taught us the limitations of our theological methods when it comes to grasping human reality. We now see the danger that theology is becoming irrelevant for the problems of the world and the problems of Europe.

So we strive to pierce the shadows of our own context; we try to find out why the lives of so many persons are being crushed by poverty while we waste the world's resources. We look for the flaws in the social systems, little and great, that grind human beings to powder. We seek new paths to follow. We begin to discover that no known established theology is of any help to us. In abstract terms, theology always pretends to have answers. But when we have to act in a risky, concrete situation, then theology falls silent.

Many questions lie open before us. We must learn what role theology plays for the handicapped, for those pushed aside by society, for those who cannot adapt to the norms, values, and pressures of an achievement-oriented capitalist society. We have to ask what meaning theology can have for the ever increasing number of the unemployed in all countries of Europe. We have to ask how theology can respond to the victims of an economy whose goal is to make the highest possible profit.

IDEAS FOR EUROPEAN THEOLOGY OF THE FUTURE

Prodded by the theology of the poor, we see we have more to learn here than ever before. A theological education that wants to come to grips with the unjust situations of our time cannot simply pass on the accumulated knowledge of scholastic theology. It must produce a new way of applying the Christian tradition to a context shaped by nontheological factors. No one would claim that this has already been done sufficiently by Third World theology; but it is astounding how little it has been attempted elsewhere.

A universal theological model that merely translates the ruling ideology into its own language or that exists in an illusionary self-confinement must be rejected. What is needed is a theology that is "on the spot," and not wafting about in empty sacred space somewhere; a theology willing to bridge life's gaps, a theology that goes to the root of life's tragedies and searches for the creative power to renew it.

God confronts us in the conflicts and tensions of society, which become the object of our theological concern. Active participation in this struggle is essential for doing theology, for it is in active obedience that we learn from God. In this way theological reflection becomes subjected to the test of life experience, and practical commitment is guided by disciplined theological thinking.[44]

Theology's place is where—to name a few examples—the consciences of individuals and small groups are beginning to wake up to the exploitation of the Third World by multinational corporations, where liberation movements combat apartheid in South Africa, and where protest is voiced against the unrestricted poisoning of the natural environment by uncontrollable industrial complexes. In these movements, in this search for justice, we perceive the ominous rumblings of a God who is once more setting out to create new manifestations of his emergent kingdom. We are present at the birth of a prophetic movement, which will shake the old church of the West out of the spell of demonic powers and false idols.

It is no coincidence, then, that the end of the quest for the historical Jesus has proved to be premature. For it is precisely the Jesus of history who is cause and starting point of our discipleship—this Jesus as he is presented by exegetes when they apply the methods of historical materialism or social history to the concrete socio-economic, political, and ideological relationships of his time. This Jesus dared to approach humankind with his God and expose himself to the destructive processes in which human beings entangle themselves. In his talk about the kingdom of God he risked a showdown with harsh reality. The Argentinean Old Testament scholar J. Severino Croatto writes:

It is the earthly Jesus who liberates human beings, it is the Jesus who died on account of the Law as structure, on account of racial and religious prejudices, on account of his servitude among people whose subversive memory of liberation had lost its bite.[45]

French theologian Georges Casalis echoes Fernando Belo when he says: "The praxis of Jesus in the flesh, in society, and in history invites other human beings to imitation, offering them both a source and a gauge for their own praxis."[46] Why? Because Jesus liberates the physically oppressed, opens up a livable future for the poor, and gets actively involved in class confrontation.

A theology that is committed to this Jesus and relates itself to the practice of discipleship must not be tailored to fit conventional measures. On the contrary, it is inspiringly, provocatively measureless. Looking back to the Christian tradition we observe, on one side, commandments of love, dogmas of faith, and procrastination; on the other there is faith that heals, faith that moves mountains. This faith centers all its concern on how human beings can find power in helplessness, how the despised of this earth can recover their dignity. The last shall not be promoted to next-to-last. They shall be first.

A theology of this quality is not concerned with regulating life; it is concerned with life's breaches and breakthroughs, with crucifixion and resurrection. It is concerned with the daily infliction of misery, and the daily proclamation of salvation. It does not rest content with the feasible. It refuses to discuss compromises. It is on the road to the kingdom of God.

Where the historical Jesus is suppressed, where he is idealized, spiritualized, or disregarded by theology, there the church is on the verge of losing its identity.

In the long run, theology in Europe will not scrape out of this uneasiness and this upset without taking a clear position. It is going to have to make decisions appropriate to concrete situations, decisions against exploitation and repression, against capitalism and imperialism, and in favor of a socialistic form of society that is just, sustainable, and participatory. The alternative? The New Delhi conference states:

> To proclaim a God who does not see the plight of the poor and does not act in their favor is to preach a God of death, a dead God. When the forces of death are free to kill, God's reality is not recognized. When life is ignored or cruelly crushed, false gods are set up. This is idolatry (Exod. 20:2–6).[47]

The credibility of our church and theology, thrown into confusion and crises by this indictment by the Third World, depends on our arriving at a point where we can make an admission:

> Christian existence is a revolutionary existence, and . . . the duty of the church to the world is to champion every social reform without demanding anything for Christianity, without attempting to christianize the revolution.[48]

The task of the theologians, as the church fights for humankind's full humanity, will be to unmask the "metaphysics of death" inherent in the capitalist system.[49] It penetrates all areas of life, degrading men and women to one-dimensional creatures. It threatens to become a totalitarian social system, so rigid and immovable in its irrational, self-destructive "rationality" that all expressions of life are more and more repressed and laid waste, until nothing is left but dead tissue, existence without life, creativity, or spirit—a death-culture, a society without strength to renew itself.

Latin American theologian Hugo Assmann therefore asks:

Are we really all convinced that the demand for work, bread, and shelter . . . in the countries held in a state of underdevelopment brings with it a break with the capitalist system? Or do we still believe that, after correction of some of the faults of the system, a capitalist solution could successfully meet the basic needs of the majority of the human race?[50]

Theology is confronted with the task of reshaping its tradition. This tradition has become the victim of the death-producing capitalist system. Now theology must step in on the side of life, the side of phil-anthropy against necro-philia. It must fight the lust for the power of domination and subjugation that ends by stifling life altogether.

It must be the goal of theological theory and praxis to strike out against the transformation of God's creation into a rotting death camp, to resist the hatred of life that is visible in the attempt of the mighty to gain possession of the world.

It is time to look at social reality with the eyes of life again, to test the power of the gospel, whether it is mighty enough to counterbalance the history of prevailing evil, or whether it is ensnared in that history. It has come time to test a faith that breaks apart when it cannot deliver a person to a future worth living, thus opposing the "no future" view of life of today's insecure, disillusioned youth in Europe.

To see reality means to see men and women in their vulnerability and human worth. This implies the willingness to fight against the mentality that human beings may be treated as disposable commodities and taken into account only as useful material.

This is why the theology of the poor demands that we enter upon a "new Reformation" and develop from the Scriptures a new, sound militant praxis that will put an end to a theology that ignores social, political, and economic as well as cultural and religious realities. Traditional theology is in danger of becoming an apathetic and sterile science that, in the words of systematic theologian Werner Schneider, "knows no victims and no executioners, has no words for the voicelessness and nonpersonhood of the masses, and no scientific terms for feelings of degradation and outrage."[51]

He contrasts this sort of science with a new model:

Science, when it is in the service of true life and living truth, has primarily a negative task: that of describing as exactly as possible all situations and relationships in which truth is negated and untruth reigns, in which life dies and death triumphs. Criticism of the church, of religion, of capitalism, and of bureaucracy, as well as research into peace, are constitutive parts of a science that is truly free. It puts sand into the well-oiled machinery of lies and death, and casts a veto in the name of the victims and the poor whose right to truth and life science ought to defend.[52]

This is the only approach to theology that can give European theology back its character as a sign of God's solidarity with human beings, a sign of the beginning of God's reign.

What this means for our churches is again something we can learn from Third World theologians:

The cross shows that the disciple is called to participate in the painful and constant effort of God, until his reign finally comes, to reinstate the ways of justice which men have distorted and destroyed through love of wealth and greed for power. This means we must become incarnate (as God was incarnate in Jesus Christ), identifying ourselves with the victims of injustice, who hope for a better tomorrow. For these, there is no glory, but the persistent reality of the cross. In other words, those who claim to be disciples of Jesus cannot participate in the social processes of our time with the perspective of triumphalism, but with the openness of the Suffering Servant, the true poor of Yahweh. As Gustavo Gutiérrez says, Jesus does not assume the condition of poverty and its tremendous consequences with the purpose of idealizing it, but because of love for and solidarity with men who suffer in it. It is to redeem them from their sin and to enrich them with his poverty. It is to struggle against human selfishness and everything that divides men and causes there to be rich and poor, possessors and dispossessed, oppressors and oppressed![53]

SUMMING UP

These massive, excruciating questions, aimed at the self-understanding of the church and theology, have had the effect of a concave mirror, reflecting the tradition of European theology and the effects it has had down through history. They constitute a challenge to share the burden of responsibility for the history of Christianity. And they constitute a challenge to switch over to new patterns of theological thinking and behavior. European theologians have generally reacted evasively up to now, with ecumenical demeanor or provincial criticism.

And yet a general consciousness is taking hold that the 1980s will be a decade that theology and the church will survive only by a thoroughgoing revision of the prevailing order. The realization that the catastrophe we all fear has already struck elsewhere, and has just not reached us yet, is beginning to release forces for change.[54]

We see some changes in the area of theology. The mentality of dominance, with its notion of a universal theology of European provenience, is beginning to be corrected. Social and cultural minorities, together with the victims of sex discrimination, begin to be taken into theological account. It remains to be seen whether these small steps can stop the march of our Western society toward its own self-destruction and that of the Third World in its wake.

At the present moment the task of European theology can only consist in helping churches and their local congregations to express—in their theology, their lifestyle, and their organizational structures—solidarity with the struggle of the poor and the oppressed.[55]

We speculated at the beginning of this paper that the irruption of the theology of the Third World into our own theological models might yet take on the proportions of a "second Reformation." Whether this estimate is a correct one or not—that is, whether it will be a reformation in the shape of a theology of the poor that will carry the day—or whether instead it will be a restoration, probably will not depend on theological or exegetical arguments. During the age of the Reformation, the course of events was determined by the victory of certain material interests rather than by religious convictions. The world was twisted to benefit those interests.[56]

Today will be no different. Whether a second reformation, spurred by a theology of the poor, can prevail in Europe depends on the course of the crises of the 1980s, and "on their effects upon the Third World in the First World and the First World in the Third World."[57]

The task of the Ecumenical Association of Third World Theologians seems comparable to that of the prophets in the Old Testament who, although proclaiming disaster, called attention to God's still valid demand for justice in this world.

NOTES

1. Jürgen Moltmann's characterization of black theology, expressed in the terminology of the Communist Manifesto, is equally applicable to the new Third World theology as developed by the Ecumenical Association of Third World Theologians; see *Evangelische Theologie,* 34/1 (1974): 1.

2. Trutz Rendtorff's description in his article "Universalität oder Kontextualität der Theologie: Eine 'europäische Stellungnahme,' " *Europäische Theologie herausgefordert durche die Weltökumene* (Geneva: Konferenz Europäischer Kirchen, 1976), Studienheft, no. 8.

3. Moltmann, in his open letter to José Míguez Bonino, *EPD-Dokumentation,* 18 (1976): 103.

4. Julio de Santa Ana, ed., *Towards a Church of the Poor* (Maryknoll, N.Y.: Orbis, 1980), pp. 98, 101.

5. See Georges Casalis, *Die richtigen Ideen fallen nicht vom Himmel: Grundlagen einer induktiven Theologie* (Stuttgart, 1980), p. 29; English translation of French original forthcoming from Orbis Books.

6. Ludwig Rütti, "Westliche Identität als theologisches Problem," *Zeitschrift für Mission,* 4/2 (1978): 97.

7. Rendtorff, "Universalität," p. 69.

8. Cited by Rütti, "Westliche Identität," p. 105.

9. Final Statement, nos. 33, 32.

10. Sergio Torres and Virginia Fabella, eds., *The Emergent Gospel* (Maryknoll, N.Y.: Orbis, 1978), p. 269.

11. Virginia Fabella, ed., *Asia's Struggle for Full Humanity: Towards a Relevant Theology* (Maryknoll, N.Y.: Orbis, 1980), pp. 157–58.

12. Frantz Fanon, *The Wretched of the Earth* (New York, 1963), p. 295.

13. Rendtorff, "Universalität," p. 73.

14. Wilhelm Dantine, *Schwarze Theologie: Eine Herausforderung der Theologie der Weissen* (Vienna, 1976), p. 103.

15. Ibid., p. 104.

16. Ibid., p. 106.

17. Ibid., p. 108.

18. Ibid., p. 104.

19. Rütti, "Westliche Identität," p. 105.

20. Ibid., pp. 105–6.

21. Ibid., p. 106.

22. Helmut Gollwitzer, "Why Black Theology?," *Black Theology: A Documentary History, 1966–1979,* Gayraud S. Wilmore and James H. Cone, eds. (Maryknoll, N.Y.: Orbis 1979), p. 155.

23. Torres and Fabella, eds., *The Emergent Gospel,* p. 266.

24. Richard Sorg, *Marxismus und Protestantismus in Deutschland* (Cologne, 1974), p. 34.

25. Ibid.

26. Wolf-Dieter Marsch, *Institution im Übergang: Evangelische Kirche zwischen Tradition und Reform* (Göttingen, 1970), pp. 38–39.

27. Erich Graesser, "Die politische Herausforderung an die biblische Theologie," *Text und Situation: Gesammelte Aufsätze zum Neuen Testament* (Gütersloh, 1973), p. 265.

28. Ibid., p. 277.

29. Ibid.

30. See Wolfhart Pennenberg, "Stellungnahme zu dem Papier der CCPD. 'Für eine mit den Armen solidarische Kirche' " (unpublished MS), p. 5.

31. Ibid., p. 4.

32. Ibid., p. 6.

33. Cited by Erhard Kamphausen, "Südafrika heute—Hoffnung um welchen Preis?," *ISSA Archiv Aktuell,* 13 (1979): 5.

34. Hans-Dieter Bastian, "Vom Wort zu den Wörten: Karl Barth und die Aufgabe der Praktischen Theologie," *Evangelische Theologie,* 27 (1968): 29.

35. *Wie stabil ist die Kirche? Bestand und Erneuerung: Ergebnisse einer Umfrage,* H. Hild, ed. (Berlin, 1974).

36. Sorg, *Marxismus,* p. 83.

37. Ibid., p. 130.

38. Ibid., p. 204.

39. Ibid., pp. 204–5.

40. Eberhard le Coutre, "Anfragen zum Klima," *Der Überblick,* 4 (1981): 194.

41. Sorg, *Marxismus,* p. 207.

42. Wolfgang Huber, *Kirche und Öffentlichkeit* (Stuttgart, 1973), p. 123.

43. Casalis, *Die richtigen Ideen,* p. 18.

44. See "Europäische Konsultation über theologische Ausbildung, Herrnhut, 9–14. Oktober 1980," *EMW-Informationen,* 20 (Hamburg, 1981): 6.

45. J. Severino Croatto, "Befreiung und Freiheit," *Weltmission heute: Zum Thema Theologie in der Dritten Welt* (Hamburg, 1979), p. 43.

46. Casalis, *Die richtigen Ideen,* p. 125.

47. Final Statement, no. 63.

48. Richard Shaull, "Die revolutionäre Herausforderung an Kirche und Theologie," *Protestantische Theologie,* K. M. Beckmann, ed. (Düsseldorf, 1971), p. 230.

49. Typewritten transcription of an address delivered by Hugo Assmann for a seminar organized by Evangelisches Missionswerk (EMW), Sept. 1980, Bossey (Geneva), Switzerland.

50. Ibid.

51. Werner Schneider, "Bermerkungen zu 'Wissenschaftskritik als theologische Aufgabe' " (unpublished MS), p. 2.

52. Ibid., p. 4.

53. Julio de Santa Ana, *Good News to the Poor* (Maryknoll, N.Y.: Orbis 1977), p. 33.

54. See Werner Ustorf, "Angst und Hoffnung in der Bundesrepublik," *Protokoll, 459* (Mülheim/Ruhr: Evangelische Akademie, 1980), 42.

55. See "Für eine mit den Armen solidarische Kirche," *EPD-Dokumentation,* 25A (1980): 1.

56. See Kristian Hungar, "Führe uns nicht in Versuchung (Lk. 11, 4)" (unpublished MS), p. 4.

57. Ibid. EATWOT has made a definite impact on a considerable number of theologians in Europe. This became clear when about a hundred persons gathered at Woudschoten, Dec. 10 to 14, 1981, to hold a symposium with the title: "The Future of Europe: A Challenge to Theology." The history and the findings of this symposium in its relation with the EATWOT conferences has been analyzed by Erhard Kamphausen: "Eigenständigkeit und Dialog. Zum Weg kontextueller Befreiungstheologien in Süd und Nord," *Ökumenische Rundschau,* 31/2 (April 1982): 205–22.

21

Hope for the Future

Emílio J.M. de Carvalho

I went to New Delhi for the first time in my life, and as a neophyte to an EATWOT conference. I had mixed feelings, being someone from an under-developed Third World country, belonging to an oppressed people, and bearing within me the vestiges of despised cultural and religious traditions.

What a "salad" of theologies! Happily, as I became lost in the maze of theological discourses from Asia, Africa, Latin America, and minorities in the U.S.A. and the Caribbean, I found out that in our ecumenical dialogue we were dealing with the same issues and realities: the oppressed peoples of our continents, now making their voices heard, and irrupting into a world long dominated by their oppressors.

There is always hope for the future. Five years have now elapsed since Dar es Salaam. They have taught us that Third World theology is not something that we have to do in order to show that something good and fruitful can come from "backwardness" and "underdevelopment." The experiences of faith and biblical reflection have been on our continents since the gospel of Jesus Christ was first incorporated by Third World peoples. We thank EATWOT for helping us break away from our multiform secular theological consumerism, by making explicit and communicable what has always been implicit in our search for God and full humanity.

In New Delhi the hope for the future of the mission of the church in our countries was vivid. EATWOT turns its eyes to the future, to be at the service of Third World theologies, by helping to make them more objective, more relevant, and more open to the real aspirations of our struggling peoples. Such theologies will eventually replace the inadequate and foreign traditional Western theology.

How Europe and North America will respond to our theological approach, and acknowledge our right to think and to express our thought in our own forms, idioms, images, symbols, mental and verbal categories, is not the issue at stake. Nor is even our rereading of the Bible from our specific socio-historical contexts and perspectives. The real issue for the future is the passage of theological reflection from the elitist circles of professional theologians to the oppressed masses of our societies, so that the message of the gospel can become relevant to their lives.

From EATWOT there will come another sign of hope: comradely dialogue with First and Second World theologians, as well as a response to the claims of the oppressed of other faiths and religions.

In a word, hope for the future does not emerge from a vacuum. It is a hope emerging from the struggle of the poor and oppressed, a source of a new experience of God, and of a redefinition of the role of our theologies in and from situations of struggle.

Contributors

Abraham, K. C.: director of the Ecumenical Christian Center in Whitefield, Bangalore, India.

Alvarez Calderón, Jorge: Latin American chaplain for the Christian Worker Movement and a member of the Centro de Estudios Bartolomé de las Casas.

Carvalho, Emílio J. M. de: Methodist bishop from Angola and president of the Ecumenical Association of Third World Theologians.

Chandran, J. Russell: principal and professor of theology and ethics at the United Theological College, Bangalore, India.

Cone, James H.: Charles A. Briggs Professor of Systematic Theology at Union Theological Seminary, New York.

Croatto, J. Severino: professor of Old Testament at the Instituto de Estudios Teológicos, Buenos Aires.

Dias, Zwinglio: pastor of the Lutheran Church of Rio de Janeiro and a member of the Ecumenical Center of Documentation and Investigation.

Döring, Dirk: pastoral assistant at the Academy of Mission at the University of Hamburg.

Duraisingh, J. C.: professor of systemic theology at the United Theological College, Bangalore, India.

Elizondo, Virgil: president of the Mexican-American Cultural Center, San Antonio, Texas.

Gebara, Ivone: professor of philosophy and theology at the Theological Institute of Recife, Brazil.

Goba, Bonganjalo: ordained minister of the United Congregational Church of Southern Africa and lecturer of systematic theology at the University of South Africa.

Gutiérrez, Gustavo: professor of theology at the Catholic University in Lima, Peru, and author of *A Theology of Liberation.*

Kamphausen, Erhard: director of studies at the Academy of Mission at the University of Hamburg.

Mveng, Engelbert: Jesuit priest and executive secretary of the Ecumenical Association of African Theologians.

Oduyoye, Amba: originally from Ghana, teacher in the religious studies department of the University of Ibadan, Nigeria.

Park, Sun Ai: ordained minister of the Disciples of Christ, editor of *Korea Scope,* and researcher of Asian women's theology.

Pieris, Aloysius: Jesuit priest, director of the Tulana Research Centre, Kelaniza, Sri Lanka, and visiting professor of Asian religions and philosophies at the East Asian Pastoral Institute, Manila.

Rayan, Samuel: Jesuit priest and professor of theology at the Vidyajyoti Institute of Religious Studies, Delhi, India.

Roy, Ajit: editor of the *Marxist Review* and member of the Permanent People's Tribunal, Rome.

Tamez, Elsa: professor of Old Testament at the Seminario Bíblico Latino-americano in San José, Costa Rica.

Torres, Sergio: Chilean priest and executive director of EATWOT.

Also in the EATWOT series:

AFRICAN THEOLOGY EN ROUTE

Edited by Kofi Appiah-Kubi and Sergio Torres

"These papers, presented at the Pan-African Conference of Third World Theologians, do not attempt to 'adapt' European thought to Africa, but show Africans thinking for themselves about the sources, presuppositions, and priorities of their faith, using literature, art, traditional religion, and current events, as well as the Bible, as resources. The contributors write; not primarily as Catholics or Protestants, but as African Christians, concerned with community, healing, and liberation from poverty, racism, sexism, and elitism. They do not announce conclusions as much as they exhibit participation in a process. This is an important collection which should be read by students of Christian theology and of contemporary African thought."

Religious Studies Review

"Well written and, where necessary, well translated. It adds to a growing literature on the subject and is recommended for libraries seriously concerned with theology in Africa." *Choice*

224pp. Paper $9.95

ASIA'S STRUGGLE FOR FULL HUMANITY

Edited by Virginia Fabella

"Christians in Asia are an insignificant minority today, a mere two percent of the Asian masses, despite centuries of missionary activity. Christianity is considered an unwelcome foreign import. This indicates that there is a tremendous need then for a theological awakening among all Christian elements in Asia for a contextualization impetus that will result in the Christian message and the non-Christian environment having an impact on each other. *Asia's Struggle for Full Humanity* is the official report of an Asian Theological Conference held in Sri Lanka, attended by eighty participants mostly from Asian countries (Bangladesh, Indonesia, India, the Philippines, Taiwan, Hong Kong, Japan, Pakistan, Thailand and Sri Lanka) convened in response to an awareness of that need. The book details the preparations for and implementation of the declared task of the Conference, viz., the continuing search for a relevant theology in Asia. The conference was an ecumenical venture of Catholics and Protestants jointly building together on what had previously been done by seperate groups." *Review for Religious*

"This book doesn't require previous knowledge of Asian theology to be appreciated. It would be an excellent introduction for people who have been intending to acquaint themselves with current Christian thinking by Asians but have never found the right place to start." *Mission Focus*

192pp. Paper $8.95

THE CHALLENGE OF BASIC CHRISTIAN COMMUNITIES

Edited by Sergio Torres and John Eagleson
Preface by Jorge Lara-Braud

"A grass-roots 'people's church' movement has emerged in the last two decades, especially in Latin America among Roman Catholics. The fourth meeting of the Ecumenical Association of Third World Theologians attempted to evaluate this development. The addresses, papers and reports of the meeting in São Paulo, Brazil, are published in this book. The significance of this new form of church life is analyzed, along with the challenge it poses to historic churches—especially in light of the formal declarations of many Christian assemblies of solidarity with the poor and oppressed." *The Disciple*

352pp. Paper $9.95